SECRETS *of a* Jewish Baker

Secrets of a Jewish Baker

Authentic Jewish Rye and Other Breads

by

George Greenstein

The Crossing Press
Freedom, CA 95019

Acknowledgments

I wish to thank the following people without whom this book would not have been possible:

My publisher, Elaine Goldman Gill, and Dennis Hayes, Barbara Feller-Roth (editor), Sheryl Karas, Julia Greenstein Bleicher, Lucy Natkiel, Annette Bleicher, Gertrude Downing, Bertha Steinhauer, Bob Schild, Alan B. Posner, Manny (from Food of All Nations Bakery), Aaron Wenzelberg, Erica Marcus, and Naph Waxman. Special thanks to Marcia Pudalov who convinced me I could write it, and Elaine Greenstein who supplied me with motivation whenever it was lacking.

Cover design and illustrations by Anne Marie Arnold
Cover photograph by Amy Sibiga
Book design by Sheryl Karas

Printed in the U.S.A.

Library of Congress Cataloging-in-Publication Data

Greenstein, George.
Secrets of a Jewish Baker : Authentic Jewish Rye and Other Breads / by George Greenstein.
p. cm.
Includes index.
ISBN 0-89594-631-9 — ISBN 0-89594-630-0 (pbk.)
1. Bread. I. Title.
TX769.G734 1993
641.8'15—dc20 92-41639
CIP

For my wife, Adele,
with love
for her patience, assistance,
and perception.

Contents

How to Make the Rye Bread Sing

There is something sensual about kneading dough. Touching and molding it is a true hands-on experience. Savor the yeasty aroma. It's exciting to start with flour and water and feel the mixture come to life with an almost magical quality, stimulated by the gentle pressure of your hands.

The author of this book is a master baker who has spent his life working with his hands in pursuit of the perfect loaf. What is the perfect bread? How does one know when it has been found? Who is qualified to judge?

One night, working alone while the others were asleep, a baker was standing in front of a huge oven. Behind him was an wire rack containing more than 200 loaves, hot, just removed from the oven. All was still in the bakery that very first time when he heard the rye bread sing. He turned, stood listening, at first without comprehension, then he smiled, recognizing the sound—for him, a melody!

Occasionally when making bread everything comes together in harmony. The dough is flawless and the surrounding conditions are ideal. When the rye bread is removed from the oven, the crust begins to crack in the cooler air and form a finely veined alligator-like appearance. To the baker's ear the almost imperceptible crackling, multiplied a hundredfold, is a song of praise for the perfect loaf.

Chapter One

Basic Materials

In all my years as a professional baker, one of the most satisfying tasks has always been bread baking. What a wonderful reward there is when freshly baked loaves are placed on the dinner table, still warm from the oven. One often sees a look of awe on people's faces when told that the bread before them is homemade.

It has been my experience that many excellent cooks and bakers are intimidated by the thought of making bread at home. Yet bread baking can be made simple to understand for both the novice and experienced baker. Errors can be easily corrected so that beginners' first attempts are successful and, with a little practice, professional results can be achieved.

This book is more than just another collection of recipes. It is all about getting professional results using bread-baking methods made simple and foolproof, while utilizing modern, time-saving systems without the need for expensive equipment. Whether this is your first attempt at bread making or you are an old hand, this book can be used as a complete bread-baking manual that will produce results sure to delight.

Nutrition and a balanced diet are continually taking on more important roles in our lives. Baking your own bread allows you to take more control of your family's dietary requirements. You can use natural foods and salt-free, low-fat, and low-cholesterol ingredients in your family's meals. Fiber-rich grains are easily added to breads. Many breads can be produced without sweeteners. Most assuredly, baking bread is one way to improve your family's nutrition and add to the enjoyment of their daily meals.

In the ensuing pages I share with you many of my hard-won and dearly paid-for professional secrets. The old European bakers jealously guarded their recipes and methods. I remember an elderly hunchbacked giant of a man grudgingly permitting a novice to weigh out the ingredients for a recipe that was about to be mixed. When it came to the critical ingredients, such as leavening, salt, spices, or flavoring, the master baker always seemed to find an excuse to send the novice to the storeroom for supplies or to the sink for a clean utensil. While the young man was gone, the baker would furtively add the important ingredients so that the newcomer would not be able to memorize the complete recipe.

A friend who taught me much always cautioned me never to take a recipe from another baker unless I mixed it and baked it myself while the baker stood by and instructed. Otherwise, much to my sorrow, I would belatedly learn that some key ingredient had "accidentally" been omitted from the recipe.

Not many young people are coming into the baking industry. Oddly, in this time of increased awareness for good foods, we are threatened with the loss of the natural flavor of many foods. Mass production and chemical additives pervade our food supply. For example, years ago my father made wine at home. He began with the grapes, crushed them in a wine press, and fermented the mash naturally, without additives. Today, one buys a grape concentrate in a kit that comes complete with a chemistry set.

I foresee many of our wonderful breads disappearing from the marketplace. I hope that those interested in real food and real bread will find in this book some of the joy of creating a variety of good breads in their own kitchens.

Getting Started

The bread recipes that follow require very little equipment. Most or all of it can be found in your home. The doughs can be mixed and kneaded by hand, although each recipe is also formulated for use with a dough-mixing machine or a food processor. I do not recommend that you purchase a machine when beginning. If you already own one, you may find working by hand at first more informative and more fun. It is also possible to gain valuable experience mixing by machine and finishing the kneading by hand for the last few minutes.

Here is a list of the basic equipment necessary for getting started.

Oven Thermometer

This is of premier importance, because other than the oven itself, this is the instrument that you will need most to become a successful baker. It is the only tool that you should certainly purchase before beginning. I suggest a good oven thermometer made of stainless steel with a glass tube filled with a mercury-like substance. The round dial type that uses a metal coil tends to be very inaccurate after some use. I strongly recommend using a thermometer every time you bake. Oven thermostats take a lot of abuse from the prolonged heat and become inaccurate with time. Accurate baking temperatures are critical for a properly baked loaf. The oven should be preheated and checked with a thermometer each time you bake.

Mixing Bowls

Several large bowls should be on hand. Stoneware or earthenware bowls are the best, since they are heavy and make mixing easier. They retain heat well, so that the temperature remains consistent and the dough rises easily. Other ceramic or heavy plastic bowls are also good. Stainless steel bowls can also be used, but I find that they transfer heat too quickly and might slow down the rising time.

Wooden Spoons

Several large wooden spoons make mixing easier.

Rubber Spatula

Several rubber spatulas of different sizes are handy. If you can, seek out the real rubber ones instead of the plastic ones that are found in most houseware shops. The spatulas I have are made in France and do a wonderful job. Better cookery shops carry them.

Plastic Bowl Scraper

A plastic bowl scraper with one straight edge across the bottom and a curved edge on top is an inexpensive tool of a hundred uses that is good for scraping dough from a mixing bowl (using the curved edge); it can also be used as an inexpensive dough cutter and work-top scraper (using the straight edge). It is handy for scraping the dough together in the initial stages of kneading. Scrapers can be purchased in kitchen or gourmet cooking shops or restaurant supply houses. Some scrapers have multiple curves and no straight edge. The straight-edge type is much more functional (these are used in the bakery); it pays to search them out.

Dough Cutter (optional)

A dough cutter (also called a bun dough cutter) is a rectangular metal scraper with a wooden or plastic grip. Bakers use it for many cutting and scraping chores; it can be used as a bench-top scraper. The plastic bowl scraper (above) and a wide putty knife can suffice. Dough cutters are available in restaurant supply houses and some cooking catalogues. They are not expensive, and a good one should last a lifetime. In the bakery, we use the Dexter brand.

Measuring Cups

Have on hand two or more graduated measuring cups, one for liquid ingredients and one for dry ingredients.

Measuring Spoons

A set of measuring spoons is essential. If you own two sets, use one for wet ingredients and one for dry.

Pastry Brush

A small, 2-inch-wide paint brush, preferably natural bristle, is used to brush (paint) the bread with liquid, such as water or eggs, before baking. The process is called washing. In a pinch you can use your fingers.

Rolling Pin

A rolling pin is rarely used in bread making. Unless you have one at home, do not purchase one when you begin baking. Most of the breads can be shaped with your hands. A broomstick cut about 16 inches long makes a perfect rolling stick (lightly sandpaper the ends). We do this in the bakery, using the stick for rolling out small pieces of dough or pastry. A similar length of hardwood dowel can be purchased in a hardware store or lumberyard. A pie rolling stick, a commercially available wooden stick that is thicker in the center and tapers toward each end, does a nice job on small items.

Work Top

Large hardwood boards are convenient for kneading and molding dough and they are easy to clean. The kitchen counter, table, or a piece of Formica or composite board will suffice. It is most important to work at a comfortable height. I have a hardwood board that I set aside exclusively for baking. After each use I apply a light coat of vegetable oil to keep the wood from drying out after washing. Most bakers scrape their wooden workbenches with a bench scraper (see Dough Cutter, above) and avoid using water on the wood as much as possible.

Loaf Pans

Two to four loaf pans are recommended, approximately 8 1/2 inches by 4 1/2 inches by 2 1/2 inches (sizes may vary). Inexpensive steel meat-loaf pans bake better than aluminum but require seasoning (page 27). Black metal or Teflon-coated pans are also fine but do not warrant the expense of purchasing new ones. A shiny pan tends to keep the bread crust from baking to a rich dark color. If a shiny pan is used, when the bread is almost done remove it from the pan for the last 5 minutes of baking and return the bread to the oven rack to finish baking. This will allow the crust to brown nicely.

Baking Sheets

One or two baking (cookie) sheets are helpful for baking bread and rolls. See the recommendations for Loaf Pans (above). Buy the heaviest gauge metal for uniform baking.

Muffin Tins

Have on hand several muffin or cupcake tins of a size that suits you, whether standard, jumbo, or miniature.

Getting Serious

Baskets

Reed or cloth-lined wicker baskets are used as forms for rising bread. When turned over they leave a distinctive pattern that is baked into the crust of the bread.

Bread Pans

French Bread Pan. The serious French bread devotee may wish to purchase a set of baguette pans, each of which looks like the bottom half of a split tube or stovepipe. They are usually made up in two or four sections and help bake perfectly formed loaves of French bread. They can also be used to achieve a uniform shape for French rolls. The bread or rolls are allowed to rise directly in the lightly greased pans in which they are baked. Perforated pans are preferred in the bakery but the plain ones are more than adequate.

Pullman pan. This long, straight-sided bread pan has a cover that slides onto the top, locking the dough inside. It bakes a square loaf useful for sandwiches and party loaves. Without the cover it can be used for a square-sided pound cake.

Oven Stones or Tiles

Bread bakes best with radiant (indirect) heat. In my bakery we had special brick-lined ovens, which radiated heat evenly throughout the oven. At home we seek to duplicate these conditions by using clay tiles (quarry tiles) or an oven stone on a shelf placed in the oven. There is no need to purchase this when you begin. Later, if you bake often, tiles or a stone allow you to bake crusty bread as is done in many bakeries, by placing the bread directly on the floor of the oven, called the hearth. Oven or pizza stones are sold in cookery shops or department stores. I use ordinary red clay quarry tiles that can be purchased at a well-stocked ceramic tile distributor. I brought my wire oven rack to the store with me and they graciously cut the tiles to fit. These tiles are very inexpensive and can be left in the oven during regular cooking and baking. Leave a bit of space on the sides and front so that the heat can circulate better. Another method is to place the tiles on a baking sheet and slide the sheet in and out of the oven with the bread directly on the tiles.

Peel

A baker's peel—a wooden pallet with or without a handle—is convenient for sliding bread directly onto the oven hearth (or onto an oven stone or clay tiles—baking on the oven hearth always produces a better crust than baking bread in a pan). Sometimes you can allow the bread to rise directly on the cornmeal-dusted peel before sliding the loaf into the oven. A suitable substitute for a peel is a piece of heavy corrugated cardboard box. I once saw an artist using a clean painter's pallet as a makeshift peel.

Dough-Mixing Machine

In the bakery we mix bread in a dough-mixing machine. I do not recommend purchasing a mixing machine in the beginning unless you are going to use the mixer for cake baking and batter whipping or intend to make bread regularly. When you feel that you are ready for a mixer and are purchasing one, make sure that it is guaranteed to mix up to 8 cups of flour when making bread dough. Standard equipment should include a wire whip, a flat beater (paddle), and a dough hook. I use a Kitchen Aid, Model K5SS, with a 5-quart capacity bowl.

Better breads can be produced with the mixer than by hand, although most people do not know how to use the full kneading power and capacity of their machines. Until now, one merely took a recipe for making bread by hand and processed it in the machine. In this book the proper methods for using a dough-mixing machine are fully explained, and recipes are given for its use. A dough-mixing machine allows the baker to work out the full elasticity of the dough by kneading heavier doughs for longer periods of time than is reasonable by hand. The pros know that kneading is more effective when the proper capacity of the mixer is utilized. In the smallest bakery, it would be unusual to find less than three different-sized mixing bowls being used. The capacity of a good kitchen mixer requires larger amounts of dough than most hand recipes call for. Accordingly, the recipes for a machine mixing are written for larger yields.

Food Processor

I like to call the food processor the whiz; it can whiz through many tedious chores in the kitchen. Many people like to use it for bread, and I have adapted my recipes accordingly. Nothing matches the speed of the processor. The capacity of the machine is limited by the size of the work bowl. Most processors have a 4-cup capacity, limiting the baker to one loaf of bread. Larger processors are available that allow for bigger batches. If you own one of the larger machines, simply adjust the recipes. Some mixing techniques can double processor yields. I usually make two loaves of bread in my standard machine, and most of the recipes here reflect this practice.

Thermometer

An instant-reading mini chef's, or baker's, thermometer with a 1-inch round dial has innumerable uses for the baker. Utilize it to check dough temperatures, liquids, even refrigerator or freezer temperatures quickly. If left in the oven while cooking a roast, for example, no more than an inch of the probe should be exposed. My thermometer reads

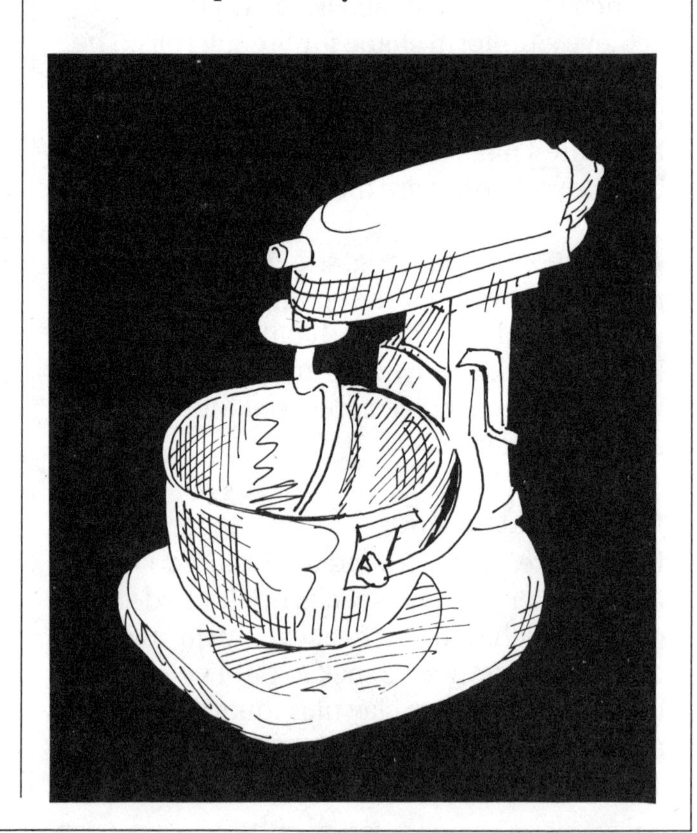

from 0°F to 220°F. It has a 5-inch metal probe and stores in a plastic sheath with a handy clip for keeping in a pocket or an apron. These thermometers are available in restaurant supply houses and gourmet cookery shops.

Yardstick

A yardstick is perfect for measuring dough on the work top; the thickness of the stick can often be used as a guide when rolling out thin doughs.

Ingredients

The following brief descriptions of essential ingredients used by professionals will help you produce quality breads with ease and confidence. Beginning with the ingredients available in the bakery, we discuss the way the baker makes use of them and the way they differ from those available at home. Included are substitutions and suggestions for locating local sources for hard-to-obtain ingredients. There are tips for storage, some shortcuts that bakers use, a few secrets, and corrections for a list of common misconceptions .

Flour

Flour, even the same brand, differs in various sections of the country. The amount of flour called for in a bread recipe is always variable: 3 to 4 cups, for example. The reason is that the amount of moisture the flour absorbs depends upon many factors, including the age of the flour, when and where the wheat was grown and stored, the amount of humidity in the air, and temperature, altitude, and so on. The baker adjusts for these variables by altering the amount of flour while mixing or kneading the dough. This requires a little experience, which you will quickly acquire as you bake. Once the proper measure of flour is established for a recipe, based upon using the same brand, the amount of flour employed will stay fairly constant throughout any given season.

Modern flour, when used for making bread, does not have to be sifted. Sifting flour is done by professionals only in certain cake recipes where it is necessary for very light and tender results. Breads are basically flour and water, and sifting will make no difference in the final product. Bakers adjust for differences in weight due to settling and moisture absorption by varying the amount of flour when mixing. Most flour is clean and free from foreign matter. If for any reason the purity of the flour is in question, sifting would certainly be in order. Otherwise, in all the recipes flour is not sifted unless so specified.

The main differences between baking at home and in a bakery are found in the flour. The flours in the bakery are not generally available to the home cook. Most consumer markets carry two types of flour—all-purpose flour and cake flour. Bread flour is now becoming readily available in many parts of the country. Specialty flours, such as stone-ground whole wheat, rye, and pumpernickel flour, are occasionally found. Cake flour is generally unsuitable for yeast-raised bread doughs. Keeping extra flour on hand is a good practice.

BAKER'S SECRET. When fresh bread flour is allowed to age for 5 to 6 weeks, its potency is increased and color improved.

All-purpose flour. This is a hard wheat flour either combined with a small proportion of soft wheat flour or milled with a lower protein content than the high-gluten flour in the bakery. This flour is in general use for home bread recipes. While in some recipes its use is a compromise, it excels in others (see short patent flour, below). All-purpose flour is available bleached and unbleached; the unbleached has a slightly higher protein content. Most of the recipes in this book are formulated for use with unbleached all-purpose flour. Some recipes suggest the appropriate bakery flour if available. When no specific type of flour is called for in a recipe, use all-purpose flour.

High-gluten flour. This flour has the highest gluten or protein content of all the flours. It is milled from hard wheat and is used for light-textured rolls, breads, and yeast cakes. In the bakery I use high-gluten flour milled from hard wheat grown in Montana and North Dakota, since I consider these the finest available. In the olden days, bakers called this king, or strong, flour. It is now available in many supermarkets labeled as bread flour. Ask the local store manager to order it for you.

Short-patent flour. Lower in gluten content than high-gluten flour, short-patent flour is used where the bread requires a denser texture. All-purpose flour falls in between the high-gluten and short-patent flours in protein content and can be substituted in place of either. All-purpose flour is not used in the bakery. Years ago bakeries chauvinistically called short-patent flour weak, or queen, flour. (The terms king, queen, and common—see below—allowed the flour bins to be labeled without regard to brand names. I suspect that many bakers could not read or write well and were able to memorize K, Q, and C, or the number of letters in the words. This type of labeling was seen as late as the 1950s.)

Some French and Italian breads are formulated with a blend of high-gluten and short-patent flour, lowering the gluten content to avoid large air pockets and to give a denser texture. All-purpose flour gives similar results.

First Clear or Clear Flour. Often referred to as common flour, this is the least refined of the bread flours. Lower in gluten content and darker in color than other flours, it is used primarily in rye breads. Rye flour has no gluten and has to be mixed with a wheat flour in order to rise. The common flour keeps the desired dark color of the rye while providing enough gluten for the bread to rise. The lower protein content allows for the dense texture, which makes it a good sandwich bread and gives it the chewy bite sought for in rye bread. Use of common flour is one of the secrets of making real Jewish rye bread. The best source is a local bakery, or try specialty shops that carry flour made from different grains. Perhaps they will even order it for you.

Whole wheat flour. Milled from the whole kernel of the wheat, this flour includes the outer husk, which is rich in nutrients. Stone-ground whole wheat flour is preferable because it is roughly ground and therefore coarsely textured, which makes a better-eating loaf. Stone-ground milling causes less destruction of the desirable nutrients in the hull of the wheat kernel. This flour is now widely available in specialty stores and by mail order. Ethnic markets and natural foods stores that sell loose flour by weight are the best sources in terms of freshness and price. Refrigerate or store this flour in a cool place, since the wheat germ in the whole kernel contains the fat found in wheat and can spoil quickly in hot, humid weather.

Rye flour. Often call white rye, this flour is milled from rye grain, not wheat. Off-white or slightly gray in color, it is used mainly for rye breads and rye rolls. As has been noted, rye flour has no gluten and will not rise unless combined with other flour. Rye flour is available from gourmet or wholesale supply houses, but the best sources are a friendly local baker, natural foods store, or food cooperative.

Pumpernickel flour. This is a medium-ground rye flour, somewhat course and light brown in color, similar to bran in appearance. Pumpernickel is labeled medium rye, not pumpernickel, in commercial packaging.

Cake flour. Also called high-ratio cake flour, this flour is used in fine, light cakes and batters. It allows a higher ratio of sugar to shortening or fat to be absorbed, making for a richer, lighter cake. When short-patent flour is not available for breads, the baker often uses a scoop or two of cake flour to lower the gluten content of the high-gluten flour. Sometimes this is done at home to lower the gluten content in all-purpose flour.

Pastry flour. Used in short doughs with a low sugar-to-shortening ratio, this flour makes fine pie crusts, pastry doughs, and cookie doughs.

Cornmeal. Milled in fine to coarse granules, cornmeal is used for southern-style corn bread, muffins, corn sticks, and New England johnnycakes. It is available as yellow or white cornmeal; most bakers used the yellow variety, which is less costly. There is no difference in flavor. New Englanders seem to prefer white cornmeal in many of their recipes. An extrafine grind, known as corn flour, is used in some recipes.

Semolina flour. This pale yellow flour, made from fine durum wheat, is used for Italian semolina bread and in better pastas.

Dusting flour or meal. We dust a baking pan or peel so that the unbaked loaf of bread does not stick. Fine granular yellow cornmeal is most often used for dusting.

BAKER'S SECRET. For rye breads, some bakers dust with rye flour, which adds its own flavor to the bottom crust when baked. Italian bakers dust with semolina flour for the same reason. In an emergency, I have used finely ground bread crumbs to dust the peels in the bakery. Crumbs tend to burn in the oven and can generate smoke. They have, however, gotten us through a day when no dusting meal was available.

Yeast

Active Dry Yeast. Active dry yeast packets need no refrigeration, have a long shelf life, and will work properly if not outdated. The life of the packets can be further extended by refrigerating or freezing. I always keep dry yeast packets in the refrigerator or freezer. In very warm or tropical climates, dry yeast (rather than fresh compressed yeast) should always be used. Active dry yeast is available in bulk packages, which must be refrigerated. If you do a good deal of bread baking, the savings gained by using bulk yeast are phenomenal and worth the effort to locate a source. Try a wholesale yeast or bakery distributor, or natural foods stores.

Brewer's Yeast. Brewer's yeast cannot make dough rise, but it is sometimes added to enrich bread.

Fresh Compressed Yeast. In the bakery we use fresh compressed bricks of yeast, delivered twice weekly to ensure freshness. Although most bakers feel that fresh yeast is more powerful than the dry type—that it creates a livelier dough with a yeasty aroma—I do not generally recommend using it in home baking. Fresh yeast is extremely perishable. It must be kept under refrigeration and I do not like to store it for more than a week. If you use it, be wary of purchasing it in a supermarket, because it may have been there a long time. Try to persuade your friendly local baker to sell you some. Unless you take a full cake of yeast, you may be given a small precut piece that may have been kept too long and has begun to dry out. The yeast should be smooth looking and of even color, without many streaks in it. The edges will start to brown lightly after several days. This is perfectly all right. One ounce of fresh yeast is equivalent to two envelopes of active dry yeast.

Since dry yeast is more expensive than fresh, if a great amount of baking is being done I would consider using fresh yeast. I have taken a 1-pound cake of compressed yeast, crumbled it up, and kept it in the freezer, well wrapped. The evening before I intend to use it, I break off a small bit and refrigerate it for use the next morning. It keeps quite well frozen. If you freeze fresh yeast, or are unsure of any yeast you use, I recommend proofing it by adding a pinch of sugar and dissolving it in a small portion of the warm liquid called for in the recipe. After 5 to 10 minutes it should begin to foam or bubble and is safe for use in the dough.

Rapid Rise Yeast. Rapid rise yeast, which supposedly acts twice as fast as regular yeast, in my opinion will give you breads that are half as good. Bread with full-bodied flavor and aroma requires dough that has been fully aged. Like good wine it should not be rushed; it requires slow, full rising, as described in the recipes. I feel that the higher temperatures called for in rapid rise yeast are too hot and adversely affect the finished product. If you do use rapid rise yeast, use it in the same way as the regular type.

Bakeries sometimes rush a dough with the addition of extra yeast; the results are never superior. Sometimes people suggest double or more amounts of yeast for quick results. Save your precious time and energy and bring home a loaf of store-bought bread. Having gone through the effort of mixing, kneading, rising, baking, and cooling, you are entitled to a quality result for your efforts. Even if you have never baked before, your very first attempt will result in a wonderful bread if you follow directions carefully.

Eggs

When added to bread dough, eggs enrich the dough, add flavor and color, and soften and expand the bread as it rises, making it more tender. In the bakery we use fresh eggs, shelled frozen eggs available as whole eggs, enriched eggs (one extra yolk to two or more whole eggs), egg whites, and sugared yolks. In a bread recipe, when one egg is used for each cup of liquid, two egg whites or a cholesterol-free egg substitute may replace one whole egg. This does not necessarily hold true when a greater proportion of eggs to liquid is called for. Do not be afraid to experiment.

Salt

When used in yeast doughs, salt retards the growth of yeast cells. This allows you to control the aging of the dough in addition to adding flavor to the bread. In most recipes a ratio of 1 to 1-1/2 teaspoons salt to each 3 cups flour is maintained. Recognizing the need to reduce the amount of sodium in the diet, I have cut back salt in most of the bread recipes to the minimum ratio of 1 teaspoon salt to 3 cups flour. Of course, you can vary these amounts to suit your own taste.

Skim Milk Powder

The addition of milk in bread doughs imparts flavor, adds color to the crust, and acts as a tenderizer. Milk is high in protein, calcium, and important vitamins. In this book, and in the bakery, skim milk powder is used. Among its many advantages are that it is easy to store and can be mixed dry. Nutritionally, it is more desirable than whole milk, since it provides all the benefits without the fat. It's also economical. There is no discernible difference in flavor between skim milk powder or whole milk in the finished bread.

Buttermilk is available as a powder. Use 4 tablespoons to 1 cup water. It can be added dry and mixed with the rest of the ingredients. See page 22 for an easy way to make your own buttermilk using skim milk powder.

Shortenings and Oils

Shortenings, fats, or vegetable oils, when used in bread dough, tenderize the bread, make it soft or flaky, add flavor (especially with butter

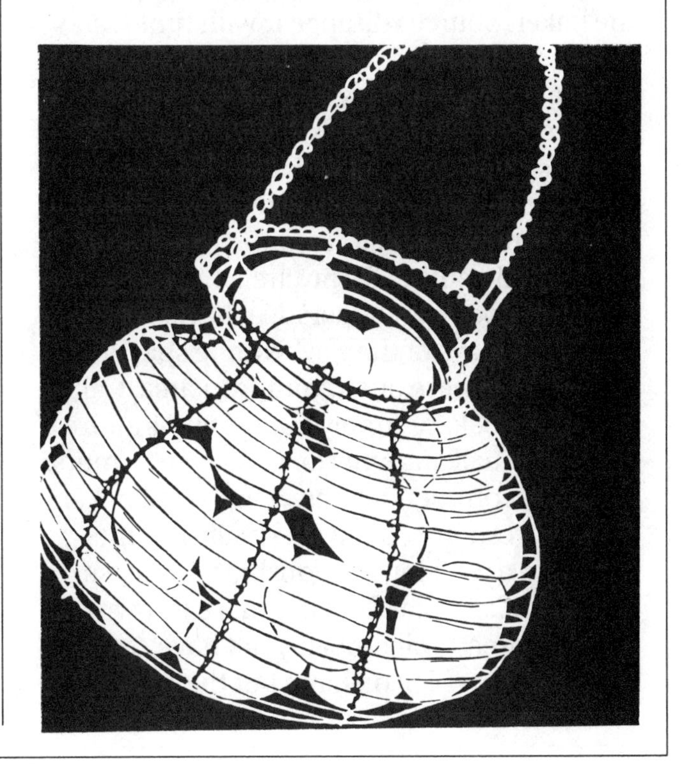

or olive oil), improve texture and bite, and add keeping qualities (due to moisture retention) to the finished bread. A hard fat or hydrogenated shortening as opposed to liquid produces a finer texture and more tolerance in the rising. As people are becoming more conscious about consuming liquid vegetable oils, for dietary considerations I have tried to substitute liquid vegetable oils for hard fats, both vegetable and animal. Often you can substitute measure for measure. Those recipes that are much better with hard fats can generally be changed to half hard, half liquid. Experiment—that is one of the bonuses of baking your own bread.

Sources

It is somewhat fruitless to try to include specific information about sources of supply for the baker. Sources disappear with time, sales policies are altered, and what is available in one part of the country is not in another. Some national flour mills merchandise their flour using different brand names in different areas. Conversely, flours with the same label coming from one mill can differ between one region and another. In my area there is a wholesale bakers' cooperative that sells retail on certain days of the week during specific hours. Seek these out in your own area. Call wholesale bakery supply houses and inquire if they sell small amounts to walk-in customers. Ask for recommendations. Many retail bakers will sell fresh ingredients in small amounts. Cultivate a working relationship with these folks. A bakery that does not make its own sour rye bread will probably not have common flour (page 8) on hand but they might be able to put you in touch with someone who does. Neighborhood food co-ops often have ingredients not found elsewhere. Natural foods stores and gourmet shops are good sources. Large markets in rural areas are sometimes as well stocked as wholesale suppliers. Some urban supermarkets carry more bakers' supplies than others. Seek them out. Markets in ethnic areas are always excellent sources. Network—ask friends who bake or those who are gourmet cooks. If you find a flour that is hard to come by, take home an extra supply, because it may not be available in warm weather, or the supplier may receive only one or two shipments per year. Ask the store manager when in doubt. Flour can be stored for months in a cool, dry area and can be refrigerated or frozen.

Correcting Misconceptions

Over the years, neighborhood bakeries have adapted many modern techniques and labor-saving devices, making many traditional steps and old ways unnecessary. This book gives you the benefit of the best of small-bakery recipes presented in the simplest and most efficient form.

Proofing Yeast

In years past we always proofed the yeast—proved that it was active— before it was added to the mix. This was accomplished by dissolving the yeast in a portion of water, with a pinch of sugar added, to see if the yeast began to bubble upon standing. With modern yeast, unless the potency is suspect, we no longer proof. This holds true for the active dry yeast packets used in the home kitchen. If the yeast is not outdated, there is no need to proof it. One must, however, activate the dry yeast by dissolving it first in warm water (105°F to 115°F). Mixing can then proceed at once. If the water feels warm to your fingertips, it will be fine for the yeast. Use a thermometer the first few times and you will quickly learn to judge the proper temperature by feel.

Another mistaken practice is to add sugar to the warm water when dissolving yeast in the normal mixing process. It was thought that the yeast had to be fed to begin activation. Warm water alone will awaken the yeast, which will feed on natural sugars in the flour. Nothing additional is required.

Scalding Milk

I am often surprised to see a modern recipe that calls for scalding whole milk in a yeast dough. When a formula specifies skim milk powder, it is used as a dry ingredient and the dough is made in the normal manner. The reason for this is very simple. There is an enzyme present in whole milk that is able to destroy the yeast cells, causing the dough to rise poorly or preventing it from rising at all. Bakers very quickly learned that by scalding the milk, the enzyme was destroyed. Thinking this through, it should become apparent that the powdered milk has been manufactured with a heat process that destroys the enzyme. All processed whole milk is pasteurized. Most whipping cream now available is ultrapasteurized, meaning sterilized. Pasteurization and sterilization are heat processes, and the enzymes in question are no longer present in our milk, so there is no reason to scald it. Unless raw whole milk is being used, you may safely ignore a requirement for scalding milk in any bread recipe you may be using.

Vinegar in Sourdough Bread

Sourdough breads are made from a sour, or starter, which is a batter of flour and water allowed to ferment under controlled conditions and used as a base for making the breads. I am appalled by recipes that call for vinegar to be incorporated into the dough to create sourdough bread or rolls. Sourdough breads and rolls made from a proper sour, or starter, have no vinegary flavor. The sourdough process adds a prefermented base to the bread dough, which results in aging the dough and developing a crumb with more moisture. It creates better texture and produces superior flavor.

Sour, fermented by wild yeast present in the air, was used as leavening to make breads rise as far back as ancient Egypt. It often produced erratic results. With the advent of modern yeast we use the sour for flavor and aging and rely on yeast for controlled leavening. Hand a baker a slice of bread and he or she will most likely smell the bread before tasting. Smell the aroma of real sour rye or sourdough wheat bread and you will instantly become expert at recognizing it.

Chapter Two

Bread Making A to Z

This chapter contains everything you need to know about bread making, from an all-but-forgotten secret about making pumpernickel bread (see Altus, page 15) to common mistakes that even the pros make and how to avoid or correct them, from mixing and rising the dough to understanding oven techniques.

Also included in this chapter are directions for the preparation of ingredients such as cereals or grains, homegrown sprouts, toasted nuts, pumpernickel color, and homemade buttermilk. Illustrations give complete directions for shaping the loaves. Important in baking professional-looking bread, proper shaping has a vital effect on the quality of the finished bread. Some of the examples shown include free-form loaves, French baguettes, and pan loaves.

Almond Paste

Almond paste has many uses in baking and pastry making. In the bakery it is often replaced by kernel paste, made from apricot pits, or macaroon paste, a mixture of almond paste and kernel paste. Almond paste is expensive; the supermarket variety is not comparable with the commercial product. Try to purchase this at a local bakery, but make sure that if you are buying kernel paste you are not paying for pure apricot paste. Make your own almond paste as follows.

1/2 pound (about 1 3/4 cups) whole blanched almonds
4 tablespoons water
1 cup sugar
2 tablespoons light corn syrup
1 teaspoon almond extract

In a food processor grind the almonds with 2 tablespoons of the water until smooth when rubbed between your fingers.

In a heavy saucepan heat the remaining 2 tablespoons water. Add the sugar and corn syrup; heat slowly until the sugar melts, then bring to a boil. Cover and boil for 3 minutes.

Remove the lid but do not stir. Heat the mixture to 240 ° F (soft ball stage). Remove the pan from the heat and add the almond extract.

With the processor running, slowly add the hot syrup to the almonds until the paste forms a ball and tries to ride up on the blade.

Refrigerate in a sealed plastic bag or tightly covered container. Allow to season for 1 week. Bring to room temperature before use.

Yield
Makes about 1 pound.

Altus

European in origin, altus is little known outside of the bakery establishment. Newcomers to the bakery think of it as a method of using up stale bread. However, as with many old-fashioned techniques, bakers find that it enhances the desirable qualities of certain breads. Its use seems to have begun in the making of pumpernickel doughs, and the best of these breads often contain altus.

Altus is a mash made by slicing and trimming the crusts from leftover sour rye bread, soaking the trimmed bread in water for several hours or overnight under refrigeration, squeezing it dry, and adding small amounts to the bread dough. Altus intensifies the distinctive flavor of pumpernickel and rye bread and helps them retain moisture. When using altus, allow for a little extra flour in the recipe. The mash keeps well, covered, in the refrigerator.

Butter Substitutes

Although butter imparts a special flavor to baked goods, in recipes for cakes or pastries commercial bakers often substitute shortening for butter, measure for measure. In delicate pastries such as croissants, shortening is often substituted for half the butter to make them flakier, or less fragile, in order to package and transport them safely. This substitution lowers cholesterol by 50 percent, enough reason for many bakers to make the change.

Oils often do not give the same results as hard fats and cannot be substituted indiscriminately. In most cases, however, when baking breads or yeast cakes, half of the fat can safely be replaced with liquid oils. In the bakery, butter flavors are often used to enhance the flavor or aroma of some baked goods. For the home baker, butter-flavored shortenings, oils, and sprays are becoming more widely available.

Cut and Stipple

When most breads are ready for the oven, the tops are either scored with a sharp knife or razor blade, or they are stippled (docked)

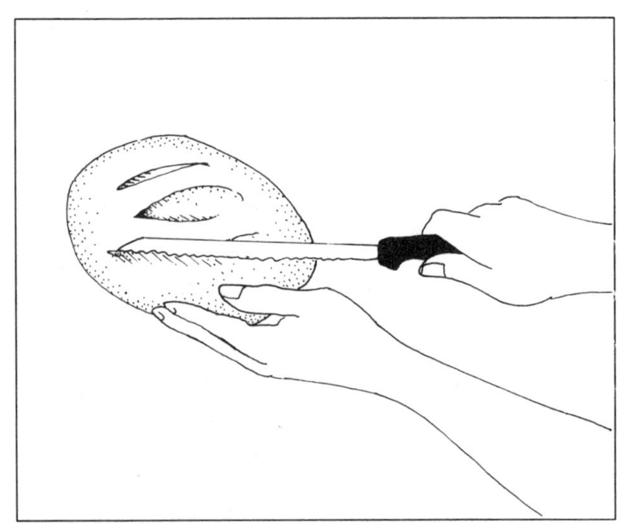

Figure 1

with a series of small holes made with a skewer or pointed blade, allowing the expanding gases in the loaf to escape without causing the crust to burst. Each recipe has a suggested method or pattern.

The fashion in which the cuts are made influences the appearance and often the flavor of the bread. In cutting French or Italian bread, the slash is not made vertically. The blade is held at an angle of not more than 20 to 30 degrees and the cut is made as if slitting under the skin of the bread (Figure 1). When the bread rises in the oven, this type of slash swells and the crust thickens along the lip. The thickening of the swollen crust is referred to as bloom, which gives the bread its traditional appearance and makes the bread crisp and chewy. French bread may have from three to ten slashes, the number determined by the length of the bread.

Other cuts or holes, while allowing the bread to expand, form a design, sometimes quite intricate. Round breads may have a tic-tac-toe pattern; others may be stippled with a series of holes. Most breads are cut in an orthodox manner, which serves to identify them. Others might be cut in an interesting signature motif of the baker. When you have a bit of experience, you should feel free to try some ideas of your own.

Occasionally, the crust will burst regardless of your best efforts. Do not despair. When we baked our European Corn Bread in the bakery, knowledgeable shoppers would seek out a bread with a split crust. This part of the bread is remarkably crunchy. It was often selected by the bakers, myself included, for their own table.

INSIDER'S JOKE. A bread that is both cut and stippled is like a man's trousers that are held up with a belt and suspenders.

Dough, Mixing and Kneading

All of the yeast-raised breads in this book can be mixed by hand. I suggest that your first efforts be done by hand, which will provide you with a basic feeling for the doughs. Choose one of two methods—a straight dough method or a sponge method. Neither is difficult.

Straight Dough Method

In a large bowl dissolve the yeast in warm water (105°F to 115°F). The exact temperature is not critical. If the water feels warm to the touch, the yeast will activate. Add the ingredients as specified in the recipe. The precise amount of flour will be determined while kneading. Stir with a wooden spoon until the dough forms up into a ball and begins to come away from the sides of the bowl. Turn out onto a lightly floured board. Scrape down the sides of the bowl and add the scrapings to the dough. Knead as described below.

Sponge Method

This method pre-ferments part of the dough, resulting in a moister and more flavorful loaf. The sponge doubles in volume in 20 to 45 minutes, depending upon room temperature, and takes the place of the first rise. Dissolve the yeast in warm water and stir in a portion of the flour until smooth. Cover and set aside until the mixture doubles in volume or appears bubbly or spongy. Stir in the balance of the ingredients and mix the dough as in the method above. When the dough is fully kneaded, allow it to rest, then shape it into loaves. The sponge process replaces the first rising (see page 26) of the bread. The amount of time from start to shaping the loaf is often less than required in the straight dough method.

Kneading

Kneading may be done on any clean, flat surface, such as a countertop, worktable, or kitchen table. It is important to work at a convenient, comfortable height—one that allows you to knead with arms extended so that you can press down from the shoulders without bending excessively. I prefer working with a hardwood board placed on the countertop. Wood makes a good work surface and is easily cleaned. A marble slab is excellent and is always cool.

After mixing as above, turn out the dough onto a lightly floured work top. The dough will be wet and sticky. Keep your hands dusted with flour. With your palms, push down from the shoulders, turn the dough a quarter turn, fold it in half, press away, turn, fold, turn, fold, press—working the dough up into a ball. Use a plastic or metal dough scraper to keep the surface of the board clean. Work the scrapings back into the dough. When the dough is no longer sticky to the touch, pick it up and stretch it to develop the elasticity. Knead once or twice and stretch again. Repeat this several times. Then lift the dough and drop it down onto the work surface, lift once more, turn

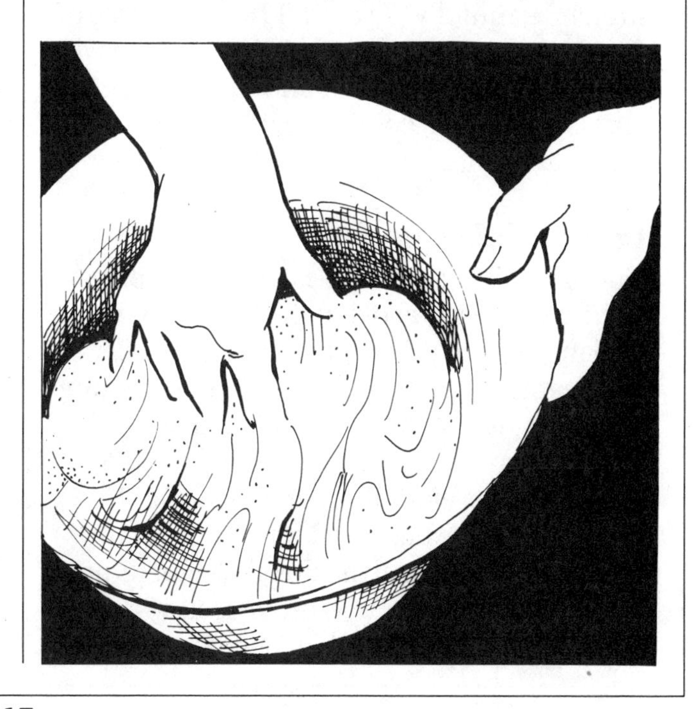

over, and drop it again. Repeat—stretching, dropping, and kneading. This serves to aerate the dough. Some folks say that this also helps work out tensions. Don't be afraid to slam it down. If the dough is still too sticky, more flour can be added 1/4 cup at a time. If the dough is stiff and unyielding, soften it with cool water added 1 teaspoon at a time. Extra time is required to incorporate the water into the dough, so be patient. Press your hand down on the dough; if it comes away clean it contains sufficient flour. Continue to turn, fold, press until the dough feels smooth and elastic (8 to 10 minutes or more). As the dough becomes fully developed, it should come to life and push back, not feel limp.

The kneading process can be a relaxing and personally satisfying endeavor. It's fun! Tear off a small piece of dough as you begin kneading. Try to stretch it and it will tear. Repeat when the dough is ready and it will stretch beautifully. If you hold a small piece of dough, fully stretched, up to the light, you will see a pattern of fine, even lines in the dough. This is the gluten, coming to life under the pressure of your hands.

Dough-Mixing Machine

A dough-mixing machine is capable of producing a better bread dough than is possible by hand or with a food processor. You will find that the recipes in this book often require more mixing time with the machine. Kneading by machine allows bakers to mix a stiffer dough and develop the gluten to its full strength. This results in a larger, better-textured loaf. To control the dough temperature in the bakery, ice water is often used so that the dough may be kneaded longer and developed further. In summer and in hot climates, do this at home by using ice water and cold ingredients. The goal is to maintain a 78°F dough temperature while mixing for 10 to 15 minutes. In the bakery it is not unusual to mix some doughs for 25 minutes.

It is important when mixing bread dough by machine to use only a heavy-duty machine with a minimum capacity of 8 cups of flour. Mixing machines do a better job of kneading when operated at their ideal capacity. Whereas recipes in most books call for the same volume of ingredients as those used for hand mixing, here you will find separate recipes for using a dough-mixing machine, producing larger yields. You will quickly find out for yourself how much better your breads are when using these methods. As a bonus you will often get three loaves for the same effort as you previously expended for only two.

In the bakery most bread doughs are mixed with a dough hook, but I have found that with most home mixers the hook is not able to stir the liquid and dry ingredients together until they are combined or are solid enough for the kneading process to begin. That's why in some recipes I specify starting to mix with the flat beater until the ingredients

ADVICE FROM A PRO. Do not walk away and leave the mixer unattended while mixing. The bowl is liable to jump off the saddle or the beater could come loose if not properly installed. When mixing a heavy dough, you sometimes have to hold the machine down with your hand to keep it from walking or jumping.

are mixed into a dough solid enough to knead with the hook. The flat beater is then removed, the dough scraped back into the bowl, and the dough hook inserted. The batch is mixed until it is fully developed. Begin noting the mixing time when the dough stops flopping around and the dough hook bites into the mass.

Kitchen Aid has a new dough hook that kneads bread doughs without having to use the flat beater. It also develops the dough more quickly and is worthwhile having.

Some of the recipes for stiff doughs may strain your mixing machine. Always begin with the smallest amount of flour called for in the recipe. Hold back 2 cups of flour. Mix until the flour is barely absorbed, then add the reserved amount in several additions. The mixer can get very warm but it is safe to continue mixing. If necessary keep the dough a little softer than called for. When in doubt refer to the manufacturer's recommendations. You can always process part of the dough separately. You also have the option of finishing kneading by hand. With experience, if you determine that the recipe is too large for your mixer, use the amounts called for in the smaller hand-mixed recipe.

BAKER'S SECRET. When the dough is fully kneaded, trickle some vegetable oil down the side of the bowl while the mixer runs at slow speed until the dough is coated and flops around the sides of the bowl. Use care, keeping your fingers away from the edge of the bowl. Coated, the dough can be turned out, or left in the bowl, covered, and allowed to rise.

Food Processor

The basic procedure for mixing bread with a food processor is as follows. Yeast is dissolved in warm water in the work bowl by pulsing. Dry ingredients, including half the flour and ice water, are added. The machine is run until a dough forms. The rest of the flour is added 1 cup at a time, pulsing until the dough is thoroughly mixed. At the speed of this machine, often the mixing time is a minute or less.

If the dough is overprocessed, in baker's terminology the dough becomes burned; that is, so much heat is built up from friction that the yeast cells and enzymes present in the dough are destroyed and the dough becomes useless. Here's how to overcome this problem.

BAKER'S SECRET. Each cup of water in the recipe is divided into 2 parts: 1/4 cup warm water and 3/4 cup ice water. Dry yeast requires warm water (105°F to 115°F) to become activated. Ice water brings down the temperature of the dough, allowing it to be processed for 2 to 3 minutes or longer.

Ordinarily, a standard 4-cup food processor has the capacity to mix one loaf of bread. Following the method used in these recipes, it is possible to produce two loaves. If the machine strains and overheats, it will stop automatically. After cooling down for several minutes, the machine can be restarted without any harm. When mixing a large batch of dough, if the machine begins to labor, stop, remove the dough, divide it in half, and process each half separately. When mixed, turn out onto a work surface and knead the two pieces together.

Glazing Bread

Cornstarch Solution

Before slashing the top of the bread and placing it in the oven, the tops may be brushed (painted) with a pastry brush dipped in a cornstarch solution made as follows: While bringing 1 cup water to a boil, dissolve 2 tablespoons cornstarch in 1/4 cup cold water; then whisk into the boiling water until it thickens. This solution may be kept for several days. For a high shine, brush a second time as soon as the bread emerges from the oven. I use the cornstarch solution for breads that should have a glaze, such as Sour Rye Bread; I use water for French- and Italian-style breads.

Egg Wash

Egg wash is applied on certain breads, rolls, and yeast cakes, such as egg-roll knots, egg twist breads, and brioche, when a dark, mahogany-hued gloss is called for. Breads that are brushed with a whole egg or egg yolk solution are baked without steam. An egg wash glaze is made by lightly beating a whole egg or yolk with 1 to 2 teaspoons water. The solution is brushed (painted) over the bread with a pastry brush. If yolks are used, the color will be deeper, but care must be taken so that the glaze does not burn. Often these types of baked goods will be brushed twice—once before the bread is proofed and a second time before it goes into the oven. The first coating is always allowed to dry before the second coating is applied.

Water

The simplest bread wash is tap water used at room temperature. This is used when a high shine is not desirable or as a substitute for the cornstarch solution, above. Water brushed on the bread before baking aids the steaming process in the oven, which enhances the development of the final color of the crust. Brushing the bread when it emerges from the oven imparts a slight sheen to the finished product. When baking several breads, you might try brushing one a second time when it comes from the oven and leaving the other one dry. Compare the difference and use the method you prefer. Some breads, such as country breads, which are dusted with flour before baking are not brushed at all.

Egg White Glaze

Some recipes call for a glaze of lightly beaten egg white with or without the addition of a small amount of water. This glaze is not used often in the bakery for oven baking. The results are somewhat similar to the cornstarch solution described above. I find that the cornstarch solution gives superior results and is economical to use. If you are curious about the difference, try them both and compare.

Greasing Pans

Pans should be greased thoroughly so that the baked goods will not stick to them when done. The pans should be clean and completely dry before greasing. You may use a brush or a rag, or even your fingers. Shortening, vegetable oils, butter, margarine, or other cooking fats may be used. Oils work well with most breads and rolls; if you encounter any sticking problems use a hardened shortening. Cake pans require a heavier greasing; hard fats are best to use. Butter is often applied to impart extra flavor to the baked goods. Antistick sprays work well; they allow you to get into hard-to-reach corners, ensure full coverage, and apply a thinner coat than possible by hand. Pans that have a nonstick coating require less grease. I do like to coat them lightly. Often a few drops of oil spread out with a paper towel or a quick spray will be sufficient. Steel and iron pans that have been properly seasoned (page 27) also require very little grease. Aluminum can be seasoned but does not hold the glaze well and generally requires a heavier greasing. In the bakery, special pan greases are available that have better releasing properties and can be used frugally. Many bakers mix their own. Here is my recipe for pan grease for use in the home kitchen. It will keep indefinitely when stored the same way as shortening.

1/4 cup vegetable shortening
1/4 cup vegetable oil (see Note)
1/4 cup unbleached all-purpose flour, or more
1/4 teaspoon lecithin (optional, see Note)

Mix the shortening, oil, and 1/4 cup flour together in a mixer or with a wire whisk. Add more flour if the mixture is runny. Lecithin gives the fats better releasing qualities and allows you to use a thinner coat. When lecithin is used, grease the pans sparingly.

Yield: Makes about 3/4 cup.

Note: If the oil separates out on standing, it can be stirred back in and a little more flour added.

Lecithin is available in a bakery in an emulsified form. Check local natural foods stores. A little lecithin goes a long way.

Measuring

Always measure carefully. All measurements should be level. Most recipes can be doubled or cut in half to change the yield. A common mistake often made by professionals is to multiply or divide mentally instead of writing out the new measurements. Invariably the baker forgets to double or divide one ingredient or will omit one entirely. I always write down the entire converted recipe, then check it against the original before beginning to mix.

Microwave Tricks

Here are several shortcuts using the microwave oven in the bread-making process.

Sour, in the Refrigerator

Several hours can be saved waiting for the first stage of sourdough bread to rise by microwaving the sour. Keep it in the refrigerator in a microwavable container. When needed, microwave on medium or on the defrost cycle for 10 to 30 seconds to bring it to room temperature (68°F to 70°F). Check the temperature after 10 seconds with a chef's instant-reading thermometer; if the temperature gets too high, the sour will die.

Proofing

Use the microwave oven as a steam box, where the loaves will rise in half the usual time. Bring 1 to 2 cups water to a boil in the microwave oven. Place the water in a corner of the oven and put in the bread. Keep the oven turned off. The hot water generates steam.

The microwave without the steam makes an effective sealed cabinet to dry-proof some yeast goods.

Defrosting

Frozen unbaked bread can be defrosted following the microwave oven manufacturer's instructions. Once the bread is defrosted, use the steaming method, above, to proof. The steaming method can also be used for the initial defrosting.

Milk

Skim Milk Powder

Dry skim milk powder is easy to store and use and can be mixed into the dough in its dry stage. For 1 cup whole milk, substitute 1/3 cup skim milk powder and 1 cup water. Buttermilk is available as a powder; use 4 tablespoons to 1 cup water.

Buttermilk

Buttermilk or sour milk tenderizes yeast breads and makes them lighter. Buttermilk is called for in many quick-bread and muffin recipes. When preparing several baked goods that require buttermilk, it is convenient to make your own buttermilk. My method is fast to do at home with little fuss. To 4 cups water at room temperature (70° to 80°F), add 1 1/3 cups dry skim milk powder and 1 cup prepared buttermilk (70° to 80°F). You will have to use store-bought buttermilk the first time. Stir until dissolved. Leave uncovered at room temperature until clabbered (12 to 18 hours), then refrigerate and use as needed. Always reserve 1 cup as the starter for the next batch. If buttermilk is not available, substitute quick sour milk, below.

Quick Sour Milk

Sour milk is also made by a clabbering process, but for our purpose quick sour milk for baking can be made by adding 1 teaspoon vinegar or lemon juice to 1 cup skim milk. Allow to stand until clabbered (about 10 minutes). This sour milk can be substituted for buttermilk in any recipe.

Nuts, Toasting

In the bakery, we have found that toasting nuts before adding them to a cake or bread significantly enhances the flavor of the finished product. Even when we grind nuts to be used in batters, we toast them before grinding. It is very simple to toast nuts in one of two ways.

A small amount can be toasted quickly on the stovetop by tossing or shaking in a dry, heavy sauté pan at medium heat until lightly browned (about 10 minutes).

Larger amounts can be spread out on a baking sheet and baked in a 350°F oven, shaking or lightly stirring once or twice, for 10 to 15 minutes. We do it this way in the bakery.

Filberts, or hazelnuts, are skinned by swirling them in a sieve after toasting, or placing them on a towel and rubbing until most of the skins fall away.

Onion Filling and Topping

Use this recipe in onion white bread, pumpernickel, rye, onion rolls, sticks, Foccacia, pizza, and wherever your imagination leads you.

Mix together:
1/2 cup yellow onions, chopped
1 green onion (white part only), chopped
1-2 teaspoons poppy seeds
1-2 teaspoons vegetable oil, try olive oil
Salt to taste, optional

Peel

A peel is a long-handled, paddle-shaped wooden instrument used mainly by bakers for inserting or removing something, such as bread or pies, from the oven hearth (see below). When you have become comfortable with your bread-baking ability, you may want to begin baking on the oven hearth and using a peel. (Bread and rolls are better when baked directly on the oven hearth. Development of the bottom crust is enhanced and the bread rises higher.)

You will need an oven stone or tiles to serve as the hearth. Dust the peel well with cornmeal or flour, place the proofed bread carefully on the end of the peel, insert the peel into the oven, and sheave (shove) the bread off the peel onto the hearth. The action is like snatching a tablecloth out from under a full set of tableware. I jiggle the bread around on the peel before inserting it into the oven to make sure that the bread is not sticking, then with the back of the peel slightly elevated, sheave the bread onto the hearth.

A good way to learn about sheaving is to use a peel for inserting your loaf pan breads into the oven. This will allow you to get a feel for sheaving without damaging your free-form breads.

When first learning how to pick up and place a proofed free-form bread onto the peel, do not let the bread rise fully. When is it too soft it will collapse while being lifted. If this happens, reshape the bread and try again. It is possible to proof some breads directly on the peel, making sure that the bottom of the loaf is not stuck to the peel before sheaving.

Proofing Bread

The final rising of the bread just before baking is called proofing. This should not be confused with the term used to describe the proofing of yeast discussed elsewhere (page 12). Full proof means the maximum growth that the loaf can attain without collapsing in the oven.

Overproofed Bread

If the bread is overproofed, all the nutrients in the dough that feed the yeast cells have been used up or not enough are left to provide for the final burst of growth that allows the bread to spring up in the oven. If this occurs, the bread will fall in the oven. It will come out flat, improperly baked, and poor or raw tasting. Sometimes the overproofed dough can be saved prior to baking if it is punched down, reshaped, and allowed to rise once more.

Underproofed Bread

Underproofed bread will burst or split in the oven. It may be misshapen, come out too small, be too heavy, or the texture will not be right. Each recipe will give you the general amount of growth necessary—for example, "the bread should come up slightly over the top of the pan," or "set aside until the loaf doubles in size." A great deal of leeway is allowed by the dough. Using a moderate amount of care will always produce a satisfactory loaf.

Determining Proof

For those who wish to have more control over the proofing process, this is how the pros determine the amount of proof. They do it by eye, touch, and experience, which is almost never discussed in books on home baking and is generally ignored. There is no great mystery involved. With experience anyone can quickly become competent at judging. Each time you bake, gently touch the side of the loaf with one finger. The fully proofed loaf will yield slightly to the delicate touch. In the beginning, gauge the proof by the amount of growth suggested in the recipe (double in size, for example). With every test observe the finished result. You will quickly gain experience and in a short time will have taught yourself. Producing a loaf of bread that has risen to the point of perfection will give you a great deal of satisfaction.

Not all breads require full proof. Occasionally a recipe will call for half proof, or some similar instruction. There will be an explanation in the recipe helping you to make this judgment. With experience, you will be able to alter the amount of proof to suit yourself.

Pumpernickel Color

Pumpernickel color, also known as caramel color or burnt sugar, is used in the bakery to give pumpernickel its dark, or sometimes black, color. You might ask your friendly local baker to sell you some pumpernickel color, or make it yourself with the recipe given below. (Or you may substitute 2 tablespoons molasses, 2 tablespoons cocoa powder, or 2 tablespoons instant coffee for color.) Pumpernickel color will keep indefinitely stored at room temperature in a covered jar or plastic container.

3 tablespoons sugar
1 tablespoon water
Pinch cream of tartar
1/4 cup boiling water

In a heavy saucepan over low heat, melt the sugar in the 1 tablespoon water. Increase the heat to medium-high, cover the pan, bring to a boil, and boil for 2 minutes. Add the cream of tartar and continue to boil, uncovered, until the sugar is almost black in color. Remove the pan from the heat. The sugar will continue to cook and darken. Allow it to begin to cool. Using extreme care, add the boiling water (the sugar will boil up and may spatter). Stir to dissolve, then let cool to room temperature.

Whenever you use pumpernickel color, wet the measuring spoon or cup with cold water for easier cleanup. Soaking the saucepan and the utensils in hot water will dissolve the caramelized sugar remaining on them.

Putting Bread By

There are many good ways of keeping and storing breads. Crusty bread can be harder to store, since the crust tends to soften when enclosed in an airtight wrap. Crusty bread will keep for several days in the bread box when placed in a paper bag or a waxed bakery-type bag. By allowing the bread to breathe, these bags help maintain some of the original crispness. In the retail bakery, breads are kept unwrapped on the display shelves so that the crusts remain crisp.

Some people prefer day-old bread. Stale bread can always be toasted. Wrap crispy bread in aluminum foil to refresh, and warm in a preheated oven or toaster oven at 325° F. Microwave ovens, when used at medium heat for a very short time, will soften or defrost bread but the crust will not crisp. Bread kept in a sealed plastic bag will stay soft longer but the crust will soften quickly. Warm, humid air increases the probability of mold forming on the bread. Bread kept wrapped and refrigerated will resist molding.

Freezing is an excellent way to store bread without compromising quality. When only several slices are needed each day, the bread can be presliced and frozen. Defrost as many slices as desired. The slices come to room temperature quickly or can be toasted while frozen. Well-wrapped loaves keep for up to 6 months in the freezer, although they taste better if used sooner.

Freezing unbaked bread allows you to prepare extra loaves at one mixing and bake fresh hot breads whenever desired. For best results, allow the frozen unbaked loaves to thaw slowly overnight in the refrigerator. Alternatively, you can defrost them at room temperature or place them in a warm enclosed space—a cabinet or a warm empty oven, for example—and allow them to thaw and rise slowly over a period of several hours. For quicker results, place the bread in a warm, moist place (see Proofing Bread, above), and defrost and proof in one operation.

Unbaked frozen bread can be defrosted in the microwave oven following instructions in the manufacturer's handbook. (See Microwave Tricks, page 21.)

Before refrigeration in the home, most cooks made bread once a week. Breads were kept longer by baking very large loaves, as much as 5 pounds in weight. These breads baked slower and retained more moisture. Years back, we sold 3-pound loaves of table rye. They were wide, stubby loaves, and very flavorful. They made he-man-sized sandwiches. If you bake large loaves—2 pounds or more—at home, they require longer baking and will be tastier than smaller breads. Try it!

Raisins, Soaking

Many people prefer the flavor and texture of plump raisins in their bread. Raisins plump up when soaked. To soak in water, measure the required amount of raisins, cover with hot water, and let soak for 15 to 20 minutes. Drain well before use. When mixing dough by machine, be careful when adding the plumped raisins to the dough. They are delicate and can be crushed easily. When in doubt, knead them in by hand after the dough has been mixed.

For a gourmet touch soak raisins overnight in enough rum or brandy to cover.

Refrigeration

Refrigerating retards the growth of yeast doughs, slowing down the rising process.

Dough and unbaked loaves can be retarded at almost any stage of the bread-making process. Rising at a slow rate, they can be kept for many hours, even overnight. The baker is free to leave or attend to other tasks.

When yeast dough is fully risen, it can be punched down and frozen or made up into loaves. The loaves are then proofed and baked or frozen before proofing for future use. Unbaked bread can also be left overnight in the refrigerator to proof slowly and may be baked the following day. Raw dough or bread should not be kept for more than a day. When frozen, after a week at home freezer temperatures, it begins to lose some strength. Although frozen dough can be kept for 3 to 6 months, many years of experience have taught me that there is some loss of flavor. Wrap well when freezing for long periods.

Any dough that has been frozen can be thawed, shaped into a loaf, and baked in the normal manner. Previously shaped loaves, rolls, croissants, and other ready-to-proof items can be made at a convenient time, frozen, then baked as desired. Slow defrosting, overnight in the refrigerator, yields the best results.

Rising

First Rise

After kneading, the bread dough is allowed to rise. Rising is caused by the action of enzymes in the yeast cells, which feed upon the sugar and starch present in the flour. In the first rise the sugar feeds the yeast cells, which give off carbon dioxide gas. The gas is trapped in cells formed by gluten in the flour and the bread dough begins to rise.

The dough is left to rise until it doubles in size. When left too long, the yeast will use up the sugar upon which it feeds and the dough will collapse. Test by pressing a finger into the risen dough. If the dough is still young (not risen enough), the indent from the fingers will begin to rise and disappear. If the indent remains, the dough is ready. If the indent shrinks and begins to collapse, the dough is old. A ready dough is preferable, although one that is a little young is acceptable. A dough that has become old may often be revived by kneading out all the air and allowing the dough to rise until it is puffed up, then shaped.

Punching Down

Punching down the dough forces out all the old gases and prepares the dough for the next rise. Press down with your hand into the center of the dough so that it collapses. Grasp both sides, bring them into the center of the dough, and press down again. Turn a quarter turn and repeat. Turn out onto a lightly floured surface and press out all the remaining air with your palms. Shape into a ball once more, cover, and let the dough rest for 5 to 10 minutes.

Second Rise (Proofing)

At this point the dough is shaped and allowed to rise before baking. During the second rise, starches in the flour are converted into food for the yeast, allowing the bread to rise once more. When the bread doubles in size (see Steam, for Proofing, page 30), it is ready for the oven. Some breads, such as country loaves, require a third rise to give the bread a large-holed texture and chewy quality.

Seasoning Pans

I always season my baking pans so that they require very little grease or oil and the breads slip out of the pans without sticking.

The method we use in the bakery is to wash and scrub the pans thoroughly, then dry and place them in a preheated oven at 425°F for 25 minutes. They are then removed from the oven and while still hot a thin coat of vegetable oil is applied with a brush or rag to the entire interior surface, carefully getting into the corners and the rim. Caution should be used to avoid getting burned. When the pan cools it is wiped dry with a paper towel.

Seasoned pans reserved for baking should merely be wiped dry with a clean, soft cloth or paper towel after each use. Avoid washing except with water and a soft brush or pad. Do not scour or use soap. Dry-scrubbing with salt works well for stuck-on crumbs. Eventually, if the bread begins to stick the pan must be reseasoned.

Pans that have lost their shine and are black from a great deal of use produce baked goods with a richer color and better crust.

Seasoning works best with steel pans. Aluminum pans are also seasoned but they have to be redone sooner. Do not season Teflon or similar coated pans.

Shaping a Loaf

Shaping a loaf is a critical step in producing a professional-looking loaf with the proper texture. Most instructions merely tell you to roll into a tube shape, or roll up like a jelly roll. This type of instruction will prevent you from achieving a perfect loaf. The dough must be molded tightly and have the appropriate shape to bake correctly. A little extra time spent in shaping the loaves will result in baking ideal breads every time.

We begin with four basic shapes, the Pan Loaf, Vienna Loaf, French/Italian Loaves, and the Round Loaf. Other shapes will be discussed as needed.

Pan Loaf

This loaf is baked in a rectangular bread pan of the type discussed on page 4. With your hands or a rolling pin, press a piece of dough into a rectangular shape (Figure 1) and fold it in thirds, right over left, two-thirds of the way (Figure 2), then left over right (Figure 3). Flatten out with your hands.

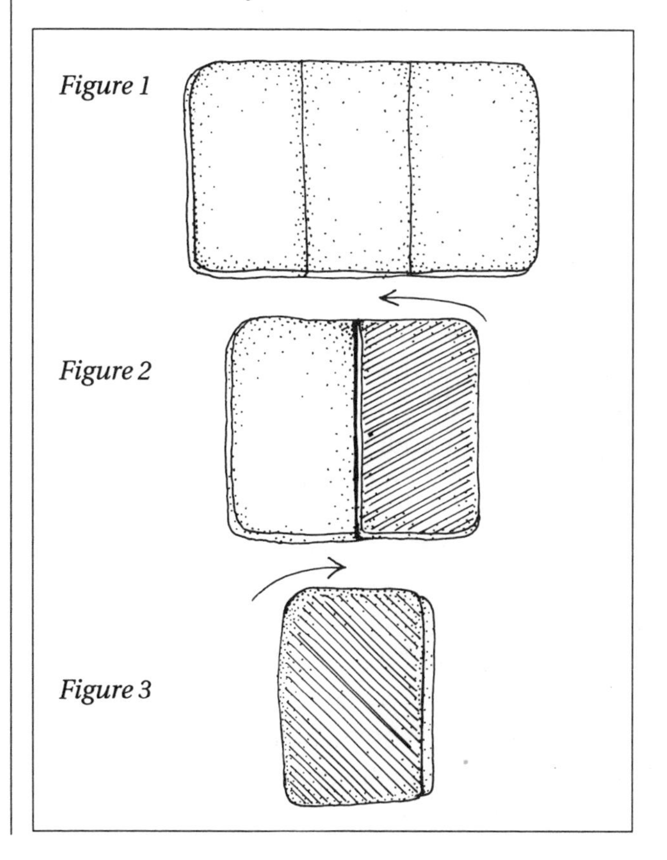

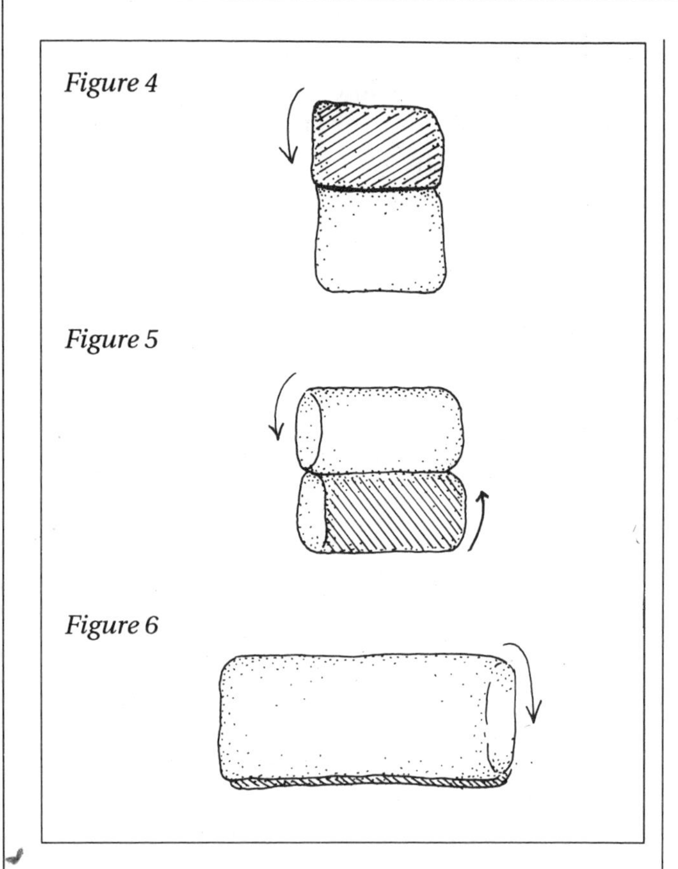

Without turning the dough, fold the top down to the center (Figure 4). With your knuckles or the heel of your palm, press a seam down into the center of the dough. Turn the bottom half up to the center and seal the edge with your knuckles or the heel of your palm (Figure 5). Now roll and fold the top half over the bottom and seal the seam again. Squeeze and roll back and forth (Figure 6) to elongate. If necessary lengthen the loaf further with a back-and-forth motion, working from the center of the loaf to the ends. Roll the seam around so that it is centered on the bottom. The loaf should be tight and extend the length of the baking pan. Keep the seam down when the bread is placed in the pan so that it cannot crack open while baking.

The pan loaf may also be baked as a free-form loaf either on an oven stone or tile hearth or a baking sheet. In the bakery we use this shape for sandwich rye or pumpernickel bread.

Vienna Loaf

The Vienna shape is a free-form loaf baked on the hearth or on a baking sheet; it is wide in the center and narrows to a point on both ends. It can be molded as a pan loaf (see above), then, with one hand on either end, the tips are rolled down with the palms in a back-and-forth motion until a pointed end is achieved. Years ago rye bread was molded in this fashion, and the ends made wonderful eating. We currently bake rye loaves with a blunt end to give more uniform slices and to get more sandwich slices from the loaf. The Vienna loaf can also be made jelly roll fashion as in French/Italian Loaves, below.

French/Italian Loaves, Baguettes

The shorter French and Italian shapes can be made up as pan loaves (see above) and then elongated with a rolling, pressing motion of the palms beginning in the center of the loaf and working out toward the ends. The ends can be left blunt or pointed.

A second version, necessary for longer loaves, is made in jelly roll fashion. The dough is pressed out or rolled with a pin into a long rectangular shape. Starting from the top, a short roll or lip is formed along the entire length, then it is pressed down with the fingertips. Rolling or folding, and pressing down a seam with each roll, is continued. As the roll gets bigger the knuckles or heel of the hand are used. Rolling is continued, with the last turn sealed firmly. The loaf may be elongated with a rolling, stretching, back-and-forth motion, working from the center to the ends. The seam, or closure, should be centered at the bottom of the formed loaf when done.

If you begin by pressing or rolling the dough out into a circular shape instead of a rectangle, then proceeding in jelly roll fashion, you can create the classic Vienna bread shape (wide, high center and low, pointed ends) or a longer Italian bread version.

Round Loaf

The loaf is shaped into a smooth, tight ball.

Sprouts, Wheat Berry

It's easy to sprout seeds or beans in your own kitchen. Wheat berries can be purchased in natural foods stores and some markets. Don't buy the variety found in garden or pet supply stores. These are chemically treated and are not fit for human consumption. The same berries that you sprout can be used for Cracked Wheat Bread (page 91) or cooked up into a hearty hot breakfast cereal.

For every cup of sprouts you will need 1/4 cup wheat berries, a clean mason jar, and some cheesecloth or a clean nylon stocking, or a commercially available sprouting jar. Place the wheat berries in the jar with water to cover and soak overnight covered with the cheesecloth secured with a rubber band. In the morning spill out the water through the cloth and allow the jar to drain well. Place the jar on its side in a dark, warm cupboard or closet. In the evening pour in tepid water to cover, swish around, and drain. Reserve the drained water for use in any bread recipe.

The next day change the water twice, morning and evening, saving the drained water if desired. Drain well each time. When the sprouts burst forth in 1 to 2 days, you may begin to make your bread. Some bakers prefer to allow the sprouts to grow until they are the length of the berry, which takes about a day and provides additional nutrients. Either way works well in bread making. If you spread out the ready sprouts on a dish or tray and leave them in the sunlight for 20 minutes or so, they will manufacture their own chlorophyll and begin to turn green, adding to the nutrient value of the sprouts.

Stales

What does the baker do with leftover bread in the bakery? The successful baker converts or recycles stales into fresh products. Here are a few ways to recycle stale bread in the home kitchen.

Bread Crumbs

Dry bread may be grated in a hand or an electric grinder, food processor, or blender. If you use a blender, prepare small amounts at a time. Add your favorite herbs while processing.

Bread Pudding

Use a favorite recipe.

Bruschetta

These are thick slices of Italian or French country bread, toasted, rubbed with garlic and olive oil, and doused with thick tomato sauce. Use them as an appetizer or a snack.

Croutons
Trim the crusts from sliced bread and dice the bread. Place on a baking sheet and brown in a 375° F oven, or lightly fry until golden brown in color. For a variation, sauté garlic in oil, discard the garlic, and sauté the croutons in the garlicky oil. Alternatively, soak the croutons in oil and vinegar and toss with a salad.

Fines Herbes
I sprinkle a mixture of 1 tablespoon each dried chives, tarragon, parsley, and chervil on garlic bread (see below) and top with grated Parmesan or Romano cheese.

French Toast
Make French toast with thick slices of Challah (see page 73). This is a delicious Sunday brunch.

Garlic Bread
Split a long loaf of French or Italian bread most of the way through, then spread with a mixture of half and half melted butter and oil. Sprinkle with sautéed minced garlic. (Granulated or powdered garlic may substituted.) Wrap in aluminum foil and freeze, or bake immediately at 350°F for 15 to 20 minutes. The wrapped bread can also be grilled on the barbecue. Try toasting the cut side on the grill before buttering. Make several pieces per person.

Rusk
Place thin slices of hard bread on a baking sheet and bake at 250°F until lightly browned. Before baking, the rusks can be flavored by sprinkling with herbs or spices. Try drizzling them with olive oil, then sprinkling with dried rosemary before baking.

Stuffing
Tear or cube day-old bread or rolls. The pieces can be bagged and frozen for future use.

Thickening
Use stale bread to thicken soups.

Toasts
Bread that is a day or two old can be toasted and served hot. Split long French-style loaves and toast them in the oven, broiler, or toaster oven. I like to scoop out most of the soft center with a spoon before toasting. Smooth on butter, or any spread, or sprinkle with olive oil and stuff with your favorite sandwich filling. Rye toast is always a special treat.

Steam, for Proofing
Proofing is the final rise. When the shaped loaf is ready to be proofed, there are many ways to induce it to rise. The usual method is to place the loaves in a warm spot, free from drafts; but there are many alternatives, both in the home kitchen and in the bakery. An understanding of how bread is proofed commercially will help you to find your own method at home.

The oldest and best method was very simple. The bread or rolls were placed in wooden boxes approximately 30 by 30 inches and 3 to 4 inches high. The boxes were dusted with flour and the bread or rolls were spaced carefully so as not to touch one another as they grew. A second box was placed on top of the first and the process was repeated, filling the boxes and stacking them higher and higher. The warm air and moisture in the bakery was perfect for allowing the loaves to rise slowly.

Simple control over the rising time was accomplished by crisscrossing the boxes, allowing the corners of the boxes to stay open and thus slowing down the rising time. This was necessary if the bakers were backed up at the ovens, or if they were attending to other tasks.

Since no additional heat or moisture was supplied, the bread rose naturally. Bakers describe this method as "giving natural proof." Although this method takes longer than using a steam box with a burner (see below), it still produces the best results to this day.

An "improvement" to this method was the use of a special cabinet called a steam box or proofing cabinet. The cabinet was wide enough to accommodate the wooden boxes on rack-type shelves. The boxes were stacked one above the other, with several inches of space in between each shelf. At the bottom of the cabinet was a small burner and a trough or container that was filled with water, which was allowed to boil. Heat and steam circulated around the boxes, causing the breads to rise rapidly, thereby reducing the rising time dramatically. There was a penalty exacted, however, in that the breads or rolls never rose quite as much as with the natural method.

Through the years these proofing cabinets evolved until today we have cabinets that accommodate multiple rolling racks, with the baked goods on pallets or baking pans. The racks are rolled into the steam cabinets, which have sophisticated temperature and humidity controls that allow quicker rising times and are adjustable to the best conditions for the type of dough being proofed.

Fortunately, we can do as well or better in the home by using the natural proof method. The bread is placed in a warm, draft-free spot, covered with a damp or flour-rubbed cloth or towel, and allowed to rise slowly. Alternately, the bread can be placed in a closed kitchen cabinet or a home-built wooden box. I have proofed bread in an empty oven that was heated for a few minutes and then turned off.

I often allow my doughs or pan breads to rise in a microwave oven that is not turned on (page 22).

Often while baking one bread dough in the oven, I proof the next dough on top of the warm range, covering the bread with a damp cloth. Be careful not to allow a skin to develop on the bread, since this will keep it from rising. I have a friend who tells me that she proofs her bread in the dishwasher after putting it on the heat cycle for a few minutes.

Another simple method for proofing bread is to place the loaves on a wire rack over a pan filled with boiling water. The breads can be covered with a cloth or cardboard box. As you can see, the possibilities are as great as the baker's ingenuity.

Steam, in Baking

Steam introduced into the oven during the baking process is the key to developing a proper crust on bread. Essential during the first part of the baking process, steam allows for better rising in the oven and slows crust development. The crust is kept moist so that it does not split while it rises in the oven. Steam is also necessary for giving the bread its sheen.

In the bakery, steam is produced in a boiler and injected into the oven while the bread is baking. After the crust develops, the steam is shut off so that the sugars in the crust can crystallize, producing color and flavor.

In the home kitchen, the generally accepted method of introducing steam into the oven is to place a pan of boiling water in the bottom of the oven before putting in the bread. Other methods include spraying water on the bread several times during the baking process with an ordinary household spray bottle. These methods really do not give the burst of steam necessary to do a professional job, so I suggest the following method for use at home. Though still a compromise, this method results in a crustier, more professional-looking bread.

Place an empty roasting pan or other heavy pan on the floor of the oven 5 to 10 minutes before baking, so it gets hot. Before slashing the breads prior to putting them in the oven, brush the tops with water or a cornstarch solution (page 20). I prefer the cornstarch method for breads that should have a shiny crust, such as Sour Rye Bread, and the water method for French and Italian-style breads. (Breads that are brushed with a whole egg or egg yolk solution are baked without steam.)

When ready to bake, place the bread in the oven and carefully toss six to eight ice cubes into the hot pan, or pour in 1 cup boiling water and immediately close the oven door.

CAUTION: When using boiling water, wear a glove and keep your face away from the open oven door, since there will be a burst of live steam when the boiling water hits the hot pan. Do not open the door to peek or the steam will escape.

When you remove the bread from the oven, place it on a rack to cool, then brush the top with water or cornstarch solution once more. The results will astonish you: Your bread will look as professional as any that comes from a fine bakery.

What Went Wrong?

Bread Has No Flavor (Tastes Flat) or Dough Rises Too Fast

No salt. Forgetting to add salt is the most common error in bread baking. A good habit to get into is to measure the salt first and place it in a small container or on a square of waxed paper next to the work bowl. If left out, you will see it, avoiding any doubt. Salt retards the action of the yeast and, if left out, the dough will rise much faster than normal. Salt that was left out may be added later by dissolving in a little water and kneading thoroughly.

•

Dough Does Not Rise or Rise Properly

No yeast. You will note that most of the recipes in this book call for yeast and water to be the first ingredients used in mixing. This is done to ensure that the yeast is not forgotten. If it is not the first ingredient, sprinkle the dry yeast over a small amount of warm water (1/4 to 1/2 cup) and place it next to the work bowl so that it will be visible if left out. Deduct the amount of water used from the total liquid in the recipe. If forgotten, the yeast can be added to the dough by thorough kneading. Sometimes the yeast is added in the dry stage. Leave the packet next to the machine or even on the top of it so that it will be seen if forgotten.

Dough is too soft. Not enough flour was added to the mix. If the dough is too soft, it will not have enough body to rise properly or hold whatever shape you mold it into. Add flour in small amounts and knead it thoroughly into the dough. If the bread has already risen it can often be saved by squeezing or punching it down, adding flour small amounts at a time and kneading until well absorbed. The dough should rise again and bake quite well.

Dough is too stiff. When too stiff, the dough has no elasticity. It will remain a solid heavy lump, unwilling to rise or allow itself to be shaped. Add water a teaspoonful at a time and work it thoroughly into the dough.

Dough was improperly kneaded. Bread must be well worked out to develop the dough. Yeast is a living single-cell plant. It reproduces and multiplies, giving off carbon dioxide gas, which is trapped in the dough. Gluten, a wheat protein, is very malleable and continually stretches and forms thousands of little cells that entrap the gas and expand. This is how the dough rises. Kneading converts the gluten into the elastic material. You must work the dough long enough to make all of the gluten resilient. Stretching while kneading activates the gluten. Slamming the dough down on the work surface aerates the dough, making more pockets that will expand.

Yeast was not activated, or was stale or outdated. If the yeast wasn't omitted but was activated properly, and the bread rose improperly, look to the yeast itself as the source of the problem. Yeast cells can be killed by improper storage or age. If the yeast is suspect, proof it first. (See Proofing Yeast, page 12.)

•

Baked Bread Sags

The finished bread is soggy, or shows a wet, fallen section when cut.

Bread was overproofed. The loaf has been allowed to grow too much in the last rise before baking and collapses in the oven.

Gluten is undeveloped. The dough has not been kneaded long enough to develop the gluten in the flour. As a result the bread does not rise properly and falls while in the oven.

•

Bread Is Gummy or Wet When Baked

Bread is underbaked. The oven thermostat is inaccurate. Always use a good oven thermometer to ensure proper temperature. At high altitudes increase the oven temperature by 2° F for every thousand feet above sea level. To test if the bread is fully baked, tap the bottom of the loaf with your fingertips and lightly squeeze the sides. The finished loaf should emit a hollow thump and the sides should be firm. If the crust is too dark and the loaf is underbaked, use a lower oven temperature.

•

Bottom of Bread Is Burnt

Oven shelf is too low. If the bottom is burnt the oven shelf may be too low. Move it up higher.

Top of Bread Is Burnt

Oven shelf is too high. If the top is burnt or overbaked and the bottom is soft, try moving the oven shelf lower. Some breads (often those that are brushed with egg wash) tend to burn on top before the bottom is baked. When these breads first begin to brown, they can be covered with a tent made of parchment paper or a brown paper bag that has been cut open. The paper can be removed shortly before the loaves are finished baking if the tops need additional browning.

•

Crust Has Burst

Bread was underproofed. The bread was not given enough time to rise.

Top was not slashed. The loaf was not slashed or stippled on top. The crust bursts because the gases formed by the yeast cannot escape.

Seam was not sealed. The seam, or closure, when the loaf is shaped was not sealed well or was not properly positioned for the final rise, and it breaks open.

•

Crust Has Uneven Color

Oven bakes unevenly. The oven may have hot spots. Move the loaves once or twice during the baking process. You may have to turn the loaves front to back to ensure even baking. If only one loaf is being baked, center it on the shelf.

Crust Separates from Loaf

Skin allowed to form. Before baking, a skin formed on the unbaked bread. Keep the dough in a draft-free area and covered with a cloth so that the crust does not dry out.

Oven temperature too low. Check with an accurate oven thermometer or bake at a higher temperature.

•

Bread Has Too Many Holes

Dough was overmixed. The dough temperature was allowed to go too high. The ingredients were too hot or were overmixed in the processor or electric mixer. (In country-style breads, large holes are desirable and give the bread a coarse grain and chewy quality. Some recipes call for an extra rise to create this chewy quality.)

Bread was overproofed. Adjust rising time.

•

None of the Above

Sometimes whatever went wrong is not immediately obvious. The baker must put on a detective's hat. Most often the culprit turns out to be a careless baker. Measure carefully. Double-check that no ingredients have been omitted.

Chapter Three

Basic Yeast Bread

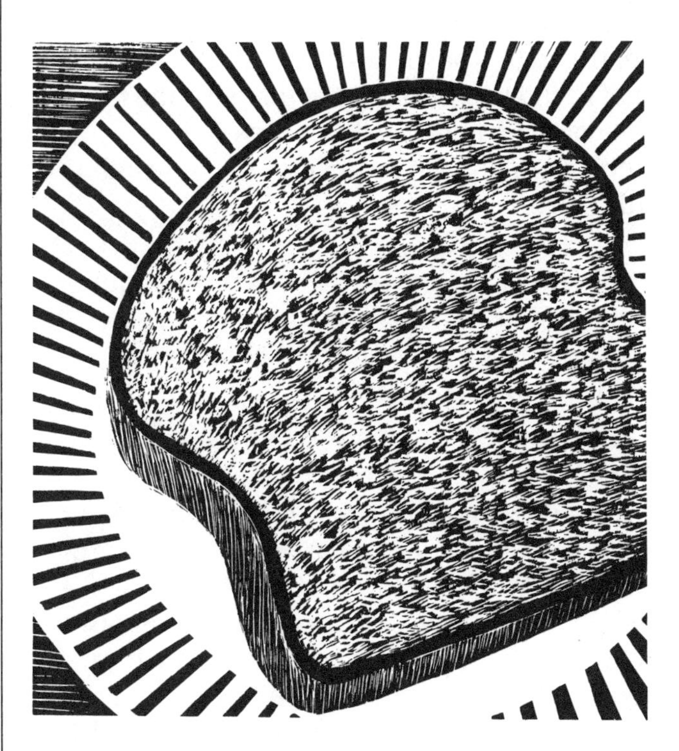

To give you a basic understanding of how bread is mixed, two methods of mixing are presented in this chapter using a recipe for Milk Bread, an easy basic yeast bread. Choose either the straight dough method or the sponge method to make this bread that you will enjoy often.

In the straight dough method, all the ingredients are combined in one step, the resulting dough is allowed to rise, and then it is shaped into a loaf and given a final rise before baking.

In the sponge method, a quick sponge that takes the place of the first rise is made from flour, yeast, and water. The bread, including the sponge, is then mixed, shaped, and given a final rise before baking.

Many bakers feel that the sponge method is a little quicker and produces a softer and better-keeping loaf. Try both methods. Decide which you prefer, while at the same time learning all you need to know about basic bread baking.

Note that for each method, recipes are given for making the bread by hand, in a food processor, or in a dough-mixing machine. For definitions of specific terms used in the recipes, consult the glossary (page 357) or Bread Making A to Z starting on page 14.

Milk Bread, Straight Dough Method

The old-time bakers with whom I once worked called this bread *milk bread* although it is actually white bread. In my opinion commercially available white bread, which is truly the staff of life and the most widely used bread that we produce, has lost that wonderful quality and flavor of years gone by. What makes white bread wonderful? The crust should be thick, rich in color, and have either a good bite or crunch to it. The bread should have a tight texture, toast evenly, slice cleanly, hold jam from oozing, and tolerate being spread with butter. Next is aroma: Hand a slice of bread to a baker and the first thing that he or she will do is take a deep whiff. The aroma of bread to a baker is like the perfume of a flower to a lady. Last of course is flavor. The bread should chew well, not taste spongy or cardboardlike, and should be bursting with rich flavor. So with respect for the old-time bakers with whom I worked, I use their name Milk Bread.

2 cups warm water
2 packages active dry yeast
4 teaspoons sugar
2 tablespoons unsalted butter or shortening, at room temperature (use cold in summer)
2/3 cup skim milk powder
5 to 6 cups unbleached all-purpose flour
2 teaspoons salt
Flour, for dusting work top
Vegetable oil, for coating bowl
Shortening, for greasing pans
Water or melted butter, for brushing loaves

In a large bowl sprinkle the yeast over the warm water to soften; stir to dissolve. Add the sugar, butter, milk powder, 5 cups flour, and salt; mix until the dough comes away from the sides of the bowl.

Turn out the dough onto a flour-dusted work top. Knead, adding more flour 1/4 cup at a time if necessary, until the dough feels smooth and silky (8 to 10 minutes).

Transfer the dough to a clean, oil-coated bowl and turn the dough top to bottom to coat. Cover and set aside until doubled in volume (40 to 60 minutes).

Shaping

Punch down the dough and cut in half. Shape each half into a ball, cover, and let rest for 15 minutes. Shape into 2 pan loaves (pages 27-28). Place the loaves, seam down, in 2 greased 8- or 9-inch loaf pans. Keep in a warm, draft-free area and allow to rise until the loaves form nicely rounded tops and rise above the tops of the pans.

Place the pans on a baking sheet. Slash lengthwise down the center of each loaf with a sharp knife or razor. Brush the tops with water or melted butter.

Baking

Bake with steam (pages 31-32) in a preheated 375°F oven until the bread has browned and the bottom emits a hollow sound when tapped lightly with your fingertips (35 to 45 minutes). The loaves can be removed from the loaf pans for the last 5 minutes of baking for crustier bread. Let cool on a wire rack.

Yield

Makes 2 loaves.

Milk Bread, Straight Dough

(Food Processor, Steel Blade)

In the recipe above, instead of 2 cups warm water use:

1/2 cup warm water
1 1/2 cups ice water

In the work bowl sprinkle the yeast over the warm water to soften; stir to dissolve. Add the ice water, sugar, butter, milk powder, 2 cups flour, and salt; mix until smooth. Add 3 cups flour, 1 cup at a time. Pulse until the dough comes together and tries to form up on top of the blade. More flour may be added 1/4 cup at a time if the dough is too soft. If necessary divide the dough in two and process each half separately, then knead together. Process for about 2 to 3 minutes. Do not allow the dough to overheat. Extra kneading by hand is sometimes necessary to make the dough elastic.

Turn out the dough and place in a clean, oil-coated bowl. Turn the dough top to bottom to coat. Cover and set aside until doubled in volume (40 to 60 minutes).

Proceed as in Shaping and Baking above.

Milk Bread, Straight Dough

(Dough-Mixing Machine, Flat Beater)

---

3 cups warm water
3 packages active dry yeast
2 tablespoons sugar
3 tablespoons unsalted butter or shortening
7 1/2 to 9 cups unbleached all-purpose flour
1 cup skim milk powder
1 tablespoon salt
Flour, for dusting worktop
Vegetable oil, for coating bowl
Shortening, for greasing pans
Water or melted butter, for brushing loaves

In the mixing bowl sprinkle the yeast over the warm water to soften; stir to dissolve. Add the sugar, butter, 7 1/2 cups flour, milk powder, and salt. Pulse with the on/off switch, so that the flour is not thrown out of the bowl, until all the flour is absorbed, then mix until the dough comes away from the sides of the bowl. More flour may be added 1/4 cup at a time if the dough is too soft.

Remove and scrape down the beater and insert the dough hook. Run at the first speed until the dough forms up on the hook and comes away from the sides of the bowl (8 to 10 minutes). You may use the second speed for the last few minutes to develop the gluten.

Remove the hook, add oil to the bowl, and turn the dough top to bottom to coat. Cover and allow to rise until doubled in volume (45 to 60 minutes). Proceed as in Shaping and Baking, above, except shape into 3 loaves.

Yield

Makes 3 loaves.

Milk Bread, Sponge Method

Sponge

2 cups warm water
2 packages active dry yeast
3 cups unbleached all-purpose flour

Dough

4 teaspoons sugar
2 tablespoons unsalted butter or shortening
2/3 cup skim milk powder
2 to 3 cups unbleached all-purpose flour
2 teaspoons salt
Flour, for dusting work top
Vegetable oil, for coating bowl
Shortening, for greasing pans
Water or melted butter, for brushing loaves

Sponge

In a large bowl sprinkle the yeast over the warm water; stir to dissolve. Add the flour and stir until smooth. Cover and set aside in a warm place until doubled in volume (30 to 45 minutes).

Dough

Stir down the Sponge. Add the sugar, butter, milk powder, 2 cups flour, and salt. Stir until the dough comes away from the sides of the bowl, adding more flour 1/4 cup at a time if necessary.

Turn out the dough onto a lightly floured work top. Knead with a turn, fold, push motion, adding more flour in small amounts if the dough is sticky. Knead until the dough is smooth, elastic and springy (8 to 10 minutes). Allow to rest, covered, for 10 minutes.

Shaping

Shape each piece into a pan loaf (pages 27-28) and place in 2 greased 8- or 9-inch loaf pans, seam down. Place in a warm, draft-free area to rise until the loaves come up above the rim of the pans. Brush the tops with water or melted butter and slash lengthwise down the center of each loaf with a sharp blade.

Baking

Bake with steam (page 31) on the middle shelf of a preheated 375°F oven until the bread has a rich color and the bottom emits a hollow sound when tapped lightly with your fingertips (approximately 35 to 45 minutes). For the last 5 to 10 minutes the bread can be removed from the pans for a crustier loaf. Brush again with water or melted butter and let cool on a wire rack.

Yield

Makes 2 loaves.

Milk Bread, Sponge Method

(Food Processor, Steel Blade)

Instead of 2 cups warm water use:

1/2 cup warm water
1 1/2 cups ice water

Sponge

In the work bowl sprinkle the yeast over the warm water; pulse to dissolve. Add the ice water and flour and process until smooth. Keep covered in place until doubled in volume (30 to 45 minutes).

Dough

Pulse once or twice to punch down the Sponge. Add the sugar, butter, milk powder, 2 cups flour (1 cup at a time), and salt. Pulse until the dough comes away from the sides of the bowl and tries to ride up on top of the blade. Add more flour if necessary 1/4 cup at a time. Process until all the flour is absorbed (1 to 2 minutes). If necessary, divide the dough in half and mix each half separately, then knead together. Do not overmix or the dough will get too hot. It may be necessary to knead by hand for a few minutes to make the dough more elastic.

Turn out the dough onto a lightly floured work top and cut it into 2 equal pieces. Shape each half into a ball. Allow to rest, covered, for 10 minutes.

Proceed as in Shaping and Baking, above.

Milk Bread, Sponge Method

(Dough-Mixing Machine, Flat Beater)

Sponge

3 cups warm water
3 packages active dry yeast
4 1/2 cups unbleached all-purpose flour

Dough

2 tablespoons sugar
3 tablespoons unsalted butter or shortening
1 cup skim milk powder
3 to 4 1/2 cups unbleached all-purpose flour
1 tablespoon salt
Flour, for dusting work top
Vegetable oil, for coating bowl
Shortening, for greasing pans
Water or melted butter, for brushing loaves

Sponge

In the mixing bowl dissolve the yeast in the warm water. Add the flour and mix at the first speed until smooth. Cover in place and let rise until doubled in volume (30 to 45 minutes).

Dough

Stir down the Sponge with one or two rotations of the beater, then add the sugar, butter, milk powder, 3 cups flour, and salt. Pulse at the first speed using the on/off switch so that the beater does not throw the flour out of the bowl. When the flour is absorbed run the machine at the first speed until the dough comes away from the sides of the bowl. If the dough is too soft, add more flour 1/4 cup at a time.

Remove and scrape down the beater and insert the dough hook. Run at the first speed until the dough forms up on the hook and comes away from the sides of the bowl (8 to 10 minutes). You may use the second speed for the last few minutes to strengthen the gluten.

Turn out the dough onto a floured surface, cut into thirds, shape into rounds, and cover. Allow the dough to rest 10 minutes. Proceed as in Shaping and Baking, above, except use 3 greased loaf pans.

Yield

Makes 3 loaves.

Chapter Four

Corn and Potatoes: Seeds of the Americas

Corn (maize) and potatoes are two of the most economically important plant crops to modern civilization and are cultivated by more nations than wheat or rice. Both corn and potatoes are native to the Americas. There is no part of North or South America that does not have its regional corn and potato breads. When Columbus returned to Europe from his first voyage of discovery in 1492, he brought examples of corn and potatoes with him.

The contemporary cuisines of the South and the West emphasize corn and potatoes, not only in the dishes that have evolved there but also in adaptations of the breads of native Americans both north and south of the border.

Anadama Bread

There are many versions of anadama bread using either white or whole grain flours. I like this recipe with half white, half whole wheat flour. The addition of cornmeal and molasses underscores the bread's Yankee character.

1 1/4 cups warm water
1 package active dry yeast
2 tablespoons unsalted butter or margarine
1/4 cup molasses
1/2 cup yellow cornmeal
2 cups whole wheat flour, preferably stone ground
1 to 2 cups unbleached all-purpose flour
1 1/2 teaspoons salt
Flour, for dusting work top
Vegetable oil, for coating bowl
Shortening, for greasing pans
Water, for brushing loaves

Dough

In a large bowl sprinkle the yeast over the warm water; stir to dissolve. Add the butter, molasses, cornmeal, whole wheat flour, 1 cup all-purpose flour, and salt. Stir until the dough comes away from the sides of the bowl, adding more all-purpose flour if necessary.

Turn out the dough onto a lightly floured work top. Knead with a turn, fold, push motion, adding more all-purpose flour in small amounts if the dough is sticky. Knead until the dough is smooth and elastic (8 to 10 minutes).

Rising

Transfer the dough to a clean, oil-coated bowl and turn the dough top to bottom to coat. Cover and set aside until doubled in volume (40-60 minutes).

Shaping

Punch down the dough, cut it in half, and shape into rounds. Cover and allow to rest for 10 minutes. Shape into 2 pan loaves (pages 27-28). Place into 2 greased 8- or 9-inch loaf pans and proof until the loaves rise up over the tops of the pans. Brush with water, then slash once down the length of each loaf.

Baking

Bake with steam (pages 31-32) on the middle shelf of a preheated 375°F oven until the loaves are browned and the bottom emits a hollow sound when tapped lightly with your fingertips (35 to 45 minutes). For the last 5 to 10 minutes the loaves can be removed from the pans for a crustier bread. Brush with water and let cool on a wire rack.

Yield

Makes 2 loaves.

Anadama Bread

(Food Processor, Steel Blade)

Instead of 1 1/4 cups warm water use:

1/4 cup warm water
1 cup ice water

In the work bowl sprinkle the yeast over the warm water; stir to dissolve. Add the ice water, butter, molasses, cornmeal, and whole wheat flour. Pulse until all the flour is absorbed. Add 1 cup all-purpose flour and pulse until the dough comes away from the sides of the bowl, adding more all-purpose flour 1/4 cup at a time if necessary. Process or pulse for 2 to 3 minutes. Do not overmix. If the machine strains, stop, remove the dough, and process in two halves, then knead together. Or turn out the dough onto a lightly floured work top and knead lightly by hand for several minutes. Shape into a ball.

Transfer the dough to an oiled bowl and turn to coat. Cover and allow to rise until doubled in volume. Proceed as in Shaping, and Baking, above.

Anadama Bread

(Dough-Mixing Machine, Flat Beater)

1 3/4 cups plus 2 tablespoons warm water
1 1/2 packages active dry yeast (1 package plus scant 1 1/2 teaspoons)
3 tablespoons unsalted butter or margarine
6 tablespoons molasses
3/4 cup yellow cornmeal
3 cups whole wheat flour, preferably stone ground
1 1/2 to 3 cups unbleached all-purpose flour
2 1/4 teaspoons salt
Flour, for dusting worktop
Vegetable oil, for coating bowl
Shortening, for greasing pans
Water or melted butter, for brushing loaves

In the mixing bowl sprinkle the yeast over the warm water; stir to dissolve. Add the butter, molasses, cornmeal, whole wheat flour, 2 cups all-purpose flour, and salt. Pulse by switching quickly on and off so that the flour is absorbed without having it thrown out of the bowl. Continue mixing at the first speed until the dough comes away from the sides of the bowl, adding more all-purpose flour if necessary.

Scrape down the beater and insert the dough hook. Mix at the first speed until the flour is completely absorbed (8 to 10 minutes). More all-purpose flour can be added in small amounts as necessary. The dough should be smooth and elastic. You can use the second speed for the last few minutes to strengthen the gluten. If the motor becomes excessively strained, use the first speed.

Remove the dough hook. Oil the bowl and turn the dough to coat, then cover and allow to rise until doubled in volume. Proceed as in Shaping and Baking, above, except shape into 3 loaves.

Yield

Makes 3 loaves.

Cornmeal Bread

Cornmeal Bread is the perfect accompaniment to barbecue or beans and anything Southern or Southwestern in origin. It is less sweet than muffins or corn sticks and toasts beautifully. For a soul-satisfying breakfast, try two thick slices of Cornmeal Bread lightly toasted and served with butter and maple syrup, pancake style. Fresh bananas or blueberries in season make a perfect side dish.

1 cup water
1 egg, beaten
1/3 cup skim milk powder
1/4 cup sugar
1/2 cup yellow cornmeal (preferably stoneground)
1 1/2 cups unbleached all-purpose flour
1 teaspoon salt
5 teaspoons baking powder
2 tablespoons shortening
Shortening, for greasing pans

In a small bowl combine the water, egg, and milk powder; set aside. In a large bowl combine the sugar, cornmeal, flour, salt, and baking powder. Cut or rub in the shortening until the mixture resembles coarse meal.

Add the egg mixture to the flour mixture and stir with a wooden spoon or rotary beater until incorporated. Drop out into a greased 8- or 9-inch loaf pan.

Baking

Bake on the middle shelf of a preheated 425°F oven for approximately 25 minutes. A toothpick or straw inserted in the center should come out clean and the top should spring back when lightly pressed with your fingertips.

Yield

Makes 1 loaf.

Cornmeal Bread

(Food Processor, Steel Blade)

Add all the ingredients to the work bowl at one time and pulse for a few seconds until fully incorporated. Drop out into a greased 8- or 9-inch loaf pan.

Baking

Bake on the middle shelf of a preheated 425°F oven for approximately 25 minutes. A toothpick or straw inserted in the center should come out clean and the top should spring back when lightly pressed with your fingertips.

Yield

Makes 1 loaf.

Cornmeal Bread

(Dough-Mixing Machine, Flat Beater)

4 cups water
4 eggs, beaten
1 1/3 cups skim milk powder
1 cup sugar
1/2 cup shortening, melted
2 cups yellow cornmeal, preferably stone ground
6 cups unbleached all-purpose flour
4 teaspoons salt
6 tablespoons plus 2 teaspoons baking powder
Shortening, for greasing pans

In the mixing bowl combine the water, eggs, milk powder, sugar, and shortening; mix at the first speed to dissolve. Add the cornmeal and flour, then add the salt and baking powder and lightly stir them through the flour with your fingertips.

Begin mixing with a few quick on and off pulses of the switch until the flour becomes wet so that it is not thrown out of the bowl. Mix at the first speed until the flour is incorporated. Drop into 4 greased 8- or 9-inch loaf pans. Proceed as in Baking, at left.

Yield

Makes 4 loaves.

Honey Oatmeal Bread

Honey for natural sweetness, oatmeal to retain moisture and add flavor, and cornmeal for texture and grain all combine to make this unusual breakfast loaf. This wholesome bread can turn eggs and breakfast meat into a Sunday treat. It is my version of a bread I found in an upstate New York mountaintop inn where people drive miles out of their way to have breakfast. They come for the view and the home-cured bacon as well as the wonderful bread. Hardly anyone leaves without a loaf of hot bread to take home. The bread is so tasty that it can stand alone, served warm from the oven or lightly toasted. Serve with butter and jam and a big cup of steaming coffee.

Sponge

2 cups warm water
2 packages active dry yeast
3 cups unbleached all-purpose flour

Dough

1/2 cup honey
2/3 cup skim milk powder
1 cup cooked oatmeal
4 tablespoons cornmeal
4 tablespoons unsalted butter or margarine, at room temperature
3 to 3 1/2 cups unbleached all-purpose flour
1 tablespoon salt
Flour, for dusting work top
Shortening, for greasing pans
Water or melted butter, for brushing loaves

Sponge

In a large bowl sprinkle the yeast over the warm water to soften; stir to dissolve. Add the flour and stir until smooth. Cover and set aside until it doubles in volume (25 to 30 minutes).

Dough

Stir down the Sponge and add the honey, milk powder, and oatmeal. In a separate bowl combine the cornmeal, 3 cups flour, and salt. Cut in the butter or rub between your fingertips until the flour resembles coarse meal. Add this mixture to the Sponge and stir until the dough comes away from the sides of the bowl.

Turn out the dough onto a floured work surface and knead. More flour can be added 1/4 cup at a time if the dough is sticky. Continue kneading until the dough becomes smooth and silky and has an elastic feel (8 to 10 minutes).

Cut the dough in half, shape into 2 rounds, cover, and allow to rest for 10 minutes.

Shaping
Shape the rounds into pan loaves (pages 27-28), then place in 2 greased 8- or 9-inch loaf pans, seam down and centered. Keep in a warm, draft-free place covered with a cloth and allow to rise until the loaves form nicely rounded tops and rise above the top of the pans.

When ready to bake, gently brush the tops with water or melted butter and slash each loaf lengthwise down the center with a sharp knife or razor blade. Place the pans on a baking sheet or oven stone.

Baking
Bake with steam (pages 31-32) in a preheated 375°F oven until the crust is golden brown (35 to 45 minutes). When done the bottom will emit a hollow sound when thumped with your fingertips. If desired, continue baking 5 to 10 minutes without the loaf pan to develop a better crust.

Yield
Makes 2 loaves.

Honey Oatmeal Bread
(Food Processor, Steel Blade)

In the Sponge, instead of 2 cups warm water use:

1/2 cup warm water
1 1/2 cups ice water

Sponge
In the work bowl sprinkle the yeast over the warm water to soften; pulse to dissolve. Add the ice water and flour; process until smooth. Allow to stand, covered, until doubled in volume. You can leave the bowl and blade in place on the machine.

Dough
Pulse once or twice to punch down the Sponge. Add the honey, milk powder, oatmeal, butter, cornmeal, 3 cups flour (1 cup at a time), and salt. Pulse until the dry ingredients are thoroughly moistened, then process until the dough forms up and tries to ride up on the blade. More flour can be added 1/4 cup at a time if the dough is too soft. Process for 2 to 3 minutes. Do not allow the dough to overheat. If the machine strains, stop and divide the dough in half. Process each half, then knead together on a floured surface. Extra kneading by hand may be necessary to make the dough elastic.

Cut the dough in half, shape into rounds, cover, and allow to rest for 10 minutes.

Proceed as in Shaping and Baking, above.

Yield
Makes 2 loaves.

Honey Oatmeal Bread

(Dough-Mixing Machine, Flat Beater)

Sponge

1/2 cup warm water
3 packages active dry yeast
2 1/2 cups ice water
4 1/2 cups unbleached all-purpose flour

Dough

3/4 cup honey
1 cup skim milk powder
1 1/2 cups cooked oatmeal
6 tablespoons cornmeal
6 tablespoons sweet butter or margarine
4 1/2 to 5 1/4 cups unbleached all-purpose flour
1 1/2 tablespoons salt
Flour, for dusting work top
Vegetable oil, for coating bowl
Shortening, for greasing pans
Water or melted butter, for brushing loaves

Sponge

In the mixing bowl sprinkle the yeast over the warm water to soften; stir to dissolve. Add the ice water and flour and stir until smooth. Cover with a cloth and allow the Sponge to rise until doubled in volume.

Dough

Stir down the Sponge with one or two rotations of the beater and add the honey, milk powder, oatmeal, cornmeal, butter, 4 1/2 cups flour, and salt. Pulse at the first speed using the on/off switch so that the beater does not throw the flour out of the bowl. When the flour is almost absorbed, run the machine at the first speed until the dough comes away from the side of the bowl. If the dough is too soft, add flour 1/4 cup at a time.

Remove and scrape down the beater and insert the dough hook. Run at the first speed until the dough forms up on the hook and comes away from the sides of the bowl (8 to 10 minutes). You can use the second speed for the last few minutes to strengthen the gluten.

Turn out the dough onto a floured surface, cut into thirds, shape into 3 rounds, and cover. Allow the dough to rest 10 minutes. Proceed as in Shaping and Baking, above, except use 3 greased 8- or 9-inch loaf pans.

Yield

Makes 3 loaves.

Portuguese Corn Bread (Broa)

When I first came upon this bread in a Portuguese bakery, I was surprised because it seemed middle European to me. Made up of a combination of flours, this loaf is heavy, moist, and crusty. Broa keeps well for a week or more in a paper bag in the bread box. Four people can easily devour an entire loaf in one sitting.

Sponge

1 cup warm water
2 packages active dry yeast
1 1/2 cups bread flour

Boil

3/4 cup cold water
1/4 cup cornstarch dissolved in
1/4 cup cold water

Dough

1 cup corn flour (see Note)
2 to 3 cups bread flour
1 tablespoon salt
Flour, for dusting work top
Flour or cornmeal, for dusting baking sheet
Potato flour, for topping

BAKER'S SECRET. Potato flour dusted onto the top of the loaf before baking cracks haphazardly in the oven, creating crisp fissures that add to the bread's unique flavor and texture.

Sponge

In a large bowl dissolve the yeast in the warm water to soften; stir to dissolve. Add the flour and stir until smooth. Cover and allow to stand until doubled in volume (about 30 to 45 minutes).

Boil

While waiting for the Sponge to rise, bring the 3/4 cup cold water to a rapid boil. Slowly add the dissolved cornstarch, stirring constantly. Bring to a second boil, remove from the heat, and set aside to cool.

Dough

When the Sponge has risen, add the cooled cornstarch solution, corn flour, 2 cups bread flour, and salt. Stir until the dough comes away from the sides of the bowl. The dough should be kept softer than usual.

Turn out the dough onto a lightly floured work top. Knead with a turn, fold, push motion, adding more bread flour in small amounts if the dough is too sticky. Knead until the dough is smooth (5 to 8 minutes). This should be a soft dough.

Shaping
Prepare a heavily floured or cornmeal-dusted baking sheet. Cut the dough in half and shape each half into a ball. Place on the baking sheet, leaving ample room for the loaves to spread. Dust the loaves well with potato flour. Cover and set aside to proof for 45 to 60 minutes. A series of fine cracks should develop in the flour if it is not disturbed.

Baking
This bread requires a hot oven and it likes a great deal of steam. Bake with steam in a preheated 475°F oven for 45 to 60 minutes. Five minutes before baking, place a heavy shallow pan on the floor of the oven. When the oven is hot, place the bread in the oven. Carefully pour 2 cups hot water into the pan to create a burst of steam; shut the door quickly. Protect your hands and face from the initial burst of steam. I wear long oven mitts. If you are using a stone or tiles, bake directly on them for the last 10 minutes. Allow the bread to bake with a hard, dark crust, almost to the point of becoming black on the edges. The top and sides should be hard when pressed. Test by tapping the bottom with your fingertips for a hollow thump when done. Let cool on a wire rack.

Yield
Makes 2 loaves.

Note: Corn flour is available in some specialty or natural foods stores. You can substitute stone-ground cornmeal by grinding it, 1/4 cup at a time, into a fine powder in a blender or food processor.

Portuguese Corn Bread (Broa)
(Food Processor, Steel Blade)

Sponge
In the work bowl dissolve the yeast in the warm water. Add the flour and pulse until dissolved. Cover and allow the Sponge to rise until doubled in volume (30 to 45 minutes).

Boil
While waiting for the Sponge to rise, bring the 3/4 cup cold water to a rapid boil. Slowly add the dissolved cornstarch, stirring constantly. Bring to a second boil, remove from the heat, and set aside to cool.

Dough
When the Sponge has risen, add the cornstarch solution, corn flour, 2 cups bread flour (1 cup at a time), and salt. Pulse until the dough tries to form up on top of the blade. More bread flour can be added 1/4 cup at a time if necessary. This dough should be softer than usual. Process for 1 to 2 minutes. If necessary divide the dough in half and process each half separately, then knead together. Proceed as in Shaping and Baking, above.

Yield
Makes 2 loaves.

Portuguese Corn Bread (Broa)

(Dough-Mixing Machine, Flat Beater)

Sponge

1 1/2 cups warm water
3 packages active dry yeast
2 1/4 cups bread flour

Boil

1 cup plus 2 tablespoons cold water
6 tablespoons cornstarch dissolved in
1/3 cup cold water

Dough

1 1/2 cups corn flour
3 to 4 1/2 cups bread flour
1 1/2 tablespoons salt
Flour, for dusting work top
Flour or cornmeal, for dusting baking sheet
Potato flour, for topping

Sponge

In the mixing bowl dissolve the yeast in the warm water; stir to dissolve. Add the flour and stir until smooth. Cover and allow to stand until doubled in volume (about 30 to 45 minutes).

Boil

While waiting for the Sponge to rise, bring the water to a rapid boil. Slowly add the dissolved cornstarch, stirring constantly. Bring to a second boil, remove from the heat, and set aside to cool.

Dough

When the Sponge has risen, add the cooled cornstarch solution, corn flour, 3 cups bread flour, and salt. Pulse with the on/off switch until the flour is absorbed so that it does not fly out of the bowl. Mix at the first speed until the dough comes away from the sides of the bowl.

Remove and scrape down the beater, insert the dough hook, and continue mixing for 5 to 8 minutes. More bread flour can be added 1/4 cup at a time if necessary, but this dough should be soft and wet.

Proceed as in Shaping and Baking, above, except shape the dough into 3 rounds.

Yield

Makes 3 loaves.

Potato Bread

Long before the invention of modern yeast, potatoes and the starchy water in which they are boiled were used to leaven bread. Today we use the potatoes and their boiling water for the flavor and tenderness they impart to the finished bread. Potato breads keep exceptionally well in the bread box or refrigerator and can be frozen. Friends in the Midwest still compete at fairs and food shows, justifiably proud of their potato breads, some of which come from family recipes handed down through the generations. My father often spoke about potato breads that were baked in Europe when he was a young man. Although we now have potato flour, starch, and instant flakes available for baking, I like this recipe using fresh mashed potatoes and the water in which they cooked. You can use instant mashed potatoes but you do not get the benefits of the potato water.

1 medium potato
2 1/2 cups boiling water
1/4 cup warm water
2 packages active dry yeast
2 tablespoons unsalted butter or shortening, at room temperature
2 tablespoons sugar
1/3 cup skim milk powder
5 to 6 cups unbleached all-purpose flour
2 teaspoons salt
Flour, for dusting work top
Vegetable oil, for coating bowl
Shortening, for greasing pans
Water or melted butter, for brushing loaves

Wash and thoroughly scrub the potato, then cook in the boiling water until soft (approximately 10 minutes). Drain, reserving 2 cups potato water. Peel the potato, mash, and set aside to cool. Extra potato water can be refrigerated and used in any yeast recipe for added nutritive value and tenderizing power.

Dough

In a large bowl sprinkle the yeast over the 1/4 cup warm water; stir to dissolve. Stir together the cooled mashed potato and butter and add to the bowl together with the 2 cups reserved potato water. Add the sugar, milk powder, 5 cups flour, and salt. Stir until the dough comes away from the sides of the bowl, adding more flour 1/4 cup at a time if necessary. Potato dough will remain a little sticky.

Turn out the dough onto a floured surface and knead, adding more flour if necessary, until the dough feels smooth and elastic (8 to 10 minutes).

Rising

Transfer the dough to a clean, oiled mixing bowl and turn to coat. Cover and set aside until the dough doubles in volume. Punch down, cut in half, shape into two balls, and allow to rest, covered, for 10 minutes.

Shaping

Press down each ball and shape into a pan loaf (pages 27-28). Place in 2 greased 8- or 9-inch loaf pans, cover, and set aside to proof until the breads come up above the tops of the pans. Dust with flour and cut a deep slash down the length of each loaf.

Baking

Bake in a preheated 375°F oven until the bread has a hollow sound when the bottom is tapped with your fingertips (about 50 minutes). The sides should feel firm. If necessary return the bread to the oven for an additional 5 to 10 minutes. If using tiles or an oven stone, finish the bread on them for an additional 5 to 10 minutes. Remove from the pans and let cool on a wire rack.

Yield

Makes 2 loaves.

Variation

Shape into 2 round loaves or 1 large one, then proof on a cornmeal-dusted baking pan, covered, until doubled in size. Dust with flour and slash the tops in a tic-tac-toe pattern. The large loaf will require extra oven time.

Potato Bread

(Food Processor, Steel Blade)

Prepare the potatoes as above. In the work bowl sprinkle the yeast over the warm water; stir to dissolve. Add the mashed potato, butter, 2 cups reserved potato water, sugar, milk powder, 3 cups flour, and salt. Process until smooth. Add 2 cups flour, 1 cup at a time. Pulse until the dough begins to clean the sides of the bowl. More flour can be added 1/4 cup at a time if necessary. Pulse or process for 1 to 2 minutes. If the machine begins to strain, stop and cut the dough in half and process one half at a time, then knead together. Do not overmix. If necessary finish kneading by hand until the dough is elastic. Turn out on a floured surface and knead into a ball.

Proceed as in Rising, Shaping, and Baking, above.

Yield

Makes 2 loaves.

Potato Bread

(Dough-Mixing Machine, Flat Beater)

3 1/2 cups water
1 1/2 medium potatoes
1/4 cup plus 2 tablespoons warm water
3 packages active dry yeast
3 tablespoons sugar
3 tablespoons butter or shortening, at room temperature
1/2 cup skim milk powder
7 1/2 to 9 cups unbleached all-purpose flour
1 tablespoon salt
Flour, for dusting work top
Vegetable oil, for coating bowl
Shortening, for greasing pans
Water or melted butter, for brushing loaves

Prepare the potatoes as above, using 3 1/2 cups water and reserving 3 cups.

In the mixing bowl sprinkle the yeast over the warm water to dissolve. Stir in the cooked mashed potato and 3 cups reserved potato water. Add the sugar, butter, milk powder, 7 1/2 cups flour, and salt. Pulse at the first speed with the on/off switch until the liquids are absorbed, then run at this speed until the dough comes away from the sides of the bowl, adding more flour 1/4 cup at a time if the dough remains too soft. Potato dough will remain a little sticky.

Remove and scrape down the beater, insert the dough hook, and run at the first speed until the dough feels smooth and silky (8 to 10 minutes), adding more flour if necessary. The last 2 minutes can be run at the second speed to further develop the gluten. If the motor strains and threatens to stop, use the first speed.

Turn out the dough and proceed as in Rising, Shaping, and Baking, above, except use 3 greased 8- or 9-inch loaf pans.

Yield

Makes 3 loaves.

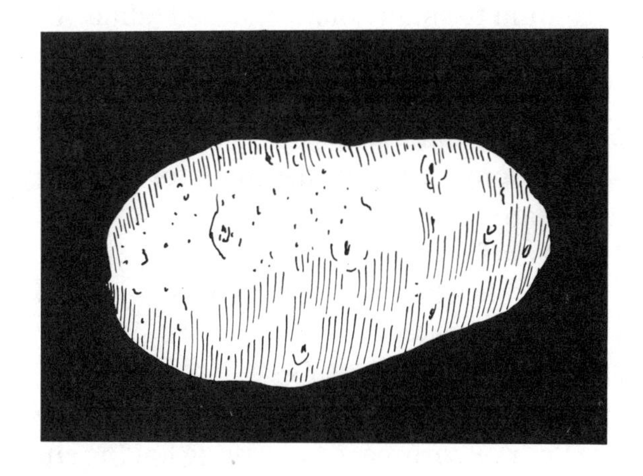

Potato Rye Bread with Onion and Caraway

My father's recipe for sourdough potato rye bread is adapted here for quick preparation, richer flavor, and a softer crust. These breads were often proofed in floured and cloth-lined baskets and tipped upside down onto peels, so that they baked with interesting designs on the crust. This bread is an excellent accompaniment for a cheese platter, roasted garlic, or hors d'oeuvres. Try it for open-faced sandwiches with cured meats and roasted bell peppers.

1 medium to small yellow onion, minced
2 tablespoons caraway seeds, or more to taste
Pinch salt
Vegetable oil or olive oil, for sautéing
1 cup warm water, preferably potato water
1 package active dry yeast
1 medium to small potato, mashed (about 1/2 cup mashed potato; see Note)
1 tablespoon sugar
1 tablespoon shortening
3 tablespoons milk powder (omit for nondairy bread)
2 cups rye flour
1 cup unbleached all-purpose flour
1 1/2 teaspoons salt
Flour, for dusting work top
Vegetable oil, for coating bowl
Rye flour or cornmeal, for dusting baking sheet

In a small skillet over medium-low heat, sauté the onion, caraway seeds, and the pinch salt in the oil just long enough to soften the onion. Set aside.

Dough

In a large bowl dissolve the yeast in the warm water. Add the mashed potato, sugar, shortening, milk powder (if used), flours, and the 1 1/2 teaspoons salt. Stir with a wooden spoon until the dough comes away from the sides of the bowl.

Turn out the dough onto a floured work surface and knead. If the dough is moist and sticky, add more all-purpose flour 1/4 cup at a time. Knead until elastic (5 to 8 minutes). The dough will be softer than usual because of the rye flour, and it will tend to feel sticky.

Transfer the dough to an oiled bowl and turn to coat. Cover and allow to rise until doubled in volume (45 to 60 minutes). Punch down, shape into 1 or 2 rounds, and allow to rest, covered, for 15 minutes. Knead in the reserved onion mixture.

Shaping
Shape into 1 or 2 round loaves. Place on a rye flour or cornmeal-dusted baking sheet. Proof until doubled in size. Dust the tops with additional all-purpose flour and cut decorative slashes.

Baking
Bake with steam (pages 31-32) in a preheated 375° oven for 35 to 45 minutes. If 1 large loaf is made, allow for additional oven time. The bread is done when tapping the bottom with your fingertips produces a hollow thump. Let cool on a wire rack.

Yield
Makes 1 or 2 loaves.

Note: Scrub the potato. Cook, quartered, in 2 1/2 cups boiling water until soft (about 10 minutes). Let cool, then peel and mash. Store extra potato water in the refrigerator for use in any bread recipe. Instant mashed potato can be used but you lose the added benefit of the potato water.

Potato Rye Bread with Onion...

(Food Processor, Steel Blade)

Dough
In the previous recipe, instead of 1 cup warm water use:

1/4 cup warm water
3/4 cup ice water, preferably potato water

In the work bowl sprinkle the yeast over the warm water to soften; stir to dissolve. Add the ice water, potato, sugar, shortening, milk powder (if used), and the 2 cups rye flour 1 cup at a time. Mix until the flour is absorbed. Blend in the all-purpose flour and salt. Pulse until the dough tries to form up on top of the blade. More all-purpose flour can be added 1/4 cup at a time if the dough is too soft. Keep in mind that this dough will be softer than usual. Process for 2 to 3 minutes. If necessary divide the dough in two and process each half separately, then knead together. Do not overmix, since the dough will get too hot. Extra kneading by hand is sometimes necessary to make the dough elastic.

Transfer the dough to an oiled bowl and turn to coat. Cover and allow to rise until doubled in volume (45 to 60 minutes). Shape into 1 or 2 balls. Cover and let rest for 15 minutes. Punch down, then knead in the reserved onion mixture.

Proceed as in Shaping and Baking, above.

Yield
Makes 1 or 2 loaves.

Potato Rye Bread with Onion...

(Dough-Mixing Machine, Flat Beater)

---

1 medium yellow onion, minced
3 tablespoons caraway seeds, or more to taste
Vegetable oil or olive oil, for sautéing
Pinch salt
1 1/2 cups warm water, preferably potato water
1 package active dry yeast
1 medium potato, mashed (3/4 cup mashed potato; see Note on previous page)
1 1/2 tablespoons sugar
1 1/2 tablespoons shortening
4 1/2 tablespoons milk powder (omit for nondairy bread)
3 cups rye flour
1 1/2 cups unbleached all-purpose flour
2 1/4 teaspoons salt
Flour for dusting work top
Vegetable oil, for coating bowl
Rye flour or cornmeal, for dusting baking sheet

In a small skillet over medium-low heat, sauté the onion, caraway seeds, and salt in the oil just long enough to soften the onion. Set aside.

Dough

In the mixing bowl sprinkle the yeast over the warm water; stir to dissolve. Add the mashed potato, sugar, shortening, milk powder (if used), flours, and salt. Pulse with the on/off switch until the flours are absorbed so that they are not thrown out of the bowl. Run at the first speed until the dough comes away from the sides of the bowl.

Remove and scrape down the beater, insert the dough hook, and run at the first speed until the dough forms up on the hook and comes away from the sides of the bowl (5 to 8 minutes). Add more all-purpose flour 1/4 cup at a time if necessary. Rye doughs are normally soft and somewhat sticky.

Transfer the dough to an oiled bowl and turn to coat. Cover and allow to rise until doubled in volume (45 to 60 minutes). Punch down, then shape into 1, 2, or 3 balls. Cover and let rest for 15 minutes. Knead in the reserved onion mixture. Proceed as in Shaping and Baking, above.

Yield

Makes 1 to 3 loaves.

Sweet Rye Bread with Potato

German bakers whom I knew made this version of rye bread. The potatoes keep the bread moist and give it a long shelf life. We made this in the bakery with stubby rounded ends to distinguish it from Sour Rye Bread, which had pointed ends. Many people like the sweet flavor that the molasses imparts to this bread.

1/4 cup warm water
1 package active dry yeast
2 cups mashed potatoes plus 1 cup water (preferably water from cooking potatoes; see Note)
1/2 cup light molasses
2 cups rye flour
2 1/4 to 3 1/4 cups common flour (page 8; see Note)
2 teaspoons salt
2 tablespoons caraway seeds (optional)
Flour, for dusting work top
Vegetable oil, for coating bowl
Water or cornstarch solution (page 20), for brushing loaves

In a large bowl sprinkle the yeast over the warm water; stir to dissolve. Add the potatoes and the 1 cup water, molasses, rye flour, 2 1/4 cups common flour, salt, and caraway seeds (if used). Stir until the dough comes away from the sides of the bowl, adding more common flour 1/4 cup at a time if necessary. Potato dough will remain a little sticky.

Turn out the dough onto a floured surface and knead until the dough feels smooth and elastic (8 to 10 minutes), adding more common flour if necessary.

Rising

Transfer the dough to a clean, oiled bowl and turn to coat. Cover and set aside until the dough doubles in volume (about 45 minutes). Punch down, cut in half, shape into rounds, and allow to rest while covered for 15 minutes.

Shaping

Mold the dough into 2 free-standing pan loaves or 1 large free-standing pan loaf (pages 27-28). Place on a cornmeal-dusted baking pan, then cover and set aside to proof until the loaves double in size. Cut each with 3 horizontal slashes. Brush with water or the cornstarch solution, or dust the tops with flour.

Baking

Bake in a preheated 375°F oven until when tapped with the fingertips the bottom of the bread emits a hollow sound (35 to 45 minutes). The large loaf will require extra oven time. The sides should feel firm. When using tiles or an oven stone, finish baking on them for the last 5 to 10 minutes. Let cool on a wire rack.

Yield

Makes 1 or 2 loaves.

Note: Wash and thoroughly scrub 2 or 3 medium to large potatoes. Cook with jackets in boiling water to cover until soft (approximately 10 minutes). Drain, reserving 2 cups potato water. Peel the potatoes, mash, and set aside 2 cups mashed potatoes to cool. Any extra potato water can be refrigerated and used in any yeast recipe for extra nutritive value and tenderizing power. You can use instant mashed potatoes but you lose the benefits of the potato water. In place of common flour, you can substitute 1 cup cake flour and 1 1/4 to 2 1/4 cups all-purpose flour.

Variation

Shape into 2 round loaves or 1 large one. Proof on a cornmeal or rye flour-dusted baking sheet, covered, until doubled in size. Dust the tops with rye flour and slash several times. Bake as above.

Sweet Rye Bread with Potato

(Food Processor, Steel Blade)

In the recipe above, use

1 cup chilled potato water

Prepare the potatoes as above. In the work bowl sprinkle the yeast over the warm water; stir to dissolve. Add the mashed potatoes, chilled potato water, molasses, rye flour, 2 1/4 cups common flour (add the flours 1 cup at a time), salt, and caraway seeds (if used). Pulse until the dough begins to clean the sides of the bowl. More common flour can be added 1/4 cup at a time if necessary. Pulse or process for 2 to 3 minutes. If the machine begins to strain, stop and cut the dough in half and process half at a time, then knead together. Do not overmix. Turn out the dough on a floured surface and knead into a ball. Proceed as in Rising, Shaping, and Baking, above.

Yield

Makes 1 or 2 loaves.

Sweet Rye Bread with Potato

(Dough-Mixing Machine, Flat Beater)

1/4 cup plus 2 tablespoons warm water
1 package plus 1 1/2 teaspoons active dry yeast
3 cups mashed potatoes plus 1 1/2 cups water from cooking potatoes (see Note)
3/4 cup light molasses
3 cups rye flour
3 1/2 to 4 1/2 cups common flour (see Note)
1 tablespoon salt
3 tablespoons caraway seeds (optional)
Flour, for dusting work top
Vegetable oil, for coating bowl
Water or cornstarch solution (page 20), for brushing loaves

In the mixing bowl sprinkle the yeast over the warm water to dissolve. Add the mashed potatoes and cooking water, molasses, rye flour, 3 1/2 cups common flour, salt, and caraway seeds (if used). At the first speed, pulse with the on/off switch until the liquids are absorbed. Continue running at the first speed until the dough comes away from the sides of the bowl, adding more common flour 1/4 cup at a time if the dough remains too soft. Potato dough will remain a little sticky.

Remove and scrape down the beater. Insert the dough hook and run at the first speed until the dough feels smooth and elastic (8 to 10 minutes), adding more common flour if necessary. The last 2 minutes can be run at the second speed to further develop the gluten. Turn out the dough and proceed as in Rising, Shaping, and Baking, above, except shape into 3 loaves.

Yield

Makes 3 loaves.

Note: Wash and thoroughly scrub 3 to 4 medium to large potatoes. Cook with jackets in boiling water to cover until soft (approximately 10 minutes). Drain, reserving 1 1/2 cups potato water. Peel the potatoes, mash, and set aside 3 cups mashed potatoes to cool. Any extra potato water can be refrigerated and used in any yeast recipe for extra nutritive value and tenderizing power. You can use instant mashed potatoes but you lose the benefits of the potato water. In place of common flour, you can substitute 1 1/2 cups cake flour and 2 to 3 cups all-purpose flour.

Potatonik

In the late 1950s we called these yeast-baked Jewish potato puddings Spudniks, a takeoff on the first Russian Sputnik space satellite. In the bakery these zesty onion and ground pepper-laced loaves were baked every week from Thursday through Sunday. It became a tradition that the first loaves out of the oven always had to be tested by the entire baking and sales staff. Often, one had to taste two or three slices before pronouncing them up to standard. One Thursday I observed a usually timid middle-aged sales clerk who appeared to be in distress. When I asked if she was feeling well, her response was, "I think there's something wrong with the potatonik today," while indicating with an unmistakable gesture that a fire was being stoked up inside her chest. A young part-timer who was standing nearby quickly turned away, doubled over with suppressed laughter. Finally, when she could no longer contain herself, the youngster turned and blurted out to the older woman, "Of course you don't feel well. If I ate two whole potatonik I wouldn't feel well either."

Potatonik can be used in place of potatoes at any meal. A side dish of applesauce makes an appealing accompaniment. Always serve warm. Potatonik can be refrigerated for several days and reheated when ready to be used. They can also be frozen.

Sponge

1 cup warm water
1 1/2 packages active dry yeast (scant 1 1/2 tablespoons)
1 1/2 cups bread flour or unbleached all- purpose flour

Dough

3/4 pound potatoes (about 1 1/2 medium potatoes), skins on
6 ounces yellow onions (1 1/4 medium onions), ground or grated
1 small stale roll or 2 slices old bread (torn or crumbs)
1/2 cup bread flour or unbleached all-purpose flour
1 1/2 teaspoons salt
Scant 1/2 teaspoon baking powder
1/4 teaspoon freshly ground black pepper, or more to taste
1/2 cup vegetable oil
1/2 cup lightly beaten egg
Shortening, for greasing pans

Sponge
In a large bowl sprinkle the yeast over the warm water; stir to dissolve. Add the flour and mix until smooth. Cover and set aside until it puffs up (20 to 25 minutes).

Dough
Stir down the Sponge. Scrub the potatoes, then grind or grate them with the skins on. Add the ground potatoes and onion to the Sponge and stir until blended. Add the stale roll, flour, salt, baking powder, and ground pepper; mix until incorporated. Add the oil and egg and mix well. Drop the mixture out into 3 well-greased 8- or 9-inch loaf pans. Each loaf should weigh about 15 ounces. Leave room for expansion—the potatonik will rise in the oven.

Baking
Bake with steam (pages 31-32) in a preheated 360°F oven until the crust is brown and feels firm when gently pressed in the center with your fingertips (about 1 hour). Let cool on a wire rack covered with a cloth for 5 minutes to allow the loaves to steam. Invert and tap out onto the rack. Serve warm. Potatonik can be refrigerated for several days or frozen for 1 to 2 weeks. Reheat at 325°F until warm. When reheating, I like to bake it for 35 to 45 minutes to develop a hard crust.

Yield
Makes 3 loaves.

Potatonik

(Food Processor, Steel Blade)

Sponge
In a medium bowl sprinkle the yeast over the warm water and stir to dissolve. Add the flour and mix until smooth. Cover and set aside until it puffs up (20 to 25 minutes).

Meanwhile, scrub the potatoes, then process the potatoes, onion, and stale roll into a coarse chop. Do not purée. Transfer to a large bowl.

Dough
Stir the Sponge into the potato/onion mixture. Add the stale roll, flour, salt, baking powder, and ground pepper and pulse only until the dry ingredients are absorbed. Add the oil and egg and mix well. Drop the mixture out into 3 well-greased 8- or 9-inch loaf pans. Each loaf should weigh about 15 ounces. Leave room for expansion—the potatonik will rise in the oven.

Proceed as in Baking, above.

Yield
Makes 3 loaves.

Potatonik

(Dough-Mixing Machine, Flat Beater)

For 3 loaves, you can use the quantities shown in the hand-mixed recipe.

Sponge

2 cups warm water
3 packages active dry yeast
3 cups bread flour or unbleached all-purpose flour

Dough

1 1/2 pounds uncooked potatoes (3 medium potatoes), skins on
12 ounces yellow onions (2 1/2 medium onions), ground or grated
1 stale roll or 3 slices old bread (torn or crumbs)
1 cup bread flour or unbleached all-purpose flour
1 tablespoon salt
3/4 teaspoon baking powder
1/2 teaspoon freshly ground black pepper, or more to taste
1 cup vegetable oil
1 cup beaten egg
1 cup water
Shortening, for greasing pans

Sponge

In the mixing bowl sprinkle the yeast over the warm water and stir to dissolve. Add the flour and mix until smooth. Cover and set aside until it puffs up (20 to 25 minutes).

Dough

Stir down the Sponge. Scrub the potatoes, then grind or grate them with the skins on. Mix in the ground potatoes, onion, and stale roll and stir until blended. Add the flour, salt, baking powder, ground pepper, oil, egg, and water. Pulse with the on/off switch until absorbed, then mix thoroughly. Drop out into 6 well-greased loaves.

Proceed as in Baking, in the hand-mixed recipe.

Yield

Makes 6 loaves.

Chapter Five

Breads of All Nations

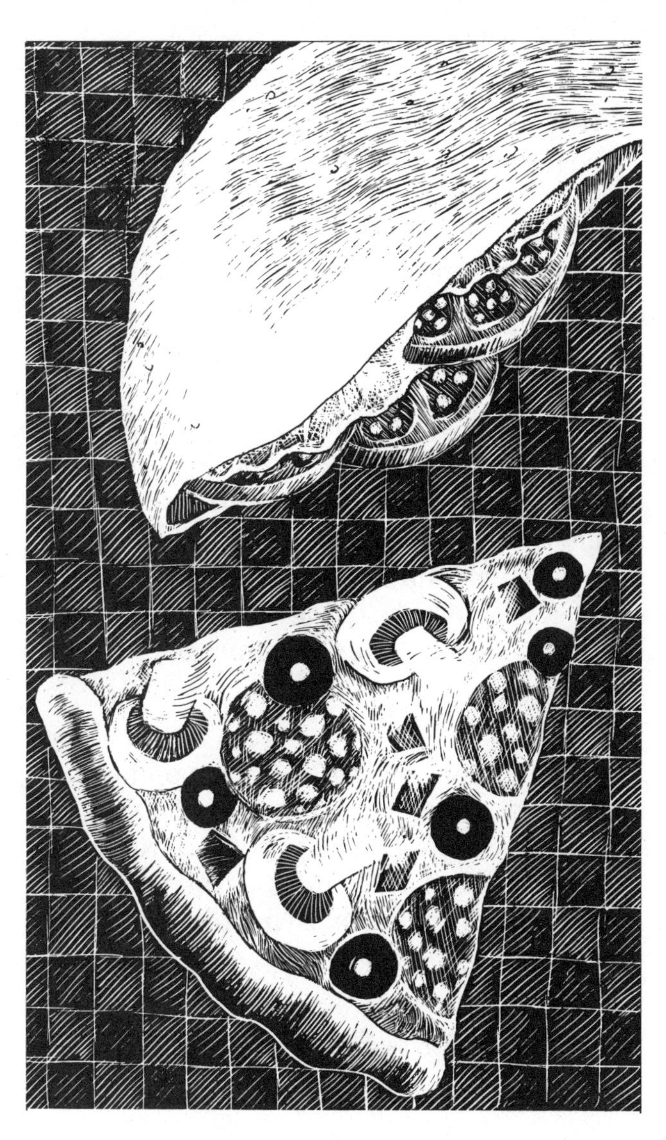

Our daily bread, as is our country's heritage, is rooted in the culture of our immigrant ancestors. Some recipes have remained intact for hundreds of years. Others are derivations that have evolved as bakers strive for perfection. Many of the new breads are in fact old breads rediscovered, or new combinations of ingredients that have been forgotten in the passage of time. The breads that grace our table are from an amalgam of ethnic recipes gathered the world over. Following are the breads of America—the breads of all nations.

Bavarian Farmer Bread

This is a light pumpernickel bread traditionally formed in a round reed basket, which gives it a beehive appearance. You can use any reed or straw basket. Heavy reed baskets need only be dusted with flour. Straw baskets should be lined with thin cloth loosely fastened to the interior with a few sewn stitches. The flour-dusted design makes for an unusually appealing country bread. This bread can also be made as a free-standing loaf or in any round form. Dust with flour and score before baking.

2 cups warm water
2 packages active dry yeast
2 tablespoons molasses
1 cup rye flour
1 cup pumpernickel flour
3 to 4 cups common flour, preferred (page 8), or all-purpose flour
1 tablespoon salt
Flour, for dusting work top
Oil, for greasing bowl
Additional rye flour, for dusting basket
Cornmeal, for dusting baking sheet

In a large bowl sprinkle the yeast over the warm water to soften; stir to dissolve. Add the molasses, rye flour, pumpernickel flour, 3 cups common flour, and salt. Mix until the dough comes away from the sides of the bowl.

Turn out the dough onto a floured work surface and knead, adding small amounts of common flour as necessary. Knead until smooth and elastic (5 to 8 minutes).

Rising

Place the dough in a clean, oiled bowl and turn several times to coat. Cover and allow to rise until doubled in size (45 to 60 minutes). Punch down and let stand, covered, until puffy (about 15 minutes).

Shaping

Shape into 1 or 2 round loaves, depending upon the basket size. Place in a basket well dusted with rye flour. Cover with a cloth and proof in a warm, draft-free place until doubled in size. Carefully tip the dough out upside down onto a cornmeal-dusted baking sheet or peel so that the textured design comes out on top.

Baking

Bake with steam (pages 31-32) in a preheated 375°F oven until the loaf emits a hollow thump when tapped on the bottom with your fingertips (about 45 minutes, or longer for 1 large bread). Let cool on a wire rack.

Yield

Makes 1 large or 2 small loaves.

Bavarian Farmer Bread

(Food Processor, Steel Blade)

In the previous recipe, instead of 2 cups warm water use:

1/2 cup warm water
1 1/2 cups ice water

In the work bowl sprinkle the yeast over the warm water to soften; stir to dissolve. Add the ice water, molasses, rye flour, pumpernickel flour, 1 cup common flour, and salt. Mix until all is absorbed. Blend in 2 cups common flour, 1 cup at a time, until the dough comes away from the sides of the bowl. More common flour can be added 1/4 cup at a time if the dough is too soft. Process for 2 to 3 minutes. If necessary divide the dough in two and process each half separately, then knead together. Do not let the dough overheat. Extra kneading by hand is sometimes necessary to make the dough elastic.

Proceed as in Rising, Shaping, and Baking, above.

Yield

Makes 1 large or 2 small loaves.

Bavarian Farmer Bread

(Dough-Mixing Machine, Flat Beater)

3 cups warm water
3 packages active dry yeast
3 tablespoons molasses
1 1/2 cups rye flour
1 1/2 cups pumpernickel flour
4 1/2 to 6 cups common flour, preferred (page 8), or all-purpose flour
1 1/2 tablespoons salt
Oil, for greasing bowl
Additional rye flour, for dusting basket
Cornmeal, for dusting baking sheet

In a large bowl sprinkle the yeast over the warm water to soften; stir to dissolve. Add the molasses, rye flour, pumpernickel flour, 4 1/2 cups common flour, and salt. Stir through the dry ingredients with your fingertips to incorporate the salt into the flours. Pulse with the on/off switch until all is absorbed so that the flour is not thrown out of the bowl. Run at the first speed until the dough comes away from the sides of the bowl. More common flour can be added 1/4 cup at a time if the dough is too soft.

Remove and scrape down the beater and insert the dough hook. Mix at the first speed until the dough forms up on the hook and comes away from the sides of the bowl (8 to 10 minutes). You can use the second speed for the last few minutes to strengthen the gluten. Proceed as in Rising, Shaping, and Baking, above.

Yield

Makes 1 large, 2 medium, or 3 small loaves

Bran Bread

The addition of bran to whole wheat bread makes for a more healthful and tasty loaf. Use this bread anywhere that whole wheat or white is used. Substituting vegetable shortening for butter will give you a nondairy, no-cholesterol loaf.

2 cups warm water
1 package active dry yeast
2 tablespoons unsalted butter or shortening, at room temperature (use it cold in summer)
2 tablespoons honey or sugar
1 cup unprocessed bran
2 cups whole wheat flour, preferably stone ground
2 to 3 cups all-purpose flour
2 teaspoons salt
Flour, for dusting work top
Oil, for greasing bowl
Shortening, for greasing pans
Melted butter or water, for brushing loaves

In a large bowl sprinkle the yeast over the warm water to soften; stir to dissolve. Add the butter, honey, bran, whole wheat flour, 2 cups all-purpose flour, and salt; mix until the dough comes away from the sides of the bowl.

Turn out the dough onto a flour-dusted work top. Knead, adding more all-purpose flour 1/4 cup at a time if necessary. Knead until the dough feels smooth and silky (8 to 10 minutes).

Transfer to a clean, oil-coated bowl and turn the dough top to bottom to coat. Cover and set aside until the dough doubles in volume (40 to 60 minutes).

Shaping

Punch down the dough and cut in half. Shape into rounds, cover, and let rest for 15 minutes. Form into 2 pan loaves (pages 27-28). Place the loaves, seam down, in 2 greased 8- or 9-inch loaf pans. Proof in a warm, draft-free area until the loaves form nicely rounded tops and rise above the tops of the pans. Make 1 slash lengthwise down the center of each loaf with a sharp blade. Brush the tops with melted butter or water.

Baking

Bake with steam (pages 31-32) in a preheated 375°F oven until the bread has browned and the bottom emits a hollow sound when tapped lightly with your fingertips (35 to 45 minutes). The loaves can be removed from the pans for the last 5 minutes of baking to improve the crust. Let cool on a wire rack.

Yield

Makes 2 loaves.

Bran Bread

(Food Processor, Steel Blade)

Instead of 2 cups warm water use:

1/2 cup warm water
1 1/2 cups ice water

In the work bowl sprinkle the yeast over the warm water to soften; stir to dissolve. Add the ice water, butter, honey, bran, whole wheat flour, and salt. Process until smooth. Add 2 cups all-purpose flour, 1 cup at a time. Pulse until the dough comes together and tries to form up on top of the blade. More all-purpose flour can be added 1/4 cup at a time if the dough is too soft. Process for 2 to 3 minutes. Do not overheat. If necessary divide the dough in half and process each half separately, then knead together. Extra kneading by hand is sometimes necessary to make the dough elastic.

Turn out the dough and place in a clean, oil-coated bowl; turn top to bottom to coat. Cover and set aside until the dough doubles in volume (40 to 60 minutes). Proceed as in Shaping and Baking, above.

Yield

Makes 2 loaves.

Bran Bread

(Dough-Mixing Machine, Flat Beater)

3 cups warm water
1 package active dry yeast
3 tablespoons unsalted butter or shortening, at room temperature
3 tablespoons honey or sugar
1 1/2 cups unprocessed bran
3 cups whole wheat flour, preferably stone ground
3 to 4 1/2 cups all-purpose flour
1 tablespoon salt
Flour, for dusting work top
Oil, for greasing bowls
Shortening, for greasing pans
Melted butter or water, for brushing loaves

In the mixing bowl sprinkle the yeast over the warm water to soften; stir to dissolve. Add the butter, honey, bran, whole wheat flour, 3 cups all-purpose flour, and salt. Pulse with the on/off switch until all is absorbed so that the flour is not thrown out of the bowl. Mix at the first speed until the dough comes away from the sides of the bowl. More all-purpose flour can be added 1/4 cup at a time if the dough is too soft.

Remove and scrape down the beater and insert the dough hook. Run at the first speed until the dough forms up on the hook and comes away from the sides of the bowl (8 to 10 minutes). You can use the second speed for the last few minutes to develop the gluten.

Remove the hook, add oil to the bowl, and turn the dough top to bottom to coat. Cover and allow to rise until doubled in volume (45 to 60 minutes).

Proceed as in Shaping and Baking, above, except divide into 3 loaves.

Yield

Makes 3 loaves.

Buttermilk Bread

Buttermilk Bread has an old-fashioned farm flavor and just enough texture to give it a homemade taste. Make this bread with butter and honey, cut thick slices, and serve it warm for breakfast. It is also excellent for sandwiches and at a buffet lunch accompanied by a dish of apple butter.

1/2 cup warm water
2 packages active dry yeast
1 cup buttermilk (page 22)
4 teaspoons honey
2 tablespoons butter or shortening, at room temperature (use it cold in summer)
5 to 6 cups unbleached all-purpose flour
2 teaspoons salt
Flour, for dusting work top
Oil, for greasing bowl
Shortening, for greasing pans
Melted butter or water, for brushing loaves

In a large bowl sprinkle the yeast over the warm water to soften; stir to dissolve. Add the buttermilk, honey, butter, 5 cups flour, and salt. Mix until the dough comes away from the sides of the bowl.

Turn out onto a flour-dusted work top. Knead, adding more flour 1/4 cup at a time if necessary, until the dough feels smooth and silky (8 to 10 minutes).

Transfer to a clean, oil-coated bowl and turn top to bottom to coat. Cover and set aside until the dough doubles in volume (40 to 60 minutes).

Shaping

Punch down the dough and cut in half. Shape into rounds, cover, and let rest for 15 minutes. Shape into 2 pan loaves (pages 27-28). Place the loaves, seam down, in 2 greased 8- or 9-inch loaf pans. Proof in a warm, draft-free area until the loaves form nicely rounded tops and rise above the tops of the pans. Place the breads on a baking sheet. Punch 3 holes in the crust of each with an ice pick or skewer. Brush the tops with melted butter or water.

Baking

Bake with steam (pages 31-32) in a preheated 375°F oven until the bread has browned and the bottom emits a hollow sound when tapped lightly with your fingertips (35 to 45 minutes). The loaves can be removed from the pans for the last 5 minutes of baking to improve the crust. Let cool on a wire rack.

Yield

Makes 2 loaves.

Buttermilk Bread

(Food Processor, Steel Blade)

In the previous recipe, make sure that the buttermilk is cold or iced.

In the work bowl sprinkle the yeast over the warm water to soften; stir to dissolve. Add the cold buttermilk, honey, butter, 2 cups flour, and salt. Mix until smooth. Add 3 cups flour, 1 cup at a time, and pulse until the dough comes together. More flour can be added 1/4 cup at a time if the dough is too soft. Process for about 2 minutes. Do not allow the dough to overheat. If necessary divide the dough in two and process each half separately, then knead together. Extra kneading by hand is sometimes necessary to make the dough elastic.

Turn out the dough, then transfer to a clean, oil-coated bowl and turn top to bottom to coat. Cover and set aside until the dough doubles in volume (40 to 60 minutes).

Proceed as in Shaping and Baking, above.

Yield

Makes 2 loaves.

Buttermilk Bread

(Dough-Mixing Machine, Flat Beater)

1/2 cup warm water
3 packages active dry yeast
2 1/2 cups buttermilk
2 tablespoons honey
3 tablespoons butter or shortening
7 1/2 to 9 cups unbleached all-purpose flour
1 tablespoon salt
Oil, for greasing bowl
Shortening, for greasing pans
Melted butter or water, for brushing loaves

In the mixing bowl sprinkle the yeast over the warm water to soften; stir to dissolve. Add the buttermilk, honey, butter, 7 1/2 cups flour, and salt. Pulse with the on/off switch until all is absorbed so that the flour is not thrown out of the bowl. Mix at the first speed until the dough comes away from the sides of the bowl. More flour can be added 1/4 cup at a time if the dough is too soft.

Remove and scrape down the beater and insert the dough hook. Run at the first speed for 8 to 10 minutes after the dough forms up on the hook and comes away from the sides of the bowl. You can use the second speed for the last few minutes to develop the gluten.

Remove the hook, add oil to the bowl, and turn the dough top to bottom to coat. Cover and allow to rise until doubled in volume (45 to 60 minutes). Proceed as in Shaping and Baking, above, except shape into 3 loaves.

Yield

Makes 3 loaves.

Carrot Bread

Carrot bread is vitamin rich and exceptionally nutritious. A slightly sweet flavor and attractive orange flecks from the carrots make this a colorful and festive bread. It is good with cheese dishes and salads and can replace whole wheat or white bread for party sandwiches.

Sponge

2 cups warm water
2 packages active dry yeast
3 cups unbleached all-purpose flour

Dough

2 teaspoons sugar
1 tablespoon unsalted butter or shortening, at room temperature
2 cups ground or shredded carrots (about 4 medium carrots)
6 tablespoons skim milk powder
1 cup whole wheat flour, preferably stone ground
1 to 2 cups unbleached all-purpose flour
1 tablespoon salt
Flour, for dusting work top
Oil, for greasing bowl

Sponge

In a large bowl sprinkle the yeast over the warm water to soften; stir to dissolve. Add the flour and mix until smooth. Cover and allow to stand until doubled in volume (30 to 45 minutes).

Dough

Stir down the Sponge and add the sugar, butter, carrots, milk powder, flours, and salt. Mix until the dough comes away from the sides of the bowl.

Turn out the dough onto a floured work top and knead, adding more all-purpose flour 1/4 cup at a time if necessary. Knead until the dough is soft and elastic (8 to 10 minutes).

Transfer to an oiled bowl and turn to coat. Cover and allow to rise until doubled in bulk (35 to 45 minutes). Cut the dough in thirds, shape into rounds, and cover. Allow to rest for 15 minutes.

Shaping
Shape into 3 pan loaves. Place the loaves, seam down, in 3 greased 8- or 9-inch loaf pans. Cover with a flour-dusted cloth and allow to rise 1 inch above the tops of the pans (45 to 60 minutes). When the bread is fully proofed, cut 3 diagonal slashes down the length of each loaf.

Baking
Bake with steam (pages 31-32) in a preheated 425°F oven until golden brown (25 to 35 minutes). Bake the last 5 minutes on tiles or an oven stone if you have them. The bread is done when it emits a hollow sound when tapped on the bottom with your fingertips and the sides feel hard and crisp.

Yield
Makes 3 loaves.

Carrot Bread

(Food Processor, Steel Blade)

Sponge
In the work bowl sprinkle the yeast over the warm water to soften. Add the flour, then pulse to dissolve. Pulse until smooth, cover, and allow to double in volume (30 to 40 minutes). You can leave the bowl and blade in place on the machine.

Dough
Pulse to punch down the Sponge, then add the sugar, butter, carrots, milk powder, whole wheat flour, 1 cup all-purpose flour, and salt. Add the flours 1 cup at a time. Pulse until the dough comes together. More all-purpose flour can be added 1/4 cup at a time if the dough is too soft. Process for about 1 minute. If necessary divide the dough in two and process each half separately, then knead together. Do not overmix. Extra kneading by hand is sometimes necessary to make the dough elastic.

Transfer the dough to an oiled bowl and turn to coat. Cover and allow to rise until doubled in bulk (35 to 45 minutes). Cut the dough in thirds, shape into rounds, and cover. Allow to rest for 15 minutes.

Proceed as in Shaping and Baking, above.

Yield
Makes 3 loaves.

Carrot Bread

(Dough-Mixing Machine, Flat Beater)

Sponge

3 cups warm water
3 packages active dry yeast
4 1/2 cups unbleached all-purpose flour

Dough

1 tablespoon sugar
1 1/2 tablespoons unsalted butter or shortening, at room temperature
3 cups ground or shredded carrots (about 6 medium carrots)
1/2 cup plus 1 tablespoon skim milk powder
1 1/2 cups whole wheat flour, preferably stone ground
1 1/2 to 3 cups unbleached all-purpose flour
1 1/2 tablespoons salt
Flour, for dusting worktop
Oil, for greasing bowl

Sponge

In the mixing bowl sprinkle the yeast over the warm water; stir to dissolve. Add the flour and mix at the first speed until smooth. Cover and allow to rise until doubled in size (35 to 45 minutes).

Dough

Stir down the Sponge with 1 or 2 rotations of the beater. Add the sugar, butter, carrots, milk powder, whole wheat flour, 1 1/2 cups all-purpose flour, and salt. Pulse at the first speed using the on/off switch so that the beater does not throw the flour out of the bowl. When the flour is absorbed, run the machine at the first speed until the dough comes away from the sides of the bowl. If the dough is too soft, add more all-purpose flour 1/4 cup at a time.

Remove and scrape down the beater and insert the dough hook. Run at the first speed until the dough forms up on the hook and comes away from the sides of the bowl (8 to 10 minutes). You can use the second speed for the last few minutes to strengthen the gluten.

Transfer the dough to an oiled bowl and turn to coat. Cover and allow to rise until doubled in size (35 to 45 minutes). Turn out the dough onto a floured surface, cut into 4 rounds, and cover. Allow the dough to rest for 15 minutes.

Proceed as in Shaping and Baking, above, except shape into 4 loaves.

Yield

Makes 4 loaves.

Challah

Challah, or egg bread, is a sweet, egg-rich, festive-looking bread with an elegant mahogany hue. This bread was originally baked by Jewish families to grace the Sabbath or holiday table. Years ago bakery customers who were unfamiliar with the name would ask for the Friday bread.

Challah can be made up in different shapes, ranging from a sectioned pan loaf to fancy and intricate braids (see Braiding Challah, which follows). On certain holidays it is made into a round turban-shaped bread. Today its use is becoming universal. It is found in ethnic bakeries and food markets of all kinds. Challah is often used as a centerpiece at Sunday dinner and appears on many Easter tables. When the bread is baked in braided form, it is customary to break off small knobs of it rather than cutting or slicing it. One literally breaks bread with guests and family. Leftover challah makes the best French toast I've ever eaten.

Challah dough is also used as rich egg roll dough and is made into many varieties of party or dinner rolls (see page 240). In summer it's advisable to use cold ingredients to keep the dough temperature from becoming too high.

1 cup warm water
2 packages active dry yeast
1 egg, lightly beaten
2 egg yolks, lightly beaten
1/4 cup vegetable oil
1/4 cup plus 1 1/2 teaspoons sugar
4 to 4 1/2 cups bread flour (see Note)
2 teaspoons salt
Flour, for dusting work top
Oil, for greasing bowl
1 egg beaten with 1 teaspoon water, for egg wash
Cornmeal, for dusting baking pan
Poppy or sesame seeds, for topping (optional)

In a large bowl sprinkle the yeast over the warm water and stir to dissolve. Add the egg, egg yolks, oil, sugar, 4 cups flour, and salt. Stir until the dough comes away from the sides of the bowl.

Turn out the dough onto a lightly floured work top and knead, adding more flour 1/4 cup at a time if the dough is sticky or very soft. The dough should be firm. Knead until the dough is smooth and elastic and the gluten is well developed (10 to 15 minutes). When you push down, the dough should feel firm and push back.

Rising

Transfer the dough to an oiled bowl, turn to coat, and cover until the dough is tripled in volume, or when an indentation made with a finger pushed down into the center of the dough remains and does not recede. This is a fully aged, or ready, dough.

Shaping

Punch down the dough, cut in half, cover, and allow to rise for 15 minutes. Punch down again and with the palms roll out into 2 ropes. Cut each into 6 equal pieces and braid or make up into a six-section pan bread (see pages 76-81). Brush with the egg wash, using care to cover completely. Do not let excess egg drip into the crevices.

Transfer the bread to a cornmeal-dusted baking pan if you are making the braided challah. Place in a warm, draft-free area, preferably enclosed, and allow to rise until doubled in size.

> ***BAKER'S SECRET. Allow the bread to air dry, then brush a second time with the egg wash to give the bread its characteristic shine. Sprinkle lightly with the poppy or sesame seeds if desired.***

Baking

Bake in a preheated 350°F oven on the middle shelf until the bread has a rich mahogany color and the bottom has a hollow sound when tapped lightly with your fingertips (35 minutes). If the top begins to brown excessively and the bottom is raw, cover the bread with a sheet of parchment paper or a brown paper bag that has been cut open and creased down the center to form a tent. If there is a white line visible between the braids, continue baking until it disappears. To test for doneness, press lightly between the braids on the highest part of the bread; it should be firm. If you feel the creases give when lightly pressed, continue baking until they firm up. Let cool on a wire rack. Challah keeps very well for several days in the bread box. It can be frozen; defrost slowly, preferably wrapped, overnight in the refrigerator.

Yield

Makes 2 loaves.

Note: You can substitute all-purpose flour for bread flour, but the bread will not come out as light or tender.

Challah

(Food Processor, Steel Blade)

In the recipe above, instead of 1 cup warm water use:

1/4 cup warm water
3/4 cup ice water

In the work bowl sprinkle the yeast over the warm water to soften; pulse to dissolve. Add the ice water, egg, egg yolks, oil, sugar, 2 cups flour, and salt; pulse to combine. Add 2 more cups flour, 1 cup at a time. More flour can be added 1/4 cup at a time if necessary. The dough should be firm. Pulse until the dough forms up into a mass, then continue pulsing for 2 to 3 minutes. If the processor motor strains, divide the dough in half and process each half separately, then knead together. If using a dough thermometer, keep the dough at 78°F. Do not overmix. If necessary knead by hand until the dough is smooth and elastic and the gluten is well developed. When you push down, the dough should be firm and push back. Knead together and shape into a ball.

Proceed as in Rising, Shaping, and Baking, above.

Yield

Makes 2 loaves.

Challah

(Dough-Mixing Machine, Flat Beater)

---

1 1/2 cups warm water
3 packages active dry yeast
1 1/2 eggs, lightly beaten (reserve extra egg for egg wash)
3 egg yolks
1/4 cup plus 2 tablespoons vegetable oil
1/3 cup plus 1 tablespoon sugar
6 to 6 1/2 cups bread flour (see Note above)
1 tablespoon salt
Flour, for brushing work top
Oil, for greasing bowl
Cornmeal, for dusting baking pan
Poppy or sesame seeds, for topping (optional)
1/2 egg (or more) beaten with 1 teaspoon water, for egg wash

In the mixing bowl sprinkle the yeast over the warm water to soften; stir to dissolve. Add the eggs, egg yolks, oil, sugar, 6 cups flour, and salt. Pulse with the on/off switch until all is absorbed so that the flour does not fly out of the bowl. Mix until the dough comes away from the sides of the bowl, adding more flour if necessary. This bread requires a firmer dough than normal.

Scrape down the beater and insert the dough hook. Mix at the first speed for 15 minutes. Do not leave the mixer unattended. Continue as in Rising, Shaping, and Baking, above, except shape into 3 loaves.

Yield

Makes 3 loaves.

Braiding Challah

Many different braids and shapes can be used for making challah. In the bakery we make a six-strand braided challah. For the home I recommend a method using two three-strand braids, one placed on top of the other. Called Top Challah, this is a festive, professional-looking bread. We baked Top Challahs in the shop for large centerpieces, often 6 feet in length.

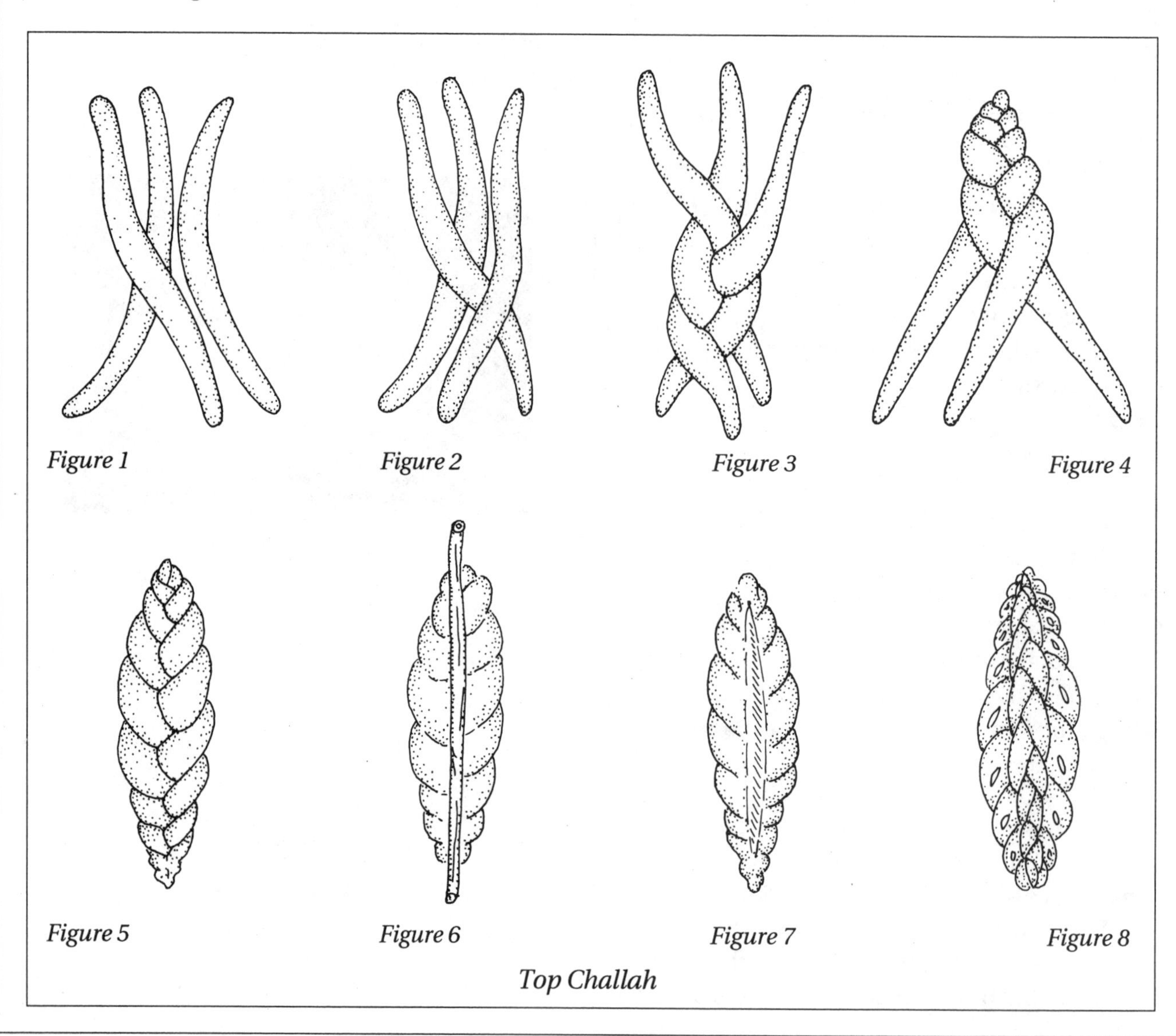

Top Challah

Top Challah

Prepare the challah dough (see previous recipe). Divide the dough into 4 pieces. (I suggest also using 4 pieces for the mixing machine recipe; you will have a larger, more beautiful table bread.)

Take 1 piece and cut it into thirds. When braided, the 3 small pieces will form the top and the large pieces will be the base. While working, keep the dough covered with a cloth. Begin with the large pieces. Using little flour, with your palms roll the pieces out into ropes about 12 inches long, thick in the center and with tapered ends. If a strip resists stretching, set aside to rest and go on to the next.

When all are rolled, start over with the first piece. Continue rolling until the desired length is achieved. Set aside, covered, and allow to rest for a few minutes.

Use little or no flour to make the braids. If the dough sticks, a very light dusting will suffice. Make two 3-strand braids.

Begin braiding from the center down to the end (Figure 1). Bring the left strand over the center, then the right over the center (Figure 2). Repeat, left over right, right over left, until you reach the end. Flip the braid over on its opposite side and turn top to bottom (Figure 3). Complete the braid (Figure 4). Pinch the ends tightly together to close (Figure 5). Braid the smaller strands in the same manner.

BAKER'S SECRET: To prevent the top braid from sliding off to one side while baking, we make a crease or an indentation down the length of the bottom braid, upon which we will place the top strand.

With your fingertips press out a straight line of indentations down the center not quite to the ends (Figure 6). Strike the indentations with the side of your hand to form one continuous line. A thin dowel or even a pencil can be used to widen the crease. Dip your fingers in some water and lightly moisten the crease throughout its length (Figure 7). Set the smaller braid on top of the moistened crease and press down gently, pinching all the ends together tightly (Figure 8). Brush with egg wash (page 20). When proofed, allow to dry and brush a second time for a high gloss.

BAKER'S SECRET. Poppy seeds can be decoratively applied (Figure 8) by wetting the thumbs, pressing them into the seeds, then pressing onto the sides of the bottom braid.

Allow to proof until not quite doubled in size and the braid feels firm when lightly touched on the sides. The bread will spring up in the oven. Bake for 45 to 60 minutes. When the top begins to brown, cover with a tent of parchment paper or an opened brown paper bag so that the top does not burn while the center is allowed to bake.

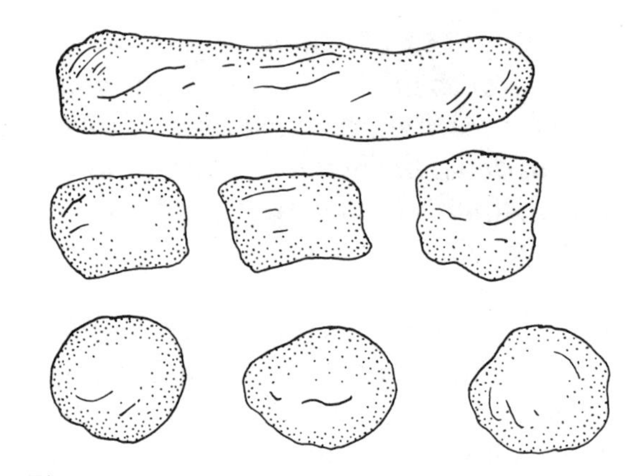

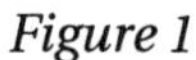

Figure 1

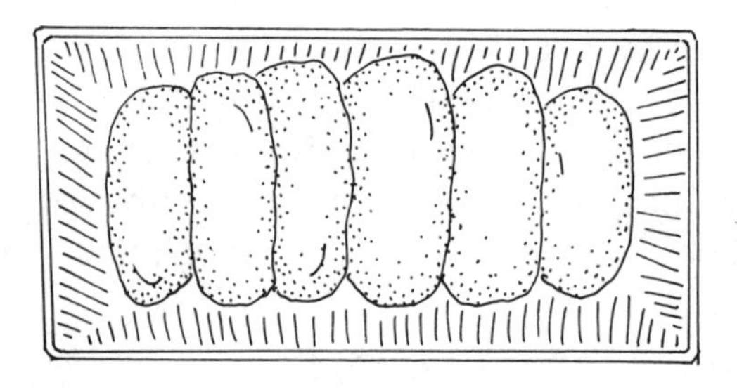

Figure 2

Section Challah

Section Challah (Pan Loaf)

One recipe will yield 2 loaves (3 in the mixing machine recipe). Divide each round into 6 equal pieces. Roll into balls (Figure 1). With your palms gently roll the balls into small oblongs not more than the width of your hand. Line up 6 of these sections in a well-greased 8- or 9-inch loaf pan (Figure 2). Brush carefully with egg wash (page 20). In the bakery we line up the oblongs on the bench top in rows of 6, brush with egg wash, then with both hands pick up all 6 pieces at once and place them in the pan. Proof until doubled in volume.

BAKER'S SECRET. Brush with egg wash a second time before baking. The bread can be topped with poppy seeds or sesame seeds.

Variation

Place a 3-strand braided challah (see Top Challah, page 77) in a well-greased 8- or 9-inch loaf pan. When baked, it will form a rectangular loaf with a braided top.

Turban (Round Challah)

These breads are generally baked for the Jewish high holidays of Rosh Hashanah (Jewish New Year) and Yom Kippur (day of atonement). They are made from a long single strand made up into a coil, which when baked rises into a turban-shaped bread.

Prepare one recipe and divide it in two. Roll each piece into a fat rope and allow to rest for several minutes. Leaving one end thick, roll once more with the palms, lengthening the strand and tapering the other end to a point. You should end up with two 18- to 24-inch lengths, thick on one end and tapered to a point on the other end (Figure 1). Alternate between the two strands to allow them to rest for several minutes.

Take the lengthened strand and, keeping the wide end on the work top, with one hand lift the tapered end and wind the entire length around the wide center to form a coil (Figures 2 and 3). Slip the tip under the coil and press down lightly so that it will not open upon rising (Figures 3 and 4). Brush with the egg wash, place on cornmeal-dusted pans, proof until doubled in volume, and brush a second time before baking. Seeds for topping are optional.

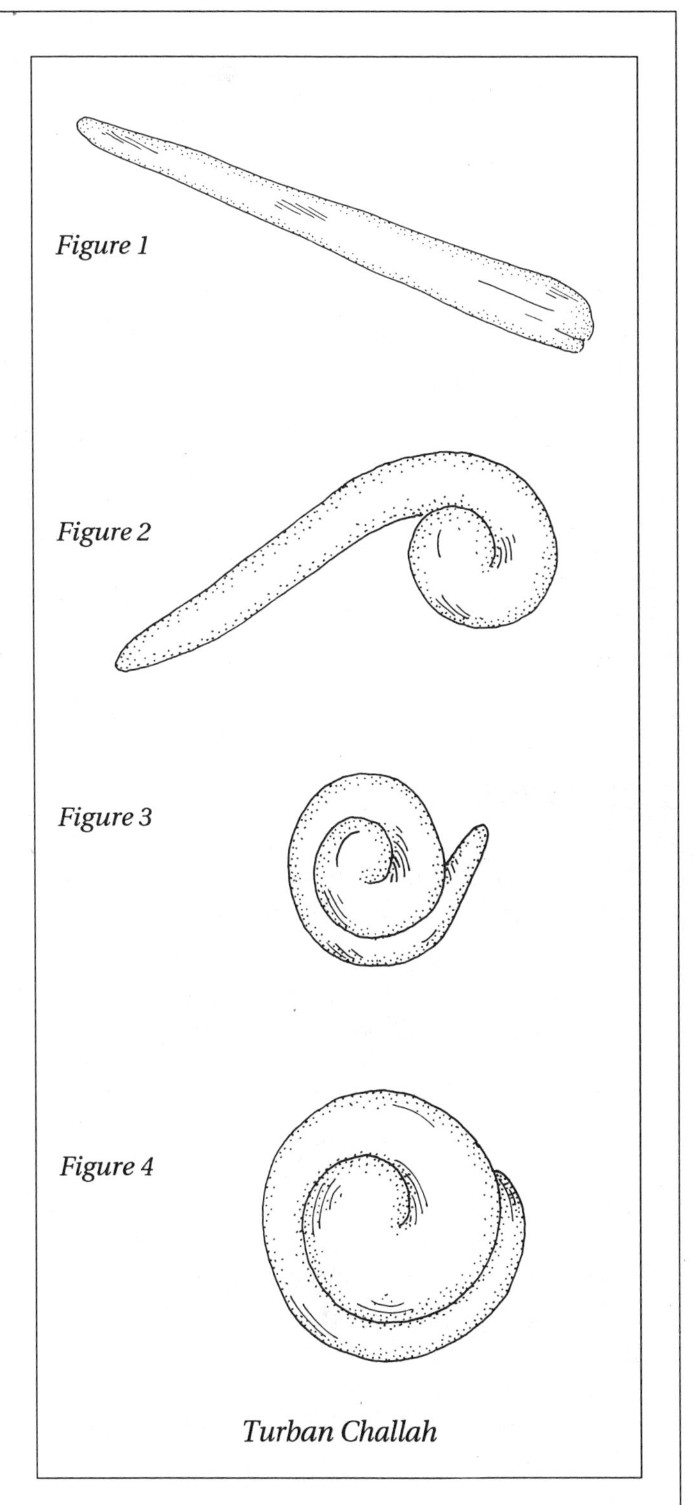

Turban Challah

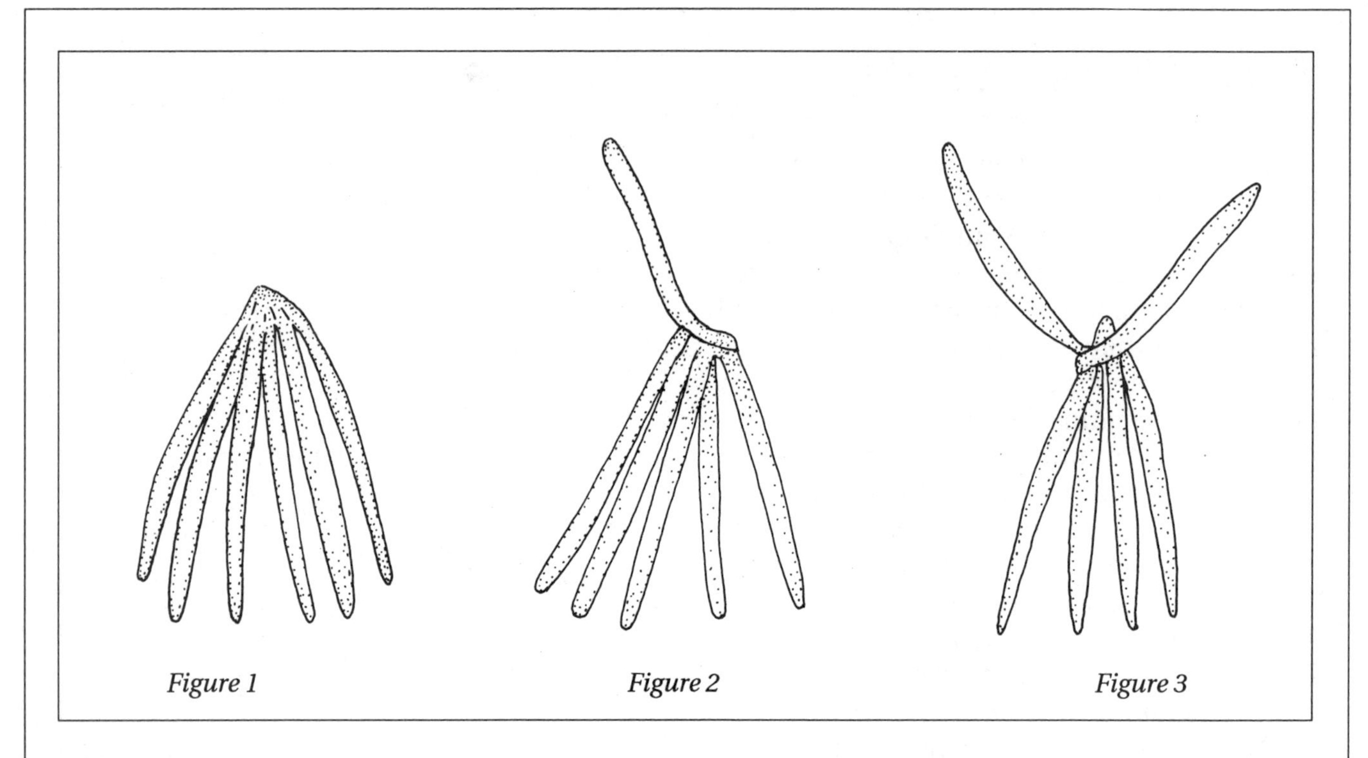
Figure 1 Figure 2 Figure 3

Six-Strand Braid

This is the standard challah braid that we use in the bakery. It is not difficult but requires practice. One cannot visualize this method from reading or studying the diagram. You must have the strips of dough in front of you and follow the directions making up the braid one step at a time. If an error is made simply open up the braid and start over.

Prepare one recipe and divide it in half. Cut each half into 6 equal pieces. Roll each piece into strands about 12 inches long, thick in the center and tapered to a point on each end. Line up the 6 strands and pinch the ends together (Figure 1).

Bring strand #6 from the right end over strand #1 and up to the left (Figure 2). Bring strand #1 from the left up to the top right (Figure 3).

You now have a four-legged creature with the arms crossed over each other. Keeping the legs spread apart in pairs, the left arm (as you face it) comes down into the center between the legs (Figure 4).

Bring the outer right leg over and up to form a new top left arm (Figure 5). The top right arm comes down between the legs (Figure 6).

Repeat the pattern. The left outer leg comes up to form the new right arm, and the left arm comes down to the center. The right leg comes up to form the left arm, and the right arm comes down to the center.

Continue by alternating, left leg up to become right arm, left arm down to the center. Right leg up to become left arm, right arm

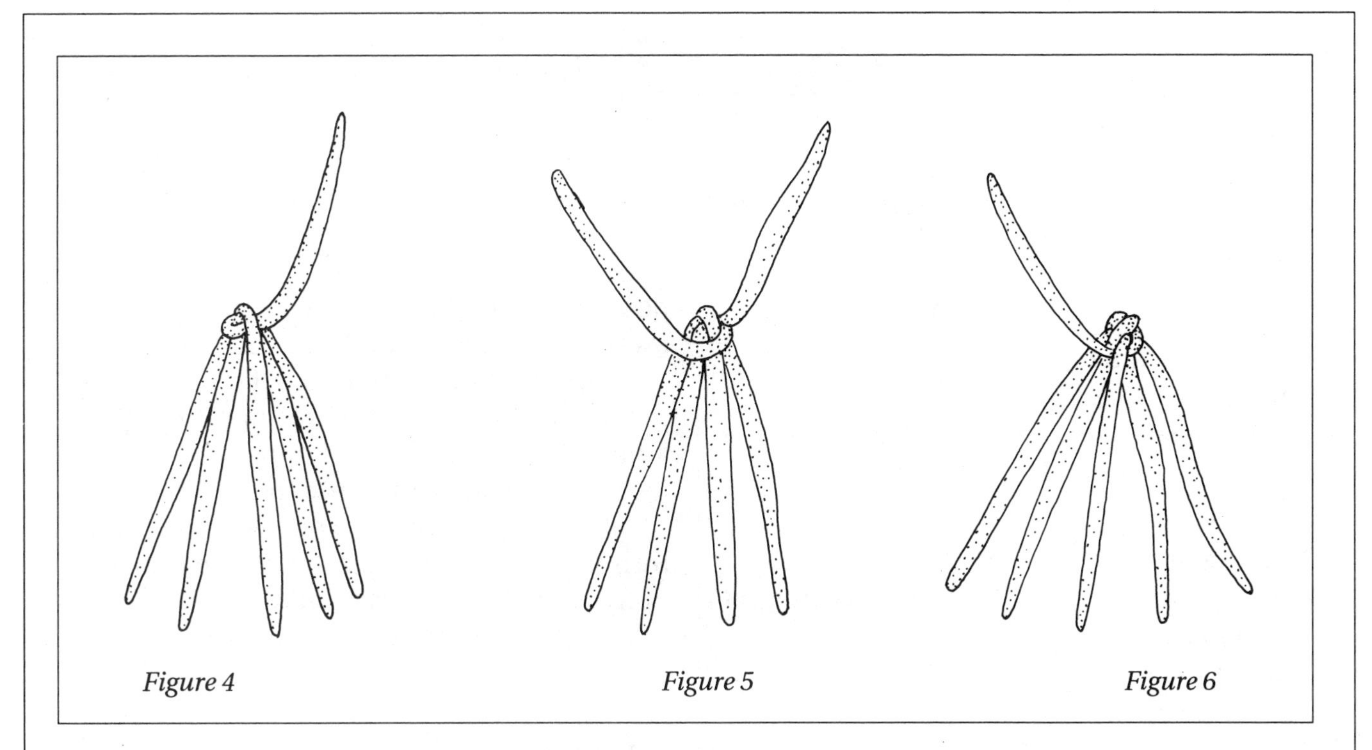
Figure 4 *Figure 5* *Figure 6*

down to the center, and so on. Finish by pinching the ends tightly closed (Figure 7).

Always keep hold of the last strand you moved so that you remember your location in the pattern. When moving strands, grasp the arms by the ends where hands would be. Grasp the legs where feet would be. Keep the legs spread in pairs so that the arms can easily be brought down to the center (Figure 6). When braiding, if you become momentarily disoriented, remember that arms come down, legs come up. If you make an error and become entirely confused, stop, open the braid, and begin again.

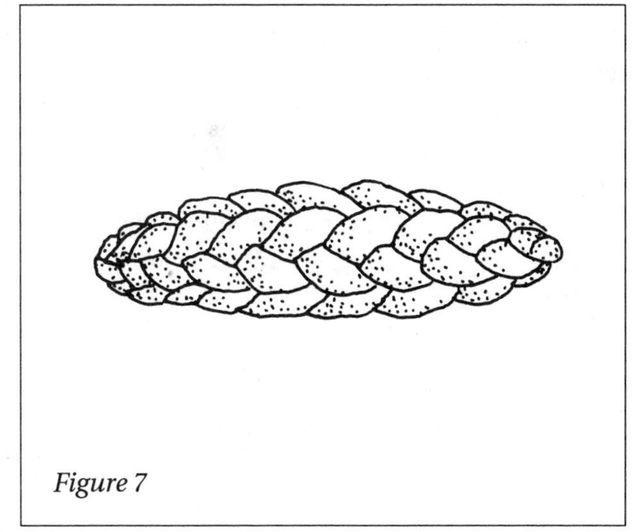
Figure 7

Cheese Bread

This rich, nutritious bread is popular with many farm families. Try making it with assorted hard cheeses to vary the flavor.

Sponge

2 cups warm water
2 packages active dry yeast
3 cups unbleached all-purpose flour

Dough

2 tablespoons sugar
2 tablespoons unsalted butter or shortening, at room temperature
2 cups grated Cheddar cheese (about 8 ounces cheese)
2/3 cup skim milk powder
3 to 3 1/2 cups unbleached all-purpose flour
2 teaspoons salt
Flour, for dusting work top
Oil, for greasing bowl
Shortening, for greasing pans
Oil or melted butter, for brushing loaves
2 tablespoons freshly grated Parmesan cheese, for topping

Sponge

In a large bowl sprinkle the yeast over the warm water to soften; stir to dissolve. Add the flour and mix until smooth. Cover and let stand until doubled in volume (30 to 45 minutes).

Dough

Stir down the Sponge and add the sugar, butter, Cheddar cheese, milk powder, 3 cups flour, and salt. Mix until the dough comes away from the sides of the bowl.

Turn out the dough onto a floured work top and knead, adding more flour 1/4 cup at a time if necessary. Knead until the dough feels soft and silky (8 to 10 minutes).

Transfer the dough to an oiled bowl and turn to coat. Cover and allow to rise until puffy (15 to 20 minutes). Cut the dough into thirds, shape into rounds, and cover. Allow to rest for 10 minutes.

Shaping

Shape the rounds into 3 pan loaves (pages 27-28). Place into 2 greased 8- or 9-inch loaf pans, seam down. Cover with a flour-dusted cloth and proof until doubled in size, or the tops rise 1 inch above the tops of the loaf pans (45 to 60 minutes). Brush with oil or melted butter and sprinkle with the Parmesan cheese. Punch 3 holes in the top of the loaves with an ice pick or a skewer.

Baking

Bake with steam (pages 31-32) in a preheated 375° F oven until the bread is golden brown and emits a hollow sound when tapped on the bottom with your fingertips (25 to 35 minutes).

Yield

Makes 3 loaves.

Variations

Substitute American cheese or any hard cheese of your choice.

Cheese Swirl

Instead of kneading the cheese into the dough, after mixing the dough, prior to shaping, flatten out the dough, sprinkle with grated cheese, and form up jelly roll style. Bake in 2 greased 8- or 9-inch loaf pans. The cheese will appear as a swirl in the finished bread. This is my favorite; it has more cheese flavor and added eye appeal.

Cheese Bread with Chives and Stuffed Olives

To the dough recipe above add:

2 teaspoons dried chopped chives
(1 tablespoon in the mixing machine recipe)
4 ounces sliced stuffed green olives
(6 ounces in the mixing machine recipe)

Knead the chives in with the dry ingredients. Before shaping the breads, flatten out the dough, sprinkle with sliced stuffed olives, and form up, jelly roll style. Bake in 2 loaf pans.

Cheese Bread

(Food Processor, Steel Blade)

Sponge

Sprinkle the yeast over the warm water to soften, then pulse to dissolve. Add the flour and pulse until smooth, then allow to stand, covered, until doubled in volume (about 30 minutes). You can leave the bowl and blade in place on the machine.

Dough

Pulse to punch down the Sponge, then add the sugar, butter, Cheddar cheese, milk powder, 3 cups flour (1 cup at a time), and salt. Pulse until the dough tries to form up on top of the blade. More flour can be added 1/4 cup at a time if the dough is too soft. Process for about 1 minute. If necessary divide the dough in two and process each half separately, then knead together. Do not overmix. Extra kneading by hand is sometimes necessary to make the dough elastic.

Transfer the dough to an oiled bowl and turn to coat. Cover and allow to rise until puffy (15 to 20 minutes). Cut the dough in half, shape into rounds, and cover. Allow to rest for 10 minutes.

Proceed as in Shaping and Baking, above.

Yield

Makes 2 loaves.

Cheese Bread

(Dough-Mixing Machine, Flat Beater)

Sponge

3 cups warm water
3 packages active dry yeast
4 1/2 cups unbleached all-purpose flour

Dough

3 tablespoons sugar
3 tablespoons unsalted butter or shortening
3 cups grated Cheddar cheese (about 12 ounces cheese)
1 cup skim milk powder
4 1/2 to 5 1/4 cups unbleached all-purpose flour
1 tablespoon salt
Oil, for greasing bowl
Flour, for dusting work top
3 tablespoons freshly grated Parmesan cheese, for topping
Shortening, for greasing pans

Sponge

In the mixing bowl sprinkle the yeast over the warm water; stir to dissolve. Add the flour and mix at the first speed until smooth. Cover and allow to rise until doubled in size (30 to 45 minutes).

Dough

Stir down the Sponge with 1 or 2 rotations of the beater, then add the sugar, butter, Cheddar cheese, milk powder, 4 1/2 cups flour, and salt. Pulse at the first speed using the on/off switch so that the beater does not throw the flour out of the bowl. When the flour is absorbed, run the machine at the first speed until the dough comes away from the sides of the bowl. If the dough is too soft, add flour 1/4 cup at a time.

Remove and scrape down the beater and insert the dough hook. Run at the first speed until the dough forms up on the hook and comes away from the sides of the bowl (8 to 10 minutes). You can use the second speed for the last few minutes to strengthen the gluten.

Transfer the dough to an oiled bowl and turn to coat. Cover and allow to rise until puffy (15 to 20 minutes).

Turn the dough out onto a floured surface, cut into four pieces, shape into rounds, and cover. Allow the dough to rest for 10 minutes.

Proceed as in Shaping and Baking, above, except shape into 4 loaves.

Yield

Makes 4 loaves.

Cinnamon Raisin Bread

This all-time breakfast favorite is good plain or toasted with butter or jam. Kids love it at snack time. (It has much less fat and fewer calories than coffee cake or cookies.)

2 cups warm water
2 packages active dry yeast
3 tablespoons sugar
2 tablespoons butter or shortening, at room temperature (see Note)
2/3 cup skim milk powder
5 to 6 cups unbleached all-purpose flour
2 teaspoons salt
Flour, for dusting work top
Oil, for greasing bowl

Filling

1/4 cup melted butter or vegetable oil
1 cup raisins, or more to taste
1/4 cup firmly packed brown sugar (optional)
1/2 cup cinnamon sugar (see Note)

In a large bowl sprinkle the yeast over the warm water to soften; stir to dissolve. Add the sugar, butter, milk powder, 5 cups flour, and salt. Mix until the dough comes away from the sides of the bowl.

Turn out the dough onto a flour-dusted work top. Knead, adding more flour 1/4 cup at a time if necessary. Knead until the dough feels smooth and silky (8 to 10 minutes).

Transfer the dough to a clean, oil-coated bowl and turn top to bottom to coat. Cover and set aside until the dough doubles in volume (40 to 60 minutes).

Shaping and Filling

Punch down the dough and cut in half. Cover and let rest for 15 minutes. Roll the dough out into a rectangle, 12 to 14 inches wide and 6 inches deep. Brush with the melted butter, then sprinkle with the raisins.

***BAKER'S SECRET.** In the bakery we spread the dough with a little Wine Cake mix (page 310) instead of melted butter before sprinkling on the raisins. This enriches the bread.*

Sprinkle lightly with the brown sugar, if desired, then with a few tablespoons cinnamon sugar. In the bakery we dust lightly with additional ground cinnamon on top of the cinnamon sugar.

Shape into 2 jelly roll-style loaves. Place the loaves, seam down, in 2 greased 8- or 9-inch loaf pans. Proof in a warm, draft-free area until the loaves rise above the tops of the pans. Stipple 3 holes down the center of each loaf.

Baking

Bake with steam (pages 31-32) in a preheated 375°F oven until the bread has browned and the bottom emits a hollow sound when tapped with your fingertips (35 to 45 minutes). Let cool on a wire rack. If desired, while the loaves are still warm, mound up the remaining cinnamon sugar on a pan, brush the breads all over with melted butter or oil, and roll them in the cinnamon sugar.

Yield

Makes 2 loaves.

Note: In summer, the butter can be used cold, cut up in small pieces. To make cinnamon sugar, use 2 teaspoons (or more) cinnamon to 1/2 cup sugar. Cinnamon varies in strength. Judge by taste and color.

Variation

Whole Wheat Cinnamon Raisin

Substitute 2 cups whole wheat flour for 2 cups all-purpose flour (3 cups whole wheat for 3 cups all-purpose flour in the dough-mixing machine recipe).

Cinnamon Raisin Bread

(Food Processor, Steel Blade)

In the recipe above, instead of 2 cups warm water use:

1/2 cup warm water
1 1/2 cups ice water

In the work bowl sprinkle the yeast over the warm water to soften; stir to dissolve. Add the ice water, sugar, butter, milk powder, 2 cups flour, and salt. Mix until smooth. Add 3 cups flour (1 cup at a time) and pulse until the dough comes together and tries to form up on top of the blade. More flour can be added 1/4 cup at a time if the dough is too soft. If necessary divide the dough in two and process each half separately, then knead together. Process for about 2 to 3 minutes. Do not allow the dough to overheat. Extra kneading by hand is sometimes necessary to make the dough elastic.

Transfer the dough to a clean, oil-coated bowl and turn top to bottom to coat. Cover and set aside until the dough doubles in volume (40 to 60 minutes).

Proceed as in Shaping and Filling, and Baking, above.

Yield

Makes 2 loaves.

Cinnamon Raisin Bread

(Dough-Mixing Machine, Flat Beater)

3 cups warm water
3 packages active dry yeast
4 1/2 tablespoons sugar
3 tablespoons butter or shortening
1 cup skim milk powder
7 1/2 to 9 cups unbleached all-purpose flour
1 tablespoon salt
Oil, for greasing bowl
Flour, for dusting work top

Filling

1/3 cup melted butter or vegetable oil
1 1/2 cups raisins, or more to taste
3/4 cup cinnamon sugar (see Note above)
1/3 cup firmly packed brown sugar (optional)

In the mixing bowl sprinkle the yeast over the warm water to soften; stir to dissolve. Add the sugar, butter, milk powder, 7 1/2 cups flour, and salt. Pulse with the on/off switch until all is absorbed so that the flour is not thrown out of the bowl. Mix at the first speed until the dough comes away from the sides of the bowl. More flour can be added 1/4 cup at a time if the dough is too soft.

Remove and scrape down the beater and insert the dough hook. Run at the first speed until the dough forms up on the hook and comes away from the sides of the bowl (8 to 10 minutes). You can use the second speed for the last few minutes to develop the gluten.

Add the oil to the bowl and turn the dough top to bottom to coat. Cover and allow to rise until doubled in volume (45 to 60 minutes).

Proceed as in Shaping and Filling, and Baking, above, except shape into 3 loaves.

Yield

Makes 3 loaves.

Cottage Cheese and Chives Bread

First served to me at a luncheon in the Culinary Institute of America, this tasty bread goes well with salads, cold dishes, vegetarian meals, and dairy dishes. Made up into little rolls, it works with appetizers, buffets, and assorted spreads. The following is my version of their recipe.

Sponge

2 cups warm water
2 packages active dry yeast
3 cups unbleached all-purpose flour

Dough

2 tablespoons sugar
2 tablespoons unsalted butter or shortening, at room temperature
1 cup cottage cheese (dry curd)
1 cup bread flour or unbleached all-purpose flour
2 to 2 1/2 cups unbleached all-purpose flour
2 teaspoons chopped chives
2 teaspoons salt
Flour, for dusting work top
Oil, for greasing bowl
Cornmeal, for dusting baking sheet

Sponge

In a large bowl sprinkle the yeast over the warm water to soften; stir to dissolve. Add the flour and mix until smooth. Cover and allow to stand until doubled in volume (30 to 45 minutes).

Dough

Stir down the Sponge and add the sugar, butter, cottage cheese, bread flour, 2 cups all-purpose flour, chives, and salt. Mix until the dough comes away from the sides of the bowl.

Turn out the dough onto a floured work top and knead, adding more all-purpose flour 1/4 cup at a time if necessary. Knead until the dough feels soft and silky (8 to 10 minutes).

Transfer the dough to an oiled bowl and turn to coat. Cover and allow to rise until doubled in bulk (about 30 minutes). Punch down and allow to rise until doubled once more. Cut the dough in half, shape into rounds, and cover. Allow to rest for 5 minutes.

Shaping

Shape into 2 Italian-shaped loaves (pages 28-29). Place the loaves on a baking sheet dusted with cornmeal. Cover with a flour-dusted cloth and allow to rise until doubled in size (45 to 60 minutes). When the bread is fully proofed, cut 3 diagonal slashes down the length of each loaf.

Baking

Bake with steam (pages 31-32) in a preheated 450°F oven until golden brown (25 to 35 minutes). Bake the last 5 minutes on tiles or an oven stone if you have them. The bread is done when it emits a hollow sound when thumped on the bottom with your fingertips and the sides feel hard and crisp.

Yield

Makes 2 loaves.

Variation

Sweet Dairy Rolls

Divide the risen dough in half. When rested as above, roll out into 2 ropes and cut each into 8 equal pieces. Roll into balls and either leave them round or taper the ends to points. Place on greased baking sheets, leaving room between each roll for expansion. Proof until doubled in size, slash once down the center of each, and bake as above until browned and crisp (15 to 20 minutes).

Cottage Cheese and Chives Bread

(Food Processor, Steel Blade)

Sponge

In the work bowl sprinkle the yeast over the warm water to soften, then pulse to dissolve. Pulse until smooth, then allow to stand, covered, until doubled in volume (about 30 minutes). You can leave the bowl and blade in place on the machine.

Dough

Pulse to punch down the Sponge, then add the sugar, butter, cottage cheese, bread flour, 2 cups all-purpose flour (1 cup at a time), chives, and salt. Pulse until the dough tries to form up on top of the blade. More flour can be added 1/4 cup at a time if the dough is too soft. Process for about 1 minute. If necessary divide the dough in two and process each half separately, then knead together. Do not overmix. Extra kneading by hand is sometimes necessary to make the dough elastic.

Transfer the dough to an oiled bowl and turn to coat. Cover and allow to rise until doubled in bulk (about 30 minutes). Punch down and allow to rise until doubled once more (30 to 45 minutes). Cut the dough in half, shape into rounds, cover, and allow to rest for 5 minutes.

Proceed as in Shaping and Baking, above.

Yield

Makes 2 loaves.

Cottage Cheese and Chives Bread

(Dough-Mixing Machine, Flat Beater)

Sponge

3 cups warm water
3 packages active dry yeast
4 1/2 cups unbleached all-purpose flour

Dough

3 tablespoons sugar
3 tablespoons unsalted butter or shortening
1 1/2 cups cottage cheese (dry curd)
1 1/2 cups bread flour or unbleached all-purpose flour
3 to 3 3/4 cups unbleached all-purpose flour
1 tablespoon chopped chives
1 tablespoon salt

Sponge

In the mixing bowl sprinkle the yeast over the warm water; stir to dissolve. Add the flour and mix at the first speed until smooth. Cover and allow to rise until doubled in size (30 to 45 minutes).

Dough

Stir down the Sponge with 1 or 2 rotations of the beater, then add the sugar, butter, cottage cheese, bread flour, 3 cups all-purpose flour (1 cup at a time), chives, and salt. Pulse at the first speed using the on/off switch so that the beater does not throw the flour out of the bowl. When the flour is absorbed, run the machine at the first speed until the dough comes away from the sides of the bowl. If the dough is too soft, add more all-purpose flour 1/4 cup at a time.

Remove and scrape down the beater and insert the dough hook. Run at the first speed until the dough forms up on the hook and comes away from the sides of the bowl (8 to 10 minutes). You can use the second speed for the last few minutes to strengthen the gluten.

Tranfer the dough to an oiled bowl and turn to coat. Cover and allow to rise until doubled in size (about 30 minutes). Punch down and allow to rise once again until doubled.

Turn out the dough onto a floured surface, cut into thirds, shape into rounds, and cover. Allow the dough to rest for 5 minutes, then proceed as in Shaping and Baking, above, except shape into 3 loaves.

Yield

Makes 3 loaves.

Cracked Wheat Bread

This whole wheat bread has a light texture and flavor. It retains the nutritional value of whole grain while the white flour allows the dough to rise better and produce a softer bread. Many people prefer this to a straight whole wheat bread because the grain adds crunch and distinction to the bite. This bread is good for sandwiches and toasts well.

Sponge

2 cups warm water
2 packages active dry yeast
1 1/2 cups unbleached all-purpose flour
1 1/2 cups whole wheat flour, preferably stone ground

Dough

1 to 2 cups unbleached all-purpose flour
1 cup whole wheat flour, preferably stone ground
4 teaspoons sugar
2/3 cup skim milk powder
2 teaspoons salt
2 tablespoons butter or shortening
2 cups wheat berries (preferred) or cracked wheat cereal, cooked (see Note)
Flour, for dusting work top

Sponge

In a large bowl sprinkle the yeast over the warm water to soften; stir to dissolve. Add the flours and mix until smooth. Cover with a cloth and place in a warm, draft-free area until doubled in size (30 to 45 minutes).

Dough

In another large bowl combine 1 cup all-purpose flour, the whole wheat flour, sugar, milk powder, and salt. Cut or rub in the butter. Add the wheat berries and the Sponge. Mix until the dough comes away from the sides of the bowl.

Turn out onto a floured work top and knead, adding more all-purpose flour if necessary, until the dough feels soft and silky (8 to 10 minutes). It should push back when pressed and your hand should come away clean. Cut the dough in half, shape into rounds, and cover. Allow to rest, covered, for 10 minutes.

Shaping

Shape into 2 pan-shaped loaves. Place the breads in 2 greased 8- or 9-inch loaf pans, seam down. Proof until the loaves form nicely rounded tops and rise above the tops of the pans. Brush the breads with water and slash once lengthwise down the center of each loaf with a sharp knife or razor.

Baking
Bake with steam (pages 31-32) in a preheated oven at 375°F on the middle shelf until the bread has a brown color and the bottom emits a hollow sound when tapped lightly with your fingertips (35 to 45 minutes). Let cool on a wire rack.

Yield
Makes 2 loaves.

Note: Wheat berries are available in some natural foods stores. Grind in small batches in a blender or grinder. The flavor derived from using freshly ground wheat berries is worth the extra work. Otherwise, use cracked wheat cereal, also available at natural foods stores. For 2 cups cooked wheat berries or cereal, use 4 tablespoons wheat berries or cracked wheat cereal to 1 1/2 cups water. Let cool before using.

Cracked Wheat Bread
(Food Processor, Steel Blade)

Sponge
In the work bowl sprinkle the yeast over the warm water to soften, then pulse to dissolve. Pulse until smooth, then allow to stand, covered, until doubled in size (about 30 minutes). Leave the bowl and blade in place on the machine.

Dough
Pulse once or twice to punch down the Sponge, then add the flours, sugar, milk powder, salt, butter, and cooked cereal. Mix until the dough comes away from the sides of the bowl. Pulse until all is thoroughly absorbed and the dough tries to form up on top of the blade. Process for about 1 minute. More all-purpose flour can be added 1/4 cup at a time if the dough is too soft. If necessary divide the dough in half and process each half separately, then knead together. Do not overmix. Extra kneading by hand is sometimes necessary to make the dough elastic. Shape into 2 rounds, cover, and let rest for 10 minutes.

Proceed as in Shaping and Baking, above.

Yield
Makes 2 loaves.

Cracked Wheat Bread

(Dough-Mixing Machine, Flat Beater)

Sponge

3 cups warm water
3 packages active dry yeast
2 1/4 cups unbleached all-purpose flour
2 1/4 cups whole wheat flour, preferably stone ground

Dough

1 1/2 to 3 cups unbleached all-purpose flour
1 1/2 cups whole wheat flour, preferably stone ground
2 tablespoons sugar
3 tablespoons butter or shortening
1 cup skim milk powder
3 cups wheat berries (preferred) or cracked wheat cereal, cooked (see Note)
1 tablespoon salt
Flour, for dusting work top

Sponge

In the mixing bowl dissolve the yeast in the warm water. Add the flours and mix until smooth. Cover and allow to rise until doubled in size (30 to 45 minutes).

Dough

Stir down the Sponge with 1 or 2 rotations of the beater, then add 1 1/2 cups all-purpose flour, whole wheat flour, sugar, butter, milk powder, wheat berries, and salt. Pulse at the first speed using the on/off switch so that the beater does not throw the flour out of the bowl. When the flour is absorbed, run the machine at the first speed until the dough comes away from the sides of the bowl. If the dough is too moist or soft, add more all-purpose flour 1/4 cup at a time.

Remove and scrape down the beater and insert the dough hook. Run at the first speed until the dough forms up on the hook and comes away from the sides of the bowl (8 to 10 minutes). You can use the second speed for the last 5 minutes to strengthen the gluten.

Turn out the dough onto a floured surface, cut into thirds, shape into rounds, and cover. Allow the dough to rest for 10 minutes.

Proceed as in Shaping and Baking, above, except shape into 3 loaves.

Yield

Makes 3 loaves.

Note: See also Note above. To make 3 cups cooked wheat berries or cracked wheat cereal, use 6 tablespoons wheat berries or cereal to 2 1/4 cups water. Let cool before using.

French Bread

Americans have a constant love affair with French foods. Among those we encounter the most are the pale, crusty loaves of real French bread. The basic loaf is made of flour, water, yeast, and salt. The procedure determines the distinctive qualities of this very special bread. Consequently, follow the procedure carefully and your breads will have that authentic French appeal.

Sponge

2 cups warm water
2 packages active dry yeast
3 cups bread flour (preferred) or unbleached all-purpose flour

Dough

2 to 3 cups unbleached all-purpose flour
1 tablespoon salt
Oil, for greasing bowl
Cornmeal, for dusting baking sheet

Sponge

In a large bowl sprinkle the yeast over the warm water to soften; stir to dissolve. Add the flour and mix until smooth. Cover, keep in a warm, draft-free area, and allow to rise until doubled in volume (45 to 60 minutes).

Dough

Stir down the Sponge, then add 2 cups flour and salt. Stir until the dough comes away from the sides of the bowl. Knead, adding 1/4 cup at a time if necessary. This dough is kept on the soft side and is easy to knead. When the dough feels good to you, knead for 15 to 20 minutes more. While kneading, pick up the dough occasionally and bang it down on the work top; this will help to aerate and strengthen the gluten so necessary for this bread. Stretching the dough will add elasticity. The finished dough will become airy and pushy under your hands and will feel very smooth.

Rising

Oil a clean bowl and turn the dough around inside to coat. Cover with a towel and set aside in a warm, draft-free area until puffed up (about 30 minutes). Punch down the dough and allow to rise a second time until doubled in volume (30 to 45 minutes). Cut the dough in half. Shape into 2 balls, cover, and let the dough rest for 5 minutes.

Shaping

Shape the balls into 2 thin baguettes (pages 28-29), about 1 inch in diameter. Place on a cornmeal-dusted baking sheet or on greased baguette pans (page 5) if available.

Proofing

Cover with a damp cloth and allow to rise in a warm, draft-free area for 45 to 60 minutes. Brush the loaves with water and cut 3 or more diagonal slashes with a razor or sharp knife. Cut with the knife held at a 20-degree angle, not straight down into the bread. This will force the crust to bloom in the oven and bake with crisp, thick edges.

Baking
Bake with steam (pages 31-32) in a preheated oven at 475°F until the bread is brown and very crusty and has a hollow sound when the bottom is thumped with your fingertips (25 to 35 minutes). If baking on an oven stone or tiles, remove the bread from the pan for the last 10 minutes of baking. The crust should feel hard when squeezed gently on the sides. If the bread still appears pale in color, bake an additional 5 to 10 minutes to develop a crustier loaf. Remove from the oven and let cool, uncovered, on a wire rack.

Yield
Makes 2 baguettes.

Variations

Whole Wheat French Bread

Use bread flour and substitute whole wheat flour, preferably stone ground, for the all-purpose flour. If bread flour is not available, use all-purpose flour in its place.

French Bread Rolls

Mix white or whole wheat dough, as above. When ready to shape up, roll out into 2 ropes (3 ropes in the mixing machine recipe) and divide each into 9 equal pieces. Let the ropes rest, then form into little baguette shapes. Place on greased baguette pans or baking sheets, allowing room for the rolls to rise. Proof, slash once down the center of each, and bake as above until crisp on all sides and light brown in color (12 to 18 minutes).

French Bread

(Food Processor, Steel Blade)

Sponge
In the work bowl sprinkle the yeast over the warm water to soften; stir to dissolve. Add the flour and pulse until smooth. Keep covered, in place on the machine, until the dough doubles in volume (45 to 60 minutes).

Dough
Pulse once or twice to punch down the Sponge, then add 2 cups flour (1 cup at a time) and salt. Pulse until absorbed. More flour can be added 1/4 cup at a time. Pulse or process for 2 to 3 minutes. Do not overheat. (If you use a dough thermometer, do not exceed 78°F). If required, divide the dough in half and process each half separately, then knead together. This dough may be softer than usual. It may be necessary to knead by hand for several minutes to make the dough more elastic and airy.

Proceed as in Rising, Shaping, Proofing, and Baking, above.

French Bread

(Dough-Mixing Machine, Flat Beater)

Sponge

3 cups warm water
3 packages active dry yeast
4 1/2 cups bread flour (preferred) or unbleached all-purpose flour

Dough

3 1/2 to 4 1/2 cups unbleached all-purpose flour
1 tablespoon salt
Oil, for greasing bowl
Cornmeal, for dusting baking sheet

Sponge

In the mixing bowl sprinkle the yeast over the warm water to soften; stir until dissolved. Add the flour and mix until smooth. Cover in place and let rise until doubled in size (45 to 60 minutes).

Dough

Punch down the Sponge by stirring at the first speed, then add 3 1/2 cups flour and the salt. Pulse with the on/off switch until the flour is absorbed so that it does not fly out of the bowl. Continue mixing at the first speed until the dough comes away from the sides of the bowl.

Remove and scrape down the beater. Insert the dough hook and mix for 12 to 15 minutes, adding more flour 1/4 cup at a time if necessary. Keep this dough a little soft. You can run the machine at the second speed for the last few minutes to strengthen the gluten.

Proceed as in Rising, Shaping, Proofing, and Baking, above, except shape into 3 or 4 baguettes.

Yield

Makes 3 or 4 baguettes.

Fougasse

This crispy flat bread originated in the south of France. Baked in a traditional oval or triangular shape, these breads are almost all crust. They can be used with any meal or as snacks. Be sure to bake more than one per person. They have been known to disappear from the table before everyone sits down to the meal. The sponge is best prepared the night before baking, or preferably 24 hours in advance, and left at room temperature.

Sponge

1/2 teaspoon active dry yeast
1/2 cup warm water
3/4 cup bread flour (preferred) or all-purpose flour

Dough

1 cup warm water
1 package active dry yeast
4 tablespoons butter (1/2 stick) or olive oil
3 to 4 cups bread flour (preferred) or all-purpose flour
2 teaspoons salt
Flour, for dusting work top
Oil, for greasing bowl
Cornmeal, for dusting baking pans

Sponge

In a large bowl sprinkle the yeast over the warm water to soften; mix to dissolve. Add the flour and mix until smooth. Cover and allow to stand overnight or for 24 hours at room temperature.

Dough

Stir down the Sponge, then add the water with yeast added, then butter, 3 cups flour, and salt. Mix until the dough comes away from the sides of the bowl.

Turn out the dough onto a floured work top and knead, adding more flour 1/4 cup at a time if necessary, until the dough feels soft and silky (8 to 10 minutes).

Transfer the dough to a large oiled bowl and turn to coat. Cover and allow to rise until doubled in volume.

Turn out the dough onto a floured surface and punch down. Cut into 6 equal pieces, shape into rounds, and allow to rest for 15 minutes.

Shaping

With a rolling pin or stick, roll out into ovals 9 to 10 inches long. Let the pieces rest until they puff up. Roll or stretch the ovals by hand. If desired you can stretch one end so that the shape is triangular. Place on 3 cornmeal-dusted baking sheets, 2 to a pan. Cover with a flour-dusted cloth and allow to rise until puffy and doubled in size (45 to 60 minutes). Press a series of indentations over the entire surface with your fingertips. Slash the tops with several inch-long incisions.

Baking

Bake with steam (pages 31-32) in a preheated 425°F oven until golden brown. These thin breads bake very quickly and must be watched carefully. The bread is done when it has good color top and bottom. Serve warm or within a few hours, since Fougasse is mostly crust and dries out quickly.

Yield

Makes 6 loaves.

Variation

Fougasse with Bac-Os®

Add 2 tablespoons Bac-Os® (3 tablespoons in the mixing machine recipe) to the dough before the final kneading.

Fougasse

(Food Processor, Steel Blade)

Sponge

Prepare the Sponge as above.

Dough

Stir down the Sponge and transfer to the work bowl. Add the yeasted water, butter, 2 cups flour, and salt. Pulse until absorbed. Add 1 more cup flour. Mix until the dough comes away from the sides of the bowl, then pulse or process for 1 to 2 minutes more. More flour can be added 1/4 cup at a time if the dough is too soft. If necessary divide the dough in half and process each half separately, then knead together. Do not overmix. Extra kneading by hand is sometimes necessary to make the dough elastic.

Transfer the dough to a large oiled bowl and turn to coat. Cover and allow to rise until doubled in volume.

Turn out the dough onto a floured surface. Cut into 6 pieces, shape into rounds, and allow to rest, covered, for 15 minutes.

Proceed as in Shaping and Baking, above.

Yield

Makes 6 loaves.

Fougasse

(Dough-Mixing Machine, Flat Beater)

Sponge

3/4 teaspoon active dry yeast (reserve the remaining for Dough, below)
3/4 cup warm water
1 cup plus 2 tablespoons bread flour or unbleached all-purpose flour

Dough

1 1/2 cups warm water
1 1/2 packages active dry yeast
6 tablespoons butter or olive oil
6 to 8 cups bread flour (preferred) or all-purpose flour
1 tablespoon salt
Oil, for greasing bowl
Flour, for dusting work top

Sponge

In a large bowl sprinkle the yeast over the warm water to soften; mix to dissolve. Add the flour and mix until smooth. Cover and allow to stand overnight or for 24 hours at room temperature.

Dough

Stir down the Sponge and transfer it to the mixing bowl. Add the water, yeast, butter, 6 cups flour, and salt. Pulse with the on/off switch until the flour is absorbed so that it does not fly out of the bowl. Mix until the dough comes away from the sides of the bowl.

Scrape down the beater and insert the dough hook. Mix at the first speed, adding more flour 1/4 cup at a time if necessary, until the dough feels soft and silky (8 to 10 minutes).

Transfer the dough to a large oiled bowl and turn to coat. Cover and allow to rise until doubled in volume.

Turn out the dough onto a floured surface. Roll out into a rope and cut into thirds. Cut each section into thirds once more, yielding 9 equal pieces. Shape into rounds, cover, and allow to rest for 15 minutes.

Proceed as in Shaping and Baking, above.

Yield

Makes 9 loaves.

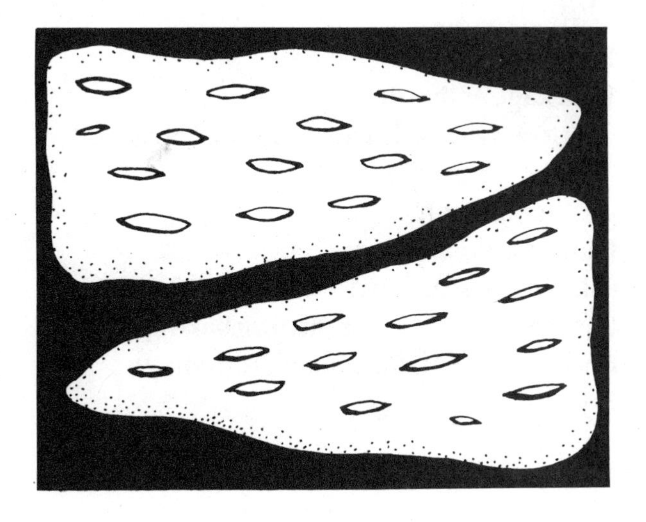

French Onion Bread

A crisp, thin-crusted bread with a rough country texture, French Onion Bread has a savory flavor that enhances soups, salads, and many meat and cheese dishes. The sponge is best prepared a day ahead.

Sponge

1 cup warm water
1/2 package active dry yeast (scant 1 1/2 teaspoons)
1 1/2 cups unbleached all-purpose flour

Onions

1 tablespoon vegetable oil
2 medium onions

Dough

1 cup warm water
1 package active dry yeast
3 1/2 to 4 1/2 cups bread flour or unbleached all-purpose flour
2 teaspoons salt
Flour, for dusting work top
Oil, for greasing bowl
Cornmeal or flour, for dusting baking sheet
Chopped onion, for topping (optional)

Sponge

In a large bowl sprinkle the yeast over the warm water; stir to dissolve. Add the flour and stir until smooth. Cover and set aside in a warm, draft-free spot until bubbly and fermented (a minimum of 4 to 6 hours or, preferably, overnight).

Onions

Thinly slice the onions, then sauté in the oil over medium-low heat until barely browned. Set aside.

Dough

Stir down the Sponge, then add the water with the yeast dissolved in it, 3 1/2 cups flour, and salt. Stir until the dough comes away from the sides of the bowl.

Turn out the dough onto a lightly floured work top. Knead with a turn, fold, push motion, adding more flour in small amounts if the dough is sticky. Knead until the dough is smooth and elastic (8 to 10 minutes). Knead in the reserved onions. If they resist inclusion into the dough, be patient. Continue kneading until incorporated.

Transfer the dough to an oiled bowl and turn to coat. Cover and allow to rise until puffy (30 to 40 minutes). Punch down, then let rise until doubled in volume (about 45 minutes).

Shaping

Punch down, then shape into 2 rounds. Place on a baking sheet that has been dusted with cornmeal or flour; proof, covered, until doubled in size (about 1 hour). Brush the tops of the loaves with water, then cut 4 slashes in the form of a square. A sprinkling of chopped onion can be placed in the center, if desired.

Baking

Bake with steam (pages 31-32) in a preheated 450°F oven until the bread has a rich color and the bottom emits a hollow sound when tapped lightly with your fingertips (30 to 35 minutes). For the last 5 to 10 minutes the loaves can be removed from the pans for a crustier bread. Brush with water and let cool on a wire rack.

Yield

Makes 2 loaves.

French Onion Bread

(Food Processor, Steel Blade)

In the recipe above, instead of 1 cup warm water in the Dough use:

1/4 cup warm water
3/4 cup ice water

Sponge

In a medium bowl prepare the Sponge with 1 cup warm water, as above.

Dough

In the work bowl dissolve the yeast in the 1/4 cup warm water, then add the Sponge. Mix in the ice water, 1 1/2 cups flour, and salt. Pulse until absorbed. Add the reserved onions. Blend in 2 more cups flour, 1 cup at a time. More flour can be added 1/4 cup at a time if the dough is too soft. Process or pulse for 2 to 3 minutes. Do not overmix or the dough will get too hot. If necessary divide the dough in half and mix each half separately, then knead together. You may have to knead by hand for a few minutes to make the dough elastic.

Transfer the dough to an oiled bowl and turn to coat. Cover and allow to rise until puffy (30 to 40 minutes). Punch down, then let rise a second time until doubled in bulk (45 to 60 minutes).

Proceed as in Shaping and Baking, above.

Yield

Makes 2 loaves.

French Onion Bread

(Dough-Mixing Machine, Flat Beater)

Sponge

1 1/2 cups warm water
scant 3/4 tablespoon active dry yeast
2 1/4 cups unbleached all-purpose flour

Onions

1 1/2 tablespoons vegetable oil
3 medium onions

Dough

1 1/2 cups warm water
1 1/2 packages active dry yeast
5 3/4 to 6 3/4 cups bread flour or unbleached all-purpose flour
1 tablespoon salt
Flour, for dusting work top
Oil, for greasing bowl
Cornmeal or flour, for dusting baking sheet
Chopped onion, for topping (optional)

Sponge

In the mixing bowl dissolve the yeast in the warm water. Add the flour and mix at the first speed until smooth. Cover in place and allow to stand until bubbly and fermented (a minimum of 4 to 6 hours or, preferably, overnight).

Onions

Thinly slice the onions, then sauté in oil at medium-low heat until barely browned. Set aside.

Dough

Stir down the Sponge with 1 or 2 rotations of the beater. Add the water with the yeast dissolved in it, 5 1/4 cups flour, and salt. Pulse at the first speed using the on/off switch so that the beater does not throw the flour out of the bowl. When the flour is absorbed, run the machine at the first speed until the dough comes away from the sides of the bowl. If the dough is too soft, add flour 1/4 cup at a time.

Remove and scrape down the beater and insert the dough hook. Run at the first speed until the dough forms up on the hook and comes away from the sides of the bowl (8 to 10 minutes). You can use the second speed for the last few minutes to strengthen the gluten. Add the reserved onions and mix until absorbed. Be patient if they resist inclusion into the dough.

Transfer the dough to an oiled bowl and turn to coat. Cover and allow to rise until puffy (30 to 40 minutes). Punch and let rise until doubled in volume (about 45 minutes).

Proceed as in Shaping and Baking, above, except shape into 3 loaves.

Yield

Makes 3 loaves.

Cholesterol-Free Irish Raisin Bread

Although cholesterol-free and reduced in fat, calories, and sodium, this bread remains sweet and rich tasting, comparable to standard Irish raisin bread but with additional flavors of its own.

1 cup warm water
2 packages active dry yeast
1/4 cup honey
2 tablespoons vegetable oil
1/3 cup skim milk powder
2 egg whites, lightly beaten, or 1/4 cup egg substitute
5 to 6 cups unbleached all-purpose flour
1 teaspoon salt (optional, see Note)
1/4 teaspoon ground coriander
1/8 teaspoon ground cardamom
Flour, for dusting work top
1 cup raisins
Oil, for greasing bowl
Cornmeal, for dusting baking sheet
1 egg white, lightly beaten, for egg wash

In a large bowl sprinkle the yeast over the warm water to soften; stir to dissolve. Add the honey, oil, milk powder, egg whites, flour, salt (if desired), coriander, and cardamom. Mix until the dough comes away from the sides of the bowl.

Turn out the dough onto a floured surface and knead, adding flour 1/4 cup at a time if the dough is sticky. Knead until the dough is smooth and elastic (about 8 minutes). The finished dough should push back when pressed down. Add the raisins and gently knead them into the dough.

Rising

Transfer the dough to an oiled bowl and turn to coat on all sides. Cover with plastic wrap or a cloth and set aside until doubled in volume. Due to the reduced salt content, this dough will rise quicker than usual (see Note). Punch down, cut in half, and shape into 2 rounds. Cover and allow to rest for about 10 minutes.

Shaping

Knead each piece lightly, then shape each into a tight ball by pulling the sides underneath and turning the dough as you work. Place on a cornmeal-dusted baking sheet, cover, and allow to rise until doubled in size. Brush with the egg wash and allow to dry.

BAKER'S SECRET. Brush with the egg wash a second time to ensure a high shine when baked.

Baking

Bake in a preheated 375°F oven until the bottom sounds hollow when tapped with your fingertips (35 to 45 minutes).

BAKER'S SECRET. After the first 10 minutes, if the top browns too quickly cover with a brown paper bag that has been cut open or with a sheet of parchment paper.

If baking on an oven stone or tiles, you can finish baking directly on them for the last 5 to 10 minutes for a better crust.

Yield

Makes 2 loaves.

Note: When salt is omitted completely, the dough will rise very quickly. Allow it to rise only until it becomes puffy (15 to 20 minutes). Shape and proof without letting it rest. The bread will proof quicker than expected. Bake immediately.

Cholesterol-Free Irish Raisin...

(Food Processor, Steel Blade)

In the work bowl sprinkle the yeast over the warm water; stir to dissolve. Add the honey, oil, milk powder, egg whites, 2 cups flour, salt (if desired), coriander, and cardamom. Pulse to combine. Add 3 more cups flour and pulse until the dough comes away from the sides of the bowl, adding more flour if necessary. Pulse for 45 to 60 seconds. Do not overmix. If necessary divide the dough in half and process each half separately, then knead together.

Turn out the dough onto a lightly floured work top. Sprinkle the raisins on top and knead them in.

Proceed as in Rising, Shaping, and Baking, above.

Yield

Makes 2 loaves.

Cholesterol-Free Irish Raisin...

(Dough-Mixing Machine, Flat Beater)

1 1/2 cups warm water
3 packages active dry yeast
1/4 cup plus 2 tablespoons honey
3 tablespoons vegetable oil
1/2 cup skim milk powder
3 egg whites, or 1/4 cup plus 2 tablespoons egg substitute
7 1/2 to 9 cups unbleached all-purpose flour
1 1/2 teaspoons salt (optional, see Note above)
Generous 1/4 teaspoon ground coriander
Generous 1/8 teaspoon ground cardamom
Flour, for dusting work top
1 1/2 cups raisins
1 egg white, lightly beaten, for egg wash
Cornmeal, for dusting baking sheet

In the mixing bowl sprinkle the yeast over the warm water and stir to dissolve. Add the honey, oil, milk powder, egg whites, 7 1/2 cups flour, salt (if used), coriander, and cardamom. Pulse with the on/off switch until the flour is absorbed. Mix at the first speed until the dough comes away from the sides of the bowl, adding more flour if necessary.

Scrape down the beater and insert the dough hook. Mix for 8 to 10 minutes at the first speed. More flour can be added in small amounts as necessary. Mix long enough so that the flour is completely absorbed. The dough should be smooth and elastic. You can use the second speed for the last 2 minutes to strengthen the dough. If the motor becomes excessively strained, use the first speed.

Turn out the dough onto a lightly floured board and knead in the raisins by hand.

Proceed as in Rising and Baking, above, except shape into 3 loaves.

Yield

Makes 3 loaves.

Irish Raisin Bread

This bread seemed to evolve in the bakery. It filled a desire for a more typical type of raisin bread but one that retained some of its ethnic origins. This is a sweet bread that goes well with many foods and is much richer than the baking soda-leavened variety. It is generally baked in a round shape with an egg wash glaze. This bread keeps well and slices easily. It goes well at breakfast or tea time. Try it with cheese, as an accompaniment to a salad entrée, or with the main course.

1 cup warm water
2 packages active dry yeast
1/2 cup plus 1 tablespoon sugar
2 tablespoons unsalted butter or margarine, at room temperature
3 tablespoons skim milk powder
1 egg, lightly beaten
5 to 6 cups unbleached all-purpose flour
1 1/2 teaspoons salt
Pinch ground cardamom (optional)
Flour, for dusting work top
1 cup raisins
1 egg beaten with 1 teaspoon water, for egg wash
Cornmeal, for dusting baking sheet

In a large bowl sprinkle the yeast over the warm water to soften; stir to dissolve. Add the sugar, butter, milk powder, egg, 5 cups flour, salt, and cardamom (if desired). Mix until the dough comes away from the sides of the bowl.

Turn out the dough onto a floured surface and knead, adding flour 1/4 cup at a time if the dough is sticky. Knead until the dough is smooth and elastic (about 8 minutes). The finished dough should push back when pressed down.

Rising

Transfer the dough to an oiled bowl and turn to coat. Cover with plastic wrap or a towel and set aside until doubled in volume. Punch down, cut in half, and shape into 2 rounds. Cover and allow to rest for 10 minutes.

Shaping

Knead each round lightly, then shape each into a tight ball. Place on a cornmeal-dusted baking sheet, cover, and allow to rise until doubled in size. Brush with the egg wash and allow several minutes to dry.

BAKER'S SECRET. Brush with the egg wash a second time to ensure a high shine when baked.

Baking

Bake in a preheated 375°F oven until the bottom of the loaf emits a hollow sound when thumped with your fingertips (35 to 45 minutes).

BAKER'S SECRET. After the first 10 minutes, if the top browns too quickly cover with a brown paper bag that has been cut open or use a sheet of parchment paper.

If baking on an oven stone or tiles, you can finish baking directly on them for the last 5 to 10 minutes.

Yield

Makes 2 loaves.

Irish Raisin Bread

(Food Processor, Steel Blade)

In the recipe above, the butter and eggs can be chilled. Instead of 1 cup warm water use:

1/4 cup warm water
3/4 cup ice water

In the work bowl sprinkle the yeast over the warm water; stir to dissolve. Add the ice water, sugar, butter, milk powder, egg, 2 cups flour, salt, and cardamom (if desired). Pulse until all is absorbed. Add 3 more cups flour, 1 cup at a time. Pulse until the dough forms up and tries to ride up on top of the blade. Add more flour 1/4 cup at a time if necessary. Pulse for 2 to 3 minutes. If necessary divide the dough in half and process each half separately, then knead together. Do not allow the dough to overheat.

Turn out the dough onto a floured surface. Sprinkle the raisins on top and knead them in. Extra kneading may be necessary to make the dough elastic.

Proceed as in Rising, Shaping, and Baking, above.

Yield

Makes 2 loaves.

Irish Raisin Bread

(Dough-Mixing Machine, Flat Beater)

1 1/2 cups warm water
3 packages active dry yeast
3/4 cup plus 1 1/2 tablespoons sugar
3 tablespoons unsalted butter or shortening, at room temperature
4 1/2 tablespoons skim milk powder
1 1/2 eggs, lightly beaten
7 1/2 to 9 cups unbleached all-purpose flour
2 1/4 teaspoons salt
1/4 teaspoon ground cardamom (optional)
Flour, for dusting work top
1 1/2 cups raisins
1 egg beaten with 1 to 2 teaspoons water, for egg wash
Cornmeal, for dusting baking sheet

In the mixing bowl sprinkle the yeast over the warm water; stir to dissolve. Add the sugar, butter, milk powder, eggs, 7 1/2 cups flour, salt, and cardamom (if desired). Pulse with the on/off switch until the flour is absorbed so that it is not thrown out of the bowl. Mix at the first speed until the dough comes away from the sides of the bowl, adding more flour 1/4 cup at a time as necessary.

Scrape down the beater and insert the dough hook. Mix for 8 to 10 minutes at the first speed. More flour can be added in small amounts as necessary. The dough should be smooth and elastic. You can use the second speed for the last 2 minutes to strengthen the gluten. If the motor becomes excessively strained, use the first speed.

Turn out the dough onto a lightly floured surface and knead in the raisins by hand. Cover and proceed as in Rising, Shaping, and Baking, above, except shape into 3 loaves.

Yield

Makes 3 loaves.

Italian Bread

On a visit to Rome I once walked into a local bread bakery where I gained admission into the kitchen. Speaking no Italian but using sign language and a few words, I conversed with the bakers, who spoke no English. I was able to establish that I was a baker. We had an extended, though wordless, conversation about their breads and managed to understand one another. With much pride, the bakers were able to show and explain to me the different grades of flour they were using; they even managed to inquire whether I used the same back home. Flours differ in each country and we can adjust the recipes but people always remember the special flavor of the breads back home. Several of the men were curious about whether or not the same equipment was available in the United States. We molded up some breads by hand to demonstrate our skill to one another. When I was ready to leave, they insisted that I take with me an assortment of breads and rolls so that I might enjoy the products of their labor.

Sponge

2 packages active dry yeast
2 cups warm water
3 cups bread flour (preferred) or unbleached all-purpose flour

Dough

3 tablespoons sugar
3 tablespoons shortening or vegetable oil, at room temperature
2 to 3 cups unbleached all-purpose flour
1 tablespoon salt
Flour, for dusting work top
Oil, for greasing bowl
Cornmeal, for dusting baking sheet
1/4 cup sesame seeds, for sprinkling (optional)

Sponge

In a large bowl sprinkle the yeast over the water to soften; stir to dissolve. Add the flour and mix until smooth. Cover and allow to stand until doubled in volume (30 to 45 minutes).

Dough

Stir down the Sponge and add the sugar, shortening, 2 cups flour, and salt. Mix until the dough comes away from the sides of the bowl.

Turn out the dough onto a floured work top and knead, adding more flour 1/4 cup at a time if necessary, until the dough feels soft and silky (8 to 10 minutes). It should push back when pressed and your hand should come away clean.

Transfer the dough to an oiled bowl and turn to coat. Cover and allow to rise until doubled in volume (35 to 45 minutes). Punch down the dough, cut it in half, shape into rounds, and cover. Allow to rest for 10 minutes.

Shaping
Form into Italian-shaped loaves (see pages 27-29). Place the loaves on a baking sheet dusted with cornmeal. Brush with water and sprinkle with the sesame seeds (if desired). Cover with a damp cloth and allow to rise until doubled in size (45 to 60 minutes). When the bread has fully proofed, cut 3 diagonal slashes or 1 long slash down the center.

Baking
Bake with steam (pages 31-32) in a preheated 400°F oven until golden brown (25 to 30 minutes). Bake the last 5 minutes on tiles or an oven stone if you have them. The bread is done when it emits a hollow sound when tapped on the bottom with your fingertips and the sides feel hard and crisp.

Yield
Makes 2 loaves.

Italian Bread

(Food Processor, Steel Blade)

Sponge
In the work bowl sprinkle the yeast over the warm water to soften, then pulse to dissolve. Add the flour and pulse until smooth. Allow to stand, covered, until doubled in size (30 to 45 minutes). You can leave the bowl and blade in place on the machine.

Dough
Pulse to punch down the Sponge, then add the sugar, shortening, 2 cups flour (1 cup at a time), and salt. Pulse until the dough begins to form up. More flour can be added 1/4 cup at a time if the dough is too soft. Process for about 1 minute. If necessary divide the dough in half and process each half separately, then knead together. Do not overmix. Extra kneading by hand is sometimes necessary to make the dough elastic.

Transfer the dough to an oiled bowl and turn to coat. Cover and allow to rise until doubled in volume (35 to 45 minutes). Punch down the dough, cut it in half, shape into rounds, and cover. Allow to rest for 10 minutes.

Proceed as in Shaping and Baking, above.

Yield
Makes 2 loaves.

Italian Bread

(Dough-Mixing Machine, Flat Beater)

Sponge

3 cups warm water
3 packages active dry yeast
4 1/2 cups bread flour or unbleached all-purpose flour

Dough

4 1/2 tablespoons sugar
4 1/2 tablespoons shortening or vegetable oil, at room temperature
3 to 4 1/2 cups unbleached all-purpose flour
1 tablespoon salt
Oil, for greasing bowl
1/2 cup sesame seeds, for sprinkling (optional)
Flour, for dusting work top
Cornmeal, for dusting baking sheet

Sponge

In the mixing bowl sprinkle the yeast over the warm water; stir to dissolve. Add the flour and mix at the first speed until smooth. Cover and allow to rise until doubled in size (30 to 45 minutes).

Dough

Stir down the Sponge with 1 or 2 rotations of the beater, then add the sugar, shortening, 3 cups flour, and salt. Pulse at the first speed using the on/off switch so that the beater does not throw the flour out of the bowl. When the flour is absorbed, run the machine at the first speed until the dough comes away from the sides of the bowl. If the dough is too soft, add flour 1/4 cup at a time.

Remove and scrape down the beater and insert the dough hook. Run at the first speed until the dough forms up on the hook and comes away from the sides of the bowl (8 to 10 minutes). You can use the second speed for the last 5 minutes to strengthen the gluten.

Transfer the dough to an oiled bowl and turn to coat. Cover and allow to rise until doubled in volume (35 to 45 minutes).

Punch down the dough, cut it into thirds, shape into rounds, and cover. Allow to rest for 10 minutes.

Proceed as in Shaping and Baking, above.

Yield

Makes 3 loaves.

Foccacia #1

Foccacia is an Italian flat bread that enjoys wide popularity. It is the forerunner of pizza as we know it and is still enjoyed all over the world. Served plain or slathered with olive oil and coarse salt, or with simple toppings, these breads make marvelous snacks and go well with most meals. Oil, salt, and rosemary are my favorite toppings. Foccacia can be split open and filled sandwich style, served either warm or cold. Try it with a melted cheese filling. Two versions follow. Don't hesitate to try both.

2 cups warm water
2 packages active dry yeast
1/4 cup vegetable oil, preferably olive oil
5 to 6 cups bread flour or unbleached all-purpose flour
2 teaspoons salt
Flour, for dusting work top
Additional oil, for coating bowl and topping
Shortening, for greasing pans
Coarse salt, sliced onions, minced garlic, rosemary, sage, or tomato paste, for topping (optional)

In a large bowl sprinkle the yeast over the warm water to soften; stir to dissolve. Add the oil, 5 cups flour, and salt; mix until the dough comes away from the sides of the bowl.

Turn out the dough onto a flour-dusted work top. Knead, adding more flour 1/4 cup at a time if necessary, until the dough feels smooth and silky (8 to 10 minutes).

Transfer the dough to a clean, oiled bowl and turn top to bottom to coat. Cover and set aside until the dough doubles in volume (40 to 60 minutes).

Shaping

Punch down the dough and cut in half. Shape into 2 rounds, cover, and let rest 15 minutes. Prepare 2 greased baking sheets or pizza pans. Roll out and stretch the dough, letting it rest when it becomes tough, until it is large enough to cover the pan. With your fingertips press indentations over the entire surface of the dough. Brush with olive oil, then sprinkle with salt and/or toppings, if desired. Cover and let stand until puffy.

Baking

Bake with steam (pages 31-32) in a preheated 375°F oven until the bread has browned top and bottom (25 to 35 minutes). Let cool on a wire rack. This bread is best when served warm.

Yield

Makes 2 breads.

Foccacia #1

(Food Processor, Steel Blade)

In the recipe above, instead of 2 cups warm water use:

1/2 cup warm water
1 1/2 cups ice water

In the work bowl sprinkle the yeast over the warm water to soften; stir to dissolve. Add the ice water, oil, 2 cups flour, and salt. Mix until smooth. Add 3 cups flour, 1 cup at a time. Pulse until the dough comes together and tries to form up on top of the blade. More flour can be added 1/4 cup at a time if the dough is too soft. If necessary divide the dough in half and process each half separately, then knead together. Process for about 2 to 3 minutes. Do not allow the dough to overheat. Extra kneading by hand is sometimes necessary to make the dough elastic.

Turn out the dough, place in a clean, oiled bowl, and turn top to bottom to coat. Cover and set aside until the dough doubles in volume (40 to 60 minutes).

Proceed as in Shaping and Baking, above.

Yield

Makes 2 breads.

Foccacia #1

(Dough-Mixing Machine, Flat Beater)

3 cups warm water
3 packages active dry yeast
1/3 cup vegetable oil, preferably olive oil
8 to 9 cups bread flour or unbleached all-purpose flour
1 tablespoon salt
Flour, for dusting work top
Additional oil, for coating bowl and topping
Shortening, for greasing pans
Coarse salt, sliced onions, minced garlic, rosemary, sage, tomato paste, for topping (optional)

In the mixing bowl sprinkle the yeast over the warm water; stir to dissolve. Add the oil, 8 cups flour, and salt. Pulse with the on/off switch until all is absorbed so that the flour is not thrown out of the bowl. Run until the dough comes away from the sides of the bowl. Add flour 1/4 cup at a time if the dough is too soft.

Remove and scrape down the beater and insert the dough hook. Run at the first speed until the dough forms up on the hook and comes away from the sides of the bowl (8 to 10 minutes). You can use the second speed for the last few minutes to develop the gluten. Remove the hook, add oil to the bowl, and turn the dough top to bottom until the dough is coated. Cover and allow to double in volume (45 to 60 minutes). Proceed as in Shaping and Baking, except shape into 3 rounds.

Yield

Makes 3 breads.

Foccacia #2

2 cups warm water
1 package active dry yeast
2 tablespoons vegetable oil, preferably olive oil
5 to 6 cups bread flour or unbleached all-purpose flour
1 tablespoon salt
Flour, for dusting work top
Additional oil, for coating bowl and topping
Shortening, for greasing pans
Coarse salt, sliced onions, minced garlic, rosemary, sage, or tomato paste, for topping (optional)

In a large bowl sprinkle the yeast over the warm water to soften; stir to dissolve. Add the oil, 5 cups flour, and salt; mix until the dough comes away from the sides of the bowl.

Turn out the dough onto a flour-dusted work top. Knead, adding more flour 1/4 cup at a time if necessary, until the dough feels smooth and silky (8 to 10 minutes).

Transfer the dough to a clean, oiled bowl and turn top to bottom to coat. Cover and set aside until the dough becomes puffy (about 30 minutes).

Punch down the dough, then allow it to rise, covered, until doubled in volume (30 to 45 minutes).

Shaping

Shape the dough into a round, then cut in half. Shape into 2 rounds, cover, and let rest for 5 minutes. Prepare 2 greased baking sheets or pizza pans. Roll out and stretch the dough, letting it rest when it becomes tough, until the dough is large enough to cover the pan. Cover and allow to proof until puffed up. Dimple the tops with your fingertips and brush with oil so that the depressions are filled with the oil. Sprinkle carefully with additional toppings if desired.

Baking

Bake with steam (pages 31-32) in a preheated 400°F oven until the bread has browned top and bottom (20 to 25 minutes). Let cool on a wire rack. This bread is best served warm.

Yield

Makes 2 breads.

Foccacia #2

(Food Processor, Steel Blade)

In the recipe above, instead of 2 cups warm water use:

1/2 cup warm water
1 1/2 cups ice water

In the work bowl sprinkle the yeast over the warm water to soften; stir to dissolve. Add the ice water, oil, 2 cups flour, and salt. Mix until smooth. Add 3 cups flour, 1 cup at a time. Pulse until the dough comes together and tries to form up on top of the blade. More flour can be added 1/4 cup at a time if the dough is too soft. If necessary divide the dough in half and process each half separately, then knead together. Process for 2 to 3 minutes. Do not allow the dough to overheat. Extra kneading by hand is sometimes necessary to make the dough elastic.

Turn out the dough, place in a clean, oiled bowl, and turn top to bottom to coat. Cover and set aside until the dough becomes puffy (about 30 minutes). Punch down the dough, then allow to rise, covered, until doubled in volume (30 to 45 minutes).

Proceed as in Shaping and Baking, above.

Yield

Makes 2 breads.

Foccacia #2

(Dough-Mixing Machine, Flat Beater)

3 cups warm water
1 1/2 packages active dry yeast
3 tablespoons vegetable oil, preferably olive oil
7 1/2 to 9 cups bread flour or unbleached all-purpose flour
1 1/2 tablespoons salt
Flour, for dusting work top
Additional oil, for coating bowl and topping
Shortening, for greasing pans
Coarse salt, sliced onions, minced garlic, rosemary, sage, or tomato paste, for topping (optional)

In the mixing bowl sprinkle the yeast over the warm water to soften; stir to dissolve. Add the oil, 7 1/2 cups flour, and salt. Pulse with the on/off switch until all is absorbed so that the flour is not thrown out of the bowl. Run until the dough comes away from the sides of the bowl. More flour can be added 1/4 cup at a time if the dough is too soft.

Remove and scrape down the beater and insert the dough hook. Run at the first speed until the dough forms up on the hook and comes away from the sides of the bowl (8 to 10 minutes). You can use the second speed for the last few minutes to develop the gluten.

Remove the hook, add oil to the bowl, and turn the dough top to bottom to coat. Cover and set aside until the dough becomes puffy (about 30 minutes).

Punch down the dough, then allow to rise, covered, until doubled in volume (30 to 45 minutes).

Proceed as in Shaping and Baking, above, except shape into 3 breads.

Yield

Makes 3 breads.

Pizza

In my lifetime I've seen the ubiquitous pizza and the bagel become universal standards, adopted and loved by all. They have gone far beyond their ethnic origins.

One pizza stands out in my memory. As a youth I patronized a restaurant on the east side of midtown Manhattan that served the most outstanding pizza in New York. It was baked in an old coal-fired tile oven with tremendous heat. The crust was thin and crisp, the hot olive oil burned the roof of your mouth, and the cheese seemed capable of stretching all the way out the front door. Although the restaurant has been gone for many years, the memory lingers on.

2 cups warm water
1 1/2 teaspoons active dry yeast
2 tablespoons vegetable oil, preferably olive oil, plus more for drizzling on pizza
5 to 6 cups bread flour
2 teaspoons salt
Flour, for dusting work top
Oil, for greasing bowl and pans
Toppings of your choice
Mozzarella or other Italian cheese, to taste

In a large bowl sprinkle the yeast over the warm water to soften; stir to dissolve. Add the 2 tablespoons oil, 5 cups flour, and salt; mix until the dough comes away from the sides of the bowl.

Turn out the dough onto a flour-dusted work top. Knead, adding more flour 1/4 cup at a time if necessary. Keep the dough somewhat soft. Knead for 10 to 15 minutes. You want to develop the gluten to be as strong as possible.

Transfer the dough to a clean, oil-coated bowl and turn top to bottom until coated. Cover and set aside until the dough doubles in volume (40 to 60 minutes).

Shaping

Punch down the dough and cut into thirds. Shape into rounds, cover, and let rest for 15 minutes. At this point the dough can be frozen or refrigerated for later use.

Roll out the dough and stretch each ball into a 14-inch round on greased pizza pans or baking sheets. Arrange the toppings and drizzle with the olive oil. Since the heat of a pizza oven cannot be duplicated in the home kitchen, wait until the pie is half baked before adding any cheese. The way I do it is to spiral a ladle full or more of pizza sauce on the dough and spread it with the bottom of the ladle. Then I add salt, pepper, and oregano, then spiral olive oil over the top from a spouted oil can. Allow to rest for a few minutes.

Baking

Bake in a preheated 500°F to 550°F oven. When the edges of the pizza begin to brown, remove it from the oven. When using a pizza stone or oven tiles, if you like at this point you can slide the pizza off the pan and onto a wooden peel. Add the cheese and additional olive oil. Return the pizza to the oven and bake until the cheese is bubbly and the edges are crisp. You might try turning the broiler on for a minute to melt the cheese. If you are lucky the edges may become slightly blackened. Carefully lift an edge and check that the bottom is baked, which should take 20 to 35 minutes depending upon the thickness of the crust.

Yield

Makes 3 pizzas.

Variation

Pizza Torte

These pies are decorative at the dinner table or buffet, and lend a party air to special occasions. A fluted 8- to 10-inch tart pan 1 inch deep is necessary. A French tart pan with a removable bottom is the easiest to use. Roll out rounds of pizza dough to about 1/8 to 1/4 inch thick and 1 inch wider than the pan. Gently transfer the dough to the greased pan. Trim the excess by rolling a stick across the top of the pan. Proceed with filling and bake as above. Several of these can be made and baked in advance, then rewarmed before serving. They are also good served cold.

Pizza

(Food Processor, Steel Blade)

In the recipe above, instead of 2 cups warm water use:

1/2 cup warm water
1 1/2 cups ice water

In the work bowl sprinkle the yeast over the warm water to soften; stir to dissolve. Add the ice water, 2 tablespoons oil, 2 cups flour (1 cup at a time), and salt. Mix until smooth. Add 3 cups flour, 1 cup at a time. Pulse until the dough comes together and tries to form up on top of the blade. More flour can be added 1/4 cup at a time if the dough is too soft. If necessary divide the dough in half and process each half separately, then knead together. Process for about 2 to 3 minutes. Do not allow the dough to overheat. A dough thermometer should read 78°F. You may need to process longer to reach this temperature. Extra kneading by hand is sometimes necessary to make the dough elastic.

Turn out the dough, place in a clean, oil-coated bowl, and turn top to bottom until the dough is coated. Cover and set aside until the dough doubles in volume (40 to 60 minutes).

Proceed as in Shaping and Baking, above.

Yield

Makes 3 pizzas.

Pizza

(Dough-Mixing Machine, Flat Beater)

---

3 cups warm water
2 1/4 teaspoons active dry yeast
3 tablespoons vegetable oil, preferably olive oil
7 1/2 to 9 cups bread flour or unbleached all-purpose flour
3 teaspoons salt
Oil, for greasing bowl and pans
Flour, for dusting work top
Mozzarella, or other Italian cheese, to taste

In the mixing bowl sprinkle the yeast over the warm water to soften; stir to dissolve. Add the oil, 7 1/2 cups flour, and salt. Pulse with the on/off switch until all is absorbed so that the flour is not thrown out of the bowl. Run at the first speed until the dough comes away from the sides of the bowl. More flour can be added 1/4 cup at a time if the dough is too soft.

Remove and scrape down the beater and insert the dough hook. Run at the first speed until the dough forms up on the hook and comes away from the sides of the bowl (8 to 10 minutes). You can use the second speed for the last few minutes to develop the gluten.

Remove the hook, add oil to the bowl, and turn the dough top to bottom to coat. Cover and allow to rise until doubled in volume (45 to 60 minutes). Proceed as in Shaping and Baking, above, except shape into 4 or 5 pizzas.

Yield

Makes 4 thick or 5 thin pizzas.

Semolina Bread

Semolina, a rich golden durum wheat flour employed in making pasta of the highest quality, is used by Italian bakers to enrich both the flavor and texture of their breads. Many of my friends travel great distances to the old ethnic neighborhoods to purchase semolina bread freshly baked in the old coal-burning ovens that were used when our parents were young. Here is my adaptation of this bread formulated for the home baker. Semolina flour is available in some Italian bakeries, natural foods stores, and gourmet and fresh pasta shops.

Sponge

2 cups warm water
2 packages active dry yeast
3 cups semolina flour

Dough

3 tablespoons sugar or malt syrup
3 tablespoons shortening or vegetable oil, preferably olive oil
2 to 3 cups bread flour or unbleached all-purpose flour
1 tablespoon salt
Flour, for dusting work top
Oil, for greasing bowl
Cornmeal, for dusting baking sheet
Sesame seeds, for sprinkling (optional)

Sponge

In a large bowl sprinkle the yeast over the warm water; stir to dissolve. Add the flour and stir until smooth. Cover and let stand in a warm spot until doubled in volume (30 to 45 minutes).

Dough

Stir down the Sponge, then add the sugar, shortening, 2 cups flour, and salt. Mix until the dough comes away from the sides of the bowl.

Turn out the dough onto a floured board and knead, adding more flour 1/4 cup at a time if the dough is sticky. Continue kneading vigorously until the dough feels smooth and elastic (10 to 12 minutes). The dough should push back when pressed down.

Transfer the dough to an oiled bowl and turn to coat. Cover and allow to rise until doubled in volume (35 to 45 minutes). Punch down, then cut the dough in half, shape into rounds, and cover. Allow to rest for 10 minutes.

Shaping
Form into 2 Italian-shaped loaves (see pages 28-29) about 18 inches long. Place the loaves on a baking sheet that has been dusted with cornmeal.

Proofing
Cover with a cloth and allow to rise until doubled in size (45 to 60 minutes). Brush the tops with water and sprinkle with sesame seeds (if desired). When the bread has proofed, cut 3 diagonal slashes with a sharp knife or single-edged razor blade. Hold the knife at a angle to the bread and try to cut inside and underneath the crust. This will cause the bread to break open, or bloom, while baking and form a thick, crunchy crust.

Baking
Bake with steam (pages 31-32) in a preheated 400°F oven until browned and the bread sounds hollow when tapped on the bottom with your fingertips (35 to 45 minutes). If baking on an oven stone or tiles, the bread can be removed from the baking pan for the last 10 minutes to firm up the crust.

Yield
Makes 2 loaves.

Semolina Bread

(Food Processor, Steel Blade)

Instead of 2 cups warm water use:

1/4 cup warm water
1 3/4 cups ice water

Sponge
In the work bowl sprinkle the yeast over the warm water to soften, then pulse to dissolve. Add the ice water and flour; pulse until smooth. Allow to stand, covered, until doubled in size (30 to 45 minutes). You can leave the bowl and blade in place on the machine.

Dough
Pulse to punch down the Sponge, then add the sugar, shortening, 2 cups flour (1 cup at a time), and salt. Pulse until the dough tries to form up on top of the blade. More flour can be added 1/4 cup at a time if the dough is too soft. Process to a dough temperature of 78°F (about 1 minute). If necessary divide the dough in half and process each half separately, then knead together. Do not overmix. Extra kneading by hand is sometimes necessary to make the dough elastic.

Transfer the dough to an oiled bowl and turn to coat. Cover and allow to double in volume (35 to 45 minutes). Punch down the dough, then cut it in half. Let it rest, covered, for 10 minutes. Proceed as in Shaping, Proofing, and Baking, above.

Yield
Makes 2 loaves.

Semolina Bread

(Dough-Mixing Machine, Flat Beater)

Sponge

3 cups warm water
3 packages active dry yeast
4 1/2 cups semolina flour

Dough

4 1/2 tablespoons sugar or malt syrup
4 1/2 tablespoons shortening or vegetable oil, preferably olive oil
3 to 4 1/2 cups bread flour or unbleached all-purpose flour
1 1/2 tablespoons salt
Flour, for dusting work top
Oil, for greasing bowl
Cornmeal, for dusting baking sheet
Sesame seeds, for sprinkling (optional)

Sponge

In the mixing bowl sprinkle the yeast over the warm water; stir at the first speed to dissolve. Add the flour and mix at the second speed until smooth. Cover and let stand until doubled in volume.

Dough

Stir down the Sponge with 1 or 2 rotations of the beater, then add the sugar, shortening, 3 cups flour, and salt. Pulse at the first speed using the on/off switch so that the beater does not throw the flour out of the bowl. When the flour is absorbed, run the machine at the first speed until the dough comes away from the sides of the bowl. If the dough is too soft, add flour 1/4 cup at a time.

Remove and scrape down the beater and insert the dough hook. Run at the first speed until the dough forms up on the hook and comes away from the sides of the bowl (10 to 12 minutes). You can use the second speed for the last 2 minutes to strengthen the gluten.

Transfer the dough to an oiled bowl and turn to coat. Cover and allow to rise until doubled in volume (35 to 45 minutes). Punch down, then cut the dough into thirds, shape into rounds, and cover. Allow to rest for 10 minutes.

Proceed as in Shaping, Proofing, and Baking, above, except shape into 3 loaves.

Yield

Makes 3 loaves.

Lavash

This Middle Eastern bread, also known as Armenian bread, Lebanese bread, and the lavash of Georgian Russia, is a large flat bread either cracker crisp or soft. Try it both ways; it is equally good depending on how it is to be used. The Georgian lavash is thick and breadlike.

1 1/2 cups warm water
1 package active dry yeast
2 tablespoons vegetable oil (preferably olive oil) or shortening
3 1/2 to 4 1/2 cups bread flour (preferred) or all-purpose flour
1 1/2 teaspoons salt
Oil, for greasing bowl
Flour, for dusting work top

In a large bowl sprinkle the yeast over the warm water to soften; stir to dissolve. Add the oil, 3 1/2 cups flour, and salt. Mix until the dough comes away from the sides of the bowl.

Turn out the dough onto a floured surface and knead, adding flour 1/4 cup at a time if necessary. The dough should be stiff, although it will soften somewhat while kneading. Knead until the dough is smooth and elastic (8 to 10 minutes). The finished dough should push back when pressed down.

Rising

Transfer the dough to an oiled bowl and turn to coat. Cover with plastic wrap or a damp towel and set aside until doubled in volume (45 to 60 minutes). Punch down the dough, then divide into 10 equal pieces. Shape into rounds with your palms while cupping them over the dough. Coat with oil or melted butter, cover, and allow to rest for 15 minutes.

Shaping

On a clean, floured work surface, roll out each ball into a circle 10 to 12 inches or more across and as thin as possible, turning over or letting the dough rest if it resists. Cover and allow to rest for 15 minutes.

Baking

Bake in a preheated 500°F oven until flecked all over with brown spots (15 to 20 minutes). Oven tiles or a baking stone work best. If neither is available place 2 baking pans upside down on the middle shelf of the oven and let them preheat for at least 5 minutes. Drape each lavash over a rolling pin (stick type) or dowel and roll the dough off into the oven. Prick any large bubbles with a long skewer or fork.

Remove the bread with a long-handled spatula. The lavash can be left to cool and used as a crisp cracker-type bread. If soft lavash is desired, stack them one on top of another between 2 towels and cover. When all are baked, sprinkle each with a little water, fold in quarters, and keep covered until cool.

Lavash can be eaten warm, or left to cool in the toweling, then placed in plastic bags. Refrigerate or freeze in plastic bags.

Yield

Makes 10 breads.

Lavash

(Food Processor, Steel Blade)

In the recipe above, instead of 1 1/2 cups warm water use:

1/4 cup warm water
1 1/4 cups ice water

In the work bowl sprinkle the yeast over the warm water to soften; stir to dissolve. Add the ice water, oil, 2 cups flour, and salt. Pulse to combine. Add 1 1/2 cups flour, 3/4 cup at a time. Process until the dough comes away from the sides of the bowl, adding more flour 1/4 cup at a time, as required. This dough should be a little stiff. Pulse for 2 to 3 minutes. Do not overmix. If necessary divide the dough in half and process each half separately, then knead together. Extra kneading by hand may be necessary to make the dough elastic.

Proceed as in Rising, Shaping, and Baking, above.

Yield

Makes 10 breads.

Lavash

(Dough-Mixing Machine, Flat Beater)

The previous recipe also works well in the mixer.

2 1/4 cups warm water
1 1/2 packages active dry yeast
3 tablespoons vegetable oil (preferably olive oil) or shortening
5 1/4 to 6 3/4 cups bread flour (preferred) or all-purpose flour
2 1/4 teaspoons salt
Oil, for greasing bowl
Flour, for dusting work top

In the work bowl sprinkle the yeast over the warm water to soften; stir to dissolve. Add the oil, 5 1/4 cups flour, and salt. Pulse, using the on/off switch, until the flour is absorbed so that it does not fly out of the bowl. Mix at the first speed until the dough comes away from the sides of the bowl, adding more flour 1/4 cup at a time if required.

Scrape down the beater and insert the dough hook. Mix for 8 to 10 minutes at the first speed. More flour can be added in small amounts as necessary. The dough should start out stiffer than usual. It will soften somewhat while mixing. The finished dough should be smooth and elastic. Tend to the mixer bowl at all times lest it jump off the saddle or cause the machine to walk. Proceed as in Rising, Shaping, and Baking, above, except shape into 15 breads.

Yield

Makes 15 breads.

London Bloomers

British foods sometimes have extraordinary names, such as Singing Hinny, Bangers and Mash, Bubble and Squeak, or Toad-in-the-Hole (see Note). So an English bread called London Bloomers is not that unusual.

My friend Bob worked in bakeries in London for several years. He became proficient at British bread and cake baking, and was a connoisseur of fiery Indian food. This recipe is adapted from his formula. As he tells it, the bread is distinguished by 13 diagonal slashes across the top. It seems that London master bakers have been known to become violent if a baker didn't make exactly 13 cuts!

2 cups warm water
2 packages active dry yeast
2/3 cup skim milk powder
1 cup cake flour
4 to 5 cups unbleached all-purpose flour
1 tablespoon salt
Flour, for dusting work top
Oil, for coating bowl
Water or cornstarch solution (page 20), for brushing loaves
2 tablespoons poppy seeds, for sprinkling

In a large bowl sprinkle the yeast over the warm water to soften; stir to dissolve. Add the milk powder, cake flour, 4 cups all-purpose flour, and salt. Mix until the dough comes away from the sides of the bowl.

Turn out the dough onto a flour-dusted work top. Knead, adding more flour 1/4 cup at a time if necessary, until the dough feels smooth and silky (8 to 10 minutes).

Rising

Transfer the dough to a clean, oil-coated bowl and turn top to bottom until the dough is coated. Cover and set aside until the dough doubles in volume (40 to 60 minutes).

Shaping

Punch down the dough, cut in half, and shape into rounds. Cover and let rest for 15 minutes. Shape into 2 pan loaves (pages 27-28). Place each bread, seam down, in a greased loaf pan and keep in a warm, draft-free area. Proof until doubled in volume. Brush with water or a cornstarch solution, then sprinkle with the poppy seeds. Cut 13 diagonal slashes across the width of the loaves.

Baking

Bake with steam (pages 31-32) in a preheated 375°F oven until the bread has browned and the bottom emits a hollow sound when tapped with your fingertips (35 to 45 minutes). Brush the bread again after removing it from the oven. Let cool on a wire rack.

Yield

Makes 2 loaves.

Note: Singing Hinny (page 276) is a type of scone or biscuit. Bangers and Mash is fried breakfast meat and mashed potatoes. Bubble and Squeak is mashed potatoes with greens mixed in, fried into inch-thick pancakes and traditionally served on Monday with Sunday's leftovers. Toad-in-the-Hole is Yorkshire pudding with little franks or wurst baked inside.

London Bloomers

(Food Processor, Steel Blade)

Instead of 2 cups warm water use:

1/2 cup warm water
1 1/2 cups ice water

In the work bowl sprinkle the yeast over the warm water to soften; stir to dissolve. Add the ice water, milk powder, cake flour, 1 cup all-purpose flour, and salt. Mix until smooth. Add 4 cups all-purpose flour, 1 cup at a time. Pulse until the dough comes together and tries to form up on top of the blade. More flour can be added 1/4 cup at a time if the dough is too soft. If necessary divide the dough in half and process each half separately, then knead together. Process for about 2 to 3 minutes. Do not allow the dough to overheat. Extra kneading by hand is sometimes necessary to make the dough elastic. Proceed as in Rising, Shaping, and Baking, above.

Yield

Makes 2 loaves.

London Bloomers

(Dough-Mixing Machine, Flat Beater)

---

3 cups warm water
3 packages active dry yeast
1 cup skim milk powder
1 1/2 cups cake flour
6 to 7 1/2 cups unbleached all-purpose flour
1 1/2 tablespoons salt
Oil, for coating bowl
Flour, for dusting work top
Water or cornstarch solution (page 20) for brushing loaves
3 tablespoons poppy seeds, for sprinkling

In the mixing bowl sprinkle the yeast over the warm water to soften; stir to dissolve. Add the milk powder, cake flour, 6 cups all-purpose flour, and salt. Pulse with the on/off switch until all is absorbed so that the flour is not thrown out of the bowl. Mix at the first speed until the dough comes away from the sides of the bowl. More flour can be added 1/4 cup at a time if the dough is too soft.

Remove and scrape down the beater and insert the dough hook. Run at the first speed until the dough forms up on the hook and comes away from the sides of the bowl (8 to 10 minutes). You can use the second speed for the last few minutes to develop the gluten.

Proceed as in Rising, Shaping, and Baking, above, except shape into 3 loaves.

Yield

Makes 3 loaves.

Millet Rye Bread

Healthful and nourishing, millet is an age-old grain and one of the first to be cultivated by man. As used here, mixed with rye flour, it makes for a new and exotic flavor. Millet is a staple in the diet of many African peoples. It is used here toasted.

Sponge

1 cup boiling water
1 cup hulled millet, toasted (see Note)
1 package active dry yeast
1 cup rye flour

Dough

1 cup warm water
1 tablespoon honey
2 tablespoons shortening
1 1/2 cups rye flour
2 1/2 to 3 1/2 cups unbleached all-purpose flour
2 teaspoons salt
Flour, for dusting work top and pans
Oil, for greasing bowl and pans
Water or cornstarch solution (page 20), for brushing bread

Sponge

In a large bowl pour the boiling water over the millet. Let cool until lukewarm. Add the yeast and stir to dissolve. Add the flour and mix until smooth. Cover and allow to stand until tripled in volume and beginning to fall back (about 1 hour). The time will vary with room and dough temperature.

Dough

Stir down the Sponge, then add the water, honey, shortening, flours, and salt. Mix until the dough comes away from the sides of the bowl.

Turn out the dough onto a floured work top and knead, adding more all-purpose flour 1/4 cup at a time if necessary, until the dough feels soft and silky (8 to 10 minutes).

Transfer the dough to an oiled bowl and turn to coat. Cover and allow to rise until doubled in volume (30 to 45 minutes). Cut the dough in half, shape into 2 rounds, and cover. Allow to rest for 15 minutes.

Shaping

Shape into 2 long pan-shaped loaves (pages 27-28). Place on a flour-dusted baking pan or into 2 greased and floured 8- or 9-inch loaf pans. Cover with a flour-dusted cloth and allow to rise until doubled in size (45 to 60 minutes). When the bread has fully proofed, slash with 6 to 8 deep diagonal cuts. Brush the tops with water or cornstarch solution.

Baking

Bake with steam (pages 31-32) in a preheated 425° F oven until golden brown (35 to 45 minutes). Bake the last 5 minutes on tiles or an oven stone if you have them. The bread is done when it emits a hollow sound when tapped on the bottom with your fingertips.

Yield

Makes 2 loaves.

Note: Hulled millet can be found in natural foods stores, Indian groceries, and some ethnic markets. Do not buy it in pet shops, since it will be unhulled. Toast millet on the stovetop in a dry cast iron skillet over medium heat, shaking until toasted and popping.

Millet Rye Bread

(Food Processor, Steel Blade)

Sponge

In the work bowl pour the boiling water over the millet. Let cool until lukewarm. Add the yeast and stir to dissolve. Add the flour and mix until smooth. Cover and allow to stand until tripled in volume and beginning to fall back (about 1 hour). The time will vary with room and dough temperature.

Dough

Punch down the Sponge, then add the honey, shortening, flours, and salt. With the machine pulsing add 1 cup warm water, mixing until the dough tries to form up on top of the blade. More all-purpose flour can be added 1/4 cup at a time if the dough is too soft. Process for about 1 minute. If necessary divide the dough in half and process each half separately, then knead together. Do not overmix. Extra kneading by hand is sometimes necessary to make the dough elastic.

Transfer the dough to an oiled bowl and turn to coat. Cover and allow to rise until doubled in volume (30 to 45 minutes). Punch down the dough, cut it in half, shape into 2 rounds, and cover. Allow to rest for 15 minutes.

Proceed as in Shaping and Baking, above.

Millet Rye Bread

(Dough-Mixing Machine, Flat Beater)

Sponge

1 1/2 cups boiling water
1 1/2 cups hulled millet, toasted (see Note above)
1 package plus 1 1/2 teaspoons active dry yeast
1 1/2 cups rye flour

Dough

1 1/2 cups warm water
1 1/2 tablespoons honey
3 tablespoons shortening
2 1/4 cups rye flour
3 3/4 to 5 1/4 cups unbleached all-purpose flour
1 tablespoon salt
Flour, for dusting work top and pans
Oil, for greasing bowl and pans
Water or cornstarch solution (page 20), for brushing bread

Sponge

In the mixing bowl pour the boiling water over the millet. Let cool until lukewarm. Add the yeast and stir to dissolve. Add the flour and mix until smooth. Cover and allow to stand until tripled in volume and beginning to fall back (about 1 hour). The time varies with room and dough temperature.

Dough

Stir down the Sponge, then add the water, honey, shortening, flours, and salt. Mix until the dough comes away from the sides of the bowl.

Remove and scrape down the beater and insert the dough hook. Mix at the first speed, adding more all-purpose flour 1/4 cup at a time if necessary. Knead until the dough feels soft and silky (8 to 10 minutes).

Transfer the dough to an oiled bowl and turn to coat. Cover and allow to rise until doubled in volume (30 to 45 minutes). Cut the dough into thirds, shape into rounds, and cover. Allow to rest for 15 minutes.

Proceed as in Shaping and Baking, above, except shape into 3 loaves.

Yield

Makes 3 loaves.

Millet Rye Bread, Country Style

This grain has an interesting flavor and is high in vitamins and minerals. You will receive many compliments when you serve this as the base for meat or poultry to sop up extra sauce. It also works well for hot open-faced sandwiches. Prepare the sponge 4 to 6 hours in advance or preferably overnight.

Sponge

1 cup boiling water
1 cup hulled millet, toasted (see Note)
1/2 package active dry yeast
3/4 cup warm water
2 cups rye flour

Dough

1 package active dry yeast
1/4 cup warm water
3 to 4 cups common flour (preferred) or unbleached all-purpose flour
1 tablespoon salt
Flour, for dusting work top
Oil, for greasing bowl
Cornmeal or rye flour, for dusting baking sheet
Water or cornstarch solution (page 20), for brushing
Sesame seeds, for sprinkling

Sponge

In a medium bowl pour the boiling water over the toasted millet and allow to cool. In a large bowl sprinkle the yeast over the warm water; stir to dissolve. Add the millet mixture and flour. Mix until smooth. Cover and allow to stand at room temperature for 4 to 6 hours or preferably overnight.

Dough

In a large bowl sprinkle the yeast over the warm water; stir to dissolve. Add the Sponge, 3 cups flour, and salt. Mix until the dough comes away from the sides of the bowl.

Turn out the dough onto a floured work top and knead, adding more flour 1/4 cup at a time if necessary, until the dough is soft and elastic (8 to 10 minutes).

Transfer the dough to a clean, oiled bowl and turn to coat. Cover and allow to rise until doubled in volume (30 to 45 minutes). Cut the dough in half, shape into 2 rounds, and cover. Allow to rest for 15 minutes.

Shaping

Shape the dough into 2 rounds or loaves. Place the loaves on a baking sheet dusted with cornmeal or rye flour. Cover with a damp cloth and allow to rise until doubled in size

(45 to 60 minutes). Brush with water or the cornstarch solution, sprinkle with the sesame seeds, and cut 3 slashes in each loaf.

Baking

Bake with steam (pages 31-32) in a preheated 400°F oven until golden brown (25 to 30 minutes). Bake the last 5 minutes on tiles or an oven stone if you have them. The bread is done when it emits a hollow sound when tapped on the bottom with your fingertips and the sides feel hard and crisp.

Yield

Makes 2 loaves.

Note: Hulled millet can be found in natural foods stores, Indian groceries, and some ethnic markets. Do not buy it in pet shops, since it will be unhulled. Toast millet in a heavy skillet over medium heat. Stir or shake for about 5 minutes until barely browned.

Millet Rye Bread, Country Style

(Food Processor, Steel Blade)

Sponge

Prepare the Sponge as above. Cover and allow to stand at room temperature for 4 to 6 hours or preferably overnight.

Dough

In the work bowl sprinkle the yeast over the warm water; stir to dissolve. Add the Sponge, 3 cups flour (1 cup at a time), and salt. Pulse until the dough tries to form up on top of the blade. More flour can be added 1/4 cup at a time if the dough is too soft. Process for about 1 minute. If necessary divide the dough in half and process each half separately, then knead together. Do not overmix. Extra kneading by hand is sometimes necessary to make the dough elastic.

Transfer the dough to a clean, oiled bowl and turn to coat. Cover and allow to rise until doubled in volume (30 to 45 minutes). Cut the dough in half, shape into 2 rounds, and cover. Allow to rest for 15 minutes.

Proceed as in Shaping and Baking, above.

Yield

Makes 2 loaves.

Millet Rye Bread, Country Style

(Dough-Mixing Machine, Flat Beater)

Sponge

1 1/2 cups boiling water
1 1/2 cups hulled millet, toasted (see Note above)
1/2 package active dry yeast (scant 1 1/2 teaspoons)
1 1/4 cups warm water
3 cups rye flour

Dough

1 package active dry yeast
6 tablespoons warm water
5 to 6 cups common flour or unbleached all-purpose flour
1 1/2 tablespoons salt
Oil, for greasing bowl

Sponge

In a medium bowl pour the boiling water over the toasted millet; allow to cool. In the mixing bowl sprinkle the yeast over the warm water; stir to dissolve. Add the millet mixture and flour. Mix until smooth. Cover and allow to stand at room temperature for 4 to 6 hours or preferably overnight.

Dough

In the mixing bowl sprinkle the yeast over the warm water; stir to dissolve. Add 5 cups flour and salt. Pulse at the first speed using the on/off switch so that the beater does not throw the flour out of the bowl. When the flour is absorbed run the machine at the first speed until the dough comes away from the sides of the bowl. If the dough is too soft, add more flour 1/4 cup at a time.

Remove and scrape down the beater and insert the dough hook. Run at the first speed until the dough forms up on the hook and comes away from the sides of the bowl (8 to 10 minutes). You can use the second speed for the last few minutes to strengthen the gluten.

Transfer the dough to an oiled bowl and turn to coat. Cover and allow to rise until doubled in volume (30 to 45 minutes). Cut the dough in half, shape into 2 rounds, and cover. Allow to rest for 15 minutes.

Proceed as in Shaping and Baking, above, except shape into 3 loaves.

Yield

Makes 3 loaves.

Murray's Kashi® Bread

An excellent cereal called Kashi® contains seven grains plus sesame seeds. My friend Murray discovered this cold, puffed grain cereal in his local market and enjoyed it with milk and fruit for breakfast. One day when I was visiting I found that he was being joshed by his entire family for an incident involving his breakfast cereal. It seems that there are two kinds of Kashi®. One is the cold, puffed grain and the other is a dry grain, which is cooked into a hot cereal. Unknowingly, my friend purchased the dry grain, poured it into his breakfast bowl, added milk, and attempted to eat it. "Not to worry," I told him. "Give me the cereal and I will make a bread with it." A few days later I presented him with three loaves of Murray's Kashi® Bread.

Sponge

2 cups warm water
2 packages active dry yeast
3 cups unbleached all-purpose flour

Dough

3 tablespoons honey or sugar
3 tablespoons vegetable oil
2/3 cup skim milk powder
2 cups cooked Kashi® cereal (see Note)
1 cup rye flour
2 cups whole wheat flour, preferably stone ground
1/2 to 1 cup unbleached all-purpose flour
1 tablespoon salt
Flour, for dusting work top
Shortening, for greasing pans

Sponge

In a large bowl sprinkle the yeast over the warm water to soften; stir until dissolved. Add the flour and stir until smooth. Cover and let stand until doubled in size (30 to 45 minutes).

Dough

Add the honey, oil, milk powder, cooked Kashi®, rye flour, whole wheat flour, 1/2 cup all-purpose flour, and salt. Mix until the dough comes away from the sides of the bowl. Turn out and knead, adding more all-purpose flour 1/4 cup at a time as necessary. Knead until smooth and elastic (8 to 10 minutes). Cut the dough into thirds, cover with a damp towel, and allow to rest for 10 minutes.

Shaping

Shape into pan loaves (pages 27-28). Place, seam down, in greased loaf pans. Allow to rise, covered, until doubled in size (about 45 minutes). Brush with water and slash once down the length of the loaves. Place on a baking sheet.

Baking

Bake with steam (pages 31-32) on the middle shelf of a preheated 375°F oven until golden in color and hollow sounding when thumped on the bottom with your fingertips (35 to 45 minutes). The top and sides should be firm, not soft. Remove from the pans for the last 5 to 10 minutes to improve the crust.

Yield

Makes 2 loaves.

Note: Follow the directions on the package, or cook the Kashi® in a microwave oven: Combine 1/2 cup Kashi® and 2 cups water and cook at medium-high for approximately 20 minutes. Let cool before using.

Murray's Kashi® Bread

(Food Processor, Steel Blade)

Sponge

1 cup warm water
1 package active dry yeast
1 1/2 cups unbleached all-purpose flour

Dough

1 1/2 tablespoons honey
1 1/2 tablespoons vegetable oil
1/3 cup skim milk powder
1 cup cooked Kashi® (see Note)
1/2 cup rye flour
1 cup whole wheat flour, preferably stone ground
1/4 to 1/2 cup all-purpose flour
2 teaspoons salt
Flour, for dusting work top
Shortening, for greasing pans

Sponge

In the work bowl sprinkle the yeast over the warm water to soften; stir until dissolved. Add the flour and stir until smooth. Cover and let stand until doubled in size (30 to 45 minutes).

Dough

Pulse to punch down the Sponge, then add the honey, oil, milk powder, cooked Kashi®, flours (1 cup at a time), and salt. Pulse until the dough tries to form up on top of the blade. More all-purpose flour can be added 1/4 cup at a time if the dough is too soft. Process for about 1 minute. If necessary divide the dough in two and process each half separately, then knead together. Extra kneading by hand is sometimes necessary to make the dough elastic. For a large loaf, leave the dough in 1 piece. For 2 small loaves, cut the dough in half, shape into rounds, and allow to stand, covered, for 10 minutes.

Proceed as in Shaping and Baking, above.

Yield

Makes 1 large or 2 small loaves.

Note: Follow the directions on the package, or cook in a microwave oven: Combine 1/4 cup Kashi® and 1 cup water and cook at medium-high heat for approximately 20 minutes. Let cool before using.

Murray's Kashi® Bread

(Dough-Mixing Machine, Flat Beater)

Sponge

3 cups warm water
3 packages active dry yeast
4 1/2 cups unbleached all-purpose flour

Dough

4 1/2 tablespoons honey or sugar
4 1/2 tablespoons vegetable oil
1 cup skim milk powder
3/4 to 1 1/2 cup all-purpose flour
1 1/2 cups rye flour
3 cups stone-ground whole wheat flour
3 cups cooked Kashi® (see Note)
1 1/2 tablespoons salt
Flour, for dusting work top
Shortening, for greasing pans

Sponge

In the mixing bowl sprinkle the yeast over the warm water; stir until dissolved. Add the flour and mix at the first speed until smooth. Cover and let rise until doubled in size (30 to 45 minutes).

Dough

Stir down the Sponge with 1 or 2 rotations of the beater, then add the honey, oil, milk powder, 3/4 cup all-purpose flour, rye flour, whole wheat flour, cooked Kashi®, and salt. Pulse at the first speed using the on/off switch so that the beater does not throw the flour out of the bowl. When the flour is absorbed, run the machine at the first speed until the dough comes away from the sides of the bowl. If the dough is too moist or soft, add more all-purpose flour 1/4 cup at a time.

Remove and scrape down the beater and insert the dough hook. Run at the first speed until the dough forms up on the hook and comes away from the sides of the bowl (8 to 10 minutes). You can use the second speed for the last 2 minutes to strengthen the gluten.

Turn out the dough onto a floured surface, cut into 4 pieces, shape into rounds, and cover. Allow the dough to rest 10 minutes. Proceed as in Shaping and Baking, above.

Yield

Makes 4 loaves.

Note: Follow the directions on the package, or cook in a microwave oven: Combine 3/4 cup Kashi® and 3 cups water and cook at medium-high for approximately 25 minutes. Let cool before using.

Naan

Naan is a chewy, blistered bread baked in a tandoor, a vertical clay oven commonly used in northern India. This recipe uses yeast as the leavening agent, as opposed to Sourdough Naan, which uses baking powder (see page 206).

Tandoori baking is a fine art, learned over many years. Oven temperatures exceed 700°F. The tandoori chef rolls and stretches the bread on the back of the hand and slaps it against the side of the clay tandoor, where it firmly adheres while swelling up and baking. Naan is a kissing cousin to Mideast pita or lavash. All have a common derivative.

Although the fierce heat of the tandoor cannot be duplicated in the home kitchen, naan can be baked at home. Naan is best when freshly baked and served warm, although it freezes well and can be reheated.

1/2 cup warm water
1 1/2 teaspoons (scant) active dry yeast
1 cup plain low-fat or nonfat yogurt (see Note)
2 tablespoons vegetable oil, preferably olive oil
4 to 4 1/2 cups bread flour (preferred) or all-purpose flour
2 1/4 teaspoons salt
Flour, for dusting work top
Oil, for greasing bowl and work top

In a large bowl sprinkle the yeast over the warm water to soften; stir to dissolve. Add the yogurt, oil, 4 cups flour, and salt; mix until the dough comes away from the sides of the bowl.

Turn out the dough onto a floured surface and knead, adding flour 1/4 cup at a time if the dough is sticky. Keep this dough soft. Knead until the dough is smooth and elastic (8 to 10 minutes). The finished dough should push back when pressed down.

Rising

Transfer the dough to an oiled bowl and turn to coat. Cover with plastic wrap or a damp towel and set aside for 30 minutes. Gently press all the air out of the dough and allow to rise once more until doubled in volume (20 to 30 minutes). Punch down, roll out into a rope, and divide into 12 pieces. Shape into rounds with your palms while cupping them over the dough. Coat the rounds with oil or melted butter and cover. Allow to rest for 15 minutes.

Shaping

On a clean, oiled work surface flatten the first round with your palms. Roll out or press into a 6-inch circle, turning at least once to coat with oil. Press a series of indentations with your fingertips all over the bread.

Baking

Bake in a preheated 550°F oven. A baking stone or oven tiles work best. Otherwise place 2 baking pans upside down on the middle shelf of the oven and let them preheat for at least 5 minutes. Drape the naan over the palm of your hand and flip it over onto the hot tiles. Bake for about 1 minute. With a long barbecue fork or skewer, pierce any extra large bubbles that appear. Immediately turn on the broiler. With the door closed continue baking until the tops of the naan begin to brown (1 to 1 1/2 minutes). Switch the oven back to the bake cycle. Remove the naan immediately with a long-handled spatula and cover by placing in the folds of a clean towel. Continue baking 1 or 2 naan at a time, then stack the breads 6 high in the toweling, keeping them covered. Naan is best when served warm. If desired, let cool in the toweling and freeze or refrigerate in plastic bags.

Yield

Makes 12 breads.

Note: In place of yogurt you can substitute water, milk, skim milk, or sour cream.

Naan

(Food Processor, Steel Blade)

In the recipe above make sure that the yogurt is cold.

In the work bowl sprinkle the yeast over the warm water; stir to dissolve. Add the cold yogurt, oil, 2 cups flour, and salt. Pulse to combine. Add 2 more cups flour, 1 cup at a time. Pulse until the dough comes away from the sides of the bowl, adding more flour if the dough is too sticky. Keep this dough soft. Pulse for 2 to 3 minutes. Do not overmix. If necessary divide the dough in half and process each half separately, then knead together. Extra kneading by hand may be necessary to make the dough elastic.

Proceed as in Rising, Shaping, and Baking, above.

Yield

Makes 12 breads.

Naan

(Dough-Mixing Machine, Flat Beater)

The previous recipe, which yields 12 breads, works equally well in the mixing machine.

1/2 cup warm water
1 package active dry yeast
2 1/2 cups plain low-fat or nonfat yogurt
4 tablespoons vegetable oil, preferably olive oil
8 to 9 cups bread flour (preferred) or
all-purpose flour
1 1/2 tablespoons salt
Oil, for greasing bowl and worktop

In the mixing bowl sprinkle the yeast over the warm water to soften; stir to dissolve. Add the yogurt, oil, 8 cups flour, and salt. Pulse using the on/off switch until the flour is absorbed so that it does not fly out of the bowl. Mix at the first speed until the dough comes away from the sides of the bowl, adding more flour 1/4 cup at a time if the dough is sticky.

Scrape down the beater and insert the dough hook. Mix for 8 to 10 minutes at the first speed. More flour can be added in small amounts as necessary. Keep in mind that this should be a soft dough. The finished dough should be smooth and elastic. You can mix at the second speed for the last few minutes to strengthen the gluten. If the motor strains excessively, stop and use the first speed. Proceed as in Rising, Shaping, and Baking, above, except divide the dough into 24 pieces.

Yield

Makes 24 breads.

Nine-Grain Bread

In the bakery we made a seven-grain bread, which was very popular. When I sought to duplicate this bread for the home and was looking for a source of readily available grains, I found a seven-grain cereal in many natural foods stores that proved to be economical and quite tasty. The bread I made from it has sesame seeds added and is rolled in oatmeal flakes before baking; *voilà*, Nine-Grain Bread!

2 cups warm water
2 packages active dry yeast
2 tablespoons honey or sugar
2 tablespoons shortening or vegetable oil, at room temperature
2/3 cup skim milk
3 cups unbleached all-purpose flour
2 1/2 to 3 1/2 cups stone-ground whole wheat flour
1 cup seven-grain cereal, cooked, at room temperature (see Note)
1 tablespoon salt
1/4 cup sesame seeds
Flour, for dusting work top
Oil, for greasing bowl
1 cup rolled oats, for topping
Shortening, for greasing pans

In a large bowl sprinkle the yeast over the warm water to soften; stir to dissolve. Add the honey, shortening, milk, all-purpose flour, 2 1/2 cups whole wheat flour, cooked cereal, salt, and sesame seeds. Mix until the dough comes away from the sides of the bowl.

Turn out the dough onto a flour-dusted work top. Knead, adding more whole wheat flour 1/4 cup at a time if necessary, until the dough feels smooth and silky (8 to 10 minutes).

Transfer the dough to a clean, oil-coated bowl and turn top to bottom to coat. Cover and set aside until the dough doubles in volume (40 to 60 minutes).

Shaping

Punch down the dough and cut it in half. Shape into rounds, cover, and let rest for 15 minutes. Shape into 2 pan loaves (pages 27-28), wet with water, and roll in rolled oats to coat. Place the breads, seam down, in 2 greased loaf pans. Proof until the loaves form nicely rounded tops and rise to the top of the pans or slightly above. Place the breads on a baking sheet. Slash the breads once lengthwise down the center with a sharp knife or razor.

Baking

Bake with steam (pages 31-32) in a preheated 375°F oven until the bread has browned and the bottom emits a hollow sound when tapped lightly with your fingertips (35 to 45 minutes). Let cool on a wire rack.

Yield

Makes 2 loaves.

Note: Cook cereal in boiling water until softened. Use 1/3 cup cereal to 1 cup water (1/2 cup cereal to 1 1/2 cups water in the mixing machine recipe).

Nine-Grain Bread

(Food Processor, Steel Blade)

Instead of 2 cups warm water use:

1/2 cup warm water
1 1/2 cups ice water

Sprinkle the yeast over the warm water to soften; stir to dissolve. Add the ice water, honey, shortening, milk, whole wheat flour, cooked cereal, salt, and sesame seeds. Mix until the flour is absorbed. Add 2 cups all-purpose flour and blend. Add the remaining 1 cup all-purpose flour. More whole wheat flour can be added 1/4 cup at a time if the dough is too soft. Process for about 2 to 3 minutes. Do not overmix. If necessary divide the dough in two and process each half separately, then knead together. Extra kneading by hand is sometimes necessary to make the dough elastic.

Turn out the dough, then transfer to a clean, oil-coated bowl, and turn top to bottom to coat. Cover and let stand until the dough doubles in volume (40 to 60 minutes). Proceed as in Shaping and Baking, above.

Yield

Makes 2 loaves.

Nine-Grain Bread

(Dough-Mixing Machine, Flat Beater)

3 cups warm water
3 packages active dry yeast
3 tablespoons honey or sugar
3 tablespoons shortening or vegetable oil, at room temperature
1 cup skim milk
4 1/2 cups all-purpose flour
4 to 5 cups stone-ground whole wheat flour
1 1/2 cups seven-grain cereal, cooked, at room temperature (see Note)
1/3 cup sesame seeds
1 tablespoon salt
Oil, for greasing bowl
Shortening, for greasing pans
1 cup rolled oats, for topping

Sprinkle the yeast over the warm water to soften, then stir to dissolve. Add the honey, shortening, milk, all-purpose flour, 4 cups whole wheat flour, cooked cereal, and sesame seeds. Pulse with the on/off switch until all is absorbed so that the flour is not thrown out of the bowl. Mix at the first speed until the dough comes away from the sides of the bowl. More whole wheat flour can be added 1/4 cup at a time if the dough is too soft.

Remove and scrape down the beater and insert the dough hook. Run at the first speed until the dough forms up on the hook and comes away from the sides of the bowl (8 to 10 minutes). You can use the second speed for the last 2 minutes to strengthen the gluten.

Remove the hook, add oil to the bowl, and turn the dough top to bottom until coated. Cover and allow to double in volume (45 to 60 minutes).

Proceed as in Shaping and Baking, above, except shape into 3 loaves.

Yield

Makes 3 loaves.

Oat Rye Bread, Country Style

At a renowned Boston restaurant, I once tasted an exceptionally good bread that inspired the development of this grainy, whole-cereal, crusty loaf.

Sponge

2 cups warm water
2 packages active dry yeast
3 cups unbleached all-purpose flour

Dough

3 tablespoons honey or sugar
1 to 2 cups unbleached all-purpose flour
1 cup rye flour
2 cups rolled oats (not instant)
1 tablespoon salt
3 tablespoons unsalted butter or shortening, at room temperature
Flour, for dusting work top
Cornmeal or rye flour, for dusting baking pan
Water or cornstarch solution (page 20), for brushing loaves

Sponge

In a large bowl sprinkle the yeast over the warm water to soften, then stir until dissolved. Add the flour and stir until incorporated, then cover and let stand until doubled in size.

Dough

In another large bowl combine the honey, 1 cup all-purpose flour, rye flour, oats, and salt. Cut or rub in the butter. Add the sponge and mix until the dough comes away from the sides of the bowl.

Turn out the dough onto a flour-dusted work top and knead, adding more all-purpose flour 1/4 cup at a time as necessary. Knead until the dough feels smooth and silky (8 to 10 minutes). Cover with a damp towel and let stand for 10 minutes.

Shaping

Punch down the dough, then knead into a tight ball to make 1 large loaf or cut in half for 2 regular-sized loaves. Proof on a cornmeal- or rye flour-dusted baking pan until doubled in size (30 to 45 minutes). Brush lightly with plain water or the cornstarch solution. Stipple (punch holes) in the tops of the loaves.

Baking

Bake with steam (pages 31-32) on the middle shelf of a preheated 380°F oven until golden in color and hollow sounding when thumped on the bottom with your fingertips (45 to 60 minutes, or more for a single large loaf). The top and sides should not be soft. When the top first begins to brown, after 15 to 20 minutes, brush once more with the cornstarch solution to ensure a shiny crust. Remove from the oven, brush again, and let cool on a wire rack.

Yield

Makes 1 large or 2 regular-sized loaves.

Oat Rye Bread, Country Style

(Food Processor, Steel Blade)

Sponge

In the work bowl sprinkle the yeast over the warm water to soften, then stir until dissolved. Add the flour and process until smooth. Leave the bowl and blade in place on the machine. Cover and let stand until doubled in size.

Dough

Pulse once or twice to punch down the Sponge. Add the honey, butter, 1 cup all-purpose flour, rye flour, oats, and salt. Pulse until all is absorbed and the dough tries to form a ball on top of the blade. More all-purpose flour can be added 1/4 cup at a time if the dough is too soft. Mix for about one minute. Do not allow the dough to overheat. If necessary divide the dough in two and process each half separately, then knead together. Extra kneading by hand is sometimes necessary to make the dough elastic.

Proceed as in Shaping and Baking, above.

Yield

Makes 1 large or 2 regular-sized loaves.

Oat Rye Bread, Country Style
(Dough-Mixing Machine, Flat Beater)

Sponge
3 cups warm water
3 packages active dry yeast
4 1/2 cups unbleached all-purpose flour

Dough
4 1/2 tablespoons honey or sugar
4 1/2 tablespoons butter or shortening
2 1/2 to 3 1/2 cups unbleached all-purpose flour
1 cup rye flour
3 cups rolled oats (not instant)
1 1/2 tablespoons salt
Flour, for dusting work top
Cornmeal or rye flour, for dusting pan
Water or cornstarch solution (page 20), for brushing loaves

Sponge
In the mixing bowl sprinkle the yeast over the warm water; mix until dissolved. Add the flour and mix at the first speed until smooth. Cover and allow to rise until doubled in size (30 to 45 minutes).

Dough
Stir down the Sponge with 1 or 2 rotations of the beater, then add the honey, butter, 2 1/2 cups all-purpose flour, rye flour, oats, and salt. Pulse at the first speed using the on/off switch so that the beater does not throw the flour out of the bowl. When the flour is absorbed, run the machine at the first speed until the dough comes away from the sides of the bowl. If the dough is too soft, add more all-purpose flour 1/4 cup at a time.

Remove and scrape down the beater and insert the dough hook. Run at the first speed until the dough forms up on the hook and comes away from the sides of the bowl (8 to 10 minutes). You can use the second speed for the last 2 minutes to strengthen the gluten.

Turn out the dough onto a floured surface, cut into 2 pieces for large loaves or 4 pieces for small loaves, shape into rounds, and cover. Allow the dough to rest for 10 minutes. Proceed as in Shaping and Baking, above.

Yield
Makes 2 large loaves or 4 small loaves.

Whole Wheat Oatmeal Bread

This bread is best when baked in a loaf pan and sliced for sandwiches or toasted. Oatmeal adds a distinct rough texture and nutty flavor. It keeps the bread moist, is high in fiber and low in sodium, and is rich in protein. This whole-grain bread is formulated to take advantage of the nutritional value of oatmeal, honey, vegetable oil, whole wheat flour, and nonfat milk. Salt can be omitted or a salt substitute can be used (see Note).

Sponge

2 cups warm water
2 packages active dry yeast
2 cups unbleached all-purpose flour
1 cup whole wheat flour, preferably stone ground

Dough

1/4 cup honey or sugar
1/4 cup vegetable oil
2/3 cup skim milk powder
1 to 2 cups unbleached all-purpose flour
1 cup whole wheat flour, preferably stone ground
2 cups rolled oats (not instant)
2 teaspoons salt
Flour, for dusting work top
Shortening, for greasing pans

Sponge

In a large bowl sprinkle the yeast over the warm water to soften, then stir until dissolved. Add the flour and stir until smooth, then cover and let stand until doubled in size (30 to 45 minutes).

Dough

Stir down the Sponge and add the honey, oil, milk powder, 1 cup all-purpose flour, whole wheat flour, oats, and salt. Mix until the dough comes away from the sides of the bowl.

Turn out the dough onto a flour-dusted work top and knead, adding more all-purpose flour 1/4 cup at a time as necessary. Knead until smooth and silky (8 to 10 minutes). Cover with a damp towel and let stand for 10 minutes.

Shaping

Cut the dough in half and shape into 2 pan loaves (pages 27-28). Place, seam down, into 2 greased loaf pans. Allow to rise until doubled in size, or until the tops are nicely rounded and the breads have risen slightly above the top of the pans (30 to 45 minutes). Brush with water and slash once down the length of each loaf.

Baking
Bake with steam (pages 31-32) in a preheated 380°F oven until golden in color and hollow sounding when thumped on the bottom with your fingertips (45 to 60 minutes). The top and sides should not be soft. Remove from the loaf pans for the last 10 minutes of baking time to develop a better crust. Remove from the oven, brush again with water, and let cool on a wire rack.

Yield
Makes 2 loaves.

Note: If salt is omitted, the final rise will take place quite rapidly. Do not allow the breads to overproof.

Whole Wheat Oatmeal Bread

(Food Processor, Steel Blade)

Sponge
In the work bowl sprinkle the yeast over the warm water to soften, then pulse to dissolve. Add the flour and pulse until smooth. Allow to stand, covered, until doubled in size (about 30 minutes). Leave the bowl and blade in place on the machine.

Dough
Pulse once or twice to punch down the Sponge, then add the honey, oil, milk powder, 1 cup all-purpose flour, whole wheat flour, oats, and salt. Pulse until all is thoroughly absorbed and the dough tries to form up on top of the blade. Process for about 60 seconds. More all-purpose flour can be added 1/4 cup at a time if the dough is too soft. If necessary divide the dough in two and process each half separately, then knead together. Do not overmix. Extra kneading by hand is sometimes necessary to make the dough elastic.

Proceed as in Shaping and Baking, above.

Yield
Makes 2 loaves.

Whole Wheat Oatmeal Bread

(Dough-Mixing Machine, Flat Beater)

Sponge

3 cups warm water
3 packages active dry yeast
3 cups unbleached all-purpose flour
1 1/2 cups whole wheat flour, preferably stone ground

Dough

1/4 cup plus 2 tablespoons honey or sugar (6 tablespoons)
1/4 cup plus 2 tablespoons vegetable oil (6 tablespoons)
1 cup skim milk powder
1 1/2 to 3 cups unbleached all-purpose flour
1 1/2 cups whole wheat flour, preferably stone ground
3 cups rolled oats (not instant)
1 tablespoon salt
Flour, for dusting work top
Shortening, for greasing pans

Sponge

In the mixing bowl sprinkle the yeast over the warm water; mix until dissolved. Add the flour and run at the first speed until smooth. Cover and allow to rise until doubled in size (30 to 45 minutes).

Dough

Stir down the Sponge with 1 or 2 rotations of the beater, then add the honey, oil, milk powder, 1 1/2 cups all-purpose flour, whole wheat flour, oats, and salt. Pulse at the first speed using the on/off switch so that the beater does not throw the flour out of the bowl. When the flour is absorbed, run the machine at the first speed until the dough comes away from the sides of the bowl. If the dough is too soft, add more all-purpose flour 1/4 cup at a time.

Remove and scrape down the beater and insert the dough hook. Run at the first speed until the dough forms up on the hook and comes away from the sides of the bowl (8 to 10 minutes). You can use the second speed for the last 2 minutes to strengthen the gluten.

Turn out the dough onto a floured surface, cut into thirds, shape into rounds, and cover. Allow the dough to rest for 10 minutes. Proceed as in Shaping and Baking, above.

Yield

Makes 3 loaves.

Pastrami Bread

Adapted from Italian prosciutto bread, this bread uses a slice of pastrami about 1/4 inch thick. See if the deli has an end or scraps to sell at a reduced price.

Sponge

2 cups warm water
2 packages active dry yeast
1 cup leftover dough, fermented (optional, see Note)
3 cups bread flour (preferred) or unbleached all-purpose flour

Dough

3 tablespoons sugar
3 tablespoons shortening or vegetable oil, at room temperature
2 to 3 cups unbleached all-purpose flour
1 tablespoon salt
Flour, for dusting work top
1/2 cup or more diced pastrami (1/4-inch slice, see Note)
Oil, for greasing bowl
Cornmeal, for dusting baking sheet

Sponge

In a large bowl sprinkle the yeast over the warm water to soften; stir to dissolve. Add the fermented dough and flour and mix until smooth. Cover and let stand until doubled in volume (30 to 45 minutes).

Dough

Stir down the Sponge and add the sugar, shortening, 2 cups flour, and salt. Mix until the dough comes away from the sides of the bowl.

Turn out the dough onto a floured work top and knead, adding more flour 1/4 cup at a time if necessary. Knead until the dough feels soft and silky (8 to 10 minutes). It should push back when pressed and your hand should come away clean.

Rising

Transfer the dough to an oiled bowl and turn to coat. Cover and let rise until doubled in volume (35 to 45 minutes). Punch down the dough, cut it in half, and shape into rounds. Allow to rest for 10 minutes.

Shaping

Roll out the dough to about 1/4 inch thick. Spread the diced sautéed pastrami over the top. Roll up jelly roll fashion into narrow Italian-shaped loaves (pages 28-29). Place the loaves on a baking sheet dusted with cornmeal. Cover with a damp cloth and let rise until doubled in size (45 to 60 minutes). When the bread has fully proofed, cut 3 diagonal slashes or 1 long slash down the center.

Baking
Bake with steam (pages 31-32) in a preheated 400°F oven until golden brown (25 to 35 minutes). Bake the last 5 minutes on tiles or an oven stone if you have them. The bread is done when it emits a hollow sound when thumped on the bottom with your fingertips and the sides feel hard and crisp.

Yield
Makes 2 loaves.

Note: To ferment leftover dough, thin it out with a little water and allowed to stand at room temperature for 4 to 6 hours, or overnight.

Dice the 1/4-inch slice pastrami and sauté gently over low heat. Do not brown. Set aside to cool.

Variations

You can substitute corned beef, salami, or wurst for the pastrami.

Pastrami Bread with Roasted Peppers
When ready to shape the bread as above, in addition to the diced meat, spread a handful of diced roasted red bell peppers over the dough.

Pastrami Bread
(Food Processor, Steel Blade)

Instead of 2 cups warm water use:

1/4 cup warm water
1 3/4 cups ice water

Sponge
In the work bowl sprinkle the yeast over the warm water to soften, then pulse to dissolve. Add the ice water, fermented dough, and flour, and pulse until smooth. Allow to stand, covered, until doubled in size (30 to 45 minutes). You can leave the bowl and blade in place on the machine.

Dough
Pulse to punch down the Sponge, then add the sugar, shortening, 2 cups flour (1 cup at a time), and salt. Pulse until the dough tries to form up on top of the blade. More flour can be added 1/4 cup at a time if the dough is too soft. Process for about 2 to 3 minutes. If necessary divide the dough in two and process each half separately, then knead together. Extra kneading by hand is sometimes necessary to make the dough elastic.

Proceed as in Rising, Shaping, and Baking, above.

Yield
Makes 2 loaves.

Pastrami Bread

(Dough-Mixing Machine, Flat Beater)

Sponge

3 cups warm water
2 packages active dry yeast
1 1/2 cups leftover fermented dough (optional, see Note)
4 1/2 cups bread flour (preferred) or unbleached all-purpose flour

Dough

4 1/2 tablespoons sugar
4 1/2 tablespoons shortening or vegetable oil, at room temperature
3 1/2 to 4 1/2 cups unbleached all-purpose flour
1 1/2 tablespoons salt
3/4 cup or more diced pastrami (1/4-inch slice, see Note)
Oil, for greasing bowl
Cornmeal, for dusting baking sheet

Sponge

In the mixing bowl sprinkle the yeast over the warm water to soften; stir to dissolve. Add the fermented dough and flour and mix until smooth. Cover and allow to stand until doubled in volume (30 to 45 minutes).

Dough

Stir down the Sponge with 1 or 2 rotations of the beater, then add the sugar, shortening, 3 1/2 cups flour, and salt. Pulse at the first speed using the on/off switch so that the beater does not throw the flour out of the bowl. When the flour is absorbed, run the machine at the first speed until the dough comes away from the sides of the bowl. If the dough is too soft, add more flour 1/4 cup at a time.

Remove and scrape down the beater and insert the dough hook. Run at the first speed until the dough forms up on the hook and comes away from the sides of the bowl (8 to 10 minutes). You can use the second speed for the last few minutes to strengthen the gluten. Proceed as in Rising, Shaping, and Baking, above, except shape the dough into 3 loaves.

Yield

Makes 3 loaves.

Note: To ferment leftover dough, thin it out with a little water and allowed to stand at room temperature for 4 to 6 hours, or overnight.

Dice the 1/4-inch slice of pastrami and sauté gently over low heat. Do not brown. Set aside to cool.

Pita

Also known as pocket bread, pita has become universal in use. A soft, chewy bread, it opens up to form a pocket that can be conveniently stuffed with all kinds of sandwich fillings. Its origin is in the Mideast, where small pieces of pita are torn off and used in place of utensils to scoop up bits of food or dips. Vegetarians and health food proponents have adopted these breads as their own and bake them with whole wheat flour for additional flavor and nutritive value. For an all-white pita you can substitute bread flour for the whole wheat flour called for in this recipe.

2 cups warm water
2 packages active dry yeast
4 tablespoons vegetable oil (preferably olive oil) or shortening
2 cups whole wheat flour, preferably stone ground
3 to 4 cups bread flour (preferred) or all-purpose flour
2 teaspoons salt
Flour, for dusting work top
Oil, for greasing bowl

In a large bowl sprinkle the yeast over the warm water to soften; stir to dissolve. Add the oil, whole wheat flour, 3 cups bread flour, and salt. Mix until the dough comes away from the sides of the bowl.

Turn out the dough onto a floured surface and knead, adding more bread flour 1/4 cup at a time if the dough is sticky. Keep this dough soft. Knead until the dough is smooth and elastic (8 to 10 minutes). The finished dough should push back when pressed down.

Rising

Transfer the dough to an oiled bowl and turn to coat. Cover with plastic wrap or a damp towel and set aside until doubled in volume (45 to 60 minutes). Punch down and divide into 12 equal pieces, then shape into rounds with your palms while cupping them over the dough. Cover and allow to rest for 15 minutes.

Shaping

On a clean, floured work surface, press or roll out the rounds into 6-inch circles. Cover and allow to rest for 15 minutes.

Baking

Bake in a preheated 500°F oven. Oven tiles or a baking stone work best. If neither is available place 2 baking pans upside down on the middle shelf of the oven and let them preheat for at least 5 minutes. Slide the pita into the oven one or two at a time using a board or peel. An alternate method is to drape them one at a time over a rolling pin (stick type) or dowel and roll them off into the oven. A third method would be to place them on cornmeal-sprinkled baking sheets. Do not open the oven door for the first 10 minutes so that the breads can puff up. Bake until they are lightly browned. Remove the bread with a long-handled spatula and keep covered by placing between 2 towels. Continue baking one or two at a time, and stack the finished breads 6 high in the towels. The breads will collapse as they cool, forming a pocket. Pita can be eaten warm, or let them cool in the toweling, then place them in plastic bags to refrigerate or freeze.

Yield

Makes 12 breads.

Pita

(Food Processor, Steel Blade)

Instead of 2 cups warm water use:

1/2 cup warm water
1 1/2 cups ice water

In the work bowl sprinkle the yeast over the warm water; stir to dissolve. Add the ice water, oil, 2 cups whole wheat flour, and salt. Pulse to combine. Add 3 cups bread flour, 1 cup at a time. Mix until the dough comes away from the sides of the bowl, adding more bread flour if needed. Keep this dough soft. Pulse for 2 to 3 minutes. Do not overmix. If necessary divide the dough in half and process each half separately; then knead together. Extra kneading by hand may be necessary to make the dough elastic. Proceed as in Rising, Shaping, and Baking, above.

Yield

Makes 12 breads.

Pita

(Dough-Mixing Machine, Flat Beater)

The previous recipe also works well in the mixing machine.

3 cups warm water
3 packages active dry yeast
6 tablespoons vegetable oil (preferably olive oil) or shortening
3 cups whole wheat flour, preferably stoneground
4 1/2 to 6 cups bread flour (preferred) or all-purpose flour
1 tablespoon salt
Flour, for dusting work top
Oil, for greasing bowl

In the mixing bowl sprinkle the yeast over the warm water; stir to dissolve. Add the oil, whole wheat flour, 4 1/2 cups bread flour, and salt. Pulse with the on/off switch until the flour is absorbed so that it does not fly out of the bowl. Mix at the first speed until the dough comes away from the sides of the bowl, adding more bread flour 1/4 cup at a time if the dough is sticky.

Scrape down the beater and insert the dough hook. Mix for 8 to 10 minutes at the first speed. More flour can be added in small amounts as necessary. Keep in mind that this should be a soft dough. The finished dough should be smooth and elastic. You can mix at the second speed for the last 2 minutes to strengthen the gluten. If the motor strains excessively, stop and use the first speed. Proceed as in Rising, Shaping, and Baking, above.

Yield

Makes 18 breads.

Psomi Bread

I first heard about Psomi bread (pronounced sew-me) in a small bakery in New Hampshire. Sort of a kissing cousin to New England's anadama bread, it has an interesting flavor and texture. Sesame seed lovers will enjoy this bread. This is my own version.

Sponge

1/2 cups warm water
2 packages active dry yeast
1 1/2 cups buttermilk or sour milk (see Note), at room temperature
3 cups whole wheat flour, preferably stone ground

Dough

4 tablespoons honey
2 tablespoons butter or shortening
2 to 3 cups unbleached all-purpose flour
2 teaspoons salt
1/2 cup toasted sesame seeds (see Nuts, Toasting, page 22)
Flour, for dusting work top
Oil, for greasing bowl
Additional sesame seeds, for topping (optional)
Shortening, for greasing pans

Sponge

In a large bowl sprinkle the yeast over the warm water to soften; stir to dissolve. Add the buttermilk and flour; mix until smooth. Cover with a cloth or plastic wrap and set aside until doubled in volume (about 45 minutes).

Dough

Add the honey, butter, 2 cups flour, salt, and toasted sesame seeds. Stir until the dough comes away from the sides of the bowl, adding more flour if necessary.

Turn out the dough onto a lightly floured work top. Knead with a turn, fold, push motion, adding more flour in small amounts if the dough is sticky. Knead until the dough is smooth and elastic (8 to 10 minutes).

Note: To make sour milk, combine 1 1/2 cups skim milk and 1 1/2 teaspoons vinegar. Let stand until clabbered (about 10 minutes).

Rising

Transfer the dough to an oiled bowl and turn to coat. Cover and allow to rise until doubled in volume.

Shaping

Punch down the dough, cut it in half, then let it rest, covered, for 10 minutes. Shape into pan loaves (pages 27-28) and roll in the sesame seeds (if desired). Place, seam down, in greased loaf pans or leave free form on dusted baking sheets. Cover and proof until the loaves double in size. Score each loaf with 3 diagonal cuts and brush with water. Place on a baking sheet or directly on tiles or an oven stone.

Baking

Bake in a preheated 375°F oven on the middle shelf until the bread has color and the bottom emits a hollow sound when tapped lightly with your fingertips (35 to 45 minutes). For the last 5 to 10 minutes the bread can be removed from the forms for a crustier loaf. After removing from the oven, brush again with water and let cool on a wire rack.

Yield

Makes 2 loaves.

Psomi Bread

(Food Processor, Steel Blade)

Sponge

In the work bowl sprinkle the yeast over the warm water to soften; stir to dissolve. Add the buttermilk and flour. Mix until smooth. Allow to stand, covered, until doubled in volume (about 45 minutes).

Dough

Pulse once or twice to stir down the Sponge, then add the honey, butter, 2 cups flour (1 cup at a time), salt, and toasted sesame seeds. Pulse until all is absorbed, then continue pulsing until the dough comes away from the sides of the bowl, adding more flour 1/4 cup at a time if necessary. Process or pulse until the dough reaches 78°F (about 1 minute). Do not overmix. If necessary, turn out and knead lightly by hand for several minutes. If the machine strains, stop, remove the dough, and process in 2 halves, then knead together.

Turn out the dough onto a floured work top and shape into a ball.

Proceed as in Rising, Shaping, and Baking, above.

Yield

Makes 2 loaves.

Psomi Bread

(Dough-Mixing Machine, Flat Beater)

Sponge

3/4 cup warm water
3 packages active dry yeast
2 1/4 cups buttermilk or sour milk (see Note), at room temperature
4 1/2 cups whole wheat flour, preferably stone ground

Dough

1/4 cup plus 2 tablespoons (6 tablespoons) honey
3 tablespoons butter or margarine
3 to 4 1/2 cups unbleached all-purpose flour
3 teaspoons salt
3/4 cup toasted sesame seeds (see Nuts, Toasting, page 22)
Additional sesame seeds, for topping (optional)
Shortening, for greasing pans

Sponge

In the mixing bowl sprinkle the yeast over the warm water to soften; stir to dissolve. Add the buttermilk and flour. Mix until smooth. Cover with a cloth and allow to rise until doubled in volume (about 45 minutes).

Dough

Add the honey, butter, 3 cups flour, salt, and toasted sesame seeds. Mix until the dough comes away from the sides of the bowl, adding more flour if necessary.

Scrape down the beater and insert the dough hook. Mix for 8 to 10 minutes at the first speed. More flour can be added in small amounts as necessary. The dough should be smooth and elastic. You can use the second speed for the last 2 minutes to strengthen the gluten. If the motor becomes excessively strained, use the first speed. Remove the dough hook, cover, and proceed as in Rising, Shaping, and Baking, above, except shape into 3 loaves.

Yield

Makes 3 loaves.

Note: To make sour milk, combine 2 1/4 cups skim milk and 2 teaspoons vinegar. Let stand until clabbered (about 10 minutes).

100% Whole Wheat Bread

Most recipes for whole wheat bread are formulated using part whole wheat and part white flour, although they are called whole wheat bread. Some will actually be labeled all wheat or 100% wheat bread. The following recipe uses all whole wheat flour. If you like whole-grain breads, the exceptional flavor of these loaves will appeal to you. They are made with wholesome ingredients, sweet dairy butter, unrefined sweeteners, and low-fat milk. For a cholesterol-free bread, use vegetable shortening or oil instead of butter. When using all whole wheat flour, it is important that all the flour not be added at one time. This is essential for the proper development of the dough.

Sponge

1/2 cup warm water
2 packages active dry yeast
1 1/2 cups buttermilk or sour milk (see Note), at room temperature
3 cups whole wheat flour, preferably stone ground

Dough

4 tablespoons honey
2 tablespoons unsalted butter or shortening, at room temperature
2 to 3 cups whole wheat flour, preferably stone ground
2 teaspoons salt
Flour, for dusting work top
Shortening, for greasing pans

Sponge

In a large bowl sprinkle the yeast over the warm water to soften; stir to dissolve. Add the buttermilk and flour. Mix with a wooden spoon until smooth. Cover with a cloth and place in a warm area until doubled in volume (approximately 45 minutes).

Dough

Add the honey, butter, 2 cups flour (stir in 1 cup at a time), and salt. Stir until the dough comes away from the sides of the bowl.

Turn out the dough onto a lightly floured work top. Knead, adding more flour in small amounts until the dough is firm. Because it is made of all whole wheat flour, the dough will tend to be heavier than usual and may remain a bit sticky. Dust lightly with flour as necessary. Knead for about 8 minutes.

Note: To make sour milk, combine 1 1/2 cups skim milk and 1 1/2 teaspoons vinegar. Let stand until clabbered (about 10 minutes).

Shaping

The dough will be heavy, tend to tear easily, and will not rise as readily as a regular dough. This is normal. Cut in half, shape into rounds, and allow to rest, covered, for 10 minutes. Punch down and shape into 2 pan loaves (pages 27-28).

Proofing

Place into 2 greased loaf pans, cover loosely, and allow to rise until the dough reaches above the rim of the pan (45 to 60 minutes). Brush with water or melted butter.

Baking

Bake with steam (pages 31-32) in a preheated 375°F oven until the loaves are well browned, sound hollow when tapped on the bottom with your fingertips, and the sides feel firm (about 45 minutes). The loaves can be removed from the pans for the last 5 to 10 minutes to firm up the crust. Let cool on a wire rack.

Yield

Makes 2 loaves.

Variations

Cracked 100% Whole Wheat Bread

Cracked wheat bread is a whole-grain, all-whole-wheat bread with a coarse texture and farm-fresh flavor. All natural ingredients, including unprocessed sweeteners, are used. The cereal adds moisture, enhances the flavor, and provides a different bite or texture. This bread is an excellent choice for sandwiches; it toasts well and is good with butter and jam or served with cheese.

Bulgur, a precooked grain, is available in many supermarkets. Cracked wheat or cracked wheat cereal is most easily found in natural foods stores. To soften bulgur, soak in boiling water for 40 minutes, then drain. Cracked wheat must be cooked as a cereal until soft. Use 1/3 cup cereal to 1 cup water. Let cool before using.

To the Dough, add:

1 cup bulgur or cracked wheat, softened (1 1/2 **cups in the dough-mixing machine recipe**)

Sprouted Whole Wheat Bread

This bread is fun to make. It comes out crunchy and is filled with nutrients that taste good. If desired, you can substitute almost any small sprouts, either homegrown or purchased, but try it with sprouted wheat berries for a natural, all-wheat bread.

To the Dough, add and mix as usual:

1 cup sprouted wheat berries or any small sprouts (page 29)
1 teaspoon salt
Pinch ground ginger
1/2 cup sesame seeds, for topping (optional)

Roll the shaped loaves in the sesame seeds before placing in the baking pans.

For the dough-mixing machine, add:

1 1/2 cups sprouts
1 1/2 teaspoons salt
1/8 teaspoon ground ginger

100% Whole Wheat Bread

(Food Processor, Steel Blade)

Sponge

In the work bowl sprinkle the yeast over the warm water to soften; pulse to dissolve. Add the buttermilk and flour and process until smooth. Keep covered and allow to rise until doubled in volume (approximately 45 minutes).

Dough

Stir down the Sponge with 1 or 2 pulses, then add the honey, butter, 2 cups flour (stir in 1 cup at a time), and salt. More flour can be added 1/4 cup at a time if the dough is sticky. Pulse until the dough comes away from the sides of the bowl, then continue to pulse for about 1 minute to knead. Do not overmix. If necessary the dough can be cut in two and processed one half at a time.

Turn out the dough onto a lightly floured board or work top and knead together then proceed as in Shaping, Proofing, and Baking, above.

Yield

Makes 2 loaves.

100% Whole Wheat Bread

(Dough-Mixing Machine, Flat Beater)

Sponge

3/4 cup warm water
3 packages active dry yeast
2 1/4 cups buttermilk or sour milk (see Note), at room temperature
4 1/2 cups whole wheat flour, preferably stone ground

Dough

1/4 cup plus 2 tablespoons (6 tablespoons) honey
3 tablespoons butter or shortening
3 to 4 1/2 cups whole wheat flour, preferably stone ground
3 teaspoons salt
Flour, for dusting work top
Shortening, for greasing pans

Sponge

In the mixing bowl sprinkle the yeast over the warm water to soften, then stir at the first speed to dissolve. Add the buttermilk and flour. Mix until smooth. Cover with a cloth and allow to rise until doubled in volume (approximately 45 minutes).

Dough

Add the honey, butter, 3 cups whole wheat flour (stir in 1 cup at a time), and salt. Run at the first speed until the dough comes away from the sides of the bowl.

Scrape down the beater and insert the dough hook. Mix at the first speed for 8 to 10 minutes, adding more whole wheat flour 1/4 cup at a time if the dough is sticky or refuses to clean the sides of the bowl and gather up around the dough hook.

BAKER'S SECRET. If after 2 to 3 minutes the dough hook does not bite into the dough but rather pushes it up along the sides of the bowl, increase to the second speed until the dough comes away from the sides, then resume mixing at the first speed and add several minutes to the mixing time.

Turn out the dough onto a floured work top, cut into 3 pieces, and proceed as in Shaping, Proofing, and Baking, above.

Yield

Makes 3 loaves.

Note: To make sour milk, combine 2 1/4 cups skim milk and 2 teaspoons vinegar. Let stand until clabbered (about 10 minutes).

Nutted Whole Wheat Cocktail Bread

The appearance of this bread on the table will bring ohs and ahs from all present. It goes exceptionally well with a cheese tray, and can be served with cocktails or after the meal in place of dessert. When served with cream cheese and a beverage, it makes a complete meal. The presence of several of these polished mahogany-hued breads on the table turns any meal into an instant occasion.

Use the list of ingredients for 100% Whole Wheat Bread (page 154). Shape as below, after kneading.

Dough

To the hand-mixed recipe, add:

1/2 cup walnuts (or more to suit), preferably toasted (page 22)

For the dough-mixing machine, add:

3/4 cup walnuts (or more to suit), preferably toasted (page 22)

Glaze

1 egg, lightly beaten with 1 teaspoon water, for brushing loaves

Shaping

Flatten the dough with your palms, then sprinkle the top with the nuts and knead until well distributed. Cut in half, shape into rounds, and allow to rest, covered, for 10 minutes. Punch down and shape into 2 narrow pan loaves 10 to 12 inches long (pages 27-28).

Set on a cornmeal-dusted baking sheet, cover loosely, and allow to rise until doubled in size (about 45 to 60 minutes). Brush with the egg mixture and cut a series of diagonal slashes 1/4 inch deep and 1/2 inch apart, taking care to cut from edge to edge (not just the tops).

BAKER'S SECRET:* *Allow to dry for several minutes and brush a second time to ensure a shiny crust.

Baking

Bake in a preheated 375°F oven until the bread has a deep mahogany color and the bottom has a hollow sound when tapped with your fingertips (about 45 minutes). If baking on tiles or a stone, after the first 25 minutes transfer the breads from the baking sheet to tiles or an oven stone and continue baking. Let cool on a wire rack.

Yield

Makes 2 loaves

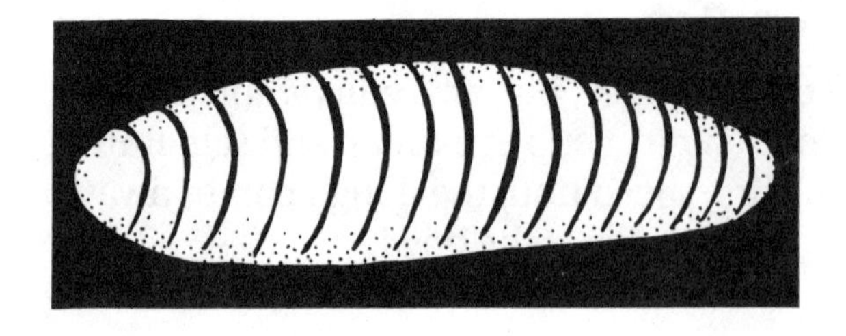

Whole Wheat Nutted Raisin Bread

This bread can accompany any light meal and also goes well with salads or cheese and fruit. The way I like it best is to make thinly sliced nutted cream cheese sandwiches served with an apple and chocolate milk.

Sponge

1/2 cup warm water
2 packages active dry yeast
1 1/2 cups buttermilk or sour milk (see Note)
2 1/2 cups whole wheat flour, preferably stone ground

Dough

4 tablespoons honey
2 tablespoons unsalted butter or shortening, at room temperature
2 1/2 to 3 1/2 cups unbleached all-purpose flour
2 teaspoons salt
1 cup raisins
1/2 cup walnuts, preferably toasted (page 22)
Flour, for dusting work top
Shortening, for greasing pans

Sponge

In a large bowl sprinkle the yeast over the warm water to soften; stir to dissolve. Add the buttermilk and flour and mix until smooth. Cover and allow to rise until doubled in volume (about 45 minutes).

Dough

Stir down the Sponge, then add the honey, butter, 2 1/2 cups flour, salt, raisins, and walnuts. Mix until the dough comes away from the sides of the bowl.

Turn out the dough onto a floured surface and knead, adding flour 1/4 cup at a time if the dough is sticky. Knead until the dough is smooth and elastic (8 to 10 minutes). The finished dough should push back when pressed down. Cut the dough in half, shape into rounds, cover, and allow to rest for about 10 minutes.

Shaping

Shape into 2 pan loaves (pages 27-28). Place in greased loaf pans, seam down and centered. Allow to rise, covered, until the breads come up over the top of the pans (about 45 minutes).

Baking

Bake with steam (pages 31-32) in a preheated 375°F oven until nicely browned and the bread sounds hollow when tapped on the bottom with your fingertips (40 to 45 minutes). The loaves can be removed from the pans for the last 5 minutes to firm up the crust.

Yield

Makes 2 loaves.

Note: To make sour milk, combine 1 1/2 cups skim milk and 1 1/2 teaspoons vinegar. Let stand until clabbered (about 10 minutes).

Whole Wheat Nutted Raisin...

(Food Processor, Steel Blade)

Sponge

In the work bowl sprinkle the yeast over the warm water to soften; pulse to dissolve. Add the buttermilk and flour and pulse until smooth. With the cover in place, allow to rise until doubled in volume (about 20 minutes).

Dough

Pulse to stir down the Sponge, then add the honey, butter, 2 1/2 cups flour, and salt. Pulse until the dough comes away from the sides of the bowl and rides up on top of the blade. Add more flour 1/4 cup at a time if the dough is sticky. Pulse until the dough is smooth and elastic (about 1 minute). You may have to divide the dough in half and process in 2 batches. The finished dough should push back when pressed down.

Turn out the dough onto a lightly floured work top. Sprinkle with the raisins and nuts, then knead them into the dough. Cut the dough in half, shape into rounds, cover, and allow to rest for about 10 minutes.

Proceed as in Shaping and Baking, above.

Yield

Makes 2 loaves.

Whole Wheat Nutted Raisin...

(Dough-Mixing Machine, Flat Beater)

Sponge

1 cup warm water
3 packages active dry yeast
2 cups buttermilk or sour milk (see Note)
4 cups whole wheat flour, preferably stone ground

Dough

1/4 cup plus 2 tablespoons (6 tablespoons) honey
3 tablespoons unsalted butter or shortening
4 to 5 cups unbleached all-purpose flour
3 teaspoons salt
1 1/2 cups raisins
1 cup walnuts, preferably toasted (page 22)
Flour, for dusting worktop
Shortening, for greasing pans

Sponge

In the mixing bowl sprinkle the yeast over the warm water to soften; stir to dissolve. Add the buttermilk and flour and mix until smooth. Cover and allow to rise until doubled in volume (about 40 minutes).

Dough

Stir down the Sponge by running the machine, then add the honey, butter, 4 cups flour, and salt. Pulse with the on/off switch to absorb, then run at the first speed until the dough comes away from the sides of the bowl, adding more flour 1/4 cup at a time if the dough is sticky.

Remove and scrape down the beater. Insert the dough hook and knead at the first speed until the dough is smooth and elastic (8 to 10 minutes). The finished dough should push back when pressed down. Turn out, sprinkle with the raisins and nuts, and knead into the dough. Cut the dough into thirds. Shape into rounds, cover, and allow to rest for about 10 minutes. Proceed as is Shaping and Baking, above.

Yield

Makes 3 loaves.

Note: To make sour milk, combine 2 cups skim milk and 2 teaspoons vinegar. Let stand until clabbered (about 10 minutes).

Chapter Six

Sourdough Breads

In the following recipes for sourdough breads, reference is made to *sour*, as in Sour Rye Bread, and *sourdough*, as in San Francisco Sourdough Bread. Both terms are more or less identical; they differ mainly in ethnic origin. In the bakery we use the term *sour* when the ferment, or starter, is part of Middle European breads; we use the term *sourdough* when the starter is part of French or American breads. In these recipes the two terms are often used interchangeably.

Rye Sour

My father, a Hungarian baker, told me stories about cooks in Europe whose culinary ability was determined by the quality of their bread. He related that when a young woman married, included in her dowry was some bread starter from her mother. These starters were passed on from mother to daughter and, as master yeast is today, the culture was never allowed to die. Small quantities were always kept with which to begin anew.

When I began to work in the bakery, sour was still made by hand, three times daily, each time doubled in volume and fermented in huge wooden troughs. Someone would have to tend to the sour whenever the bakery was closed. Thanks to modern refrigeration, we make sour at our leisure and refrigerate it at any stage in its development. The first time sour is made, it is begun with a starter. After that, enough is always left behind to begin the next batch.

Starter

(Prepare 48 hours in advance)

Caraway seeds can be ground in a coffee or spice grinder or with a mortar and pestle. In the bakery we crush the seeds with a rolling pin. The crushed seeds disappear in the ferment and add a distinctive flavor to the sour. The minced onion helps to hasten the fermentation and adds flavor.

1/2 cup rye flour
1/8 teaspoon active dry yeast (see Note)
1 cup warm water
1 tablespoon crushed caraway seeds (optional)
1 teaspoon minced onion

Combine all the ingredients in a large bowl and mix until smooth. The mixture should have a thin, soupy consistency. Cover and allow to stand in a warm spot until bubbly and fermented. It can be left up to 24 hours.

Note: Save the rest of the packet for the first dough.

Rye Sour, Developing and Fortifying

In making sour use approximately 3/4 to 1 cup flour to each 1/2 cup water. (Notice that Stage One calls for a higher ratio. This is done to adjust for the initial consistency of the starter.) The object is to make a thick consistency as close as possible to that of a soft dough. It is not necessary to thicken to the point that the mixing becomes burdensome. If the mixture is too soupy, add more flour 1/4 cup at a time. Mix until smooth.

BAKER'S SECRET. Rye Sour is made in three stages—the secret of its success. The flavor and leavening power are increased, but the fermentation is controlled. The sour is never allowed to become old or rancid.

Stage One

(Prepare 24 hours in advance.)

1/2 cup water
1 1/4 cups rye flour
All of the Starter, above
1/4 cup rye flour for sprinkling

In a large bowl or container, combine the water, 1 1/4 cups of the flour, and the Starter; stir until smooth. The dough should pull slightly and may start to come away from sides of the bowl. Wipe down the sides of the bowl with wet hands or a bowl scraper. Sprinkle 1/4 cup flour over the entire surface of the sour. Let stand, covered with a cloth or clear plastic wrap, until doubled in size and the floured top appears cracked with fissures spread widely apart. This may take 4 to 8 hours. Avoid letting the sour collapse.

Stage Two

If a double recipe is desired, this can be increased to 1 cup warm water and 2 cups rye flour.

1/2 cup warm water
1 cup rye flour

To the Stage One sour add the water and 3/4 cup of the flour; mix until smooth. Wipe down the sides of the bowl. Sprinkle the remaining 1/4 cup flour over the entire surface of the sour. Allow to rise in a warm area 4 to 8 hours. Proceed with Stage Three.

As the sour begins to rise, you can refrigerate it at any stage for later use or overnight for mixing the following day. Refrigeration retards the rate of growth of the sour, which continues to rise slowly. Whenever time permits, I prefer to make two stages the day before, refrigerating the second stage overnight and preparing the third stage the morning of baking. If the dough is to be mixed first thing in the morning, the third stage is prepared the evening before, so it can rise slowly all night and be ready in the morning.

Stage Three

1/2 cup water (see Note)
1 cup rye flour, or more

To the Stage Two sour add the water and the 1 cup flour. Mix until smooth. Additional flour can be added to attain a dough-like consistency. The sour, when fully risen in Stage Three, is ready for use in the dough. When the third stage is mixed, set aside 1/4 to 1/2 cup and refrigerate in a covered container with a light film of cold water floated over the top. I have kept sour under refrigeration for months at a time.

Note: Use warm water if the sour has been refrigerated.

It is best to stir down the starter every 3 to 4 days if unused. Periodically (every 10 to 12 days) dispose of half and refresh it by mixing in equal amounts of flour and water. If there is some discoloration on the top, it can safely be skimmed off and the sour used as normal. When going away for long periods of time, I freeze a small amount of sour. When preparing a new starter from scratch, I add the frozen sour to preserve my original culture.

To ensure the proper strength of the sour, in each stage you can only double the amount of starter you begin with. For example, if beginning with 1/4 cup starter, you can add up to 1/2 cup water plus flour to thicken. If Stage One contains 1 cup sour, Stage Two can be prepared with up to 2 cups water plus flour. If a large amount of sour is required, extra stages can be added.

BAKER'S SECRET.Some bakers like to add crushed caraway seeds each time they prepare Stage One.

Sometimes the process goes awry. Perhaps there is insufficient sour left to start the next batch, or the sour might have been forgotten and was left standing to get old or dry. There is a remedy. The bakers call it an *einfrisch,* meaning to refresh. A small amount of sour is thinned down with water to a soupy consistency. Swishing 1/4 cup water around in what remains clinging to the sides of the empty bowl can yield enough to restart the sour. Let this *einfrisch* stand, covered, at room temperature or in a warm spot until bubbly. If desperate, add a pinch of yeast. When ready, add enough flour to make a first stage, allow to rise, and proceed with two more stages.

BAKER'S SECRET: Sour can be said to be a prefermented dough or base. In some recipes, such as Sour Rye Bread, I use what I like to call the Instant Dough Method. This is also used in many of my sponge recipes. Many recipes contain enough sour or sponge in the dough that it is not necessary to wait for the dough to rise. The bread is mixed, allowed to rest a few minutes to enable it to be shaped properly, and immediately shaped into loaves.

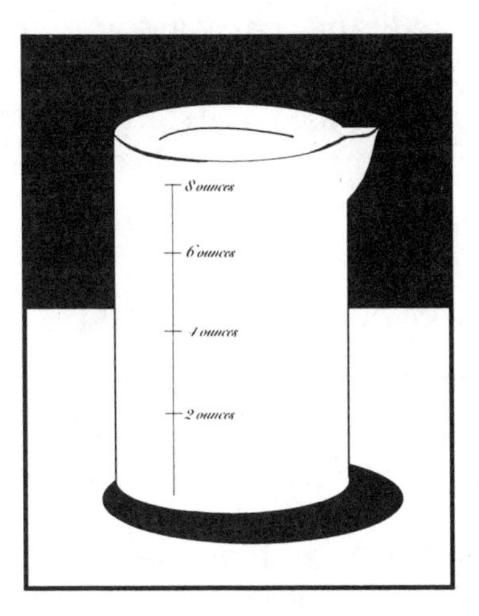

White Sour

Some sponges called starters or sourdough starters are allowed to ferment to add flavor to the bread. Fermentation times ranging from 6 hours to several days are not unusual.

In the United States during the gold rush, prospectors were often called sourbellys. They carried with them a mixture of flour and water kept in a packet wrapped around their waists. The wild yeast in the air and the heat from their bodies would allow the mixture to ferment and provide them with the leavening for their biscuits and flapjacks. These sourdoughs were the basis for San Francisco sourdough breads.

The same sours were used in Europe long before the gold rush days. There is evidence of bread having been leavened with fermented dough in ancient Egypt. However, the controlled yeast and other leavening agents we use today did not exist. The baker had only the wild yeast present in the air, and results were never uniform. By combining natural sour for flavor and commercially prepared yeast for control, we can now enjoy the best of both worlds. There is no reason to resort to the older and less reliable methods except in special circumstances for distinct flavor or just for the fun of trying them.

San Francisco-style sourdough breads and French and Italian sourdough breads are all begun with a basic sourdough starter, which in the recipes will be referred to as White Sour. Once the basic starter is made, a small amount is always saved with which to begin the next sour. If properly cared for, it will keep indefinitely (see Rye Sour, page 163).

Starter

(Prepare 24 hours in advance.)

1 cup warm water
1/2 cup unbleached all-purpose flour
1/8 teaspoon active dry yeast (see Note)

In a large bowl combine all of the ingredients and mix until smooth. Cover loosely with a cloth and let stand until bubbly and fermented. It should be left to rise and fall in a warm spot overnight (or 12 to 24 hours). The longer it is left to ferment, the tastier the breads will be.

If you wish to try making a wild yeast ferment, omit the yeast and let the mixture stand at room temperature for up to 72 hours. When the mash begins to bubble, rise, and fall, it is ready. After 72 hours if it has not fermented, discard it and try anew.

Note: Save the rest of the packet for the first dough.

White Sour: Developing and Fortifying

White Sour is made like Rye Sour—in three stages, which intensifies the flavor and strength of the sourdough. In each stage the amount of water can be doubled. In making sour, I use approximately 3/4 to 1 cup flour to each 1/2 cup water. (Notice that Stage One calls for a higher ratio. This is done to adjust for the initial consistency of the starter.) If your time is limited, the sour can be refrigerated at any stage and continued later or kept overnight. To refrigerate overnight, leave it at room temperature after mixing until it begins to rise slightly, then refrigerate. It will generally rise slowly and be ready in the morning. The bakers refer to this as a ready sour. I prefer to make the third stage just prior to mixing my dough (see above).

Stage One

1/2 cup warm water
1 1/4 cups unbleached all-purpose flour
All of the Starter, above
1/4 cup rye flour for sprinkling

In a large bowl or container, combine the water, 1 1/4 cup of the flour, and the Starter; mix until smooth. Wipe down the sides of the bowl using a bowl scraper or your wet hand. Sprinkle 1/4 cup flour over the entire surface of the sour. Let stand, covered, until doubled in size and the flour topping is cracked with wide fissures showing. This may take 4 to 8 hours, depending upon the air temperature and humidity.

Stage Two

If a double recipe is desired, these measurements can be increased to 1 cup warm water and 2 cups flour.

1/2 cup warm water
1 1/4 cups unbleached all-purpose flour

To Stage One add the water and 1 cup of the flour; mix until smooth. Scrape down the sides of the bowl. Cover with the remaining 1/4 cup flour and let rise as before.

Stage Three

If larger batches of bread are desired, the amount of water and flour can be doubled.

1/2 cup warm water
1 cup unbleached all-purpose flour, or more

To the Stage Two sour add the water and flour; mix until smooth. Additional flour can be added to attain a dough-like consistency. I prefer to make the third stage when I'm ready to mix my bread. When the third stage is ready, before it is mixed into the dough, set aside a small amount (1/4 to 1/2 cup) to be used as the starter for the next batch. Refrigerate it in a covered nonreactive container with a light film of cold water floated over the top. It is best to stir it down every 3 to 4 days. When ready to use, proceed with Stage One, above.

I have kept sour refrigerated for months, refreshing every 10 to 12 days with a few spoonfuls of water and flour. If there is some discoloration on the top, it can safely be skimmed off and the sour used as normal. Remember that in each stage you can only double the amount you have left. Should you need more, keep making extra stages until there is sufficient sour for the task.

***BAKER'S SECRET.** It is always better to let your dough rise slowly and naturally; however, when there is not enough time, the process can be hastened by putting the mixed sour in the microwave oven next to a cup of just-boiled water. The microwave is not operating; the steam and heat from the boiled water make the inside of the oven an effective steam cabinet.*

Sour Rye Bread

This is real Jewish rye bread, written by a Jewish baker, made for the most demanding audience in the world, the New York consumer. This bread transcends its ethnic boundaries due to its universal appeal. To my knowledge an authentic version of this recipe has never been published. Bakers, like chefs, are reluctant to part with their recipes and invariably try to hold something back. Few breads offer such a distinct flavor coupled with a unique crust.

The secret of great rye bread is the sour, or ferment, that gives the bread its outstanding qualities. Sour is the product of the controlled fermentation of rye flour and water. Once it is begun, the baker always saves a small amount of sour each time he or she bakes. This becomes the starter to begin the next batch.

Sour Rye Bread is made up of water, flour, yeast, and salt. There is no sugar or fat added to this pure bread. Rye bread is ideal for deli sandwiches and as an accompaniment to meat dishes. It is excellent with cheese. A favorite of mine is cream cheese and olives on rye toast. A real Jewish treat (high in cholesterol) used to be a roast beef sandwich on rye with Bermuda onion and chicken fat (*shmaltz*). My grandmother would take afternoon tea with toasted rye that had the crust rubbed with garlic while still warm. She lived well into her nineties and I always attributed it to the tea and garlic, but now I firmly believe that it was the rye bread.

1 cup warm water
1 package active dry yeast
3 cups Rye Sour (pages 163-165; see Note)
1/2 cup altus (optional, page 15)
4 to 5 cups common flour (page 8; see Note)
3 teaspoons salt
Rye flour, for dusting work top
Oil, for greasing bowl
1/2 tablespoon caraway seeds, or more to taste (optional)
Cornstarch solution (page 20) or water, for brushing loaves

BAKER'S SECRET. Some European bakers use altus to retain additional moisture and add flavor to the bread.

In a large bowl dissolve the yeast in the warm water and add the sour. Add the altus, if desired. Without stirring add 3 cups of the flour and salt. Gently stir the dry ingredients with your fingertips to incorporate, then stir with a wooden spoon, adding more flour as necessary until the dough comes away from the sides of the bowl.

Turn out the dough onto a floured work surface and knead. If the dough is moist and sticky, add more flour 1/4 cup at a time. Knead until the dough feels soft and silky (5 to 8 minutes). Rye dough will be softer than usual and tend to feel sticky.

Transfer the dough to an oiled bowl and turn several times to coat. Cover and allow to rest for 15 to 20 minutes. Punch down, sprinkle with the caraway seeds (if desired).

Shaping

Shape the balls into 2 free-standing pan loaves (pages 27-28). Place on a rye flour- or cornmeal-dusted baking sheet. In the bakery we proof the loaves and bake them on the oven hearth using a wooden peel. Cover and allow to rise until doubled in size. Brush with the cornstarch solution, then cut 3 horizontal slashes on the top of each loaf.

Baking

Bake with steam (pages 31-32) in a preheated 375°F oven until tapping the bottom with your fingertips produces a hollow sound (35 to 45 minutes). The top and sides should feel hard to the touch. Brush again with the cornstarch solution, then let cool on a wire rack.

Yield

Makes 2 loaves.

Note: Common flour, called first clear or clear flour, must be obtained from a bakery. You can substitute 3 1/4 cups all-purpose flour plus 3/4 cup cake flour, but the bread won't taste as good.

2 cups Rye Sour can be used instead of 3 cups for a milder taste.

Variations

Onion Rye

Omit the caraway seeds. Knead Onion Filling and Topping (page 23) into the dough immediately after mixing. The tops of the shaped loaves should be rolled in additional onion topping before the final rise.

Marble Rye

1/2 recipe Sour Rye Bread, unbaked
1/2 recipe Pumpernickel Bread, unbaked (page 178)

Cut each dough in half. Flatten out with your hands or a small rolling pin. Place one pumpernickel half on top of a rye half. Shape jelly roll fashion into a short loaf. For further variety, shape the second loaf with the pumpernickel on the bottom. This will yield 2 combination breads, 1 rye with pumpernickel swirled inside and the other a brown bread with the rye inside.

Cocktail Rye

This can be served plain or with either or both of the fillings and toppings below.

Fillings:
Caraway seeds
Onion Filling and Topping (page 23)

Knead one of the fillings into the dough after mixing. Roll the dough into thin baguette shapes about 1 inch in diameter and 12 inches long. Roll the tops in fillings before the final rise.

Toppings:
Caraway seeds with Kosher salt
Onion Filling and Topping (page 23)
Kosher salt (see Note)

Note: In the bakery we use pretzel salt; coarser than Kosher salt, it does not dissolve into the crust when baked. If pretzel salt cannot be found through your usual sources, try a bagel shop.

Sour Rye Bread

(Food Processor, Steel Blade)

Instead of 1 cup warm water use:

1/4 cup warm water
3/4 cup ice water

In the work bowl sprinkle the yeast over the warm water; stir to dissolve. Add the sour and mix until absorbed. Add the altus, if desired. Add the ice water, then mix in 1 cup of the flour and the salt. Next, mix in 3 cups of the flour, 1 cup at a time. Pulse until the dough tries to form up on top of the blade. More flour can be added 1/4 cup at a time if the dough is too soft. Keep in mind that this dough will be softer than usual. Process for 2 to 3 minutes. If necessary divide the dough in half and process each half separately, then knead together. Do not overmix or the dough will get too hot. Shape the dough into 2 balls, cover, and let rest for 10 minutes. Proceed as in Shaping and Baking, above.

Yield

Makes 2 loaves.

Sour Rye Bread

(Dough-Mixing Machine, Flat Beater)

1 1/2 cups warm water
1 package active dry yeast
4 1/2 cups Rye Sour (pages 163-165)
3/4 cup altus (optional, page 15)
6 to 7 1/2 cups common flour (page 8; see Note)
1 1/2 tablespoons salt
Rye flour, for dusting worktop
Oil, for greasing bowl
2 teaspoons caraway seeds, or more (optional)
Cornstarch solution (page 20) or water, for brushing loaves

In the mixing bowl sprinkle the yeast over the warm water to soften; stir to dissolve. Add the Rye Sour, altus (if desired), flour, salt, and caraway seeds (if desired). Pulse with the on/off switch until all is absorbed so that the flour is not thrown out of the bowl. Run at the first speed until the dough comes away from the sides of the bowl. More flour can be added 1/4 cup at a time if the dough is too soft.

Remove and scrape down the beater and insert the dough hook. Run at the first speed until the dough forms up on the hook and comes away from the sides of the bowl (5 to 8 minutes).

Turn out the dough and shape into 3 balls. Cover and let the dough rest for 15 minutes. Proceed as in Shaping and Baking, above.

Yield

Makes 3 loaves.

Note: Common flour must be obtained from a bakery. You can substitute 5 cups all-purpose flour plus 1 cup cake flour but the bread won't taste as good.

3 cups Rye Sour can be used instead of 4 1/2 cups, for a milder flavor.

Laszlos' Sourdough Potato Rye Bread with Caraway

This is my father's recipe that he brought with him from Hungary. He often reminisced about the Old World potato breads, which were evidently in wide use throughout Europe where he traveled as a journeyman baker.

Sourdough potato rye has the flavor of fine rye plus the texture and moisture retention properties of potato bread. The result is a rye bread that will remain soft and tender for more than a week under normal storage conditions.

1 cup warm water, preferably potato water
1 package active dry yeast
1/2 medium potato, mashed (1/2 cup mashed potato; see Note)
2 cups Rye Sour (pages 163-165)
3 cups common flour (page 8; see Note)
1 tablespoon salt
Flour, for dusting work top
Oil, for greasing bowl
2 tablespoons caraway seeds, or more to taste (optional)
Additional rye flour, if needed (see Baker's Secret)
Cornmeal or rye flour, for dusting baking sheet
Water or cornstarch solution (page 20), for brushing loaves

In a large bowl dissolve the yeast in the warm water. Blend in the mashed potato and Rye Sour. Add the common flour and stir in the salt with your fingertips to incorporate. Mix with a wooden spoon until the dough comes away from the sides of the bowl.

Turn out the dough onto a floured work surface and knead. Add rye flour 1/4 cup at a time if necessary. The rye dough will be softer than usual and tend to feel sticky. Knead the dough until it is elastic (5 to 8 minutes).

Place the dough on an oiled work surface. Cover and let rest for 15 minutes. Punch down, sprinkle with caraway seeds (if desired).

Shaping

Shape into 1 or 2 round loaves. Place on a baking sheet dusted with cornmeal or rye flour. Proof until doubled in size. In the bakery we proof the loaves and bake them on the oven hearth using a wooden peel. Brush the loaves with water or the cornstarch solution. Stipple with 10 to 12 holes using a skewer or an ice pick.

Baking

Bake with steam (pages 31-32) in a preheated 375°F oven until tapping the bottom with your fingertips produces a hollow sound (35 to 45 minutes). If 1 large loaf is made, allow for additional oven time. The top and sides should feel hard to the touch. Let cool on a wire rack.

Yield

Makes 1 large or 2 small loaves.

Note: Scrub the potato jackets thoroughly, then quarter the potatoes. Cook in 2 1/2 cups boiling water until soft (about 10 minutes). Let cool, then peel. Store extra potato water in the refrigerator for use in any bread recipe. Instant mashed potatoes can be used, but you lose the added benefit of the potato water.

You can substitute 2 1/2 cups all-purpose flour plus 1/2 cup cake or pastry flour for common flour, although the bread will not taste as good.

> *BAKER'S SECRET. If additional flour is required, the sour was too thin. Add rye flour 1/4 cup at a time to compensate.*

Variation

Onion-Potato Rye Bread

Before shaping the bread, knead in the Onion Filling and Topping (page 23) made with caraway seeds instead of poppy seeds.

Laszlos' Sourdough Potato Rye...

(Food Processor, Steel Blade)

Instead of 1 cup warm water use:

1/4 cup warm water
3/4 cup ice water, preferably iced potato water

In the work bowl sprinkle the yeast over the warm water to soften; stir to dissolve. Add the ice water, mashed potato, and Rye Sour; pulse until absorbed. Blend in 1 cup common flour and salt, then mix in the remaining 2 cups common flour, 1 cup at a time; pulse until absorbed. More rye flour can be added 1/4 cup at a time if the dough is too soft. Keep in mind that this dough will be softer than usual. Process for 2 to 3 minutes. If necessary divide the dough in two and process each half separately, then knead together. Do not overmix or the dough will get too hot. Extra kneading by hand is sometimes necessary to make the dough elastic.

Shape the dough into 1 or 2 balls. Cover and let rest for 15 minutes. Press down, sprinkle with the caraway seeds (if desired), and proceed as in Shaping and Baking, above.

Yield

Makes 1 large or 2 small loaves.

Laszlos' Sourdough Potato Rye...

(Dough-Mixing Machine, Flat Beater)

1 1/2 cups warm water, preferably potato water
1 package active dry yeast
1 medium potato, mashed (3/4 cup mashed potato; see Note)
3 cups Rye Sour (pages 163-165)
4 1/2 cups common flour (see Note)
1 1/2 tablespoons salt
Flour, for dusting work top
Oil, for greasing bowl
3 tablespoons caraway seeds, or more to taste (optional)
Additional cornmeal or rye flour, if needed (see Baker's Secret)
Water or cornstarch solution (page 20), for brushing loaves

Sprinkle the yeast over the warm water to soften; stir to dissolve. Add the mashed potato, Rye Sour, common flour, and salt. Pulse with the on/off switch until all is absorbed so that the flour is not thrown out of the bowl. Run at the first speed until the dough comes away from the sides of the bowl. More rye flour can be added 1/4 cup at a time if the dough is too soft. Keep in mind that this dough tends to be softer than usual and somewhat sticky.

Remove and scrape down the beater and insert the dough hook. Run at the first speed until the dough forms up on the hook and comes away from the sides of the bowl (5 to 8 minutes).

Turn out the dough and shape into 1, 2, or 3 round balls. Cover and let the dough rest for 10 minutes. Proceed as in Shaping and Baking, above. (Try 1 large loaf. Large breads take longer to bake and hold more moisture.)

Yield

Makes 1 large to 3 small loaves.

Note: Scrub the potato jackets thoroughly, then quarter the potatoes. Cook in 2 1/2 cups boiling water until soft (about 10 minutes). Let cool, then peel. Store extra potato water in the refrigerator for use in any bread recipe. Instant mashed potatoes can be used, but you lose the added benefit of the potato water.

You can substitute 3 3/4 cups all-purpose flour plus 3/4 cup cake or pastry flour for the common flour, although the bread will not taste as good.

BAKER'S SECRET. If additional flour is required, the sour was too thin. Add rye flour 1/4 cup at a time to compensate.

Seven-Grain Bread

This bread has become the most popular of the grain breads in the specialty bakery. Rye sour is the secret of its success. High fiber and a crunchy, nutlike flavor add to this bread's appeal. It is especially good when toasted.

1 cup warm water
1 package active dry yeast
2 tablespoons pumpernickel color (page 24; see Note)
1 cup Rye Sour (pages 163-165)
1 cup seven-grain cereal, softened and drained (see Note)
2 1/2 to 4 cups all-purpose flour
2 teaspoons salt
Flour, for dusting work top
Oil, for greasing bowl
Rolled oats or sesame seeds, for topping
Shortening, for greasing pans

In a large bowl dissolve the yeast in the warm water. Add the pumpernickel color, Rye Sour, cereal, 2 1/2 cups flour, and salt. Stir until thoroughly combined and the dough comes away from the sides of the bowl.

Turn out the dough onto a lightly floured board and knead until it feels soft and silky (5 to 8 minutes). More flour can be added 1/4 cup at a time if necessary. This dough should be on the soft side and does not require extra kneading.

Shape the dough into a ball and place in a clean, oiled bowl, turning several times to coat. Cover with a cloth and let the dough stand until doubled in volume (about 45 minutes).

Shaping

Punch down the dough to expel all the air, then divide in two. Shape into 2 pan loaves (pages 27-28). Roll in oatmeal flakes or sesame seeds. Place in greased 8- or 9-inch loaf pans, seam down. Proof in a warm, draft-free spot until the bread comes over the top of the rim. Slash once down the length of each loaf.

Baking

Bake with steam (pages 31-32) in a preheated 380°F oven until tapping the bottom produces a hollow sound (35 to 45 minutes). Remove from the pans for the last few minutes to get a crusty bottom. The top should feel firm when pressed in the center. Let cool on a wire rack.

Yield

Makes 2 loaves.

Note: You can substitute molasses or instant coffee for pumpernickel color. To soften the cereal, chop or grind and let soften overnight covered with water, or boil for 5 minutes, or cook in the microwave oven for 5 minutes at high power. Use 1/3 cup cereal to 1 cup water (1/2 cup cereal to 1 1/2 cups water in the mixing machine recipe). Seven-grain cereal can be found in natural foods stores.

Seven-Grain Bread

(Food Processor, Steel Blade)

Instead of 1 cup warm water use:

1/4 cup warm water
3/4 cup ice water

In the work bowl sprinkle the yeast over the warm water and stir to dissolve. Add the ice water, pumpernickel color, Rye Sour, cereal, 2 1/2 cups flour, 1 cup at a time, and salt. Pulse until the dough tries to form up on top of the blade. More flour can be added 1/4 cup at a time if the dough is too soft. Process for 2 to 3 minutes. If necessary divide the dough in half and process each half separately, then knead to combine. Do not all the dough to overheat. Extra kneading by hand is sometimes necessary to make the dough elastic.

Turn out the dough, cover, and allow to rise until doubled in volume (about 45 minutes). Proceed as in Shaping and Baking, above.

Yield

Makes 2 loaves.

Seven-Grain Bread

(Dough-Mixing Machine, Flat Beater)

1 1/2 cups warm water
1 package active dry yeast
3 tablespoons pumpernickel color (page 24; see Note)
1 1/2 cups Rye Sour (pages 163-165)
1 1/2 cups seven-grain cereal, softened and drained (see Note, above)
4 to 6 cups all-purpose flour
Oil, for greasing bowl
1 tablespoon salt
Flour, for dusting worktop
Rolled oats or sesame seeds, for topping
Shortening, for greasing pans

Dissolve the yeast in the warm water in a small bowl and set aside.

In the mixing bowl combine the pumpernickel color, Rye Sour, cereal, 3 3/4 cups flour, and salt. Stir through the dry ingredients with your fingertips to incorporate the salt into the flour. Add the reserved dissolved yeast. Pulse with the on/off switch until all is absorbed so that the flour is not thrown out of the bowl. Run at the first speed until the dough comes away from the sides of the bowl. More flour can be added 1/4 cup at a time if the dough is too soft.

Remove and scrape down the beater and insert the dough hook. Run at the first speed until the dough forms up on the hook and comes away from the sides of the bowl (5 to 8 minutes). You can use the second speed for the last few minutes to strengthen the gluten.

Transfer the dough to a clean, oiled bowl and turn several times to coat. Cover and allow the dough to rise until doubled in volume (about 45 minutes). Proceed as in Shaping and Baking, above, except shape into 3 loaves.

Yield

Makes 3 loaves.

Whole Wheat Sour Rye Bread

This unique bread has a flavor all its own. The sour in the recipe keeps the bread moist and gives it a long shelf life. Your family will enjoy it toasted or plain with sandwiches and meat entrees. Cheese, lettuce, and tomato provide new flavor experiences when layered between the slices.

2 cups warm water
2 package active dry yeast
1 cup Rye Sour (pages 163-165)
3 cups whole wheat flour, preferably stone ground
2 1/2 to 3 1/2 cups rye flour
3 teaspoons salt
Flour, for dusting work top
Oil, for greasing bowl
Rye flour or cornmeal, for dusting baking sheet
Cornstarch solution (page 20) or water, for brushing loaf

In a large bowl dissolve the yeast in the warm water. Add the Rye Sour, whole wheat flour, 2 1/2 cups rye flour, and salt. Mix until the dough comes away from the sides of the bowl.

Turn out the dough onto a floured work surface and knead. If the dough is moist and sticky, add rye flour 1/4 cup at a time. Knead until the dough is soft and elastic (5 to 8 minutes). This dough tends to feel sticky.

Transfer the dough to an oiled bowl and turn several times to coat. Cover and allow to rise until doubled in volume (30 to 45 minutes). Punch down and cut in half, then shape into rounds, cover, and let rest for 15 minutes.

Shaping

Shape into 2 free-standing pan loaves (pages 27-29). Place on a rye flour- or cornmeal-dusted baking sheet. Cover with a floured cloth and allow to rise until doubled in size. Brush with the cornstarch solution, then cut 4 diagonal slashes into the top of each loaf.

Baking

Bake with steam (pages 31-32) in a preheated 375°F oven until tapping the bottom produces a hollow sound (35 to 45 minutes). The top and sides should feel hard to the touch. Brush again with the cornstarch solution. Let cool on a wire rack.

Yield

Makes 2 loaves.

Whole Wheat Sour Rye Bread

(Food Processor, Steel Blade)

Instead of 2 cups warm water use:

1/4 cup warm water
1 3/4 cups ice water

In the work bowl sprinkle the yeast over the warm water to soften; stir to dissolve. Add the ice water, Rye Sour, and whole wheat flour. Blend until absorbed. Add 2 1/2 cups rye flour, 1 cup at a time. Pulse until the dough tries to come away from the sides and ride up on top of the blade. More rye flour can be added 1/4 cup at a time if the dough is too soft. Keep in mind that this dough will be softer than usual. Process for 2 to 3 minutes. If necessary divide the dough in half and process each half separately, then knead together. Do not overmix or the dough will get too hot. Extra kneading by hand is sometimes necessary to make the dough elastic.

Transfer the dough to an oiled bowl and turn several times to coat. Cover and allow to rise until doubled in volume (30 to 45 minutes). Punch down and cut in half, then shape into rounds, cover, and let rest for 15 minutes.

Proceed as in Shaping and Baking, above.

Yield

Makes 2 loaves.

Whole Wheat Sour Rye Bread

(Dough-Mixing Machine, Flat Beater)

---

3 cups warm water
3 packages active dry yeast
1 1/2 cups Rye Sour (pages 163-165)
4 1/2 cups whole wheat flour, preferably stone ground
3 3/4 to 5 1/4 cups rye flour
1 1/2 tablespoons salt
Flour, for dusting work top
Oil, for greasing bowl
Rye flour or cornmeal, for dusting baking sheet
Cornstarch solution (page 20) or water, for brushing loaf

In the mixing bowl sprinkle the yeast over the warm water to soften; stir to dissolve. Add the water, Rye Sour, whole wheat flour, and 3 3/4 cups rye flour. Pulse with the on/off switch until all is absorbed so that the flour is not thrown out of the bowl. Run at the first speed until the dough comes away from the sides of the bowl.

Remove and scrape down the beater and insert the dough hook. Run at the first speed until the dough forms up on the hook and comes away from the sides of the bowl (8 to 10 minutes). More rye flour can be added 1/4 cup at a time. Keep in mind that this dough tends to be sticky.

Transfer the dough to an oiled mixing bowl and turn several times to coat. Cover and allow to rise until doubled in volume (30 to 45 minutes). Punch down and cut into thirds, then shape into rounds, cover, and let rest for 15 minutes. Proceed as in Shaping and Baking, above, except shape into 3 loaves.

Yield

Makes 3 loaves.

Pumpernickel Bread

Pumpernickel is a tan, coarse flour made from the first milling of the rye kernel; it is similar in texture to unprocessed bran or course whole wheat flour. Thinly sliced pumpernickel bread makes wonderful cheese and cold-cut sandwiches. Try it with rich soups. I can make a meal out of raisin pumpernickel with butter or cream cheese. Real pumpernickel bread is made with rye sour.

BAKER'S SECRET: The best pumpernickel bread is made with altus (see page 15).

1 cup warm water
1 package active dry yeast
1 cup Rye Sour (pages 163-165)
1 cup altus (optional, page 15)
4 tablespoons pumpernickel color (page 24)
1 cup pumpernickel flour (see Note)
2 1/2 to 3 1/2 cups common flour (see Note)
1 tablespoon salt
Flour, for dusting work top
Oil, for greasing bowl
Cornmeal, for sprinkling baking sheet
Cornstarch solution, for brushing loaf (page 20)
1 tablespoon caraway seeds (optional)

In a large bowl sprinkle the yeast over the warm water to soften; stir to dissolve. Add the Rye Sour, altus (if desired), pumpernickel color, pumpernickel flour, 2 1/2 cups common flour, and salt. Mix thoroughly until the dough pulls away from the sides of the bowl.

Turn out the dough onto a floured work surface and knead, adding small amounts of flour as needed. Make the dough a bit stiffer that normal, since this dough softens as it is kneaded. Knead the dough until it feels smooth and silky (5 to 8 minutes).

Rising

Shape the dough into a ball, place in a large oiled bowl, and turn to coat. Cover and let rise until doubled in size. Punch out all the air, cut in half, shape into rounds, and let rest for 10 minutes.

Shape into 2 round loaves. Place on a baking sheet lightly sprinkled with cornmeal. Keep in a warm, draft-free spot covered with a damp cloth and proof until doubled in size. Brush with the cornstarch solution. Punch 5 times with an ice pick or skewer, 1 hole in the center and 4 holes in a circle around the center. With a wet finger push all the way down in the center hole, leaving a large indent in the middle of the loaf. Sprinkle the top of the loaf with caraway seeds, if desired.

Baking

Bake with steam (pages 31-32) in a preheated 375°F oven until tapping the bottom of the loaf with your fingertips produces a hollow sound (30 to 45 minutes). If you are using an oven stone, remove the breads from the pan for the last 10 minutes and bake on the stone to develop a crusty loaf. If the top of the crust feels soft, return to the oven for 5 to 10 minutes more. After baking, brush again with the cornstarch solution to ensure a shiny crust. Let cool on a wire rack.

Yield

Makes 2 loaves.

Note: Get pumpernickel flour (medium rye) from a local bakery. If unavailable, use rye meal, unprocessed bran, or coarse stone-ground whole wheat flour, or grind some rye cereal by chopping in a blender, processor, or coffee mill. Common flour, also called clear flour or first clear flour, may be available from a local bakery. All-purpose flour can be substituted, but the bread will not taste as good.

Variations

Marble Bread

Follow the directions for Marble Rye on page 169.

Raisin Pumpernickel

Omit the caraway seeds. Plump 1 cup raisins (1 1/2 cups in the dough-mixing machine recipe) in hot water for 30 minutes. Knead into the dough immediately after mixing it.

Raisin Pumpernickel, Pullman Style

Prepare this bread as in Raisin Pumpernickel, above. This square-shaped bread lends itself to thin slicing. The Pullman pan in which it is baked creates a dense texture that is exceptionally moist.

Shape the dough into a large pan loaf (pages 27-28). Place in a greased 12-inch Pullman loaf pan (page 5) and allow to rise until almost to the top of the pan. Slide on the cover and bake at the temperature in the recipe. After 35 minutes, remove the top of the pan and bake until done.

An alternate method is to put the bread in a long loaf pan, cover with a baking sheet, and lay a weight on top while baking. Allow extra baking time for large Pullman loaves.

Onion Pumpernickel

Omit the caraway seeds. Knead Onion Filling and Topping (page 23) into the dough before shaping. Roll the top of the loaves in the onion topping before the final rise.

Cocktail Pumpernickel

Knead caraway seeds or Onion Filling and Topping (page 23) into the dough, or leave it plain. Roll the dough into thin baguette shapes about 1 inch in diameter and 12 inches long. Roll the top of the loaves in your choice of toppings (caraway seeds and Kosher salt, Onion Filling and Topping, sesame seeds, or Kosher salt—see Baker's Secret) before the final rise, or leave plain.

BAKER'S SECRET. In the bakery we use pretzel salt; coarser than Kosher salt, it does not dissolve into the crust when baked. Pretzel salt is not easily obtained. If it cannot be found through your usual sources, try a bagel shop or pretzel maker.

Pumpernickel Bread

(Food Processor, Steel Blade)

Instead of 1 cup warm water use:

1/4 cup warm water
3/4 cup ice water

In the work bowl sprinkle the yeast over the warm water to soften; stir to dissolve. Add the Rye Sour and mix until absorbed. Add the altus (if desired), ice water, pumpernickel color, and pumpernickel flour. Mix in 1 cup common flour and salt; pulse until absorbed. Mix in the remaining 1 1/2 cups common flour, 1 cup at a time. Pulse until the dough tries to form up on top of the blade. More common flour can be added 1/4 cup at a time if the dough is too soft. Process for 2 to 3 minutes. If necessary divide the dough in half and process each half separately, then knead together. Do not overmix or the dough will get too hot. Extra kneading by hand is sometimes necessary to make the dough elastic. Proceed as in Rising, Shaping, and Baking, above.

Yield

Makes 2 loaves.

Pumpernickel Bread

(Dough-Mixing Machine, Flat Beater)

---

1 1/2 cups warm water
1 package active dry yeast
1 1/2 cups Rye Sour (pages 163-165)
1 1/2 cups altus (optional, page 15)
6 tablespoons pumpernickel color (page 24)
1 1/2 cups pumpernickel flour (see Note above)
3 3/4 to 5 1/4 cups common flour (see Note above)
1 1/2 tablespoons salt
Flour, for dusting work top
Oil, for greasing bowl
Cornmeal, for sprinkling baking sheet
Cornstarch solution (page 20) for brushing loaf
1 1/2 tablespoons caraway seeds (optional)

In a small bowl sprinkle the yeast over the warm water to soften; stir to dissolve.

In the mixing bowl combine the Rye Sour, altus (if desired), pumpernickel color, pumpernickel flour, 3 3/4 cups common flour, and the salt; pulse until absorbed. Stir through the dry ingredients with your fingertips to incorporate the salt into the flour. Pulse with the on/off switch until all is absorbed so that the flour is not thrown out of the bowl. Run at the first speed until the dough comes away from the sides of the bowl. More common flour can be added 1/4 cup at a time if the dough is too soft.

Remove and scrape down the beater and insert the dough hook. Run at the first speed until the dough forms up on the hook and comes away from the sides of the bowl (8 to 10 minutes). Proceed as in Rising, Shaping, and Baking, above, except shape into 3 loaves.

Yield

Makes 3 loaves.

Note: You can substitute either 3 tablespoons molasses, 3 tablespoons cocoa powder, or 3 tablespoons instant coffee for color; however, try to purchase pumpernickel color at your local bakery.

Bavarian Pumpernickel Bread

This 100% rye flour bread—gourmet Bavarian pumpernickel at its best—has no wheat, no gluten, no kneading, and no proofing. Rye flour, water, salt, and yeast are all it takes to produce this healthy all-grain loaf. Made of rye sour, medium rye flour (pumpernickel), rye berries or kernels, and rye flour, it is an ancient and flavorful bread good with thick soups, cheese, cold cuts, hearty wursts, and deli meats, or anywhere you would use pumpernickel.

1 cup warm water
1 package active dry yeast
1 cup Rye Sour (pages 163-165)
1 cup altus (optional, page 15)
2 cups cooked rye berries (see Note)
3 to 4 tablespoons pumpernickel color (optional, page 24)
3 cups pumpernickel flour (medium rye) or rye meal
1 tablespoon salt
Additional rye flour, as needed
Oil, for greasing work top
Shortening, for greasing pan

In a large bowl sprinkle the yeast over the warm water; stir to dissolve. Add the Rye Sour, altus (if desired), cooked rye berries, pumpernickel color, pumpernickel flour, and salt. Stir until the dough comes away from the sides of the bowl, adding rye flour 1/4 cup at a time if necessary. This dough will remain wet, with the consistency of heavy clay. Turn out onto an oiled work top.

Shaping

Grease a Pullman pan (page 5) or loaf pan (about 8 inches by 4 inches by 3 inches). Knead the dough into a ball and form into a cylinder the length of the pan. Place the dough in the pan. The dough should be pressed down evenly and come within a 1/4 inch of the top. If you use a Pullman pan, grease the inside of the cover, slide in place, and bake. In lieu of a Pullman pan, place the loaf pan on a baking sheet, grease a second baking sheet, and invert it over the top of the bread. Place in the oven and lay a heavy ovenproof weight or a brick on top. Do not proof.

Baking

Bake in a preheated 375°F oven on the middle shelf for approximately 45 to 55 minutes. After the first 35 minutes, carefully remove the cover, turn out the bread, and finish baking with the bread inverted directly on an oven stone or clay tiles, or on the baking sheet. The loaf is done when the bottom emits a hollow sound when tapped lightly with your fingertips. Let cool on a wire rack, wrap in plastic or aluminum foil, and refrigerate overnight. The next day, slice the loaf paper thin. Wrap well with plastic wrap and freeze or refrigerate if not used immediately.

Yield

Makes 1 loaf.

Note: To cook rye berries, to 3 cups boiling water add 1 cup rye berries (kernels) or chopped rye berries. (Chop them in a blender or food processor.) Return the water to a boil and cook, covered, stirring occasionally over low heat, until the cereal is tender (about 45 minutes). Leftovers can be used as a breakfast cereal or mixed with cooked rice.

Bavarian Pumpernickel Bread

(Food Processor, Steel Blade)

In the work bowl sprinkle the yeast over the warm water; stir to dissolve. Add the Rye Sour, altus (if desired), cooked rye berries, pumpernickel color, pumpernickel flour, and salt. Pulse until thoroughly blended, adding rye flour 1/4 cup at a time if necessary. This dough will remain wet, with the consistency of heavy clay. Turn out the dough onto a lightly oiled work top.

Proceed as in Shaping and Baking, above.

Yield

Makes 1 loaf.

Bavarian Pumpernickel Bread

(Dough-Mixing Machine, Flat Beater)

1 1/2 cups warm water
1 package active dry yeast
1 1/2 cups Rye Sour (pages 163-165)
1 1/2 cups altus (optional, page 15)
3 cups cooked rye berries (see Note)
4 to 5 tablespoons pumpernickel color (optional, page 24)
4 1/2 cups pumpernickel flour (medium rye)
1 1/2 tablespoons salt
1/2 to 1 1/2 cups rye flour, as needed
Oil, for greasing work top
Shortening, for greasing pan

In the mixing bowl sprinkle the yeast over the warm water; stir to dissolve. Add the Rye Sour, altus (if desired), cooked rye berries, pumpernickel color (if desired), pumpernickel flour, and salt. Mix until blended. Continue mixing at the second or third speed long enough for all to be absorbed completely. Add more rye flour 1/4 cup at a time if necessary. This dough will remain wet, with the consistency of heavy clay.

Turn out the dough onto a lightly oiled work top. Proceed as in Shaping and Baking, above, except shape into 2 loaves.

Yield

Makes 2 loaves.

Note: To 3 cups boiling water add 1 cup chopped rye berries. (Chop them in a blender or food processor.) Bring the water to a second boil, then cook, covered, over low heat until the cereal is tender (about 45 minutes). Leftovers can be used as a breakfast cereal or mixed with rice.

Hutzelbrot

This German black bread with either diced citron or dried apricots and prunes makes for table talk when company comes. Serve as a snack with a beverage and cheese or with cocktails. Try it buttered or just plain.

1 cup warm water
1 package active dry yeast
1 cup Rye Sour (pages 163-165)
1 cup altus (optional, page 15)
4 tablespoons pumpernickel color (page 24)
1 1/2 cups pumpernickel flour
2 to 3 cups common flour (page 8) or all-purpose flour
1 tablespoon salt
Flour, for dusting work top
1/2 cup diced citron or quartered dried apricots and prunes, or more as desired
Oil, for greasing bowl
Cornmeal, for sprinkling on baking sheet
Cornstarch solution (page 20), for brushing loaf
Rye flour, for *maszda* (paste) topping, optional

In a large bowl sprinkle the yeast over the warm water to soften; stir to dissolve. Add the Rye Sour, altus (if desired), pumpernickel color, pumpernickel flour, 2 cups common flour, and salt. Mix thoroughly until the dough comes away from the sides of the bowl.

Turn out the dough onto a floured work surface and knead, adding small amounts of common flour as necessary. Keep this dough a bit soft. Knead until the dough is smooth and elastic (5 to 8 minutes). Knead in the citron.

Rising

Roll the dough into a ball and place in a large oiled bowl, turning several times to coat. Cover and let rise until doubled in size. Punch out all the air and shape into a round. Let the dough rest for 10 minutes.

Shaping

Shape the dough into 1 large free-standing pan loaf (pages 27-28). Place directly on a baking sheet sprinkled with cornmeal. Keep in a warm, draft-free spot, covered with a cloth, and proof until doubled in size. Brush with the cornstarch solution. In the bakery we mix rye flour with enough water to make a thin paste called *maszda*. This is spread with the hands carefully over the top and sides of the proofed loaf before slashing. Cut a series of diagonal slash marks along both sides of the bread, then stipple a line of holes down the length (see Figure 1). The *maszda* bakes into a gray crusty topping, which complements the dark bread.

Baking

Bake with steam (pages 31-32) in a preheated 375°F oven until the loaf emits a hollow sound when the bottom is tapped with your fingertips (45 to 60 minutes). If you are using an oven stone, place the bread directly on it for the last 10 minutes to develop a crusty loaf. If the top crust feels soft, return the bread to the oven for 5 to 10 minutes more. After baking, brush the top again with the cornstarch solution to ensure a shiny crust. Let cool on a wire rack.

Yield

Makes 1 large loaf.

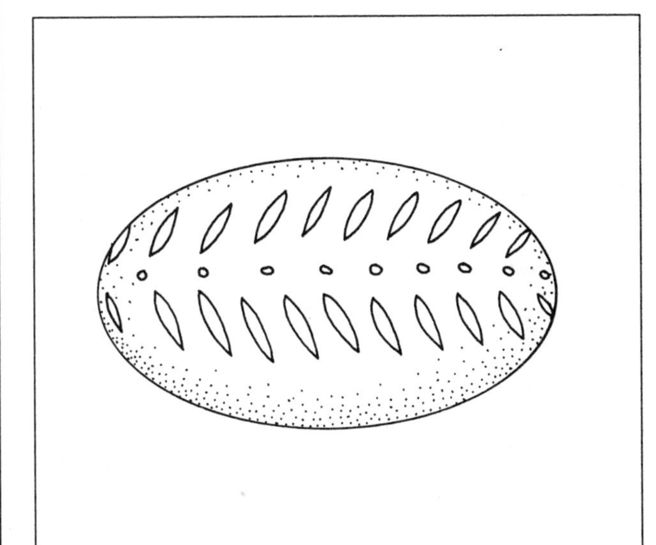

Figure 1

Hutzelbrot

(Food Processor, Steel Blade)

Instead of 1 cup warm water use:

1/4 cup warm water
3/4 cup ice water

In the work bowl sprinkle the yeast over the warm water to soften; stir to dissolve. Add the Rye Sour and altus (if desired); mix until absorbed. Add the ice water, pumpernickel color, and pumpernickel flour. Mix in 1 cup common flour and salt; pulse until absorbed. Mix in the remaining cup common flour. Pulse until the dough tries to form up on top of the blade. More common flour can be added 1/4 cup at a time if the dough is too soft. Pulse for 2 to 3 minutes. If necessary divide the dough in half and process each half separately, then knead together. Do not overmix or the dough will get too hot. Knead in the citron by hand. Extra kneading by hand is sometimes necessary to make the dough elastic.

Proceed as in Rising, Shaping, and Baking, above.

Yield

Makes 1 large loaf.

Hutzelbrot

(Dough-Mixing Machine, Flat Beater)

---

1 1/2 cups warm water
1 package active dry yeast
1 1/2 cups Rye Sour (pages 163-165)
1 1/2 cups altus (optional, page 15)
6 tablespoons pumpernickel color (page 24)
2 1/4 cups pumpernickel flour
3 to 4 1/4 cups common flour (page 8) or all-purpose flour
1 1/2 tablespoons salt
3/4 cup diced citron or quartered dried apricots and prunes, or more as desired
Oil, for greasing bowl
Cornmeal, for sprinkling on baking sheet
Cornstarch solution (page 20), for brushing loaf
Rye flour, for maszda (paste) topping, optional

In the mixing bowl dissolve the yeast in the warm water. Add the Rye Sour, altus (if desired), pumpernickel color, pumpernickel flour, 3 cups common flour, and salt. Stir the dry ingredients with your fingertips to incorporate the salt into the flour. Pulse with the on/off switch until all is absorbed so that the flour is not thrown out of the bowl. Run at the first speed until the dough comes away from the sides of the bowl. More common flour can be added 1/4 cup at a time if the dough is too soft.

Remove and scrape down the beater and insert the dough hook. Run at the first speed until the dough forms up on the hook and comes away from the sides of the bowl (8 to 10 minutes). You can use the second speed for the last few minutes to strengthen the gluten. Add the citron using the first speed or knead it in by hand.

Shape into 1 large loaf or 2 small loaves as you prefer. Allow extra baking time for the larger size. Proceed as in Rising, Shaping, and Baking, above.

Yield

Makes 1 large loaf or 2 small loaves.

Russian Health Bread

In the bakery we make a pumpernickel bread with chopped whole grains of rye. These rye "chops" are used in a bread known as Russian Health Bread. It is quite tasty and unusual in appearance. You can purchase rye grain or cereal in natural foods stores. It is easily chopped in a spice or coffee grinder, a blender (small amounts at a time), or a food processor, which takes longer.

1 cup warm water
1 package active dry yeast
1 1/2 cups Rye Sour (pages 163-165)
1 cup altus (optional, page 15)
1/2 cup rye chops
4 tablespoons pumpernickel color (page 24; see Note)
1 cup pumpernickel flour
2 1/2 to 3 1/2 cups common flour (page 8) or all-purpose flour
1 tablespoon salt
Flour, for dusting work top
Additional pumpernickel flour, for dusting pans
Oil, for greasing bowl
Shortening, for greasing pans

In a large bowl sprinkle the yeast over the warm water to soften; stir to dissolve. Add the Rye Sour, altus (if desired), rye chops, pumpernickel color, pumpernickel flour, 2 1/2 cups common flour, and salt. Mix thoroughly until the dough comes away from the sides of the bowl.

Turn out the dough onto a floured work surface and knead, adding small amounts of common flour as necessary, until the dough is smooth and silky (5 to 8 minutes).

Rising

Roll the dough into a ball and place in a large oiled bowl, turning to coat. Cover and allow to rise until doubled in volume (30 to 45 minutes).

Shaping

Punch down the dough, cut into 4 parts, and roll each into a ball. Spill pumpernickel flour into 2 greased 8- or 9-inch loaf pans. Jiggle and turn the pans so that the sides and bottoms are coated. Pour out the excess flour and reserve.

Place 2 round balls side by side in each loaf pan. This is called a saddle loaf and breaks easily into 2 breads when done. Dust the tops generously with the reserved pumpernickel flour. Proof in a warm, draft-free spot until doubled in size. Punch 1 hole in each half with a blade or skewer and indent by pushing your finger through to the bottom.

Baking

Bake with steam (pages 31-32) in a preheated 375°F oven until the loaf emits a hollow sound when the bottom is tapped with your fingertips (35 to 45 minutes). If you are using an oven stone, remove the breads from the pan for the last 10 minutes and bake on the stone to develop a crusty loaf. If the top crust feels soft, return the bread to the oven without the pan for 5 to 10 minutes more. Let cool on a wire rack.

Yield

Makes 2 large loaves.

Note: Instead of pumpernickel color, you can substitute either 2 tablespoons molasses, 2 tablespoons cocoa powder, or 2 tablespoons instant coffee, or more to suit.

Variation

Pullman Pumpernickel, German Style

This square-shaped bread is excellent for sandwiches, especially when thinly sliced. The Pullman pan in which it is baked creates a dense texture, which is exceptionally moist. Shape the dough into a large pan loaf (pages 27-28). Place in a greased 12-inch Pullman loaf pan (page 5) and allow to rise until 1/2 inch from the top of the pan. Slide on the cover and bake. After 35 minutes, remove the top and bake until done. An alternate method is to put the bread in a long loaf pan, cover with a baking sheet, and lay a weight on top while baking. Grease the bottom of the cover so that it does not stick to the rising bread.

Russian Health Bread

(Food Processor, Steel Blade)

Instead of 1 cup warm water use:

1/4 cup warm water
3/4 cup ice water

In the work bowl sprinkle the yeast over the warm water to soften; stir to dissolve. Add the Rye Sour, altus (if desired), and ice water. Mix until absorbed. Add the rye chops, pumpernickel color, pumpernickel flour, 2 1/2 cups common flour (1 cup at a time), and salt. Pulse until the dough tries to form up on top of the blade. More common flour can be added 1/4 cup at a time if the dough is too soft. Process for 2 to 3 minutes. If necessary divide the dough in half and process each half separately, then knead together. Do not overmix or the dough will get too hot. Extra kneading by hand is sometimes necessary to make the dough elastic.

Proceed as in Rising, Shaping, and Baking, above.

Yield

Makes 2 large loaves.

Russian Health Bread

(Dough-Mixing Machine, Flat Beater)

1 1/2 cups warm water
1 package active dry yeast
2 1/4 cups Rye Sour (pages 163-165)
1 1/2 cups altus (optional, page 15)
3/4 cup rye chops
6 tablespoons pumpernickel color (page 24; see Note above)
1 1/2 cups pumpernickel flour
3 3/4 to 5 1/2 cups common flour (page 8) or all-purpose flour
1 1/2 tablespoons salt
Additional pumpernickel flour, for dusting pans
Oil, for greasing bowl
Shortening, for greasing pans

In the mixing bowl dissolve the yeast in the warm water. Add the Rye Sour, altus (if desired), rye chops, pumpernickel color, pumpernickel flour, 3 3/4 cups common flour, and salt. Stir through the dry ingredients with your fingertips to incorporate the salt into the flour. Pulse with the on/off switch until all is absorbed so that the flour is not thrown out of the bowl. Run at the first speed until the dough comes away from the sides of the bowl. More common flour can be added 1/4 cup at a time if the dough is too soft.

Remove and scrape down the beater and insert the dough hook. Run at the first speed until the dough forms up on the hook and comes away from the sides of the bowl (5 to 8 minutes). You can use the second speed for the last few minutes to strengthen the gluten.

Proceed as in Rising, Shaping, and Baking, above, except shape the dough into 6 balls, two to each pan.

Yield

Makes 3 loaves.

Corn Bread

This bread should really have a chapter of its own. It's the best bread I make! The Corn Bread I write about here originated in Europe. It is made from rye and wheat flours; there is no corn at all. The word corn to many Europeans is an all-encompassing term meaning grain, such as wheat, oats, rye, barley, and maize (their word for corn). Corn as we know it is a native American grain; when we speak of corn bread in the United States we mean bread made from cornmeal, such as corn muffins, corn sticks, corn pone from the South, or johnnycake from New England. Some folks erroneously refer to my Corn Bread as corn rye, and mistakenly bake a bread that has both rye and cornmeal in the recipe. I will stick to the proper European name for this loaf—Corn Bread.

I have a lot of good things to tell about this bread. The recipe is very simple—the same as for many great breads the world over—water, flour, salt, and yeast. The procedure is different from any other bread and directions must be followed carefully. There are few bakeries left that haven't compromised this bread's real flavor, moisture, and texture. Follow the directions and success will be assured. I believe that this is the first time the recipe has been reproduced for the home baker in its proper version. Don't let the length of the instructions intimidate you. They are simple. Just go along one step at a time. Making this bread takes patience but your satisfaction will be enormous. Enjoy!

I do not recommend using the food processor for this bread. If you have a heavy-duty electric dough-mixing machine, I recommend its use, since Corn Bread is made from a soft, wet dough that can be difficult to handle.

1 1/2 cups warm water
1 1/2 packages active dry yeast (scant 1 1/2 tablespoons)
1 1/2 cups Rye Sour (pages 163-165)
1 1/2 cups rye flour
2 cups common flour, or more as needed (page 8; see Note)
1 1/2 tablespoons salt
2 1/2 tablespoons caraway seeds (optional)
Additional common flour, for dusting work top
Cornmeal or cornmeal and rye flour, for dusting baking sheet
Cornstarch solution (page 20) or water, for brushing bread

In a large bowl dissolve the yeast in the warm water. Add the Rye Sour, rye flour, common flour, and salt. Stir with a wooden spoon until thoroughly incorporated.

Turn out the dough onto a work surface covered with common flour. Use a plastic bowl scraper or dough cutter in one hand to help knead what will be a very soft, wet dough. Knead for 5 minutes by scraping, folding, pulling, and stretching. Pretend that you are pulling taffy. The dough should have some elasticity and resist being stretched. Keep the dough soft. If the dough does not feel lively or elastic, alternately add rye flour, then common flour 1/4 cup at a time, stretching and kneading with each addition. Continue for another 3 minutes. The wetter the dough, the better the bread. The amount of flour will vary depending upon how stiff you made the sour.

Transfer the dough to a clean, wet bowl. Keep a container of cold water nearby. Keeping your hands wet at all times, pat the dough down and cover with a film of water. Cover the bowl with plastic wrap and set aside. Allow the dough to rise until doubled in volume (45 to 60 minutes).

Shaping

Prepare a baking sheet sprinkled with cornmeal or a cornmeal-rye flour mixture, upon which the bread will be baked. (Or use a peel; see page 5.) Wet a clean work surface or board generously with water. When ready, cover the top of the dough with the caraway seeds, if desired. Keeping the hands wet at all times, scoop out the dough (or half the dough at a time for 2 loaves) and shape into a round by bringing the sides of the dough down to the middle and gathering it together until you have a ball of dough. Handle the dough gently so that it does not tear. Place it on the wet work top. Turn and push the sides down and underneath to further round up the bread. Work your hands underneath and gently lift the loaf, then set it down onto the prepared baking sheet. Smooth the dough down with a caressing, circular motion. Press down, flattening out the top; it will spring up in the oven. Sprinkle extra caraway seeds on top if you are using them. Allow the dough to stand no longer than 10 minutes. It can be placed in the oven without any standing time. Do not proof.

Baking

Place an empty broiler pan on the oven floor and preheat for 5 minutes at 375°F. Brush the bread with the cornstarch solution or water. Place the baking sheet holding the bread on the middle shelf of the oven, or on tiles or an oven stone if you have them. Carefully add 6 to 8 ice cubes or 1 cup hot water to the hot broiler pan and shut the door. Protect your hands and face from the burst of steam. Bake for exactly 5 minutes. Steam in the oven is not desirable after that time. In exactly 5 minutes carefully remove the hot broiler pan with the remaining water. Select a space in advance on which to set the hot pan. Observe caution with the hot water. Slide out the bread and, with a skewer or an ice pick, stipple 10 to 12 holes all around the crust; return the bread to the oven. Reduce the heat to 350°F and continue baking for 10 minutes, then stipple once more and brush again with the cornstarch solution or water.

When the bread begins to brown, turn the bread around to ensure even baking. Bake until the crust is hard and unyielding to gentle pressure. Timing will vary depending on the amount of moisture in the dough. It may take an hour or longer. The bread is done when tapping on the bottom emits a hollow sound and the top and sides are hard. If you are using tiles or an oven stone, transfer the bread from the baking sheets to the tiles and continue baking for an additional 10 to 15 minutes to make the loaves crustier.

Remove the bread from the oven, brush the top with more cornstarch solution or water, and let cool on a wire rack. The bread will keep well for more than a week in the bread box. It also freezes well.

Yield

Makes 1 large loaf or 2 small loaves.

Note: Also called clear or first clear, common flour may be available from a local bakery. You can substitute 1 1/2 cups all-purpose flour and 1/3 cup cake or pastry flour, but the bread won't taste as good.

Corn Bread

(Dough-Mixing Machine, Flat Beater)

Use the same recipe as above.

In the mixing bowl sprinkle the yeast over the warm water and stir to dissolve. Add the Rye Sour, rye flour, common flour, and salt. Mix at the first speed until the dough comes away from the sides of the bowl. Be patient. If the dough does not come away, run at the second speed for a few minutes.

Remove and scrape down the beater, insert the dough hook, and continue mixing at the second speed for 5 minutes. If the dough does not come away from the sides of the bowl, use the third speed for 2 minutes. If it still does not come away, run at the first speed and alternatively add rye flour, then common flour 1/4 cup at a time. This will be a wet, sloppy dough.

Prepare a clean mixing bowl and wet by swishing water around the inside. Transfer the dough to the prepared bowl. Keeping your hands wet at all times, remove the hook, pat down the dough, and cover with a film of water. Cover the bowl with plastic wrap, set aside, and allow the dough to rise until doubled in volume (45 to 60 minutes depending upon the humidity and room temperature). Proceed as in Shaping and Baking, above.

Yield

Makes 1 large loaf or 2 small loaves.

Sourdough French Bread

Sourdough French Bread has the thick, crisp crust of French bread plus a delightful tang that will have you devouring this loaf with gusto. It is delicious with wine and cheese, soups, meats, sandwiches—anywhere you would use a crusty bread.

2 cups warm water
2 packages active dry yeast
2 cups White Sour (pages 166-167)
5 to 6 cups all-purpose flour
1 tablespoon salt
Flour, for dusting work top
Oil, for greasing bowl
Cornmeal, for dusting baking sheet

In a large bowl sprinkle the yeast over the warm water to soften; stir until dissolved. Add the White Sour, 5 cups flour, and salt. Mix with a large wooden spoon until the dough comes away from the sides of the bowl.

Turn out the dough onto a lightly floured work surface. Knead with a push, turn, fold motion. If the dough is too soft or wet, add more flour 1/4 cup at a time while kneading. Knead until smooth and elastic (12 to 15 minutes). The dough should feel as though it is pushing back as you knead. Transfer the dough to an oiled bowl and turn to coat.

First Rise

Allow the dough to rise, covered, until puffy (about 30 minutes).

Second Rise

Punch down, shape into a ball, and allow to rise, oiled and covered, until doubled in volume (45 to 60 minutes).

Shaping

Punch down again and cut into 4 equal pieces. Shape each into a narrow baguette (pages 28-29). Place, seam down, on a baking sheet that has been sprinkled with cornmeal or in a greased and dusted baguette pan (page 5).

Proofing

Allow the bread to proof, covered with a flour-dusted cloth or towel, in a warm, draft-free area until doubled in size (45 to 60 minutes). This bread likes to be dry proofed. Do not add any moisture.

Baking

Place an empty broiler pan on the floor of a preheated 425°F oven for 5 minutes. With a razor blade or sharp knife, score 3 to 6 diagonal slashes down the center of each bread (see page 16). Place the baking sheet containing the breads on the middle shelf of the oven. Carefully pour 1 cup boiling water or place 8 or 9 ice cubes into the broiler pan in the oven. Protect your hands and face from the burst of steam. Do not open the oven door for at least 10 minutes. After 10 minutes reduce the oven temperature to 350°F. Bake until tapping with your fingertips on the bottom of the bread makes a hollow sound (about 20 minutes more). The top and sides of the bread should be hard to the touch. As long as the color of the crust remains light, an extra 5 to 10 minutes of baking will improve the crust. The bread will have a better crust if it is removed from the pan and baked on a tile hearth or baking stone for the last 5 minutes. Remove when baked and let cool on a wire rack.

Yield

Makes 4 baguettes.

Sourdough French Bread

(Food Processor, Steel Blade)

Instead of 2 cups warm water use:

1/2 cup warm water
1 1/2 cups ice water

Sprinkle the yeast over the warm water to soften; stir until dissolved. Add the ice water, White Sour, 2 cups flour, and salt. Blend, then add 3 cups flour, 1 cup at a time. Pulse until the dough tries to form up on top of the blade. More flour can be added 1/4 cup at a time if needed. Process for 2 to 3 minutes. If necessary divide the dough in half and process each half separately, then knead together. Do not overmix. Extra kneading by hand is sometimes necessary to make the dough elastic. Transfer the dough to an oiled bowl and turn to coat.

Proceed as in the First Rise, Second Rise, Shaping, Proofing, and Baking, above.

Yield

Makes 4 baguettes.

Sourdough French Bread

(Dough-Mixing Machine, Flat Beater)

1/2 cup warm water
2 packages active dry yeast
2 1/2 cups ice water
3 cups White Sour
7 1/2 to 9 cups all-purpose flour
1 1/2 tablespoons salt
Flour, for dusting work top
Oil, for greasing bowl
Cornmeal, for dusting

In a small bowl sprinkle the yeast over the warm water to soften; stir until dissolved, then set aside.

Place the ice water in the work bowl and add the White Sour, 7 1/2 cups flour, and salt. Pulse with the on/off switch until all is absorbed so that the flour does not fly out of the bowl. Add the reserved dissolved yeast. Mix at the first speed until the dough forms up into a ball.

Remove and scrape down the beater. Insert the dough hook and mix at the first speed until the dough is smooth and elastic (12 to 15 minutes). More flour can be added 1/4 cup at a time if necessary. Turn out the dough, place in an oiled bowl, and turn once or twice to coat. Proceed as in the First Rise, Second Rise, Shaping, Proofing, and Baking, above, except shape into 3 large or 6 small baguettes.

Yield

Makes 3 large or 6 small baguettes.

Sourdough Country French Bread

This round country-style bread is baked longer than a baguette and retains more moisture. A rough texture and the addition of coarse flour gives this bread a special flavor.

1 cup warm water
1 package active dry yeast
3 cups White Sour (pages 166-167)
1/2 cup whole wheat flour, preferably stone ground
2 1/2 to 3 cups bread flour or all-purpose flour
3 1/2 teaspoons salt
Flour, for dusting work top
Oil, for greasing bowl
Cornmeal or rye flour, for dusting baking sheet

In a large bowl sprinkle the yeast over the warm water to soften; stir until dissolved. Add the White Sour, whole wheat flour, 2 1/2 cups bread flour, and salt. Mix with a large wooden spoon until the dough comes away from the sides of the bowl.

Turn out the dough onto a lightly floured work surface. Knead with a push, turn, fold motion. If the dough is too soft or sticky, add more bread flour 1/4 cup at a time. Knead until the dough is smooth and elastic (8 to 10 minutes). The dough should push back when pressed.

Transfer the dough to an oiled bowl and turn to coat.

First Rise

Allow the dough to rise, covered, until puffy (about 30 minutes).

Second Rise

Punch down the dough, then shape into a round ball, cover, and allow to rise until doubled in volume (30 to 45 minutes).

Shaping

Punch down again, then shape into a ball. Place on a baking sheet that has been sprinkled with cornmeal or rye flour.

Proofing

Cover the loaf with a flour-dusted cloth or towel, place in a warm, draft-free area, and allow to rise until doubled in size (45 to 60 minutes). Dust the bread with flour or brush with water. With a razor blade or sharp knife, score the top with 4 slashes to form a square.

Baking

Place an empty broiler pan on the floor of a 475°F oven for 5 minutes. Place the baking sheet containing the bread on the middle shelf of the oven. Quickly pour 1 cup boiling water or place 8 or 9 ice cubes into the broiler pan in the oven. Protect your hands and face from the initial burst of steam. Do not open the oven door for at least 10 minutes. Bake until tapping the bottom of the loaf with your fingertips produces a hollow sound (30 to 45 minutes). The top and sides of the loaf should be hard to the touch. The bread will have a better crust if it is removed from the pan and baked on a tile or baking stone for the last 5 minutes. Let cool on a wire rack.

Yield

Makes 1 loaf.

Variations

Substitute pumpernickel flour (medium rye) for the whole wheat flour for a different flavor.

Replace the whole wheat flour with bread flour or all-purpose flour to make a smoother-textured, all-white loaf.

Use rye flour in place of the whole wheat flour.

Shape the dough into very thin, long baguettes, about 1 inch in diameter, for a crusty treat. Shorten the baking time.

Knead in Onion Filling and Topping (page 23) and shape into narrow cigar-shaped sticks about 12 inches long. Adjust the baking time.

Sourdough Country French...

(Food Processor, Steel Blade)

Instead of 1 cup warm water use:

1/4 cup warm water
3/4 cup ice water

Sprinkle the yeast over the warm water to soften; stir until dissolved. Add the ice water, White Sour, whole wheat flour, 1 cup bread flour, and salt. Blend, then add 1 1/2 cups bread flour. Pulse until the dough tries to form up on top of the blade. More bread flour can be added 1/4 cup at a time if needed. Process for 2 to 3 minutes. If necessary divide the dough in two and process each half separately, then knead together. Do not overmix. Extra kneading by hand is sometimes necessary to make the dough elastic. Turn out the dough, place in an oiled bowl, and turn to coat.

Proceed as in the First Rise, Second Rise, Shaping, Proofing, and Baking, above.

Yield

Makes 1 loaf.

Sourdough Country French...

(Dough-Mixing Machine, Flat Beater)

1 1/2 cups warm water
1 package active dry yeast
4 1/2 cups White Sour (pages 166-167)
3/4 cup whole wheat flour, preferably stone ground
3 3/4 to 4 1/2 cups bread flour or all-purpose flour
5 1/4 teaspoons salt
Oil, for greasing bowl
Flour, for dusting work top
Cornmeal or rye flour, for dusting baking sheet

Sprinkle the yeast over the warm water to soften; stir until dissolved. Add the White Sour, whole wheat flour, 3 3/4 cups bread flour, and salt. Pulse with the on/off switch so that the flour does not fly out of the bowl. Mix at the first speed until the dough comes away from the sides of the bowl.

Remove and scrape down the beater. Insert the dough hook and mix at the first speed until the dough is smooth and elastic (8 to 10 minutes). More bread flour can be added 1/4 cup at a time if necessary. Turn out the dough, place in an oiled bowl, and turn once or twice to coat. Proceed as in the First Rise, Second Rise, Shaping, Proofing, and Baking, above, but allow additional baking time for the large loaf.

Yield

Makes 1 large loaf.

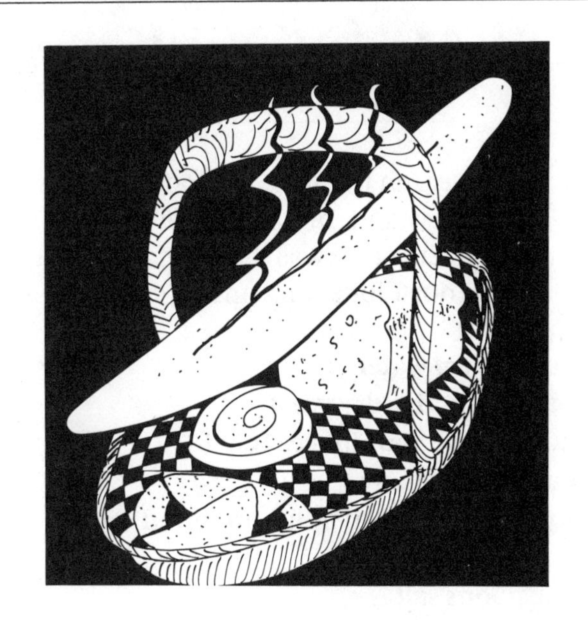

Sourdough Barley Bread

In the search for healthful foods and new flavors, I came up with a high-fiber grain bread with a new and interesting flavor. Although it may seem new to us, barley was known to the ancients and was the chief bread ingredient in Europe as late as the 1500s. This bread keeps moist for a long time and freezes well.

2 cups warm water
1 package active dry yeast
2 cups White Sour (pages 166-167)
3 cups barley flour
3 to 3 1/2 cups bread flour (preferred) or all-purpose flour
3 teaspoons salt
Additional all-purpose flour, for dusting work top
Oil, for greasing bowl
Cornmeal, for dusting baking pan

In a large bowl sprinkle the yeast over the warm water; stir to dissolve. Add the White Sour, barley flour, 3 cups bread flour, and salt. Stir until the dough comes away from the sides of the bowl, adding more bread flour if necessary.

Turn out the dough onto a lightly floured work top. Knead with a turn, fold, push motion, adding more bread flour in small amounts if the dough is sticky. The dough may be kept softer than usual. Continue until the dough is smooth and elastic (5 to 8 minutes).

Transfer the dough to an oiled bowl and turn to coat. Cover and allow to rise for 45 minutes. (This bread does not rise much.) Punch down, cut into 2 rounds, and allow to rest, covered, for 15 minutes.

Shaping

Punch down the dough, shape into 2 free-form pan loaves (pages 27-28) or 2 round loaves, and place on a cornmeal-dusted baking pan. Allow to rest, covered, for 15 minutes. Score each of the long loaves with 5 to 6 short diagonal cuts. The rounds can be stippled or slashed tic-tac-toe fashion.

Baking

Bake with steam (pages 31-32) in a 425°F oven until the bottom emits a hollow sound when tapped with your fingertips (35 to 45 minutes). Remove the bread from the pan for the last 5 to 10 minutes of baking.

Yield

Makes 2 round loaves.

Sourdough Barley Bread

(Food Processor, Steel Blade)

Instead of 2 cups warm water use:

1/2 cup warm water
1 1/2 cups ice water

In the work bowl sprinkle the yeast over the warm water; stir to dissolve. Add the ice water, White Sour, barley flour, 3 cups bread flour (1 cup at a time), and the salt. Pulse until the dough tries to form up on top of the blade. More bread flour can be added 1/4 cup at a time if the dough is too soft. Process for 2 to 3 minutes. If necessary divide the dough in half and process each half separately, then knead together. Do not overmix. Extra kneading by hand is sometimes necessary to make the dough elastic.

Transfer the dough to an oiled bowl, turn to coat, and allow to rise for about 45 minutes. (This bread does not rise much.)

Proceed as in Shaping and Baking, above.

Yield

Makes 2 round loaves.

Sourdough Barley Bread

(Dough-Mixing Machine, Flat Beater)

3 cups warm water
1 1/2 packages active dry yeast
3 cups White Sour (pages 166-167)
4 1/2 cups barley flour
4 1/2 to 5 1/4 cups bread flour (preferred) or all-purpose flour
1 1/2 tablespoons salt
Oil, for greasing bowl
Additional all-purpose flour, for dusting
Cornmeal, for dusting baking pan

In the mixing bowl sprinkle the yeast over the warm water; stir to dissolve. Add the White Sour, barley flour, 4 1/2 cups bread flour, and salt. Mix until the dough comes away from the sides of the bowl, adding more bread flour if necessary.

Scrape down the beater and insert the dough hook. Mix for 8 to 10 minutes at the first speed. This dough will be softer than usual. More bread flour can be added in small amounts as necessary. The dough should be smooth and elastic. You can use the second speed for the last 2 minutes to strengthen the gluten.

Transfer the dough to an oiled bowl and turn to coat. Cover and allow the dough to rise until doubled in volume. Proceed as in Shaping and Baking, above, except shape the dough into 3 loaves.

Yield

Makes 3 loaves.

Sourdough Bran Bread

Sourdough Bran Bread has dietary fiber, whole-grain flavor, a long shelf life, and the tang of sourdough. This dark, crusty loaf can be used for sandwiches and goes well with meat and cheese dishes. This bread is best when used one day after baking.

2 cups warm water
1 package active dry yeast
1 cup White Sour (pages 166-167)
1 cup unprocessed bran flakes
4 to 5 cups bread flour (preferred) or all-purpose flour
3 teaspoons salt
Flour, for dusting work top
Oil, for greasing bowl
Cornmeal, for dusting baking sheet
Water or cornstarch solution (page 20), for brushing loaves

In a large bowl sprinkle the yeast over the warm water; stir to dissolve. Add the White Sour, bran flakes, 4 cups bread flour, and salt. Stir until the dough comes away from the sides of the bowl, adding more flour if necessary.

Turn out the dough onto a lightly floured work top. Knead with a turn, fold, push motion, adding more flour in small amounts if the dough is sticky. Continue until the dough is smooth and elastic (8 to 10 minutes). Transfer the dough to an oiled bowl, cover, and allow to rise until doubled in volume.

Shaping

Punch down the dough and shape each round into a free-standing pan loaf (pages 27-28). Place on a cornmeal-dusted baking sheet and set aside, covered, in a warm area. Allow to proof until doubled in size (45 to 60 minutes). Brush with water or the cornstarch solution, then cut 5 or 6 diagonal slashes across the top of each loaf.

Baking

Bake with steam (pages 31-32) in a 425°F oven until the bottom emits a hollow sound when tapped with your fingertips (35 to 45 minutes). Remove the bread from the pan for the last 5 minutes of baking to improve the crust.

Yield

Makes 2 loaves.

Sourdough Bran Bread

(Food Processor, Steel Blade)

Instead of 2 cups warm water use:

1/2 cup warm water
1 1/2 cups ice water

In the work bowl sprinkle the yeast over the warm water; stir to dissolve. Add the ice water, White Sour, bran flakes, 2 cups bread flour, and salt. Blend until smooth. Add 2 more cups flour, 1 cup at a time. Pulse until the dough tries to form up on top of the blade. More flour can be added 1/4 cup at a time if the dough is too soft. Process for 2 to 3 minutes. If necessary divide the dough in half and process each half separately, then knead together. Do not overmix. Extra kneading by hand is sometimes necessary to make the dough elastic.

Transfer the dough to an oiled bowl, turn to coat, and allow to rise until doubled in volume (about 45 minutes). Punch down, shape into 2 rounds, and let rest for 15 minutes.

Proceed as in Shaping and Baking, above.

Yield

Makes 2 loaves.

Sourdough Bran Bread

(Dough-Mixing Machine, Flat Beater)

3 cups warm water
1 package active dry yeast
1 1/2 cups White Sour (pages 166-167)
1 1/2 cups unprocessed bran flakes
6 to 7 1/2 cups bread flour (preferred) or all-purpose flour
1 tablespoon salt
Oil, for greasing bowl
Cornmeal, for dusting baking sheet
Water or cornstarch solution (page 20), for brushing loaves

In the mixing bowl sprinkle the yeast over the warm water; stir to dissolve. Add the White Sour, bran flakes, 6 cups bread flour, and salt. Mix until the dough comes away from the sides of the bowl, adding more flour if necessary.

Scrape down the beater and insert the dough hook. Mix for 8 to 10 minutes at the first speed. More flour can be added in small amounts as necessary. The dough should be smooth and elastic. You can use the second speed for the last 2 minutes to strengthen the gluten.

Transfer the dough to an oiled bowl and turn to coat. Cover and allow to rise until doubled in volume. Proceed as in Shaping and Baking, above, except shape into 3 loaves.

Yield

Makes 3 loaves.

Sourdough Country Corn Bread

This is a heavy, moist, and extremely crusty country-style or peasant bread made of mixed grains. It's good with meats or soups and cold cuts or deli meats of all kinds, and goes well when toasted with cheese or jam. The crust is dusted with flour and is cracked haphazardly, creating crisp fissures that add to the bread's unique character. This bread requires a starter, which is aged for at least 6 hours. I do this very simply by mixing a yeast starter the evening before and leaving it to ferment at room temperature overnight.

Starter

1 cup warm water
1 teaspoon active dry yeast
2 cups unbleached all-purpose flour

Dough

1 1/4 cups warm water
3/4 teaspoons active dry yeast
1 cup Starter (see above)
1 cup cornmeal, preferably fine cornmeal
2 3/4 to 3 3/4 cups unbleached all-purpose flour
1 tablespoon salt
Flour, for dusting work top
Oil, for greasing bowl
Cornmeal, for dusting baking sheet
Rye flour or potato starch (preferred) or all-purpose flour, for dusting bread

Starter

In a large bowl sprinkle the yeast over the warm water to soften; stir to dissolve. Add the flour and stir until smooth. Cover with plastic wrap or a cloth and set aside at room temperature for at least 6 hours, or overnight.

Dough

In a large bowl sprinkle the yeast over the warm water; stir to dissolve. Add the Starter, cornmeal, 2 3/4 cups flour, and salt. Stir until the dough comes away from the sides of the bowl, adding more flour if necessary.

Turn out the dough onto a lightly floured work top. Knead with a turn, fold, push motion, adding more flour in small amounts if necessary. This dough should be soft. Continue until the dough is smooth and elastic (8 to 10 minutes).

Rising

Transfer the dough to an oiled bowl, turn to coat, cover, and allow to rise until puffed up (about 30 minutes). Punch down and allow to rise again until doubled in bulk (30 to 45 minutes). Shape into a ball and place on a cornmeal-dusted baking sheet. Set aside, covered, and allow to rest until puffy (about 30 minutes). Brush with water and dust with rye flour, potato starch, or all-purpose flour. Cut 5 or 6 diagonal slashes across the top of the loaf.

Baking

Bake in a 425°F oven until the bottom emits a hollow sound when tapped with your fingertips (35 to 45 minutes). Remove the bread from the pan for the last 5 minutes of baking to improve the crust.

Yield

Makes 1 loaf.

Sourdough Country Corn Bread

(Food Processor, Steel Blade)

In the Dough recipe above, instead of 1 1/4 cups warm water use:

1/4 cup warm water
1 cup ice water

Prepare the Starter as above.

To make the Dough, in the work bowl sprinkle the yeast over the warm water; stir to dissolve. Add the Starter, ice water, cornmeal, 2 1/2 cups flour (1 cup at a time), and salt. Pulse until the dough tries to form up on top of the blade. More flour can be added 1/4 cup at a time if needed. This dough should be soft. Process for 2 to 3 minutes. If necessary divide the dough in half and process each half separately, then knead together. Do not overmix. Extra kneading by hand is sometimes necessary to make the dough elastic.

Proceed as in Rising and Baking, above.

Yield

Makes 1 loaf.

Sourdough Country Corn Bread

(Dough-Mixing Machine, Flat Beater)

1 3/4 cups plus 1 tablespoon warm water
1 1/4 teaspoons active dry yeast
1 1/2 cups Starter (see above)
1 1/2 cups cornmeal, preferably fine cornmeal
4 1/4 to 6 1/4 cups unbleached all-purpose flour
1 1/2 tablespoons salt
Oil, for greasing bowl
Cornmeal, for dusting baking sheet
Rye flour or potato starch (preferred) or all-purpose flour, for dusting bread

In the mixing bowl sprinkle the yeast over the warm water to soften; stir to dissolve. Add the Starter, cornmeal, 4 1/4 cups flour, and salt. Mix until the dough comes away from the sides of the bowl.

Remove and scrape down the beater, insert the dough hook, and continue mixing at the first speed for 8 to 10 minutes. More flour can be added in small amounts as necessary. This dough should be soft. You can use the second speed for the last 2 minutes to strengthen the gluten.

Transfer the dough to an oiled bowl and turn to coat. Proceed as in Rising and Baking, above, but allow extra oven time for the larger loaf (45 to 60 minutes).

Yield

Makes 1 large loaf.

Sourdough Olive Bread

Olive bread has a special zest that goes well with cheese, luncheon meats, chicken, and salads. Create new flavors with this dark-crusted loaf. Cream cheese sandwiches are one of my favorite uses for this bread.

1 cup warm water
1 package active dry yeast
2 tablespoons oil, preferably olive oil
1/2 cup White Sour (pages 166-167)
1/2 cup whole wheat flour, preferably stone ground
3/4 cup rye flour
1 1/2 to 2 1/2 cups bread flour or all-purpose flour
1 teaspoon salt
Flour, for dusting work top
4 ounces pitted olives (preferably Greek or French)
Oil, for greasing bowl

In a large bowl sprinkle the yeast over the warm water; stir to dissolve. Add the oil, White Sour, whole wheat flour, rye flour, 1 1/2 cups bread flour, and salt. Stir until the dough comes away from the sides of the bowl, adding more bread flour if necessary.

Turn out the dough onto a lightly floured work top. Knead with a turn, fold, push motion, adding more bread flour in small amounts if the dough is sticky. The dough should be kept somewhat soft. Continue kneading until the dough is smooth and elastic (8 to 10 minutes). Knead in the olives.

Transfer the dough to an oiled bowl. Cover and allow to rise until doubled in volume.

Shaping

Punch down the dough and shape into a broad baguette (page 28) or a round. Score the long bread with a series of short diagonal cuts. The round can be stippled or slashed, tic-tac-toe fashion. In the bakery we sometimes use a bicycle form—a cylindrical, ridged metal form resembling a series of wheels lined up in a continuous length. The form is greased, the dough is shaped and inserted, and the form is closed and locked. Proofing fills the form completely; when baked, you have a ridged loaf that slices into individual rounds or wheels of bread.

Baking

Bake with steam (pages 31-32) in a 425°F oven until the bottom emits a hollow sound when tapped with your fingertips (35 to 45 minutes). If a form is used, remove it for the last 5 minutes of baking.

Yield

Makes 1 loaf.

Sourdough Olive Bread

(Food Processor, Steel Blade)

Instead of 1 cup warm water use:

1/4 cup warm water
3/4 cup ice water

In the work bowl sprinkle the yeast over the warm water; stir to dissolve. Add the ice water, oil, White Sour, whole wheat flour, rye flour, and salt. Blend, then add 1 1/2 cups bread flour. Pulse until the dough tries to form up on top of the blade. More bread flour can be added 1/4 cup at a time if the dough is too soft. Process for 2 to 3 minutes. If necessary divide the dough in half and process each half separately, then knead together. Do not overmix. Extra kneading by hand is sometimes necessary to make the dough elastic.

Turn out the dough onto a lightly floured work top. Knead in the olives. Transfer the dough to an oiled bowl, turn to coat, and allow to rise until doubled in volume.

Proceed as in Shaping and Baking, above.

Yield

Makes 1 loaf.

Sourdough Olive Bread

(Dough-Mixing Machine, Flat Beater)

1 1/2 cups warm water
1 package active dry yeast
3 tablespoons oil, preferably olive oil
3/4 cup White Sour (pages 166-167)
3/4 cup whole wheat flour, preferably stone ground
1 1/4 cups rye flour
2 1/4 to 3 3/4 cups bread flour or all-purpose flour
1 1/2 teaspoons salt
Flour, for dusting work top
Oil, for greasing bowl
6 ounces pitted olives (preferably Greek or French)

In the mixing bowl sprinkle the yeast over the warm water; stir to dissolve. Add the oil, White Sour, whole wheat flour, rye flour, 2 1/4 cups bread flour, and salt. Mix until the dough comes away from the sides of the bowl, adding more bread flour if necessary.

Scrape down the beater and insert the dough hook. Mix for 8 to 10 minutes at the first speed. More bread flour can be added in small amounts as necessary. The dough should be smooth and elastic. You can use the second speed for the last 2 minutes to strengthen the gluten.

Turn out the dough onto a lightly floured work top. Knead in the olives. Transfer the dough to an oiled bowl, turn to coat, and allow to rise until doubled in volume. Proceed as in Shaping and Baking, above, except shape into 1 large or 2 small loaves.

Yield

Makes 1 large or 2 small loaves.

Sourdough Naan

In northern India naan is made using milk curds (used in cheese making), which leaven the dough by fermentation. The following dough uses baking powder and baking soda for leavening and must be allowed to ferment overnight, or better still for 24 hours. For superior results when not using curds, a starter is desirable. Once the dough is prepared, a small portion of finished dough can be saved and set aside to begin the next baking. Any leftover yeast dough will work. (A recipe for naan using yeast is on page 135.)

Starter

1 cup plain yogurt, buttermilk, or sour cream
1/2 cup bread flour or all-purpose flour
1 piece leftover dough or 1 pinch yeast

Dough

All the Starter
2 eggs, lightly beaten
1 tablespoon sugar
3 to 4 cups bread flour or all-purpose flour
1 tablespoon baking powder
1/4 teaspoon baking soda
1/2 teaspoon salt
Oil, for greasing bowl and work top
Flour, for dusting work top

Starter

Mix all the ingredients until smooth, then allow to stand, uncovered, at room temperature until the starter becomes bubbly and puffy in appearance (overnight, but preferably for 24 hours).

Dough

In a large bowl place the Starter, eggs, sugar, 3 cups flour, baking powder, baking soda, and salt. Stir the dry ingredients together with your fingertips to distribute, then mix all the ingredients together with a large wooden spoon until the dough comes away from the sides of the bowl.

Turn out the dough onto a floured work surface and knead until the dough feels smooth and silky (8 to 10 minutes). More flour can be added if necessary. Keep this dough soft.

Rising

Transfer the dough to an oiled bowl and turn to coat. Cover with plastic wrap and allow to stand for at least 3 hours. Punch down and divide into 6 equal pieces. Shape into rounds with your palms by cupping them over the dough. Coat with oil or melted butter and cover. Allow to rest for 15 minutes.

Shaping

On a clean, oiled work surface, flatten the first round with oil-coated hands. Roll or press the dough into a 6- to 8-inch circle. Turn at least once to coat with oil. Press a series of indentations with your fingertips all over the bread. Repeat with the other five rounds.

Baking

Bake in a preheated 550°F oven. Oven tiles or a baking stone work best. If neither is available, place 2 baking pans upside down on the middle shelf of the oven and let them preheat for at least 5 minutes. Drape each naan over the palm of your hand and flip it over onto the hot tiles. Bake until puffy and the bottom is flecked with brown (about 2 minutes). Pierce any extra-large bubbles with a long barbecue fork or skewer. Immediately turn on the broiler. With the door closed continue baking until the tops begin to show some brown (1 to 2 minutes). Do not overbake. Switch the oven back to the bake cycle. Remove the bread with a long-handled spatula and cover by placing in the folds of a clean towel. Continue baking 1, 2, or 3 naan at a time (whatever you are comfortable with). As the breads are removed from the oven, stack them 6 high. Keep covered with the toweling.

Naan can be eaten warm or left to cool in the toweling and frozen in plastic bags.

Yield

Makes 6 breads.

Variation

Whole Wheat Chapati, Tandoori Style

Chapati is a layered Indian bread generally baked on a griddle. This is a northern Indian version baked tandoori style.

Substitute 1 cup whole wheat flour (1 1/2 cups in the mixing machine recipe) for the bread flour. Roll out the dough as thin as possible. Brush the top with oil or melted butter. Fold one circle into fours to form a triangle. Let the dough rest for 10 minutes while rolling and folding the rest of the pieces. Beginning with the first triangle, repeat this process 2 more times. (Roll out into as round a shape as possible.) If the dough gets too tough to roll, let it rest until it softens. Bake as above.

Yield

Makes 6 breads (9 in the mixing machine recipe).

Sourdough Naan

(Food Processor, Steel Blade)

In the work bowl place the Starter, eggs, sugar, 2 cups flour, baking powder, baking soda, and salt. Pulse to combine. Mix in the remaining 2 cups flour. Pulse until the dough comes away from the sides of the bowl (2 to 3 minutes), adding more flour if the dough is too sticky. Do not overmix. Additional kneading by hand may be necessary to make the dough elastic. Keep this dough soft. Proceed as in Rising, Shaping, and Baking, above.

Yield

Makes 6 breads.

Sourdough Naan

(Dough-Mixing Machine, Flat Beater)

Starter

1 1/2 cups plain yogurt, buttermilk, or sour cream
3/4 cup bread flour or all-purpose flour
1 small piece leftover dough or 1 pinch yeast

Dough

All the Starter
3 eggs, lightly beaten
1 1/2 tablespoons sugar
4 1/2 to 6 cups bread flour or unbleached all-purpose flour
1 1/2 tablespoons baking powder
1/2 scant teaspoon baking soda
3/4 teaspoon salt
Oil, for greasing bowl and work top

Starter

Mix all the ingredients until smooth, then allow to stand, uncovered, at room temperature until the starter becomes bubbly and puffy in appearance (overnight, or preferably for 24 hours).

Dough

In the work bowl place the Starter, eggs, sugar, 4 1/2 cups flour, baking powder, baking soda, and salt. Pulse with the on/off switch until all is absorbed so that the flour does not fly out of the bowl. Run at the first speed until the dough comes away from the sides of the bowl, adding more flour 1/4 cup at a time if the dough is sticky.

Scrape down the beater and insert the dough hook. Knead for 8 to 10 minutes at the first speed. More flour can be added in small amounts as necessary. Keep this dough soft. The finished dough should feel smooth and silky. You can mix at the second speed for the last few minutes to strengthen the gluten. Proceed as in Rising, Shaping, and Baking, above, except shape into 9 rounds.

Yield

Makes 9 breads.

San Francisco Sourdough Bread

San Francisco sourdough bread had its roots in the gold rush days, when the miners, known as sourbellys, carried a starter, or sour, in a pouch wrapped around their waist. Body heat kept the starter active. It was used for cooking flapjacks and baking biscuits.

A starter can be begun naturally with 3 to 4 days of standing time. The results are never certain; I prefer to give nature a bit of assistance. The addition of a minute amount of yeast will cut this time to 12 to 24 hours.

Once the starter is prepared, it can be kept indefinitely in the refrigerator with periodic refreshing. Prepare the starter the day before you are going to bake (3 to 4 days if yeast is not used). Store the prepared starter in a covered container in the refrigerator and stir down every 2 to 3 days. Once a week add 1 teaspoon water and 1 to 2 teaspoons flour and stir until smooth (see White Sour, pages 166-167).

Starter

1 cup warm water
1/8 teaspoon active dry yeast (optional)
1/3 cup skim milk powder
1 1/2 cups unbleached all-purpose flour

Sponge

1 1/4 cups warm water
1 package active dry yeast
2 cups bread flour (preferred) or all-purpose flour

Dough

Sponge
1 cup Starter
1 to 2 1/2 cups unbleached all-purpose flour
2 teaspoons sugar
2 teaspoons salt
1/2 teaspoon baking soda
Flour, for dusting work top
Oil, for greasing bowl
Cornmeal, for dusting baking sheet

Starter

Sprinkle the yeast (if used) over the warm water to dissolve. Add the milk powder and flour; stir until smooth. Leave uncovered in a draft-free spot for 12 to 24 hours. If yeast is not used in the starter, leave it to bubble, rise, and fall for 3 to 4 days. When ready, the starter will have a fermented aroma, which is normal.

Sponge

Dissolve the yeast in the warm water; add the flour. Stir until smooth, then cover and set aside until doubled in volume (30 to 45 minutes).

Dough

Stir down the Sponge. Add the Starter, 1 cup flour, sugar, salt, and baking soda. Stir the dry ingredients together with your fingers. With a wooden spoon stir until the dough comes away from the sides of the bowl.

Turn out the dough onto a floured surface and knead. Add more flour 1/4 cup at a time if the dough remains slack. Knead until the dough is smooth and elastic (10 to 12 minutes).

Transfer the dough to an oiled bowl and turn to coat it. Allow to double in volume.

Shaping

Leave the dough in 1 piece or cut into 2 or 3 pieces. Shape into 1 large round loaf, 2 Vienna-shaped loaves (page 28), or 2 or 3 long baguettes. Cover with a cloth and let rest for 15 minutes.

Proofing

Place on a baking sheet dusted with cornmeal, or in greased baguette pans if available. Cover and allow to double in size. Brush the tops of the breads with water and slash with 3 or 4 diagonal cuts on the long loaves or 3 lengthwise and 3 crosswise slashes (tic-tac-toe fashion) on the round loaf.

Baking

Five minutes before baking, place a broiler pan on the floor of a 375°F oven. Insert the breads, then pour 1 cup boiling water into the hot pan. Use caution. The initial puff of steam can burn. Do not open the oven door for at least 10 minutes. Bake the bread for 40 to 50 minutes. Allow extra time for the larger loaf. If using a stone or tile hearth, remove the bread from the pan and bake on the hearth for the last 5 to 10 minutes for a crustier loaf. The bread is done when tapping the bottom with your fingertips produces a hollow sound. Do not hesitate to leave the bread in the oven an extra 5 to 10 minutes if you like a very crusty loaf. Let cool uncovered on a wire rack.

Yield

Makes 1 or 2 large loaves or 3 small loaves.

San Francisco Sourdough Bread

(Food Processor, Steel Blade)

Starter

Prepare the starter as above.

Sponge

Place the Sponge ingredients in the work bowl. Pulse until smooth. Allow to rise, covered, in place until doubled in volume (30 to 45 minutes).

Dough

Pulse once or twice to punch down the Sponge, then add the Starter, 1 cup flour, sugar, salt, and baking soda. Pulse until the flour is absorbed. Additional flour can be added 1/4 cup at a time if the dough is too soft. Knead by pulsing for about 60 seconds. Do not overmix or the dough will get too hot. If the machine strains, stop and divide the dough in half. Process each half separately and knead together by hand. It may be necessary to knead by hand for several minutes to make the dough elastic.

Transfer the dough to an oiled bowl and turn to coat. Cover and allow to stand until doubled in volume (30 to 45 minutes).

Proceed as in Shaping, Proofing, and Baking, above.

Yield

Makes 1 to 3 loaves.

San Francisco Sourdough Bread

(Dough-Mixing Machine, Flat Beater)

Starter

Same ingredients as above

Sponge

1 3/4 cups plus 2 tablespoons warm water
1 1/2 packages active dry yeast (scant 1 1/2 tablespoons)
3 cups bread flour (preferred) or all-purpose flour

Dough

Sponge
1 1/2 cups Starter
1 1/2 to 3 3/4 cups unbleached all-purpose flour
1 tablespoon sugar
1 tablespoon salt
3/4 teaspoon baking soda
Oil, for greasing bowl
Flour, for dusting work top
Cornmeal, for dusting baking sheet

Starter

Combine the Starter ingredients as above.

Sponge

In the mixing bowl sprinkle the yeast over the warm water to soften; stir to dissolve. Add the flour and mix until smooth. Keeping the bowl in place on the mixer, cover with a cloth and allow to rise until doubled in volume (30 to 45 minutes).

Dough

Stir down the Sponge with one or two rotations. Add the Starter, 1 1/2 cups flour, sugar, salt, and baking soda. Sift the dry ingredients together with your fingers. Pulse with the on/off switch until all is combined so that the flour is not thrown out of the bowl. Mix until the dough comes away from the sides of the bowl.

Scrape down and remove the beater. Insert the dough hook and knead at the first speed until the dough is smooth and elastic (10 to 12 minutes). More flour can be added 1/4 cup at a time if the dough is sticky. The second speed can be used for the last 2 minutes to strengthen the gluten.

Transfer the dough to an oiled bowl and turn to coat. Cover and allow to rise until doubled in volume. Turn out the dough and proceed as in Shaping, Proofing, and Baking, above, except cut into 2 or 4 pieces.

Yield

Makes 4 small or 2 large loaves.

Sourdough Italian Bread

This bread is an adaptation of a California sourdough bread recipe. I first tasted it at Fisherman's Wharf in San Francisco and enjoyed its rich flavor.

1 cup warm water
1 package active dry yeast
1 cup White Sour (pages 166-167)
1 1/2 tablespoons sugar
1 1/2 tablespoons shortening (at room temperature) or vegetable oil
1 cup bread flour (preferred) or all-purpose flour
2 to 2 1/2 cups all-purpose flour
1 1/2 teaspoons salt
Flour, for dusting work top
Cornmeal, for dusting baking sheet

In a large bowl sprinkle the yeast over the warm water; stir to dissolve. Add the White Sour, sugar, shortening, bread flour, 2 cups all-purpose flour, and salt. Mix until the dough comes away from the side of the bowl.

Turn out the dough onto a floured board or work surface and knead. More all-purpose flour can be added 1/4 cup at a time if the dough is too sticky. Knead until the dough is soft and elastic (8 to 10 minutes).

Rising

Transfer the dough to an oiled bowl and turn to coat. Allow to rise until doubled in volume (about 45 minutes). Punch down, shape into a ball, and let rest for 15 minutes.

Shaping

Shape into a round or any Italian bread shape (pages 28-29). Place on a baking sheet dusted with cornmeal and allow to rise until doubled in size. Brush the tops with water. For a round loaf cut 4 horizontal slashes followed by 4 vertical slashes, tic-tac-toe fashion. For a long loaf cut appropriately.

Baking

Bake with steam (pages 31-32) in a preheated oven at 375° until brown and crusty (35 to 45 minutes). The bread is done when tapping the bottom with your fingertips produces a hollow sound. The top and sides of the loaf should feel hard to the touch. Let cool on a wire rack. This bread keeps nicely for several days in the bread box and also freezes well.

Yield

Makes 1 large loaf.

Sourdough Italian Bread

(Food Processor, Steel Blade)

Instead of 1 cup warm water use:

1/4 cup warm water
3/4 cup ice water

In the work bowl sprinkle the yeast over the warm water; stir to dissolve. Add the ice water, White Sour, sugar, shortening, bread flour, 2 cups all-purpose flour (1 cup at a time), and salt. Pulse until the dough tries to form up on top of the blade. More all-purpose flour can be added 1/4 cup at a time if the dough is too soft. Process for 2 to 3 minutes. If necessary divide the dough in half and process each half separately, then knead together. Do not overmix. Extra kneading by hand is sometimes necessary to make the dough elastic.

Proceed as in Rising, Shaping, and Baking, above.

Yield

Makes 1 large loaf.

Sourdough Italian Bread

(Dough-Mixing Machine, Flat Beater)

2 cups warm water
2 packages active dry yeast
2 cups White Sour (pages 166-167)
3 tablespoons sugar
3 tablespoons shortening (at room temperature) or vegetable oil
2 cups bread flour (preferred) or all-purpose flour
4 to 5 cups all-purpose flour
1 tablespoon salt
Flour, for dusting work top
Cornmeal, for dusting baking sheet

In the mixing bowl sprinkle the yeast over the warm water; stir to dissolve. Add the White Sour, sugar, shortening, bread flour, 4 cups all-purpose flour, and salt. Mix until the dough comes away from the sides of the bowl, adding more all-purpose flour if necessary.

Scrape down the beater and insert the dough hook. Mix for 8 to 10 minutes at the first speed. More all-purpose flour can be added in small amounts as necessary. The dough should be smooth and elastic. You can use the second speed for the last 2 minutes to strengthen the gluten. Proceed as in Rising, Shaping, and Baking, above, except shape into 4 loaves.

Yield

Makes 4 loaves.

Sourdough Tuscan Bread

Tuscan-style country Italian bread has a broad, round, distinctive shape. Large wheels of this bread are easily recognized. Whole wheat flour is added here for color and an earthy flavor. This bread is often served when hard, and drizzled with high-quality olive oil.

1 cup warm water
1/2 package (scant 1 1/2 teaspoons) active dry yeast
2 cups White Sour (pages 166-167)
1/2 cup whole wheat flour, preferably stone ground
1/2 cup cake flour or pastry flour
2 to 2 1/2 cups unbleached all-purpose flour
2 teaspoons salt
Flour, for dusting bread and work top
Oil, for greasing bowl

In a large bowl sprinkle the yeast over the warm water; stir to dissolve. Add the White Sour, whole wheat flour, cake flour, 2 cups all-purpose flour, and salt. Stir until the dough comes away from the sides of the bowl.

Turn out the dough onto a lightly floured work top. Knead with a turn, fold, push motion, adding more all-purpose flour 1/4 cup at a time if the dough is sticky. Knead until the dough is smooth and elastic (8 to 10 minutes).

Transfer to an oiled bowl and turn to coat.

First Rise

Cover and allow to rise until puffed up (about 30 minutes).

Second Rise

Punch down and allow to rise once more until doubled in size (30 to 45 minutes).

Shaping

Shape into a ball, then flatten down with your hand.

Proofing

Carefully transfer the bread onto a floured peel or floured baking sheet. Proof until puffed up (about 20 minutes). Dust with flour. Score with a tic-tac-toe design. If using a peel, slip the bread off onto the oven tiles or a baking stone. If using the baking sheet, place it in the oven.

Baking

Bake with steam (pages 31-32) in a preheated 425°F oven on the middle shelf until the bottom of the loaf emits a hollow sound when tapped with your fingertips and the top and sides are very firm (30 to 45 minutes). With a baking sheet, bake for the last 5 to 10 minutes without the pan for a crustier loaf. Let cool on a wire rack.

Yield

Makes 1 loaf.

Variations

Whole Wheat Sourdough Tuscan Bread

Replace the all-purpose flour with whole wheat flour mixed in 1 cup at a time.

White Sourdough Tuscan Bread

Replace the whole wheat flour with all-purpose flour.

Sourdough Tuscan Bread

(Food Processor, Steel Blade)

Instead of 1 cup warm water use:

1/4 cup warm water
3/4 cup ice water

In the work bowl sprinkle the yeast over the warm water; stir to dissolve. Add the ice water, White Sour, whole wheat flour, cake flour, and salt. Pulse until all is absorbed. Add 2 cups all-purpose flour, 1 cup at a time. Pulse until the dough tries to form up on top of the blade. More all-purpose flour can be added 1/4 cup at a time if the dough is too soft. Process for 2 to 3 minutes. If necessary divide the dough in two and process each half separately, then knead together. Do not overmix. Extra kneading by hand is sometimes necessary to make the dough elastic.

Turn out the dough and shape into a round. Place in an oiled bowl and turn to coat. Proceed as in the First Rise, Second Rise, Shaping, Proofing, and Baking, above.

Yield

Makes 1 loaf.

Sourdough Tuscan Bread

(Dough-Mixing Machine, Flat Beater)

1 1/2 cups warm water
3/4 package (scant 2 1/4 teaspoons) active dry yeast
3 cups White Sour (pages 166-167)
3/4 cup whole wheat flour, preferably stone ground
3/4 cup cake flour or pastry flour
3 to 3 3/4 cups unbleached all-purpose flour
1 tablespoon salt
Oil, for greasing bowl
Flour, for dusting

In the mixing bowl sprinkle the yeast over the warm water; stir to dissolve. Add the White Sour, whole wheat flour, cake flour, 3 cups all-purpose flour, and salt. Mix until the dough comes away from the sides of the bowl.

Scrape down the beater and insert the dough hook. Mix for 8 to 10 minutes at the first speed. More all-purpose flour can be added in small amounts as necessary. The dough should be smooth and elastic. You can use the second speed for the last 2 minutes to strengthen the gluten.

Transfer the dough to an oiled bowl and turn to coat. Proceed as in the First Rise, Second Rise, Shaping, Proofing, and Baking, above, except allow extra time for the larger loaf.

Yield

Makes 1 large loaf or 2 regular. Try the large.

Chapter Seven

Rolls

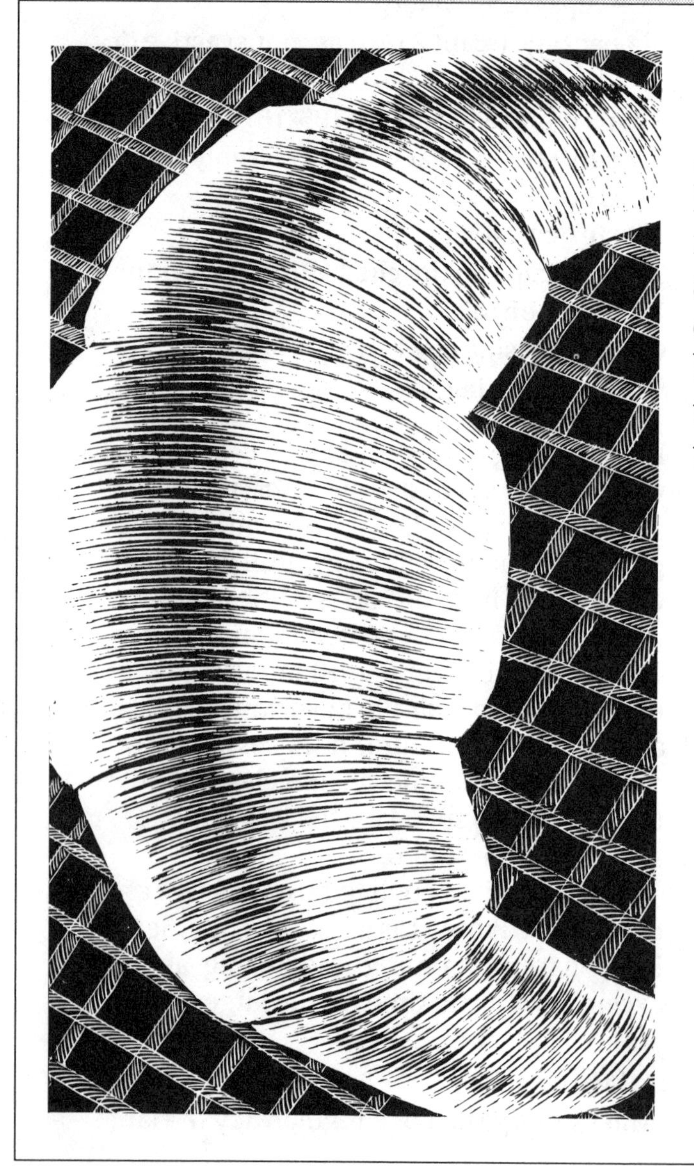

Rolls play an important part in the baker's repertoire. Sandwiches seem to become heartier and more substantial when made with a roll. Rolls can elevate the status of a particular dinner while conveying a message that the meal has been presented with extra care. Miniature dinner rolls add further elegance to holiday and party tables.

Vienna Rolls

Vienna rolls, also called Kaiser rolls or hard rolls, are known for their distinctive shape. Whatever name you know them by, authentic Vienna rolls are rich in eggs, oil, and sugar. Faithfully reproduced from my father's bakery formula, this is the recipe we used for more than 40 years. From the 1920s to the 1940s, these rolls where baked at least three times daily in very hot brick and tile ovens. The rolls had thin, hard crusts and were blown up until the interiors were feathery light. Rolls that were baked for breakfast were considered stale by lunchtime; it was not unusual for a shopper to visit a favorite local bakery several times daily for fresh rolls. Present-day demands have forced the baker to prepare rolls that will keep soft for longer periods of time. Even in quality bakeries that still use the authentic recipes, the rolls are baked so that they will remain soft inside and keep longer in the home. Bake these rolls airy and crisp the way they were meant to be enjoyed.

1/4 cup warm water
1 1/2 packages active dry yeast
3/4 cup cold water (ice water in hot weather)
2 large eggs
2 tablespoons vegetable oil
2 tablespoons malt syrup (see Note)
2 tablespoons sugar
3 1/2 to 4 cups bread flour (all-purpose flour will not work as well but can be substituted)
2 1/4 teaspoons salt
Flour, for dusting work top
Oil, for greasing bowl

In a large bowl sprinkle the yeast over the warm water; stir to dissolve. Add the cold water, eggs, oil, malt syrup, sugar, 3 1/2 cups flour, and salt. Stir until the dough comes away from the sides of the bowl, adding more flour if necessary.

Turn out the dough onto a lightly floured work top. Knead vigorously, adding more flour in small amounts if the dough is sticky. This should be a stiff dough. Knead until the dough is smooth and elastic and the gluten is fully developed (12 to 15 minutes).

Rising

Transfer the dough to an oiled bowl and turn to coat. Cover and allow to rise for 30 minutes. Punch down and allow to rise once more until doubled in volume (20 to 30 minutes).

Shaping

Punch down the dough again, divide into 3 pieces, cover, and let stand for 15 minutes. Roll out into ropes. Cut 6 equal pieces from each rope, then proceed as in Shaping Vienna Rolls on pages 221-222.

For seeded rolls, spread enough poppy or sesame seeds to cover a baking sheet. Line up the finished rolls and brush lightly with water. Arrange 9 rolls with the tops down onto a seeded pan and press down so that the seeds will adhere. Leave enough space between each roll to permit them to double in size. Cover or set in a warm, draft-free space.

For plain rolls, lay waxed or parchment paper on a baking sheet, grease or oil sparingly, and continue as with the seeded rolls, except that there is no need to brush the rolls with water.

An alternate method of seeding the rolls is to prepare them as for plain rolls, then sprinkle with seeds before baking.

Proofing

Proof the rolls upside down so that the design does not open. Allow to rise until doubled in size. In the bakery we let them rise 3 to 4 times their original size, but they must be handled very delicately or they will puncture like a balloon and collapse.

Baking

Lightly grease or oil a baking sheet, then carefully arrange each roll right side up on the pan, leaving room for them to rise in the oven. (When you become comfortable using a peel, for crusty rolls bake the rolls on an oven stone or clay tiles.) Do not puncture the rolls or they will deflate. The trick is to roll them over delicately onto your hands, palms up, and gently slide them off onto the pan. You will have no trouble handling rolls that have doubled in size. With experience you can let the rolls rise much larger.

Preheat an empty roasting pan on the floor of a 425°F oven for 5 to 10 minutes. Place the rolls in the oven, then carefully pour 2 cups hot water into the empty pan. Shield your face and hands from the burst of steam. Add more water after the first 10 minutes of baking. Bake until the rolls are golden brown (15 to 20 minutes). (If a lighter roll is desired, bake at 400°F.) Always make sure that the rolls have a browned bottom.

Yield

Makes 18 rolls.

Note: At one time malt was always used in the bakery to enhance the dough and add color. When we began to freeze unbaked dough we found it necessary to eliminate the malt. If you can find malt syrup in your supermarket or natural foods store, use it. Malt adds a special quality to the finished roll. When unavailable, omit the malt and double the sugar in the recipe.

Variations

Sweet Dairy Butter Rolls

On holidays in the bakery we couldn't keep up with the demand for these butter rolls, which are dinner roll size (half the size of a Vienna roll).

Substitute 4 tablespoons unsalted butter (6 tablespoons in the mixing machine recipe) for the vegetable oil in the above recipe. After dividing the dough into pieces, cut each piece in half to yield petite dinner-sized rolls. Shape into Vienna rolls or plain round balls like hamburger rolls. Proof as for Vienna rolls. Sprinkle with poppy seeds or sesame seeds, or leave plain. Bake, then remove from the oven and brush with melted butter or plain water.

Butter rolls can be served warm or at room temperature.

Yield

Makes 3 dozen dinner rolls.

Onion Vienna Rolls

Prepare Onion Filling and Topping (page 23) and spread on a baking sheet as for seeded rolls, above. Place the rolls, tops down, on the onion filling, then proof and bake as above.

Yield

Makes 18 large onion rolls.

Hamburger or Frankfurter Rolls

For hamburger rolls, spill a layer of sesame seeds onto a baking sheet or a clean work top. Shape the dough into balls, brush with water, and press the tops down into the seeds to make them adhere. Place the rolls right side up on two greased baking sheets, 9 rolls to a pan and evenly distributed so that they have room to rise. Proof until doubled in size, then bake as above.

For frankfurter rolls, roll out the individual pieces of dough into 6-inch ropes. Place them diagonally, in 3 rows of 3 rolls each, on two greased baking sheets and proof until doubled in size. Brush the tops with water and bake as above.

In the bakery we often use challah dough (page 73) for extra-rich hamburger or frankfurter rolls.

Vienna Rolls

(Food Processor, Steel Blade)

In the recipe above, make sure that all the ingredients are cold, and use ice water instead of cold water.

In the work bowl sprinkle the yeast over the warm water; stir to dissolve. Add the ice water, eggs, oil, malt syrup, sugar, 2 cups flour, and salt. Mix until smooth. Add 1 1/2 cups flour, 3/4 cup at a time. Pulse until the dough comes away from the sides of the bowl. More flour can be added 1/4 cup at a time if the dough is too soft. This should be a stiff dough. If necessary divide the dough in half and process each half separately, then knead together. Process for about 2 to 3 minutes. Do not allow the dough to overheat. Extra kneading by hand is sometimes necessary to make the dough elastic and to fully develop the gluten.

Proceed as in Rising, Shaping, and Baking, above.

Yield

Makes 18 rolls.

Vienna Rolls

(Dough-Mixing Machine, Flat Beater)

1/2 cup warm water
2 packages plus 1 teaspoon active dry yeast
1 cup cold water (ice water in hot weather)
3 large eggs
3 tablespoons vegetable oil
3 tablespoons malt syrup (see Note)
3 tablespoons sugar
5 1/4 to 6 cups bread flour (all-purpose flour will not work as well but can be substituted)
3 1/3 teaspoons salt
Flour, for dusting work top
Oil, for greasing bowl

In the mixing bowl sprinkle the yeast over the warm water; stir to dissolve. Add the cold water, eggs, oil, malt syrup, sugar, 5 1/4 cups flour, and salt. Mix until the dough comes away from the sides of the bowl, adding more flour if necessary.

Scrape down the beater and insert the dough hook. Mix for 15 minutes at the first speed. When using bread flour the dough will soften slightly as the gluten develops. More flour can be added in small amounts if required. This should be a stiff dough. Monitor the mixer at all times. It may be necessary to hold down the bowl while mixing. The dough should be smooth and elastic.

Rising

Transfer the dough to an oiled bowl and turn to coat. Cover and allow to rise for 30 minutes. Punch down and allow to rise once more until doubled in volume (20 to 30 minutes).

Shaping

Punch down the dough again, divide into 4 pieces, cover, and let stand for 15 minutes.

Proceed as in Shaping and Baking, above.

Yield

Makes 24 large rolls.

Shaping Vienna Rolls

In the beginning, when I first began working in the bakery, Vienna rolls were made by hand. It was not unusual to see six or more bread bakers sitting on high wooden stools or standing at long benches klopping out rolls all night long. The term *klopping* was descriptive of the knocking sound the bakers made with their karate chop blows on the work tops while molding the rolls into the distinctive Vienna roll rosettes. There was a camaraderie among the bakers which isn't found today. They all had nicknames, some exquisitely descriptive. While working they would have lively conversations, often in several languages, which sometimes turned into heated arguments about baking, politics, the weather, the boss, or whatever. The work was hard, the heat often unbearable. The bakers were likely to be working in unventilated, flour-dust-laden basements. But they all speak about those days with fondness.

Here's how to make a Vienna roll. Don't get discouraged at your first attempts. It takes time to get the hang of it, but it's fun to do and you can always eat your mistakes. They'll still taste good.

Prepare the Vienna roll dough. Shape into balls about 2 to 2 1/2 ounces each. Dust lightly with flour (preferably rye flour), or toss them in the flour to coat. Cover and allow to stand about 5 minutes.

Flatten each ball into a 3-inch circle. Put your left thumb on the circle (Figure 1). Stretch and fold a flap over your thumb. From this point on, keep your thumb in place inside the flap at all times. Seal the fold with a karate chop using the side of your hand.

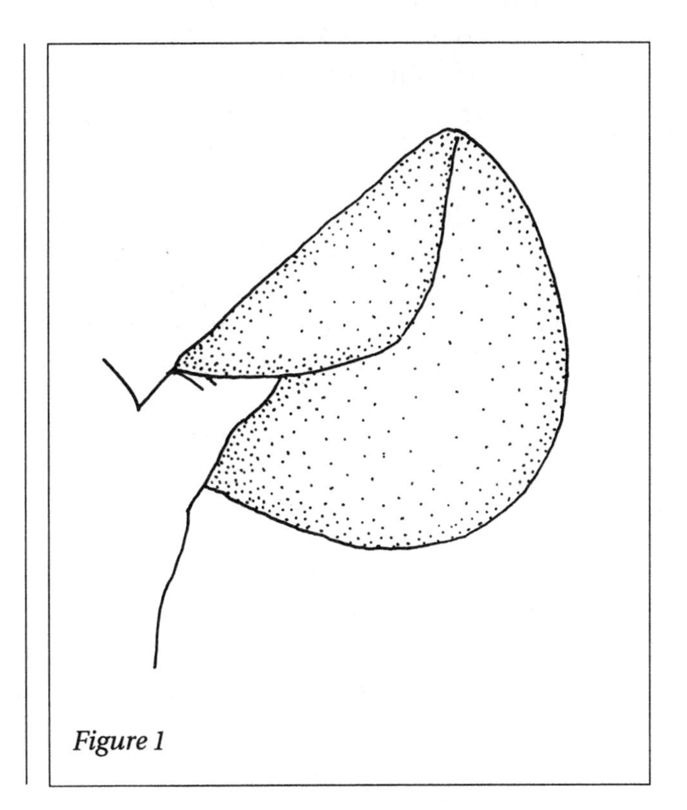

Figure 1

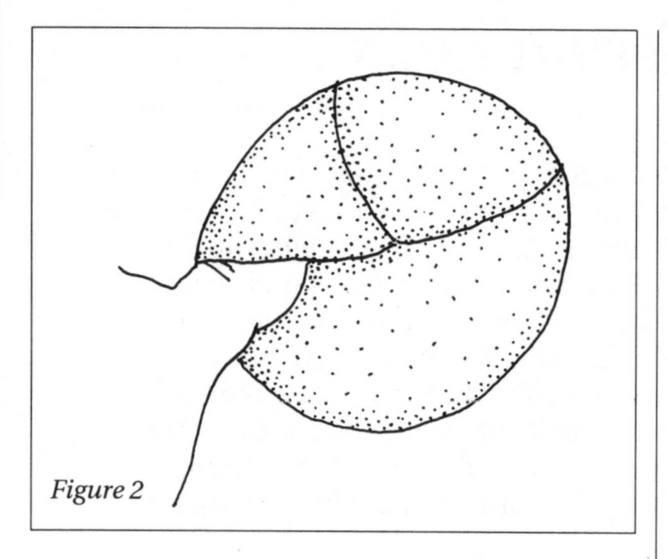
Figure 2

Begin a second flap over from the right side (Figure 2). Seal the edge with a chop as before. Turn your thumb and the dough slightly counterclockwise and pull a third flap over (Figure 3). Chop to seal. Turn just enough to bring the fourth fold comfortably in line, sealing with the side-handed chop (Figure 4).

Stretch and fold a fifth time. Simultaneously remove your left thumb while pushing the tip of the last flap with the right thumb into the hole left by the vacating thumb. You should have a five-petaled, rose-shaped design (Figure 5).

Your first attempts will be irregular but will bake up into tasty rolls. With practice you will quickly learn to make perfectly shaped Vienna rolls.

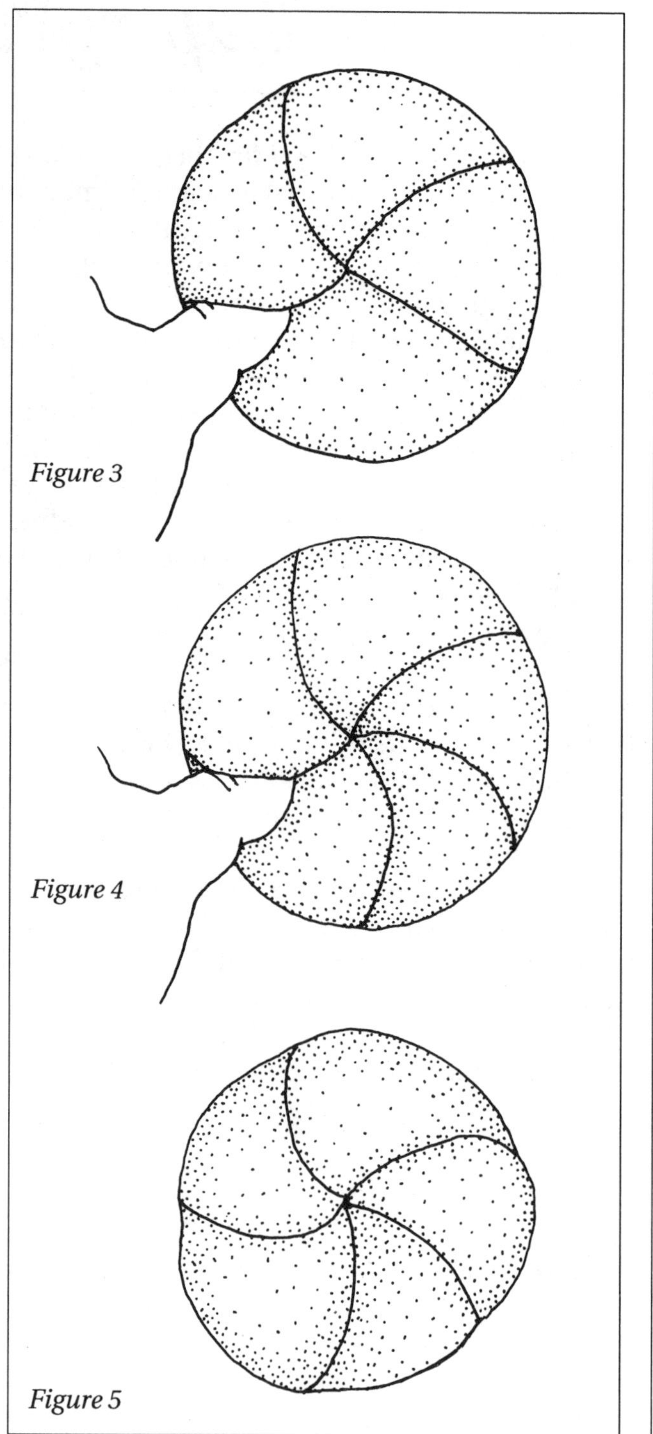
Figure 3

Figure 4

Figure 5

Hungarian Salt Sticks

My father was a member of a Hungarian fraternal organization that held an annual picnic for family and friends. Food was sold as a fund-raising adjunct and there were booths set up with hot and cold foods and beverages. Dad would work in the bakery all night prior to the picnic and bake dozens upon dozens of salt sticks, crescent rolls, and large bread-sized versions of crescents.

On the day of the picnic while everybody was having a good time he roamed about the picnic area carrying a large carton of rolls on his shoulder, singing out in Hungarian, "Salt Sticks, Fresh—Fresh Salt Sticks." Spending little time with his family, he hawked his rolls throughout the day and contributed all the money he raised to the organization. For many years after he was gone, when I met any of his friends they always made a point of mentioning the annual picnic and his wonderful rolls. I would like to share his recipe with you.

Prepare Vienna roll dough (page 217) and allow to rise for 30 minutes.

BAKER'S SECRET. Very few bakers know that a young dough yields extraordinary salt sticks.

Punch down the dough, cut into thirds, and shape into rounds. Cover and allow to rest until they begin to puff up (about 15 to 20 minutes). Press down or roll out until each round is about 1/2 inch thick. Cut 6 pie-shaped wedges from each round.

With a stick-type rolling pin or dowel, roll out 1 wedge at a time, with the wide edge held away from you, to a length of 8 to 10 inches and about 4 inches across the wide end. See diagram for Croissants (page 250). If the dough is too tough to roll, let it rest for several minutes while going on to the next wedge. Sprinkle sparingly with flour if necessary. Bakers do this without flour on the work top so that the dough adheres to the bench, making the salt stick easier to roll out.

Without lifting the triangle of dough from the work top, gently roll the dough, jelly roll fashion, from the wide ended top down to the bottom tip, stretching the tip as you roll. Seal the point by pressing it down into the edge of the roll. It should resemble a croissant 7 to 8 inches long. If necessary gently elongate it by rolling with your fingertips, outward from the center.

BAKER'S SECRET. Leave the closure on top. This will bloom in the oven, forming a chewy crust.

Line up the 18 finished salt sticks side by side, edges touching. Carefully brush the tops with water. Avoid letting the water run off onto the work surface. Sprinkle with a few tablespoons of caraway seeds, then with coarse salt, such as Kosher salt.

BAKER'S SECRET. If you know of a friendly bagel baker or pretzel maker, ask them to sell you some pretzel salt. Pretzel salt will not dissolve during proofing and baking.

Gently press with your hands to help make the seeds and salt adhere.

Evenly space the salt sticks on a lightly greased baking sheet. Let them rest for 5 to 10 minutes.

BAKER'S SECRET. Do not proof these rolls. They will spring up in the oven and bake with a dense texture.

Baking

Bake with steam (pages 31-32) in a preheated 400°F oven until well browned and crusty (15 to 20 minutes). The bottoms should have some color.

Yield

Makes 18 salt sticks.

Crescent Rolls

For crescents, follow the directions for Salt Sticks, above. Roll up into the long salt stick shape, then line up and brush with water. Sprinkle heavily with poppy seeds, preferably Dutch blue poppy seeds. Bring the ends around into a horseshoe shape and space evenly on two greased baking sheets to allow room to rise. Proof until doubled in size, then bake in the same way as salt sticks.

Yield

Makes 18 crescent rolls.

For large bread-sized crescents, divide the dough into thirds, stretch each piece into a triangular shape, and roll it out until very long and thin. Make up the same way as crescents, then proof and bake 1 or 2 to a pan. The large breads will require a longer baking time than rolls. Large crescents can make an interesting centerpiece on your dinner table.

Yield

Makes 3 large crescents.

Flat Onion Rolls

To make onion rolls the way we do in the bakery, prepare Onion Filling and Topping (page 23) and spread it onto 2 clean baking sheets. Prepare a young Vienna Roll dough (page 223), allowing it to rise for 30 minutes. The dough should have begun to rise.

Cut the dough into thirds and shape into rounds. Cover and allow to rest until they begin to puff up (about 15 to 20 minutes). Press out to about 1/2 inch thick. Cut each round into 6 wedges and shape into tight balls by cupping your palms over the pieces and rounding with a circular motion.

Evenly space 9 rolls on each onion-covered pan. Cover and allow to rise, in a warm spot if possible, until doubled in size. Flatten all the rolls by pressing down into the onion filling so that plenty of onions adhere. Expel all the air and stretch the rolls with the fingertips to about 4 inches in width. Turn, onion side up, onto greased baking pans. Cover and proof until the rolls are doubled in size. Press a single large indentation into the center of each roll with your thumb.

Bake with steam (pages 31-32) in a preheated 400°F oven until nicely browned (15 to 20 minutes). Check to make sure that the bottoms are baked.

Yield

Makes 18 rolls.

Miami Rolls

These soft, onion pockets or onion buns deliver an extra zing to the dinner table. Miamis become soft-centered from the onions and are crisp on the outside. Yum!

Prepare a young Vienna Roll dough as above. Cut the dough into thirds, roll out into ropes, and divide each rope into 6 equal pieces.

Spread the Onion Filling and Topping (page 23) on a clean baking sheet. Place all of the cut pieces of dough onto the onions (placement can be haphazard), cover, and allow to rest for 10 minutes.

Prepare a greased baking pan. Take the first piece of dough, press down into the onions so that they adhere, and turn, onion side up, on a work surface. Pull the dough and fold it into thirds, as you would a sheet of stationery for insertion into an envelope, forming a pocket with a bit of onion filling inside. Seal the seam by pressing.

With the closure on top, push the onion pocket into the onions once more. Leave it resting on top of the onions on the baking sheet and make up all of the rolls in the same manner. When all are ready, place them, onion side up, on a greased baking sheet, as evenly spaced as possible. Cover and proof until doubled in size. It's okay if the rolls touch as they rise. Bake as above. Pull apart when cooled.

Yield

Makes 18 rolls.

Onion Pletzel

Also known as onion boards, these are large flat breads rolled out into chewy, onion-flaked boards, sort of a Jewish foccacia.

Prepare a young Vienna Roll dough, as above. Cut into thirds and roll up each into a loaf pan shape. Cover and allow to rest for 15 minutes.

Prepare 3 greased baking pans or round pizza pans. Roll out and stretch the dough into a rectangular shape, allowing the dough to rest when it becomes tough, until the dough covers the pan. With your fingertips press indentations over the entire dough. Brush with vegetable oil and cover lightly with Onion Filling and Topping (page 23). Cover and proof until doubled in height.

Bake with steam (pages 31-32) in a preheated 400°F oven until the bread has browned top and bottom (20 to 30 minutes). Let cool slightly on a wire rack. This bread is best when served warm.

Occasionally we roll onion pletzels extra-thin, brush them with oil, spread a thin layer of onion filling on top, and sprinkle heavily with additional poppy seeds. Then we stipple them well and bake without proofing until crisp, allow them to cool, and cut or break them into crackerlike portions. These go equally well with appetizers or a main course. In the bakery, customers have bought lightly baked onion pletzel and used them as a base for pizza. Yummy if you love onions.

Yield

Makes 3 Onion Pletzel.

Bagels

Bagels, like pizza, have become a universal food. Glowing rings of chewy dough, bagels are common additions to breakfast tables from coast to coast. Countless numbers of people lunch on bagel sandwiches. Complex carbohydrates and low fat make bagels nutritionally desirable. The variations are unlimited.

Very few bagel bakeries still make hand-rolled bagels. In my opinion hand-rolled bagels taste better. This recipe describes an easy way to make them.

Serve bagels warm, toasted, or at room temperature. At home we like to slice them, scoop out the soft center with a spoon, and toast the remaining crust. Try these with cheese melted on top. If kept more than a day, reheat or toast them. Bagels freeze quite well and are best when defrosted slowly.

Have 2 to 4 baking sheets on hand (nonstick or perforated pans if available), a large saucepan (4-quart capacity), a skimmer or slotted spoon, and some toweling or cloths on which to drain the bagels. Several pans or plates should be prepared on which you have spread out the toppings you will use (see Note).

2 cups warm water
1/2 package (scant 1 1/2 teaspoons) active dry yeast
2 tablespoons malt syrup or sugar (see Note)
1 tablespoon vegetable oil
6 to 8 cups bread flour
1 tablespoon salt
Flour, for dusting work top
Oil, for greasing bowl and baking sheets
1 tablespoon malt syrup or sugar(see Note), to add to water when boiling

In a large bowl sprinkle the yeast over the warm water to soften; stir to dissolve. Add the 2 tablespoons malt syrup, oil, 6 cups flour, and salt. Mix thoroughly until the dough forms up and comes away from the sides of the bowl.

Turn out the dough onto a floured work surface and knead, adding small amounts of flour as necessary. Bagel dough should be stiff. Work in as much extra flour as you can comfortably knead. When using bread flour the dough will soften slightly as the gluten develops. Knead until smooth and elastic (12 to 15 minutes).

Rising

Roll the dough into a ball, place it in a large oiled bowl, and turn to coat. Cover and let fully rise until an impression made with your finger remains and does not sink into the dough (about 1 hour). Punch down, cut into thirds, and roll each piece between your palms into a rope.

Shaping

Cut each rope into 4 equal pieces and shape into balls. Roll the first ball into a rope 2 inches more than the width of your hand. Flip the rope around your fingers to form a ring, with the ends overlapping about 1/2 inch. Seal the ends by rolling with your palms on a work top. If the dough slides and resists rolling, dab on a drop of water with your fingers.

Evenly space the bagels on 2 nonstick baking pans or very lightly oiled baking sheets. I apply a thin film with my fingers. Cover and let stand until puffy (about 20 minutes).

Boiling

Bagels are boiled before they are baked. While they are proofing, fill a 4-quart saucepan two-thirds full with cold water; add the 1 tablespoon malt syrup and bring to a boil. Have ready pans or dishes containing poppy seeds, sesame seeds, coarse salt, or other toppings (see Note).

When ready to cook the bagels, drop two or three at a time into the boiling water and wait until they rise to the top. Cook for a total of 1 minute, turning once. If they have been proofed too long, they will float instead of sinking but you can continue without too much difference.

Carefully lift out each bagel with a slotted spoon or skimmer. Drain momentarily, then turn them over into the dish of prepared seeds. You may prefer to leave some plain. Evenly space the bagels on 2 baking sheets, topping side up.

Baking

Bake with steam (pages 31-32) in a preheated 500°F oven until well browned (15 to 20 minutes). Turn them over when the tops begin to brown. Continue baking until done.

Yield

Makes 1 dozen large bagels.

Note: Malt syrup adds gloss and a subtle flavor to the finished bagel. If you can find malt syrup in your supermarket or natural foods store, use it. The toppings for bagels are virtually unlimited. Try poppy seeds, sesame seeds, coarse salt, poppy seeds and coarse salt combined, minced onion flakes, or chopped or granulated garlic.

Variations

Everything Bagels

Use all of the above toppings, mixed together.

Onion Bagels

After the rise but before the dough is shaped into a rope, knead minced dehydrated onion flakes into the dough.

Cinnamon Raisin Bagels

After the dough has risen, knead in 1 teaspoon ground cinnamon mixed with 1 teaspoon sugar and 1/2 cup raisins. Knead until the cinnamon gives a marbleized appearance.

Rye Bagels

2 cups warm water
1/2 package (scant 1 1/2 teaspoons) active dry yeast
2 tablespoons malt syrup or sugar (see Note above)
1 tablespoon vegetable oil
3 cups rye flour
2 to 3 1/2 cups bread flour or all-purpose flour
1 tablespoon salt
2 tablespoons caraway seeds, kneaded in for filling (optional)

Prepare as in Bagels, above.

Onion Rye Bagels

Knead in 2 tablespoons chopped dehydrated onions.

Pumpernickel Bagels

1 3/4 cups warm water
1/2 package (scant 1 1/2 teaspoons) active dry yeast
2 tablespoons malt syrup or sugar (see Note above)
1 tablespoon vegetable oil
1/4 cup pumpernickel color (page 24)
2 cups pumpernickel flour
2 cups rye flour
1 to 3 cups bread flour or all-purpose flour
1 tablespoon salt

Prepare as in Bagels, above.

Onion Pumpernickel Bagels

Knead in 1 to 2 tablespoons minced onion flakes and 1 tablespoon poppy seeds (if desired).

Egg Bagels

2 cups warm water
1 package active dry yeast
2 tablespoons sugar
2 tablespoons vegetable oil
2 eggs, lightly beaten
6 to 6 1/2 cups bread flour
1 tablespoon salt

Prepare as in Bagels, above, except do not boil. Proof, then bake with steam (pages 31-32) in a preheated 425°F oven until browned and the bottoms have color (15 to 20 minutes).

Bagels

(Food Processor, Steel Blade)

In the basic bagel recipe above, instead of 2 cups warm water use:

1/2 cup warm water
1 1/2 cups ice water

In the work bowl sprinkle the yeast over the warm water to soften; stir to dissolve. Add the ice water, 2 tablespoons malt syrup, oil, 2 cups flour, and salt. Mix until blended. Add 3 1/2 cups flour, 1/3 at a time. Pulse until the dough tries to form up on top of the blade. More flour can be added 1/4 cup at a time if necessary. Process until the dough reaches 78°F (2 to 3 minutes). The dough should be stiff. If necessary divide the dough in half and process each half separately, then knead together. Do not overmix or the dough will get too hot. Extra kneading by hand is sometimes necessary to make the dough elastic.

Proceed as in Rising, Shaping, Boiling, and Baking, above.

Yield

Makes 1 dozen large bagels.

Bagels

(Dough-Mixing Machine, Flat Beater)

2 cups warm water
1/2 package (scant 1 1/2 teaspoons) active dry yeast
2 tablespoons malt syrup or sugar (see Note)
1 tablespoon vegetable oil
6 to 8 cups bread flour
1 tablespoon salt
Oil, for greasing bowl and baking sheets
Flour, for dusting work top
1 tablespoon malt syrup or sugar (see Note) to add to water when boiling

In the mixing bowl dissolve the yeast in warm water; stir to dissolve. Add the malt syrup, oil, 6 cups flour, and salt. Pulse with the on/off switch until all is absorbed so that the flour is not thrown out of the bowl. Run at the first speed until the dough comes away from the sides of the bowl. More flour can be added 1/4 cup at a time.

Remove and scrape down the beater and insert the dough hook. Run at the first speed until the dough is smooth and elastic (12 to 15 minutes). Bagel dough should be stiff. Add flour cautiously. Do not exceed the capacity of the machine. Do not leave the mixer running while unattended. When using bread flour, the dough will soften slightly as the gluten develops. Proceed as in Rising, Shaping, Boiling, and Baking, above.

Yield

Makes 1 dozen large bagels.

Bialys

The name Bialystocker bagels is derived from a town in Poland where it is said they orginated. I once heard them described as unbaked Jewish/English muffins. Real bialys are dense, blistered, and chewy, with a toasted flourlike taste. They taste best when slathered with cream cheese. Try them with vegetable cream cheese (see Note). Bialys have a short shelf life and should be frozen unless consumed the day they are baked. Bialys can be considered an acquired taste. Give these ugly ducklings a chance and you may become enamored of them.

2 cups warm water
3 packages active dry yeast
4 teaspoons sugar
6 to 6 1/2 cups bread flour
3 teaspoons salt
Flour, for dusting (preferably rye flour for added flavor)
Oil, for greasing bowl

Topping

3 tablespoons minced onion (see Note)
2 teaspoons poppy seeds (optional)
1 teaspoon vegetable oil
Pinch of salt

Combine the Topping ingredients and set aside.

In a large bowl sprinkle the yeast over the warm water to soften; stir to dissolve. Add the sugar, 6 cups flour, and salt. Mix thoroughly until the dough forms up and comes away from the sides of the bowl.

Turn out the dough onto a floured work surface and knead, adding small amounts of flour as necessary, for 10 to 12 minutes.

Rising

Shape the dough into a ball; place in a large oiled bowl and turn to coat. Cover and allow to rise for 30 minutes. Press out all of the air with your fingers and allow to rise until doubled in size (20 to 30 minutes).

Shaping

Punch down the dough, divide into thirds, roll out under your palms into ropes, and cut each rope in 6 equal pieces. Roll into balls. Cover and allow the dough to rest for 10 minutes.

Roll out each ball into a 3 1/2-inch circle. If the dough becomes too stiff or shrinks back, allow it to rest and go on to the next piece. When all are rolled, start again with the first.

Evenly space the circles on 2 floured or cornmeal-dusted baking pans. Cover with flour-rubbed cloths and allow to rise until puffy. Make an indentation in the center of each with 2 fingers of each hand pressing from the center outward, leaving a 1-inch rim. A shot glass with a 1-inch bottom also works well. Press with a circular motion. Dribble a bit of the reserved Topping into the hole. Dust lightly with flour. Cover with cloths and allow to proof until puffed up.

Baking

Bake *without steam* in a preheated 450°F oven for 15 to 20 minutes.

Yield

Makes 18 bialys.

Note: For vegetable cream cheese dice up small amounts of radish, cucumber, celery, green onion, or any other vegetables of your choice. Soften the cream cheese with several teaspoons of seltzer water. Mix in the chopped vegetables and slather on top of the bialys. Instead of the minced onion in the ingredients list, you can use minced onion flakes that have been soaked in water for 2 hours or longer, then the water pressed out.

Variations

Bialy Flats

Double the size of the rolls. Roll out into 6- to 8-inch circles. Allow to proof on greased baking pans. Flatten, then top the entire circle with the onion topping. Proof and bake as above, but allow extra oven time for the larger rolls. Makes 6 to 9 flats.

Bialy Loaves

Triple the size of the rolls. Roll out into hero roll shapes, cover with the onion topping, proof, and bake as above, but allow extra oven time for the larger rolls. Makes 6 loaves.

Bialys

(Food Processor, Steel Blade)

Instead of 2 cups warm water use:

1/2 cup warm water
1 1/2 cups ice water

In the work bowl sprinkle the yeast over the warm water to soften; stir to dissolve. Add the ice water, sugar, 2 cups flour, and salt. Blend until absorbed. Mix in 4 cups flour, 2 cups at a time. Pulse until the dough tries to form up on top of the blade. More flour can be added 1/4 cup at a time if the dough is too soft. Process for 2 to 3 minutes. If necessary divide the dough in half and process each half separately, then knead together. Do not overmix or the dough will get too hot. Extra kneading by hand is sometimes necessary to make the dough elastic.

Proceed as in Rising, Shaping, and Baking, above.

Yield

Makes 18 bialys.

Bialys

(Dough-Mixing Machine, Flat Beater)

Use the ingredients listed above.

In the mixing bowl sprinkle the yeast in the warm water to soften; stir to dissolve. Add the sugar, 6 cups flour, and salt. Pulse with the on/off switch until all is absorbed so that the flour is not thrown out of the bowl. Run at the first speed until the dough comes away from the sides of the bowl. More flour can be added 1/4 cup at a time if the dough is too soft. The dough should be stiffer than normal.

Remove and scrape down the beater and insert the dough hook. Run at the first speed until the dough forms up on the hook and comes away from the sides of the bowl (12 to 15 minutes). You can use the second speed for the last few minutes to strengthen the gluten.

Proceed as in Rising, Shaping, and Baking, above.

Yield

Makes 18 bialys.

Pumpernickel Rolls

Eggs and oil enrich these chewy, earthy-tasting rolls. The variations below—Raisin Pumpernickel Rolls and Pumpernickel Miami Rolls—can become habit-forming. For small, dinner-sized rolls, cut the dough balls in half before proofing.

1 cup warm water
1 package active dry yeast
1 tablespoon vegetable oil
1 egg, lightly beaten
2 tablespoons pumpernickel color (page 24)
2 tablespoons sugar
1 cup pumpernickel flour (see Note)
2 to 2 1/2 cups bread or unbleached all-purpose flour
1 1/2 teaspoons salt
Flour, for dusting work top
Oil, for greasing bowl
1 tablespoon caraway seeds (optional)
Water or cornstarch solution (page 20), for brushing

In a large bowl sprinkle the yeast over the warm water to soften; stir to dissolve. Add the oil, egg, pumpernickel color, sugar, pumpernickel flour, 2 cups bread flour, and salt. Mix thoroughly until the dough forms up and comes away from the sides of the bowl.

Turn out the dough onto a floured work surface and knead, adding small amounts of flour as needed, until smooth and elastic (8 to 10 minutes).

Rising

Shape the dough into a ball; place it in a large oiled bowl and turn to coat. Cover and let rise until doubled in size. Punch out all the air, cut in half, sprinkle with the caraway seeds (if desired), and roll each half into a ball. Cover and let the dough rest for 10 minutes.

Shaping

Shape into 3 ropes, then cut each rope in 6 pieces. Roll each piece into a round ball. The rolls can be left round or you can taper the ends to a point. Space evenly on 2 greased baking sheets. Keep in a warm, draft-free spot, covered with a damp cloth, and proof until doubled in size. Brush with water or the cornstarch solution. Slash once down the length of each roll.

Baking

Bake with steam (pages 31-32) in a preheated 400°F oven until hard to the touch and colored on the bottom (15 to 20 minutes). These rolls keep for several days and can be reheated. They freeze well baked or unbaked.

Yield

Makes 18 rolls.

Note: Pumpernickel flour, also called medium rye flour, may be available from a local bakery. If unavailable use rye flakes or rye meal, available in natural foods stores. Or grind some rye cereal or rye berries by chopping in a blender, processor, or coffee mill.

Variations

Raisin Pumpernickel Rolls

Omit the caraway seeds. Prepare 1 cup raisins (1 1/2 cups in the mixing machine recipe), preferably plumped in hot water for 30 minutes. Knead into the dough immediately after mixing. Shape into round rolls and proceed as above.

Pumpernickel Miami Rolls

Omit the caraway seeds. Prepare Onion Filling and Topping (page 23). Shape into Miami Rolls (page 226) and proceed as above.

Pumpernickel Rolls

(Food Processor, Steel Blade)

Instead of 1 cup warm water use:

1/4 cup warm water
3/4 cup ice water

In the work bowl sprinkle the yeast over the warm water to soften; stir to dissolve. Add the ice water, oil, egg, pumpernickel color, sugar, pumpernickel flour, 1 cup bread flour, and salt. Blend until absorbed. Mix in 1 cup bread flour. Pulse until the dough tries to form up on top of the blade. More bread flour can be added 1/4 cup at a time if the dough is too soft. Process for 2 to 3 minutes. If necessary divide the dough in half and process each half separately, then knead together. Do not overmix or the dough will get too hot. Extra kneading by hand is sometimes necessary to make the dough elastic.

Proceed as in Rising, Shaping, and Baking, above.

Pumpernickel Rolls

(Dough-Mixing Machine, Flat Beater)

1 1/2 cups warm water
1 1/2 packages active dry yeast
1 1/2 tablespoons vegetable oil
1 1/2 eggs, lightly beaten
3 tablespoons pumpernickel color (page 24)
3 tablespoons sugar
1 1/2 cups pumpernickel flour (see Note)
3 to 3 3/4 cups bread flour or unbleached all-purpose flour
2 1/4 teaspoons salt
1 1/2 tablespoons caraway seeds (optional)
Oil, for greasing bowl
Flour, for dusting work top
Water or cornstarch solution (page 20), for brushing rolls

In the mixing bowl dissolve the yeast in the warm water. Add the oil, egg, pumpernickel color, sugar, pumpernickel flour, 3 cups bread flour, and salt. Pulse with the on/off switch until all is absorbed so that the flour is not thrown out of the bowl. Run at the first speed until the dough comes away from the sides of the bowl. More bread flour can be added 1/4 cup at a time if the dough is too soft.

Remove and scrape down the beater and insert the dough hook. Add the caraway seeds (if desired). Run at the first speed until the dough forms up on the hook and comes away from the sides of the bowl (8 to 10 minutes). You can use the second speed for the last 2 minutes to strengthen the gluten. Proceed as in Rising, Shaping, and Baking, above, except make 3 ropes and cut each into 9 pieces.

Yield

Makes 27 rolls.

Rye Rolls

Rich rye flavor and a tender bite make these rolls a standout accompaniment to meat and dairy dishes. They can be baked as dinner-sized rolls by cutting the dough balls in half before proofing.

1 cup warm water
1 package active dry yeast
1 tablespoon vegetable oil
1 egg, lightly beaten
2 tablespoons sugar
1 cup rye flour
2 to 2 1/2 cups bread flour or unbleached all-purpose flour
1 1/2 teaspoons salt
Flour, for dusting work top
Oil, for greasing bowl
1 tablespoon caraway seeds (optional)
Water or cornstarch solution, for brushing rolls

In a large bowl sprinkle the yeast over the warm water to soften; stir to dissolve. Add the oil, egg, sugar, rye flour, 2 cups bread flour, and salt. Mix thoroughly until the dough forms up and comes away from the sides of the bowl.

Turn out the dough onto a floured work surface and knead, adding small amounts of flour as needed. Knead in the caraway seeds (if desired). Knead until smooth and elastic (8 to 10 minutes).

Rising

Shape the dough into a ball; place it in a large oiled bowl and turn to coat. Cover and let rise until doubled in size. Punch out all the air, cut the dough in half, sprinkle with caraway seeds (if desired), and roll each half into a ball. Cover and let the dough rest for 10 minutes.

Shaping

Shape the balls into 3 ropes, then cut each rope in 6 pieces. Roll each into a round ball. The rolls can be left round or you can taper the ends to a point. Space equally on 2 greased baking sheets. Keep in a warm, draft-free spot, covered with a damp cloth, and proof until doubled in size. Brush with water or cornstarch solution (page 20). Slash once down the length of each roll.

Baking

Bake with steam (pages 31-32) in a preheated 400°F oven until the rolls are hard to the touch and colored on the bottom (15 to 20 minutes). These rolls keep for several days and can be reheated. They freeze well baked or unbaked.

Yield

Makes 18 rolls.

Variations

Onion Rye Rolls

Omit the caraway seeds. Knead in Onion Filling and Topping (page 23) to taste immediately after the first rise. Sprinkle a small amount of the filling onto the tops of the rolls before baking.

Rye Rolls

(Food Processor, Steel Blade)

Instead of 1 cup warm water use:

1/4 cup warm water
3/4 cup ice water

In the work bowl sprinkle the yeast over the warm water to soften; stir to dissolve. Add the ice water, oil, egg, sugar, rye flour, 2 cups bread flour (1 cup at a time), and salt. Pulse until the dough tries to form up on top of the blade. More bread flour can be added 1/4 cup at a time if the dough is too soft. Process for 2 to 3 minutes. If necessary divide the dough in half and process each half separately, then knead together. Do not overmix or the dough will get too hot. Extra kneading by hand is sometimes necessary to make the dough elastic.

Proceed as in Rising, Shaping, and Baking, above.

Yield

Makes 18 rolls.

Rye Rolls

(Dough-Mixing Machine, Flat Beater)

1 1/2 cups warm water
1 1/2 packages active dry yeast
1 1/2 tablespoons vegetable oil
1 1/2 eggs, lightly beaten
3 tablespoons sugar
1 1/2 cups rye flour
3 to 3 3/4 cups bread flour or unbleached all-purpose flour
2 1/4 teaspoons salt
1 1/2 tablespoons caraway seeds (optional)
Oil, for greasing bowl
Flour, for dusting work top
Water or cornstarch solution, for brushing

In the mixing bowl dissolve the yeast in the warm water. Add the oil, egg, sugar, rye flour, 3 cups bread flour, and salt. Pulse with the on/off switch until all is absorbed so that the flour is not thrown out of the bowl. Run at the first speed until the dough comes away from the sides of the bowl. More bread flour can be added 1/4 cup at a time if the dough is too soft.

Remove and scrape down the beater and insert the dough hook. Add the caraway seeds (if desired). Run at the first speed until the dough forms up on the hook and comes away from the sides of the bowl (8 to 10 minutes). You can use the second speed for the last 2 minutes to strengthen the gluten. Proceed as in Rising, Shaping, and Baking, above, except shape into 3 ropes and cut each into 9 pieces.

Yield

Makes 27 rolls.

Egg Rolls

The best egg rolls are made from rich challah dough. Egg rolls add elegance to intimate dinners and festive banquet tables. In the bakery we made them several times daily and always had large orders to fill from country clubs and caterers.

Prepare a soft challah dough (page 73). Allow to rise until doubled in volume. Punch down and divide into 4 equal pieces (6 pieces for the dough-mixing machine recipe). Cover and let stand for 10 minutes. Cut each piece into thirds and roll into balls. Dust lightly with flour, cover, and let rest 5 minutes. Shape into any of the variations that follow. Then brush with egg wash (1 egg beaten, thinned with 1 to 2 teaspoons water), proof until doubled in size, brush a second time with egg wash, and bake with steam (pages 31-32) at 325°F until nicely browned and the bottoms have some color (15 to 20 minutes).

Variations

Round Knots

On a clean work surface, using little or no flour, roll out each ball into a thin rope 6 to 7 inches long. If they slide around and refuse to be shaped, too much flour has been used. As you keep rolling, the flour will become absorbed.

You can form the rolls on the work top or, as we do in the bakery, wind the rope around 2 fingers (see illustration, next page). Bring two-thirds of the right end around into a loop crossing over the opposite tip (Figure 1). Bring the end under the loop through the center as if tying a knot (Figure 2). Repeat, going over the loop a second time and into the center (Figure 3). This will produce a round double knot, very professional looking. A small piece about equal to the width of the rope should remain protruding through the center (Figure 4). If too much protrudes, adjust the length of the original loop. Evenly space 6 rolls on a baking sheet. Brush with egg wash. Proof until doubled in size.

Garlic Knots

Brush the finished Round Knots with melted butter (or margarine for a nondairy recipe). Sprinkle with garlic powder.

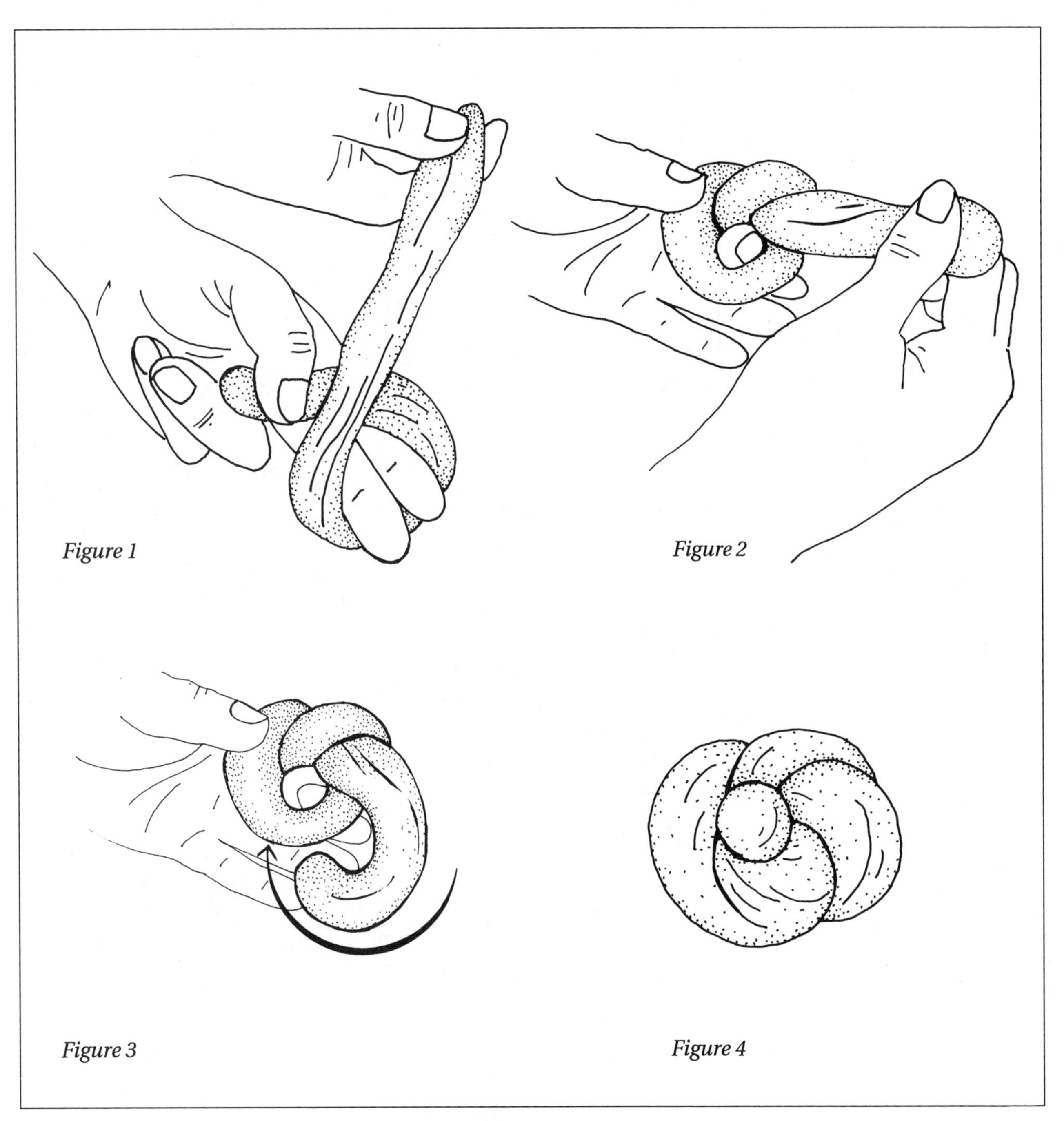

Round Knots

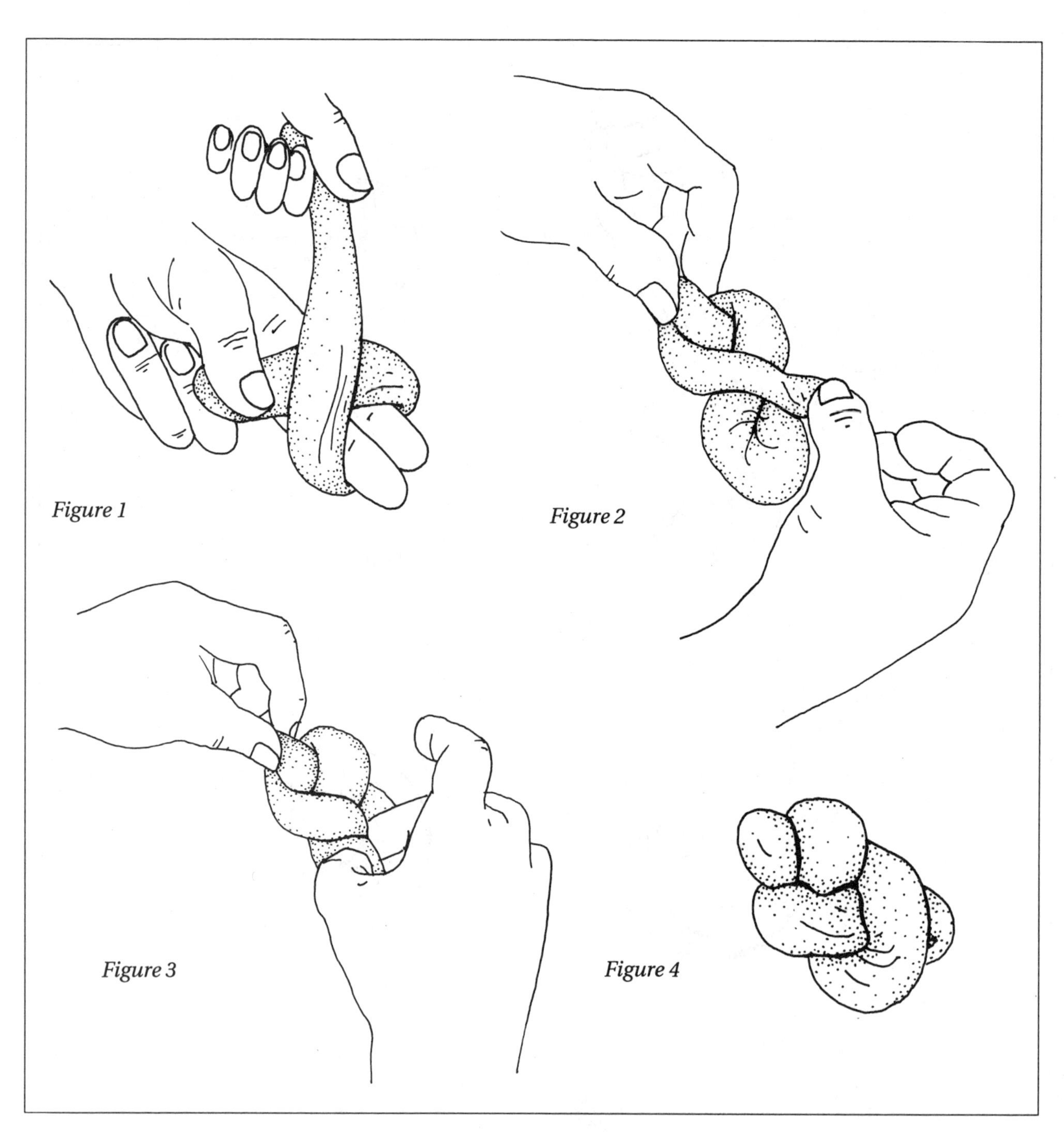

Figure 8 Knots

Figure 8 Knots

To make these figure-8 knots, roll each ball into a 9- to 10-inch rope. Bring the right end around into a loop with two-thirds of the length crossing over the opposite tip (Figure 1, page 242). Bring the long end under and over (Figure 2). The end is brought down into the center (Figure 3). The finished roll is shown in Figure 4.

Braided Knots

These knots are made on the work top. Roll each ball into a 9- to 10-inch rope. Bring one-third of the right end around into a loop crossing over the opposite end (Figure 1). Bring the long end over and through the center (Figure 2). Twist the loop into a figure-8 (Figure 3). Bring the free end over and down through the loop (Figure 4).

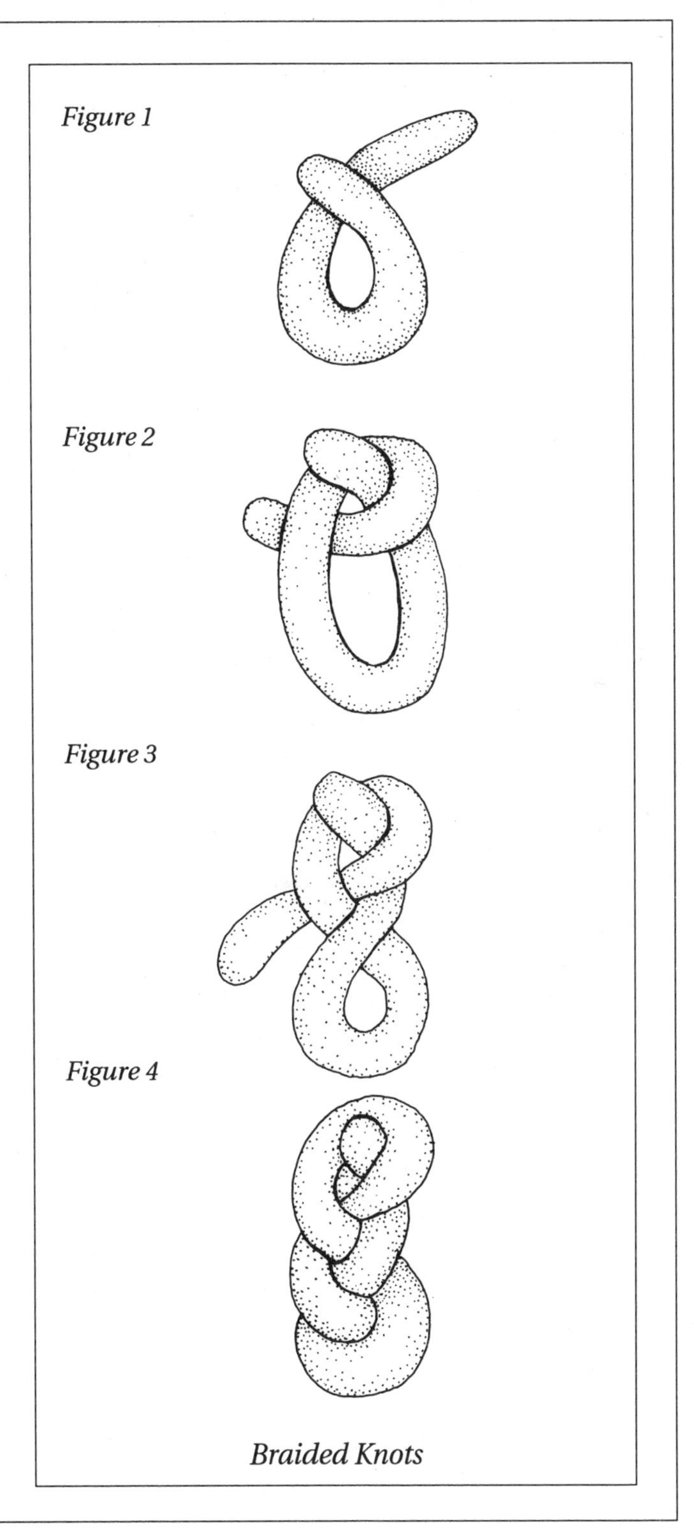

Braided Knots

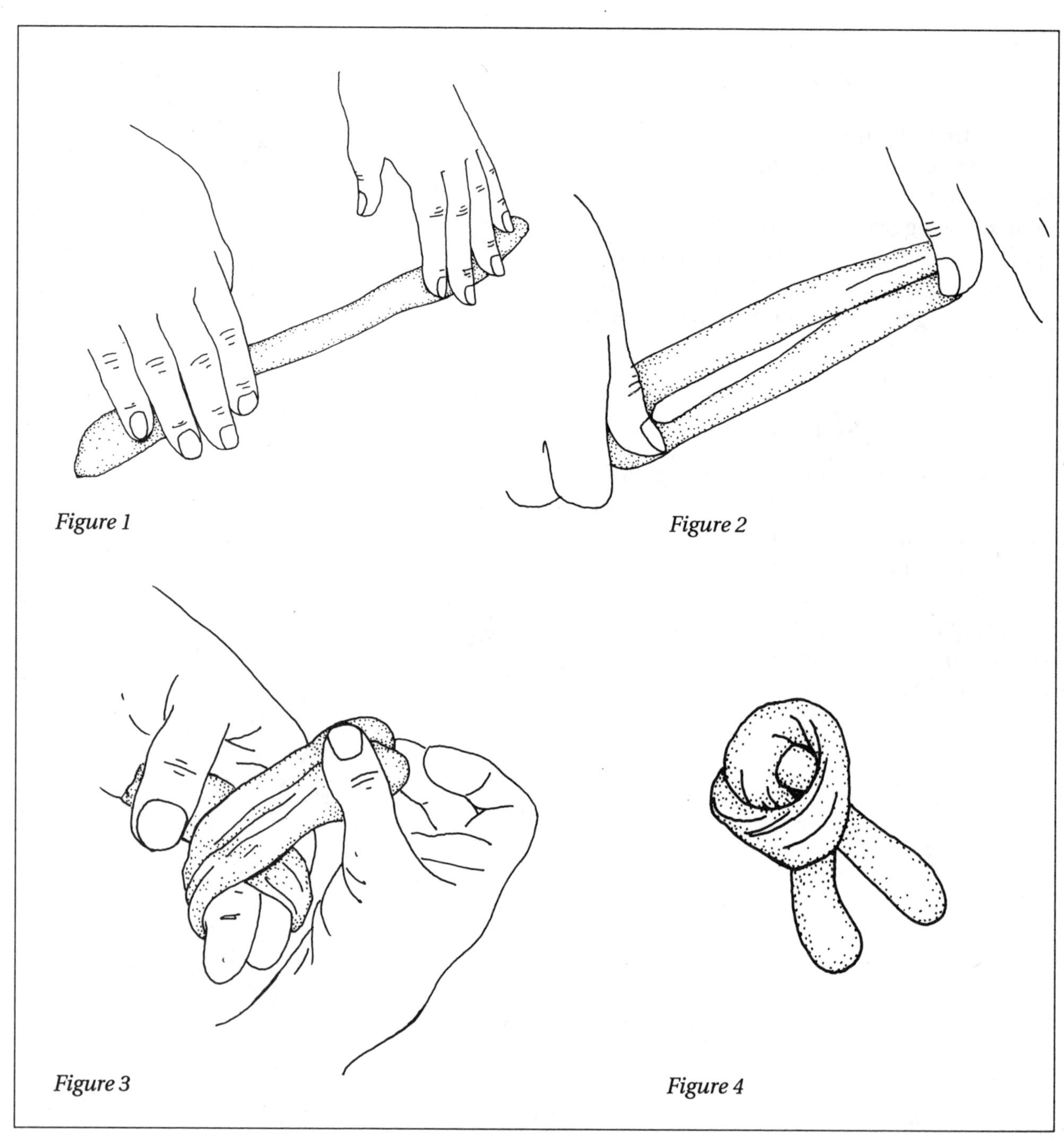

Birds of Paradise

Birds of Paradise

Roll each ball into a rope 12 inches in length (Figure 1, page 244). Bring both ends together (Figure 2). Bring the loop end around (Figure 3) and tie a slip knot (Figure 4). When the roll is fully proofed and baked, the free ends will resemble a bird's tail, the knot represents the body, and the protruding tip is the head.

Two-Strand Braided Rolls

These challah rolls, braided with 2 ropes, are individual mini challahs. Use two ropes per roll. Cross one over the other (Figure 1). Bring the ends of the bottom rope over the top (Figure 2). Repeat, crossing the bottom ends over the top (Figure 3). Continue until the braid is finished. Pinch the ends together. Bake as in Egg Rolls but allow about an extra 5 minutes oven time.

Miami Egg Rolls

Extra-rich Miami Rolls (page 226) and Onion Pletzel (page 227) can be made from egg roll dough. Make up as in Onion Pletzel. Do not brush with egg wash. Bake with steam (pages 31-32).

Sticks

To make garlic, onion, poppy, or sesame sticks, roll out the balls into ropes about 12 inches long. Brush with egg wash (page 240) and sprinkle with garlic powder or Onion Filling and Topping (page 23), or poppy or sesame seeds. Arrange the sticks across the width of a greased baking sheet, leaving enough space in between for the sticks to expand. Let rise until puffy, then bake as in Egg Rolls.

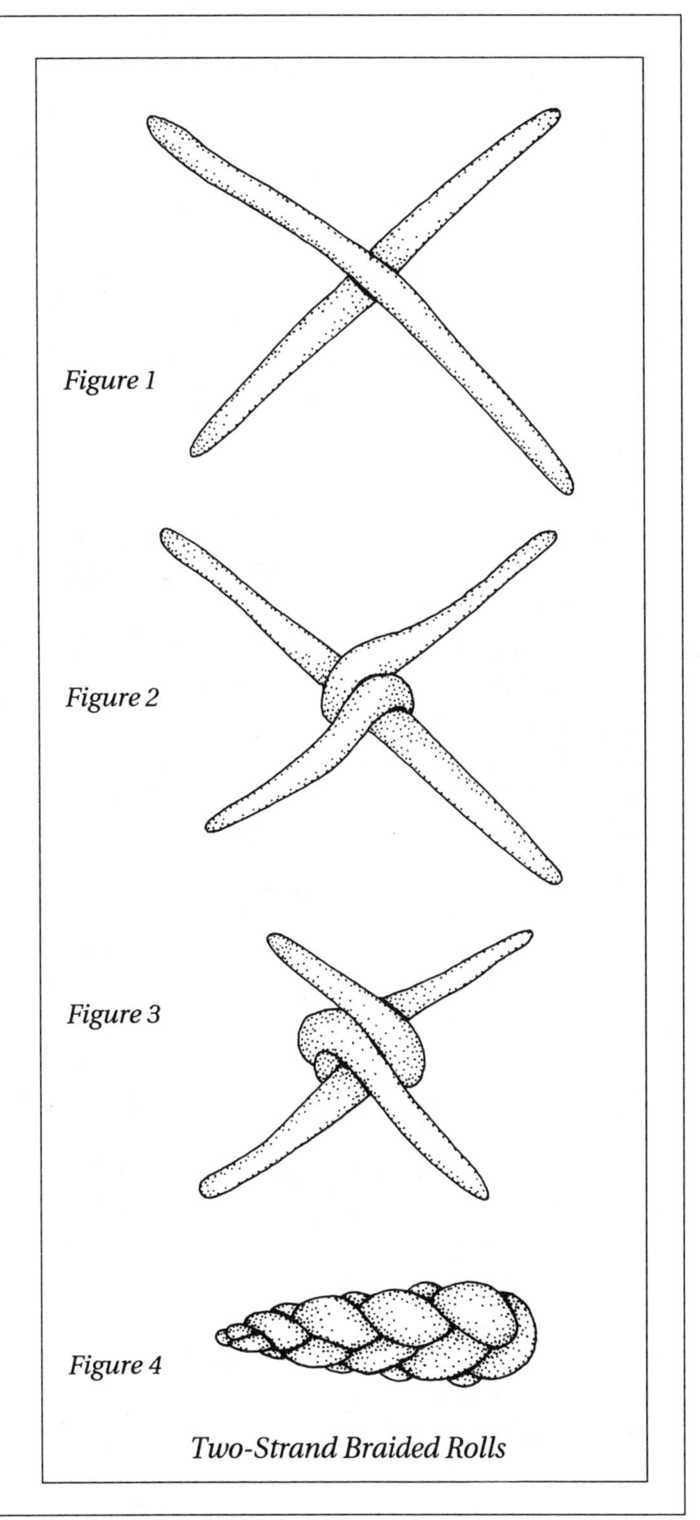

Two-Strand Braided Rolls

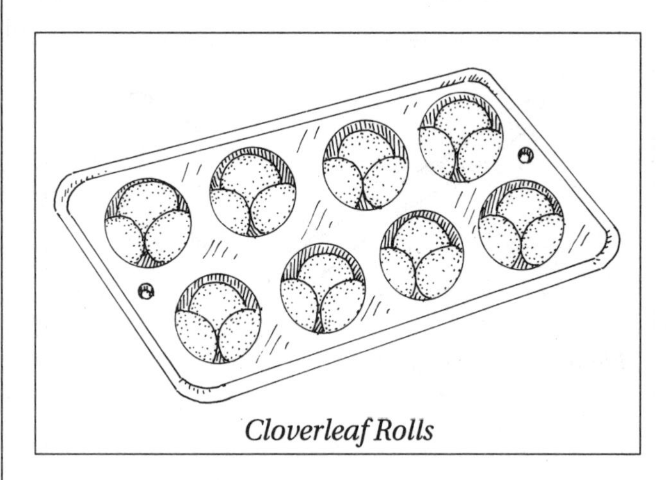
Cloverleaf Rolls

Cloverleaf Rolls

Prepare a greased muffin tin. Divide each ball into 3 equal pieces. Shape each into a small ball and squeeze side by side into a muffin cup. Proof until doubled in size. The dough balls will rise together into a 3-section cup-shaped roll. Brush sparingly with egg wash (page 240); do not allow the egg wash to drop down into the cup. Bake as in Egg Rolls.

Parkerhouse Rolls

A dough this rich is never called for in parkerhouse dough recipes. We made the rolls this way in the bakery and our customers loved them. Flatten each dough ball; with a thin dowel or the handle of a knife, lengthen and press or roll out a deep indentation across the center of the flattened ball (Figure 1). Brush the elongated center with melted butter (or margarine for a nondairy recipe). Fold over and press the fold to form a crease (Figure 2). Place on a greased baking sheet close enough together so that the rolls touch when they rise. Cover and allow to proof until doubled in size (Figure 3). Brush carefully with melted butter or margarine and bake as in Egg Rolls.

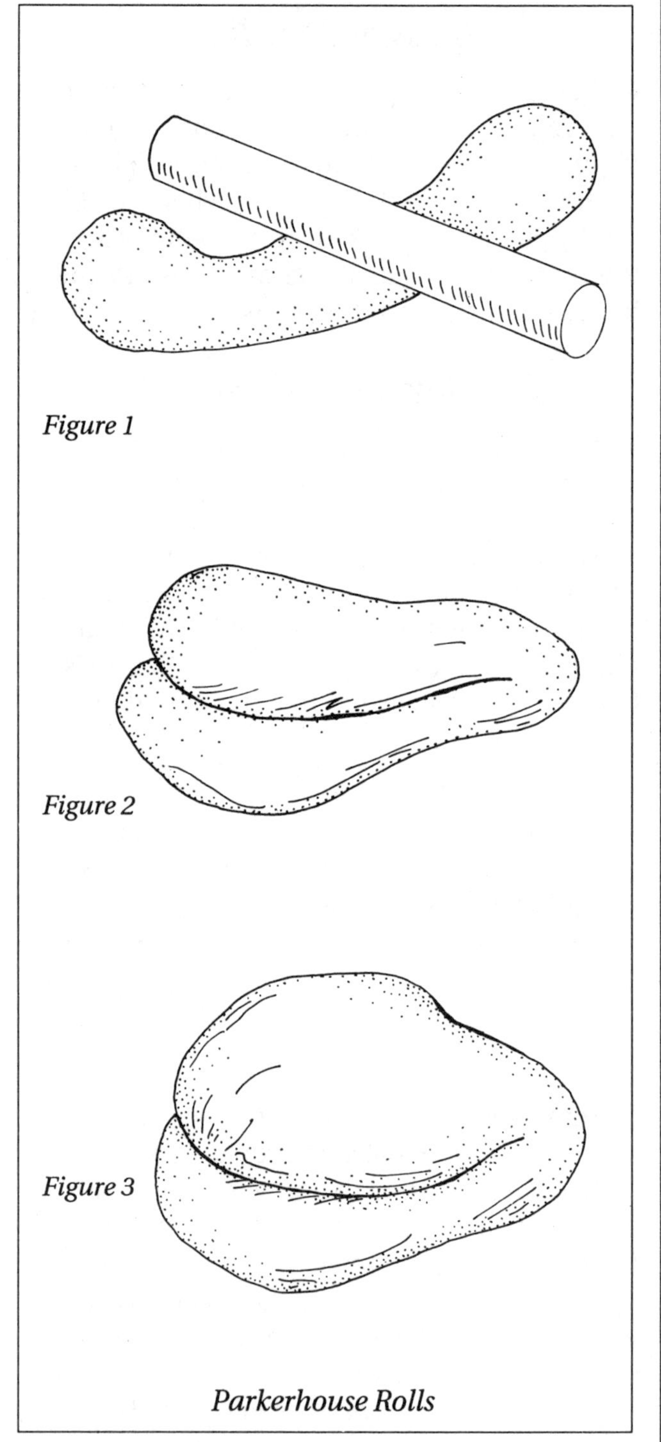

Parkerhouse Rolls

Croissants

I always associate croissants with a Continental breakfast. In Europe, they are served with hot coffee, butter, and jam or orange marmalade. Often, an egg, cheese, or cold breakfast meat may accompany the croissant. In France, the breakfast croissant is almost obligatory. At home, in both chic eateries and fast-food palaces, the buttery crescents are often served as sandwiches. When serving croissants at home, put on your best smile and announce, with justifiable pride, *voilà.*

2 cups warm water
2 packages active dry yeast
2 tablespoons sugar
3 tablespoons skim milk powder
5 cups bread flour
1 tablespoon salt
Flour, for dusting
10 ounces unsalted butter (2 sticks plus 2 tablespoons; see Note, page 251)
Egg wash (1 egg beaten with 1 tablespoon water), for brushing

In a large bowl sprinkle the yeast over the warm water to soften; stir to dissolve. Add the sugar, milk powder, flour, and salt. Mix thoroughly until the dough forms up. Mix until thoroughly combined and the dough comes away from the sides of the bowl. Knead for about 5 minutes. Do not knead to develop the gluten. This will be done during Rolling In (see below). Work with plenty of dusting flour, since this will be a soft, sloppy dough that will be refrigerated to firm it up. A scraper or bun dough cutter held in one hand while mixing is very helpful until the dough becomes cohesive.

Rolling In (Standard Method)

Turn out the dough onto a well-floured pan. Press out into a rectangular shape, cover with oiled plastic wrap or a sheet of oiled parchment paper, and chill in the refrigerator for 45 minutes or more.

Meanwhile, soften the butter just enough to enable it to be molded. Press and roll it out between 2 sheets of waxed paper into a rectangular shape about 1/4 inch thick; chill. The baker tries to have the dough and the butter (called the roll-in) at the same consistency. This generally means removing the butter from the refrigerator some time before the dough.

Using a rolling pin, roll out the croissant dough into a rectangle about 20 inches by 14 inches (Figure 1). Brush off the excess flour. The butter should be rolled out two-thirds of the width of the dough, about 13 inches by 12 inches. Place the butter on top of the dough, leaving a 1-inch border so that the butter will not run out when rolled (Figure 2). Fold over the unbuttered third of the dough (Figure 3). Brush off any excess flour, then fold the remaining third over the first 2 folds, just as if folding a letter into thirds (Figure 4). Proceed as in the First Roll, below.

The following method—called spotting in the butter—is an alternate method used by pros. It is actually easier and saves time. Try it for yourself.

Rolling In (Professional Method)

After mixing the dough, turn it out as described above and place it in the refrigerator for about 45 minutes. Soften the butter (called the roll-in). In the bakery we break up the butter and soften it in the mixer using the dough hook. Soften only until malleable. Roll out the dough as above (Figure 1). Spot the butter evenly over two-thirds of the dough, leaving a 1-inch border all around (Figure 2). Fold into thirds as above (Figures 3 and 4). Cover and refrigerate as above.

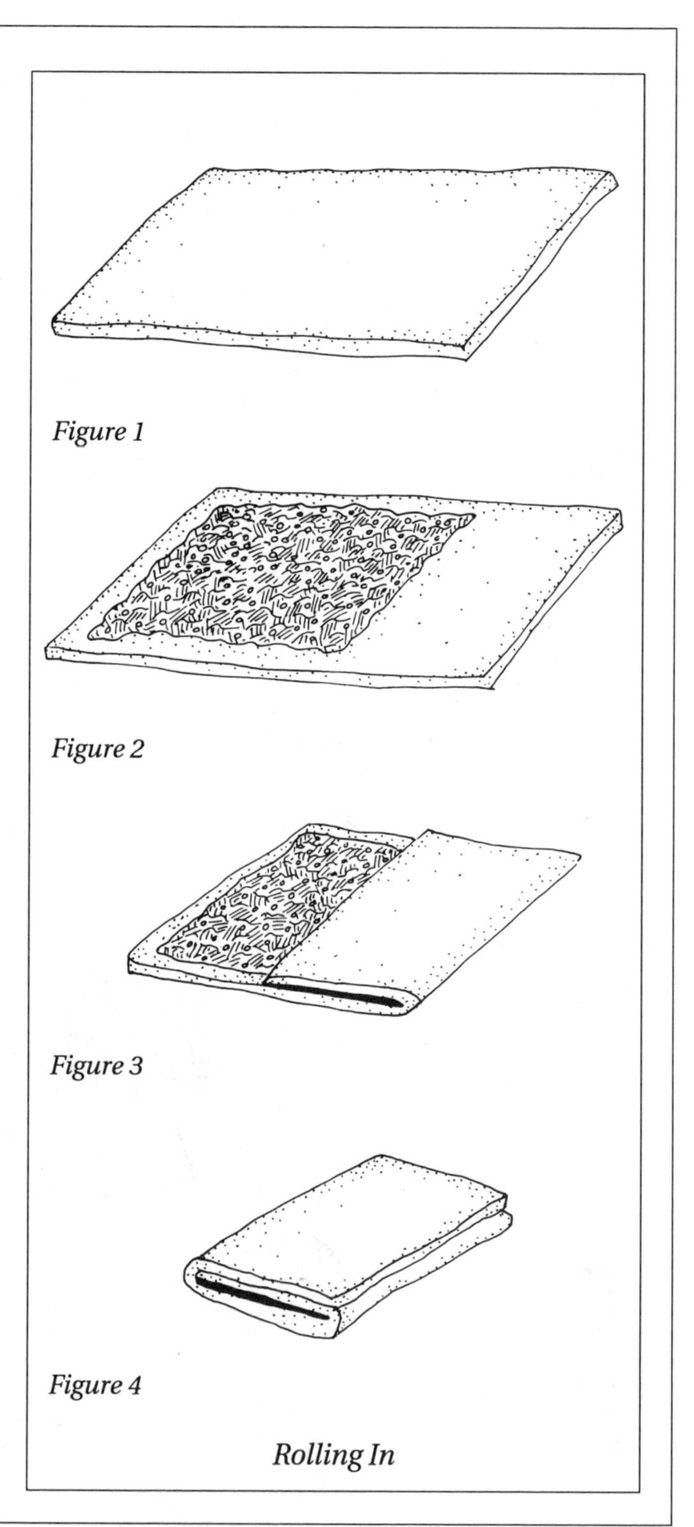

Rolling In

First Roll

Turn the dough 1/4 turn (Figure 5) and roll out as before.(Figure 6) Always roll the dough gently from the center out to each end. If the dough tears and the butter shows through, patch it by patting together with a piece of dough or sprinkling with some flour. Use plenty of dusting flour so that the dough does not stick and tear on the bottom. If the dough tends to stick on the bottom, you can flip the dough over, in half, to scrape the work top and add dusting flour. Flip back, then do the other half. Fold into thirds as above. (Figure 7) Cover on the floured pan and refrigerate to cool for about 45 minutes.

Second and Third Roll

Repeat rolling and folding into thirds two more times, letting the dough rest and refrigerating between each roll if necessary.

When finished rolling, you will have 81 alternating layers of butter and dough. Place on a floured baking pan, brush any excess flour off the top, brush with oil, and cover with parchment paper or plastic wrap. The finished dough should be refrigerated overnight. Remember, the dough was never allowed to rise after mixing. Refrigerating lets the dough age. It can also be frozen for as long as a week, then defrosted in the refrigerator overnight for use the next day.

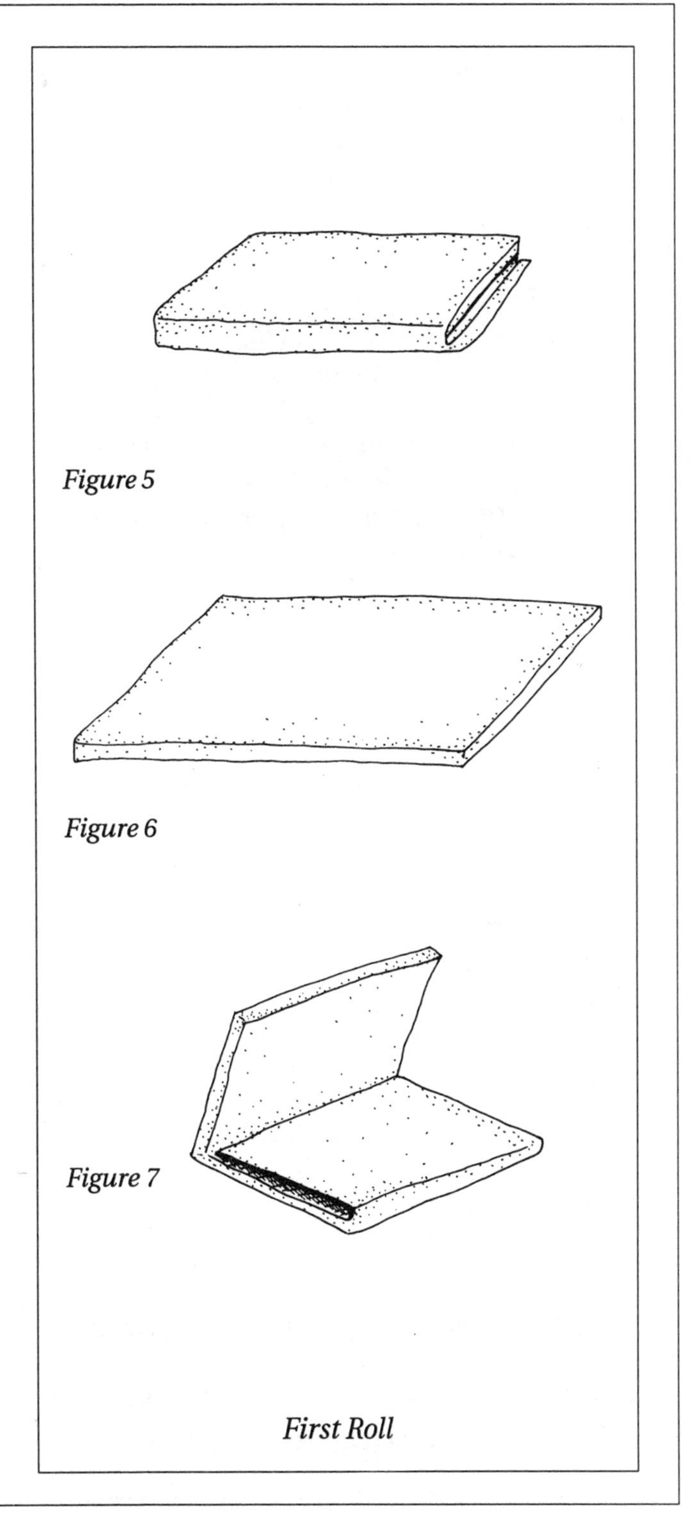

First Roll

Making Up

Prepare 3 clean baking sheets. Cover with greased waxed paper or parchment paper. Roll out the dough until 1/8 inch thick, approximately 20 inches long, and 10 inches wide.

BAKER'S SECRET: First, roll out the dough to the desired width, 20 inches. Then begin rolling until 10 inches long. Do not tear the dough. When it becomes difficult to roll, hold the rolling pin on a diagonal and roll from one end to the other. Then roll on the opposite diagonal. Return to rolling straight as in the beginning.

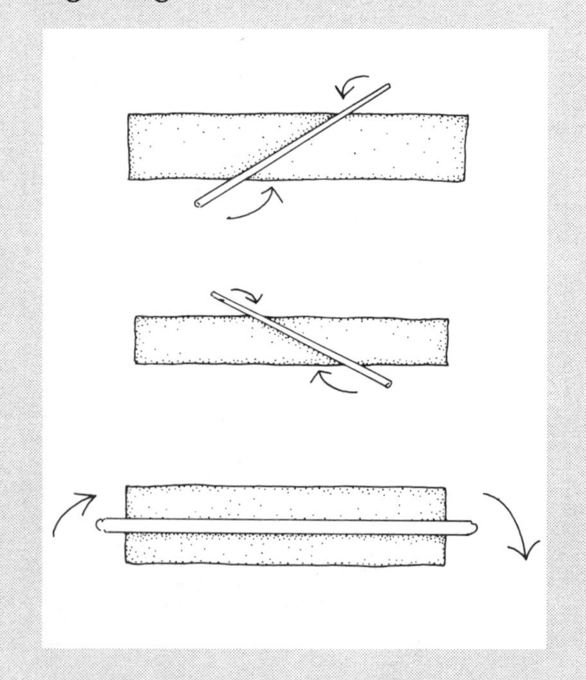

Trim the dough and cut in half horizontally with a pizza knife, bun dough cutter, or a sharp kitchen utensil. You will have 2 long strips 5 inches high (Figure 1). Cut the strips

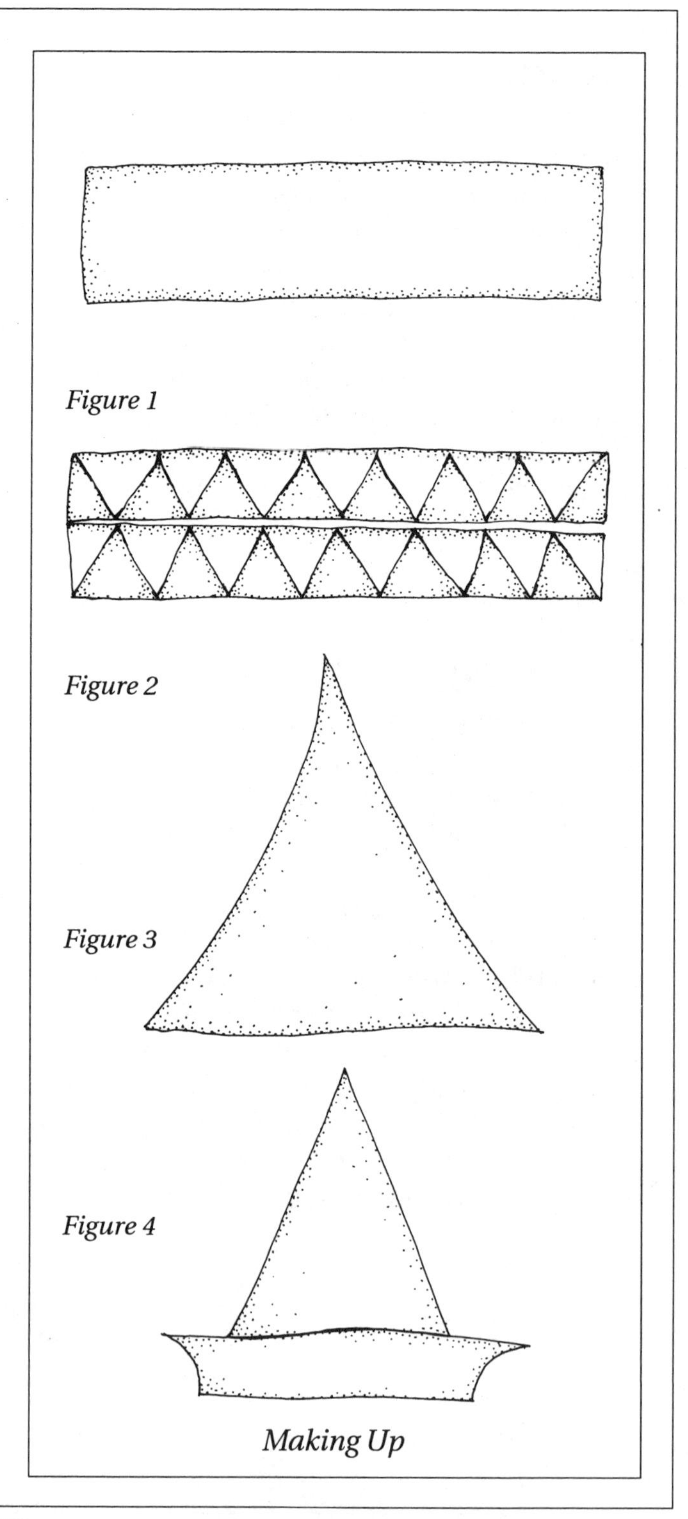

Making Up

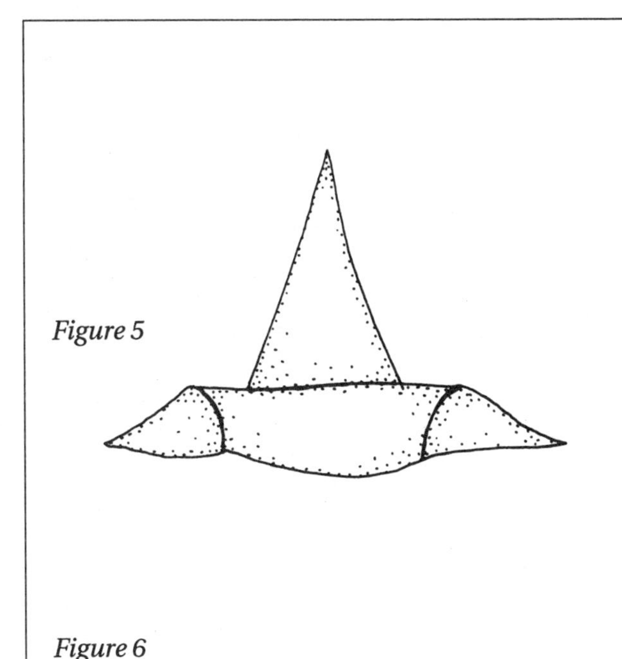

Figure 5

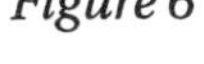

Figure 6

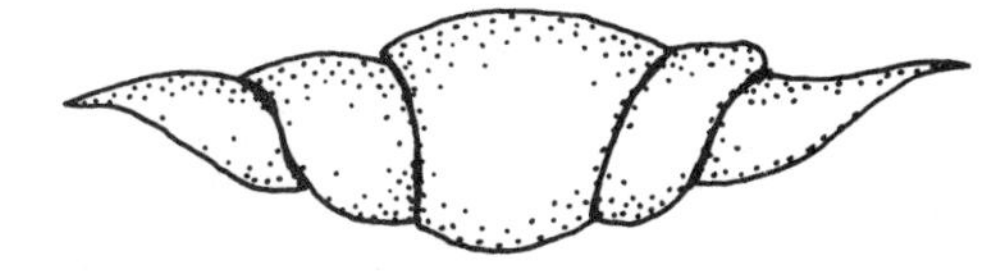

Figure 7

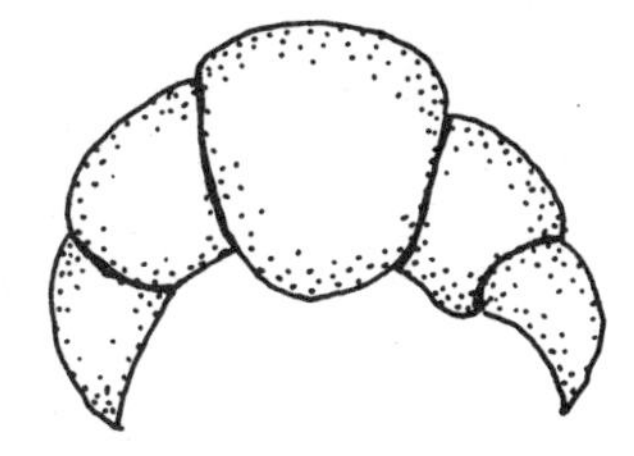

Making Up

into 5-inch triangles (Figure 2). A yardstick is helpful in measuring. Stretch the wide end of each triangle (Figure 3). Roll out each triangle with the point away from you, lengthening the croissant and making it wider (Figure 4). Roll up jelly roll style from the wide base to the tip, stretching the tip of the triangle slightly while rolling (Figure 5). Bend into a crescent shape with the tip of the triangle tucked under and facing the inside of the crescent (Figures 6 and 7). Place on a greased baking pan. The tips can be brought around until they touch or even overlap. Press the tips down with your finger so that they adhere. Leave space between the croissants to allow them to expand. The croissants can be flash frozen on the pans at this point, then wrapped for future use. Thaw overnight in the refrigerator before proofing.

Proofing

Cover the crescents and allow them to rise slowly in a dry, warm area until doubled in size (1 to 2 hours). Brush with the egg wash.

> ***BAKER'S SECRET: Allow the egg wash to dry. Brush a second time for a high gloss.***

Baking

Bake in a preheated 450°F oven until evenly browned (15 to 20 minutes). Make sure that the bottoms are well colored. Serve warm or at room temperature.

Yield

Makes 24 to 27 croissants.

Note: In the bakery we use half butter, half shortening, for a flakier croissant.

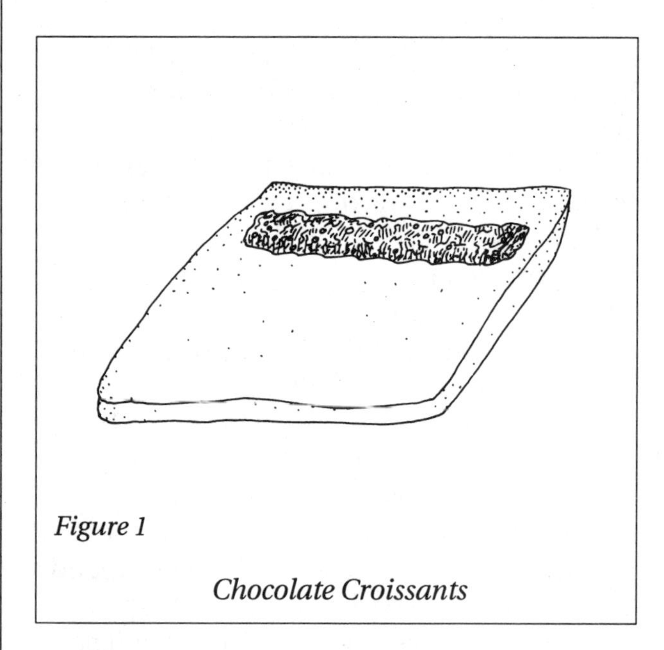

Chocolate Croissants

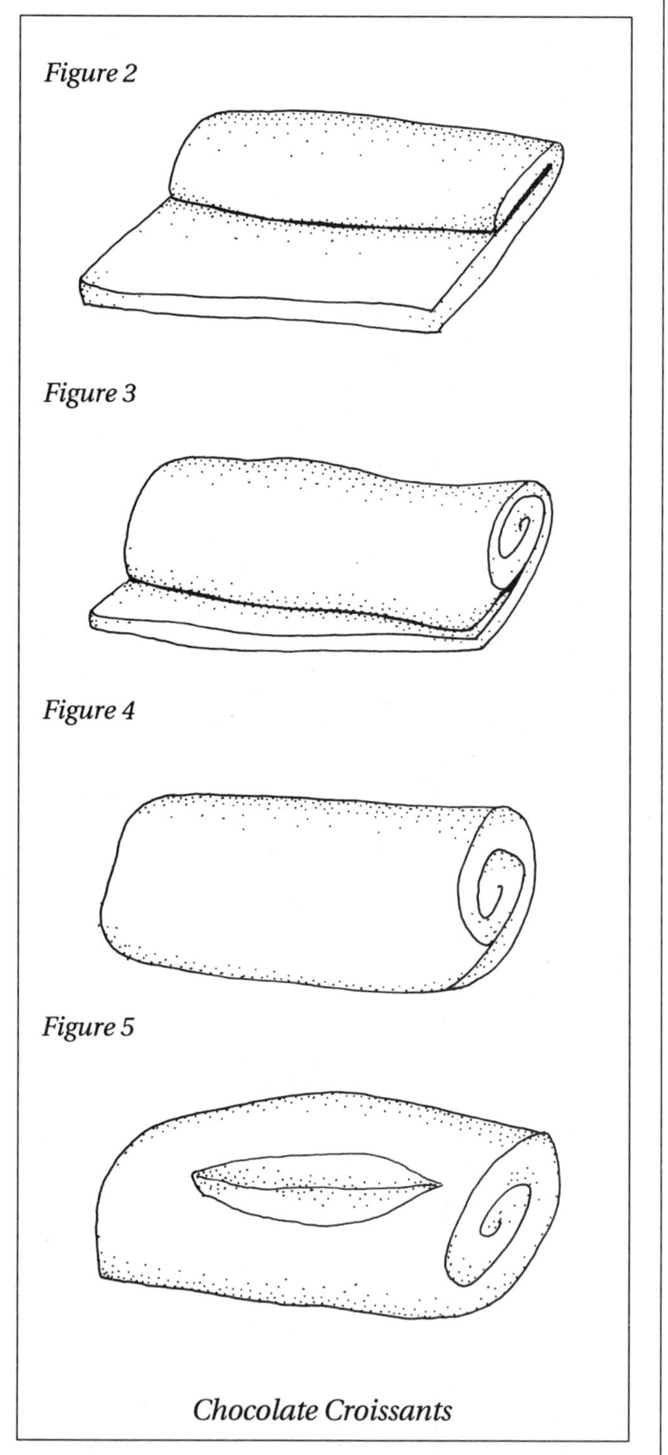

Chocolate Croissants

Variations

Chocolate Croissants

Roll out as for croissants, then cut into 4- by 6-inch rectangles. Brush the edges with the egg wash or water. Make a line of semisweet chocolate bits (about 1 tablespoon) 1/2 inch from the short edge (Figure 1). Fold the top over the chocolate (Figure 2), and roll up the dough (Figure 3), ending with the seam centered on the bottom (Figure 4). Cut a horizontal slit in the center (Figure 5). Proceed as above.

In the bakery we use a bittersweet Belgian chocolate specially formulated with a low melting point for croissants. When served warm the filling has a warm, melted texture. In place of the chocolate bits in the recipe, try using a bar of bittersweet chocolate (the best quality you can find) which has been chopped in a food processor or blender.

Cheese Croissants

Instead of cutting triangles, after rolling out, cut 4-inch squares about 1/4 inch thick. Brush the edges with egg wash. Drop 1 generous tablespoon cream cheese filling (see recipe below) into the center of each square (Figure 1). Take 2 opposite corners and stretch slightly. Form an open pocket by folding the ends over the center (Figure 2). Press the tip down hard to seal. The ends can be left open, or, to close, turn 1/4 turn and bring the remaining ends over the center. Press down to seal, forming a neat little square or pocket (Figure 3). Press hard so that the last end does not open up when baked. Proceed as above.

Cheese croissants can also be made as in Chocolate Croissants. A line of cheese filling is formed in place of the chocolate. A small amount of fruit or jam can be placed on top of the cheese. Cut 3 vertical slashes in the top to allow for expansion.

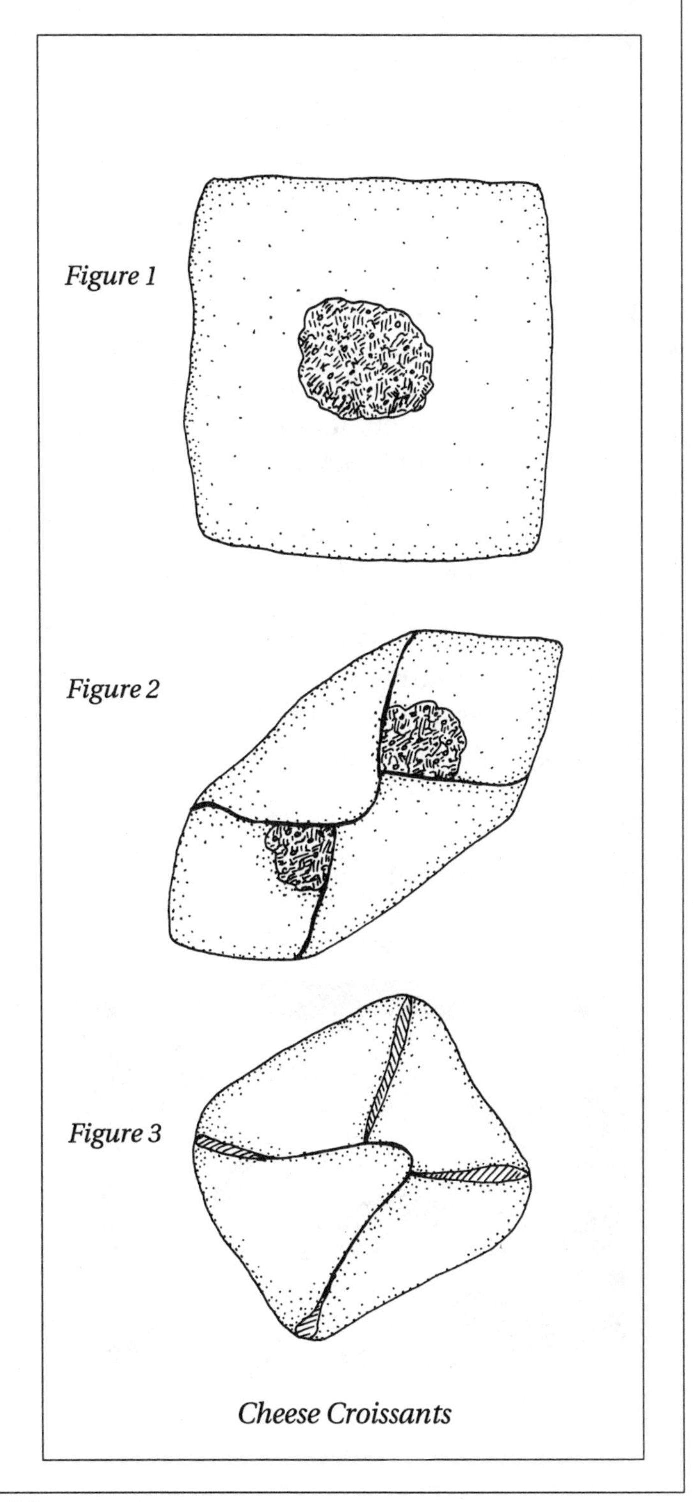

Cheese Croissants

Cream Cheese Filling

8 ounces cream cheese
1 1/2 tablespoons sugar
3 tablespoons butter
1 egg, lightly beaten
1 1/2 tablespoons flour

Cream the cheese, sugar, and butter until completely blended. Add the egg and flour and mix until smooth.

Croissants

(Food Processor, Steel Blade)

Instead of 2 cups warm water use:

1/4 cup warm water
1 3/4 cup ice water

In the work bowl sprinkle the yeast over the warm water to soften; stir to dissolve. Add the ice water, sugar, milk powder, 2 cups flour, and salt. Mix until blended. Add 3 cups flour, 1 cup at a time, and pulse only until thoroughly mixed and the dough begins to come away from the sides of the bowl. Process or pulse for 2 minutes. Do not mix to develop the gluten. This will be done during Rolling In.

Proceed as in Rolling In, Making Up, Proofing, and Baking, above.

Yield

Makes 24 to 27 croissants.

Croissants

(Dough-Mixing Machine, Flat Beater)

3 cups warm water
3 packages active dry yeast
3 tablespoons sugar
4 1/2 tablespoons skim milk powder
7 1/2 cups bread flour
1 1/2 tablespoons salt
Flour, for dusting
15 ounces unsalted butter (4 sticks less 1 tablespoon; see Note, page 251)
Egg wash (1 egg, beaten with 1 tablespoon water), for brushing

In the mixing bowl dissolve the yeast in the warm water. Add the sugar, milk powder, flour, and salt. Pulse with the on/off switch until all is absorbed so that the flour is not thrown out of the bowl. Run at the first speed until the dough comes away from the sides of the bowl. Mix only until the ingredients are thoroughly incorporated. Insert the dough hook and mix for 5 minutes. It is not necessary to fully develop the gluten. This will be accomplished during the Rolling In.

Proceed as in Rolling In, Making Up, Proofing, and Baking, above, except shape into 36 croissants.

Yield

Makes 36 croissants.

Italian Breadsticks

Place a basket of these old-fashioned breadsticks—long, knobby, and crisp—next to a steaming bowl of pasta. What could be more Italian? One batch will yield twenty fat, crusty, foot-long sticks.

1 cup warm water
1/2 package active dry yeast (scant 1 1/2 teaspoons)
1 tablespoon sugar
2 tablespoons olive oil or vegetable oil
2 1/2 to 3 1/2 cups unbleached all-purpose flour
1 1/2 teaspoons salt
Flour, for dusting work top
Oil, for greasing bowl
Cornmeal or semolina, for sprinkling and dusting

In a large bowl sprinkle the yeast over the warm water; stir to dissolve. Add the sugar, oil, 2 1/2 cups flour, and salt. Stir until the dough comes away from the sides of the bowl, adding more flour if necessary.

Turn out the dough onto a lightly floured work top. Knead with a turn, fold, push motion, adding more flour in small amounts if the dough is sticky. Knead until the dough is smooth and elastic (8 to 10 minutes).

Turn out the dough and knead into a ball.

Shaping

Transfer the dough to an oiled bowl and turn to coat. Cover and allow to rise until doubled in volume. Punch down the dough, form roughly into a rectangular shape, cover, and let the dough rest for about 10 minutes.

On a floured surface roll the dough into a long rectangle about 1/4 inch thick. Sprinkle lightly with cornmeal. With a wheel knife (pizza knife) or a thin blade and a ruler (see Note), cut 20 sticks 5 inches by 4 inches. Stretch or roll each stick to about 12 inches in length and place across the width of cornmeal-dusted baking sheets. See Toppings, below. Leave enough space between each stick to allow them to puff up and double in size in the oven. Bake immediately without allowing to rise.

Baking

Bake in a preheated 400°F oven on the middle shelf for approximately 20 minutes. It may be necessary to turn each stick over for the last 5 to 10 minutes to get an even color all around. If you are using tiles or an oven stone, turn over directly onto the stone for a crustier stick.

Yield

Makes 20 breadsticks.

Note: There are inexpensive hand-held noodle cutters available in cookware shops. These make good cutters for breadsticks.

Variations

Numerous variations of breadsticks can be made using your imagination with toppings. Here are several I like.

Sesame Seed Breadsticks

Sprinkle sesame seeds over the top of the dough before rolling. Roll the dough out on a work surface sprinkled with sesame seeds.

Garlic Breadsticks

Sprinkle 1/4 teaspoon pure garlic powder on top of the dough before rolling. In the bakery we use granulated garlic. If you want to use garlic salt, use 1/2 teaspoon and reduce the salt in the recipe by 1/4 teaspoon.

Cheese Breadsticks

Add 1/4 cup grated hard Italian cheese, such as Parmesan or Romano, to the dough before kneading. Try combining 2 such cheeses. Reduce the salt in the recipe by 1/4 teaspoon.

Olive Oil and Rosemary Breadsticks

Roll out the dough on an work surface that has been brushed with olive oil. Brush the top of the dough with oil. Sprinkle with minced fresh or dried rosemary.

Italian Breadsticks

(Food Processor, Steel Blade)

Instead of 1 cup warm water use:

1/4 cup warm water
3/4 cup ice water

In the work bowl sprinkle the yeast over the warm water; stir to dissolve. Add the ice water, sugar, oil, 2 1/2 cups flour (1 cup at a time), and salt. Mix to combine. Pulse until the dough comes away from the sides of the bowl and rides up on top of the blade, adding more flour if necessary. Process or pulse for 2 to 3 minutes. Do not overmix.

Turn out the dough and knead into a ball. Proceed as in Shaping and Baking, above.

Yield

Makes 20 bread sticks.

Italian Breadsticks

(Dough-Mixing Machine, Flat Beater)

2 cups warm water
1 package active dry yeast
2 tablespoons sugar
4 tablespoons olive oil or vegetable oil
5 to 7 cups unbleached all-purpose flour
1 tablespoon salt
Oil, for greasing bowl
Flour, for dusting work top
Cornmeal or semolina, for dusting

In the mixing bowl sprinkle the yeast over the warm water to soften; stir to dissolve. Add the sugar, oil, 5 cups flour, and salt. Pulse at the first speed using the on/off switch so that the beater does not throw the flour out of the bowl. When the flour is absorbed, run the machine at the first speed until the dough comes away from the sides of the bowl. If the dough is too soft, add more flour 1/4 cup at a time.

Remove and scrape down the beater and insert the dough hook. Run at the first speed until the dough forms up on the hook and comes away from the sides of the bowl (8 to 10 minutes). You can use the second speed for the last few minutes to strengthen the gluten.

Transfer the dough to an oiled bowl and turn to coat. Cover and allow to rise until doubled in volume. When fully risen, cut the dough in half. Refrigerate or freeze one piece of dough, since there will be too much to handle at one time. Proceed as in Shaping and Baking, above.

Yield

Makes 40 breadsticks.

Grissini

These very thin crispy breadsticks, known as grissini, have appeared in restaurants and markets of late. Here is a method for making them at home with professional-looking results. The procedure requires a hand-turned pasta-making machine, which is available inexpensively at cookware stores. Use it to make your own fresh pasta.

Prepare the dough using the hand-mixed Italian Breadstick recipe.

Shaping

Proceed as in the recipe above. When the dough is ready, roll it into a rectangle as described. Cut 5 crosswise strips and cover with a cloth. Have 2 or more cornmeal-dusted baking sheets ready for use.

Pasta Machine

Dust the dough lightly with cornmeal or semolina, top and bottom, and run one strip through the pasta machine with the rollers set at the widest opening, approximately 1/4 inch. Dust again, and roll through the wide noodle cutters (fettucine cutters). Place the strips on the work surface, dust once more, carefully separate the strips, and arrange them across the width of the baking sheet, leaving enough space between the strips so that they can puff up in the oven. Trim as necessary. The scrap pieces can be brushed off, kneaded together, and rerolled.

Baking

In a preheated 400°F oven, bake immediately without allowing to rise. Bake until barely browned (about 10 minutes). Watch carefully so that they do not burn. Turn the pans once during baking. Prepare the next baking sheet while the first is in the oven. The baking sheets cool quickly and can be reused when cool enough to touch.

Note: Inexpensive hand-held noodle cutters or truffle cutters are available in cookery shops. These make good cutters for bread sticks.

Zatar Herbed Rolls

Zatar, more or less unknown to us, is quite common in many parts of the Middle East. There are two types of zatar: One is an herb, a type of marjoram, the other an aromatic blend of sumac, thyme, and marjoram.

I first discovered zatar in the Holy Land, where the blend was used to add an exotic flavor to a dish of broiled lamb. Some time later I came upon it in Jaffa being used as a topping for rolls in an open-air Arab bakery. The oven was actually outside on the street. The bakers told me that the bakery was more than 400 years old. Some young hikers had picked fresh zatar in the hills and brought it to the bakers, who, in the space of 15 to 20 minutes, proudly produced fresh zatar-topped pita for them. Zatar can be found in Mideast ethnic markets. Here is my version of these herbed rolls.

2 cups warm water
2 packages active dry yeast
2 tablespoons sugar
2 tablespoons olive oil or vegetable oil
1/2 teaspoon dried parsley or basil
1/2 teaspoon dried tarragon
1/2 teaspoon dried chives
5 to 6 cups bread flour or unbleached all-purpose flour
2 teaspoons salt
Flour, for dusting work top
Oil, for greasing bowl
Dried zatar or marjoram, for topping

In a large bowl sprinkle the yeast over the warm water to soften; stir to dissolve. Add the sugar, oil, parsley, tarragon, chives, 5 cups flour, and salt. Mix until the dough comes away from the sides of the bowl. Add more flour 1/4 cup at a time if the dough remains sticky.

Turn out the dough onto a floured work surface and knead until smooth and elastic (8 to 10 minutes). Place the dough in a clean, oiled bowl and turn to coat. Cover and allow to rise until doubled in size.

Shaping

Punch down the dough and divide in half. Shape into 2 balls, cover, and allow to rest for 10 minutes. Roll out with your palms into 2 long ropes 1 to 2 inches in diameter. Cut each rope into 8 equal pieces and shape each into a ball. (If desired, each dough piece can be halved once more to make 16 dinner-sized rolls.) Cover and let rest for 5 minutes.

With a wooden dowel or stick, using little or no flour, roll out each ball into a disk about

4 inches wide (2 inches for small dinner rolls). Evenly space them on lightly greased baking sheets. Brush the tops with vegetable oil (preferably olive oil) and sprinkle to taste with the zatar. Cover and proof until puffy and about doubled in height. With the tips of your fingers push down and make several deep indentations in the center of each roll.

Baking

Bake with steam (pages 31-32) in a preheated 400°F oven until golden brown (about 15 minutes). Turn the baking sheets once, halfway through the baking process, to ensure even color. Let cool on the baking sheets. Serve warm or freeze for future use.

Yield

Makes 16 rolls or 32 dinner rolls.

Variation

Use zatar topping on Pita (page 149) or Naan (page 135) prior to baking.

Zatar Herbed Rolls

(Food Processor, Steel Blade)

Instead of 2 cups warm water use:

1/2 cup warm water
1 1/2 cups ice water

In the work bowl sprinkle the yeast over the warm water; stir to dissolve. Add the ice water, sugar, oil, parsley, tarragon, chives, 2 cups flour, and salt. Blend until absorbed. Add 3 cups flour, 1 cup at a time. Pulse until the dough comes away from the sides of the bowl. More flour can be added 1/4 cup at a time if the dough is too soft. If necessary divide the dough in half and process each half separately, then knead together. Process for about 2 to 3 minutes. Do not allow the dough to overheat. Extra kneading by hand is sometimes necessary to make the dough elastic and to fully develop the gluten.

Transfer the dough to a clean, oiled bowl and turn to coat. Cover and let rise until doubled in size.

Proceed as in Shaping and Baking, above.

Yield

Makes 16 rolls or 32 dinner rolls.

Zatar Herbed Rolls

(Dough-Mixing Machine, Flat Beater)

3 cups warm water
3 packages active dry yeast
3 tablespoons sugar
3 tablespoons olive oil or vegetable oil
3/4 teaspoon dried parsley or basil
3/4 teaspoon dried tarragon
3/4 teaspoon dried chives
7 1/2 to 9 cups bread flour or unbleached all-purpose flour
1 tablespoon salt
Oil, for greasing bowl
Flour, for dusting work top
Dried zatar or marjoram, for topping

In the mixing bowl dissolve the yeast in the warm water. Add the sugar, oil, parsley, tarragon, chives, 7 1/2 cups flour, and salt. Pulse with the on/off switch until all is absorbed so that the flour does not fly out of the bowl.

Scrape down the beater and replace with the dough hook. Run at the first speed for about 8 to 10 minutes, adding more flour if necessary. You can run at the second speed for the last 2 minutes to strengthen the gluten.

Turn out the dough; place in an oiled bowl and turn to coat. Cover and let rise until doubled in size.

Proceed as in Shaping and Baking, above, except form 3 ropes and cut each into 8 pieces. (16 pieces for dinner rolls).

Yield

Makes 24 rolls or 48 dinner-sized rolls.

Sweet Rolls

In many parts of the country, sweet rolls or buns, called *schnecken,* are served along with bread or rolls to be consumed during the meal. I always approve of serving dessert first because it can be the best part of the meal.

1 1/4 cup warm water
1 package active dry yeast
1/2 cup sugar
4 tablespoons butter or margarine
2 large eggs
1/3 cup skim milk powder
4 to 4 1/2 cups unbleached all-purpose flour
1 teaspoon salt
Flour, for dusting work top
Oil, for greasing bowl
Melted butter or margarine, for brushing
Ground cinnamon, for dusting
Brown sugar or cinnamon sugar, for sprinkling
1/2 cup raisins, or more to taste, for sprinkling
Egg wash (1 egg beaten with 1 tablespoon water), for brushing (optional)

Icing (optional)

1 cup confectioners' sugar
2 tablespoons melted butter or margarine (optional)
1/8 teaspoon vanilla extract
Hot water, as needed

In a large bowl sprinkle the yeast over the warm water; stir to dissolve. Add the sugar, butter, eggs, milk powder, 4 cups flour, and salt. Stir until the dough comes away from the sides of the bowl, adding more flour if necessary. The dough should be softer than for bread.

Turn out the dough onto a lightly floured work top. Knead until the dough is smooth and elastic and the gluten fully developed (8 to 10 minutes).

Rising

Transfer the dough to an oiled bowl. Cover and allow to rise until doubled in volume.

Shaping

Punch the air out of the dough. Shape into a long, narrow rectangle, cover, and allow to rest for 15 minutes. Roll out into a rectangle, 24 inches long and about 1/8 inch thick. Brush the dough clean of any flour.

Brush the top with the melted butter or margarine, then sprinkle with a light dusting of the ground cinnamon. A little goes a long way. Sprinkle with the brown sugar or cinnamon sugar and the raisins. Roll up, jelly roll style. Cut into 1-inch slices and place the slices on a greased or buttered baking sheet close enough that they will touch when they rise. Cover and allow to proof until doubled in size. Brush with the egg wash if the optional icing is not desired.

To make the Icing (if desired), combine the confectioners' sugar, melted butter, and vanilla; mix in enough hot water, a little at a time, to make it smooth and spreadable. Keep warm until needed.

Baking

Bake in a preheated 375°F oven until nicely browned and the bottom has an even color (20 to 30 minutes). Let cool on a wire rack. Apply the warm icing before the rolls are completely cooled.

Yield

Makes 24 Sweet Rolls.

Variations

Sticky Buns

Chopped pecans
Softened butter or margarine, for greasing pan

Topping
3/4 cup firmly packed brown sugar
2 tablespoons melted butter or margarine
Corn syrup, to thin out
About 1/2 cup honey

Roll out as for Sweet Rolls (omitting the raisins, if desired), then sprinkle with the chopped pecans, brown sugar and cinnamon. Roll up jelly roll style. Line a greased baking sheet with parchment or waxed paper. Grease with the softened butter or margarine. Prepare the Topping, adding enough corn syrup to make it spreadable. Distribute a thin coating of Topping over the pan. Sprinkle additional halved or chopped pecans over the Topping.

Place the rolls close together on the baking sheet. Proof and bake as above. While still hot, invert onto another tray to serve. Carefully peel off the paper.

To make individual sticky buns cut the Sweet Roll dough into 1-inch slices. Place them in muffin tins greased with the Sticky Bun topping. A pecan half or chopped pecans can be placed on the topping before inserting the dough. Bake as above and invert while still warm. In the bakery we made minibuns using miniature cupcake pans.

Rum Buns

In many parts of the South, rum buns are frequently served. In the recipe for Sweet Rolls, substitute 1/4 cup dark rum for 1/4 cup of the warm water, then proceed as above. Frost with rum-flavored icing: Add 2 tablespoons dark rum to the icing recipe above. The frosting should be applied while the rolls are still warm. In the bakery we used Meyer's brand dark rum.

Sweet Rolls

(Food Processor, Steel Blade)

Instead of 1 cup warm water use:

1/4 cup warm water
1 cup ice water

In the work bowl sprinkle the yeast over the warm water; stir to dissolve. Add the ice water and 2 cups flour. Mix until smooth. Add 2 more cups flour, 1 cup at a time. Pulse until the dough comes away from the sides of the bowl. More flour can be added 1/4 cup at a time if the dough is too soft. (It should be softer than bread dough, however.) If necessary divide the dough in two and process each half separately, then knead together. Process for about 2 minutes. Do not allow the dough to overheat. Extra kneading by hand is sometimes necessary to make the dough elastic and to fully develop the gluten.

Proceed as in Rising, Shaping, and Baking, above.

Yield

Makes 24 Sweet Rolls.

Sweet Rolls

(Dough-Mixing Machine, Flat Beater)

2 cups warm water
1 1/2 packages active dry yeast
3/4 cup sugar
6 tablespoons butter or margarine
3 large eggs
1/2 cup skim milk powder
6 to 6 3/4 cups unbleached all-purpose flour
1 1/2 teaspoons salt
Oil, for greasing bowl
Flour, for dusting work top
Melted butter or margarine, for brushing
Ground cinnamon, for dusting
Brown sugar or cinnamon sugar, for sprinkling
3/4 cup raisins, or more to taste, for sprinkling
Egg wash (1 egg beaten with 1 tablespoon water), for brushing (optional)

In the mixing bowl sprinkle the yeast over the warm water; stir to dissolve. Add the sugar, butter, eggs, milk powder, 6 cups flour, and salt. Mix until the dough comes away from the sides of the bowl, adding more flour if necessary.

Scrape down the beater and insert the dough hook. Mix for 8 to 10 minutes at the first speed. More flour can be added in small amounts if required. Keep the dough on the soft side. The dough should be smooth and elastic. Proceed as in Rising, Shaping, and Baking, above.

Yield

Makes 36 Sweet Rolls.

Quick Whole Wheat Rolls with Raisins and Walnuts

Because these rolls use baking soda for leavening, they can be whipped up from start to finish in a half hour or less. They have a country-style look and go well with most foods. Raisins or walnuts can be omitted according to taste. For a quick start preheat the oven to 375°F before you begin mixing.

2 1/2 cups whole wheat flour, preferably stone ground
1/2 to 1 cup unbleached all-purpose flour
4 teaspoons sugar
1/4 cup (4 tablespoons) shortening or vegetable oil
1 teaspoon baking soda
1/2 teaspoon salt
1 cup buttermilk or sour milk (see Note)
1 egg, beaten
1/2 cup raisins
1/2 cup chopped toasted walnuts
Flour, for dusting work top

In a large bowl combine the flours and sugar. Cut or rub in the shortening with your hands until the mixture feels course. Add the baking soda and salt and gently stir through with your fingers. Add the buttermilk and the egg. Stir, then add the raisins and walnuts and mix until all the flour is absorbed.

Lightly dust your hands with flour. Turn the dough out onto a floured work surface and knead lightly until smooth.

Shaping

Scrape down the work surface, dust with flour, and roll out the dough into a rectangular shape about 1/2 inch high. Cut to form 4 strips horizontally and 5 vertically. Dust or sift flour over the top and space evenly on a baking sheet.

Baking

Bake in a preheated 375°F oven until browned (15 to 20 minutes). The crust should feel firm. If the center feels soft, continue baking for 5 minutes more.

Yield

Makes 20 rolls.

Note: To make sour milk, combine 1 cup skim milk and 1 teaspoon vinegar. Let stand until clabbered (about 10 minutes).

Quick Whole Wheat Rolls with...

(Food Processor, Steel Blade)

In the work bowl combine the flours, sugar, baking soda, and salt. Pulse several times until the mix resembles coarse meal. Combine the milk and the beaten egg; with the machine running slowly add the egg mixture. Run for a minute or less, just long enough for a smooth dough.

Turn out the dough onto a floured surface, flatten the dough, and spread the raisins and walnuts over the top. Cut the dough in half and place one half on top of the other. Flatten the dough again to distribute the raisins and walnuts.

Proceed as in Shaping and Baking, above.

Yield

Makes 20 rolls.

Quick Whole Wheat Rolls with...

(Dough-Mixing Machine, Flat Beater)

2 cups buttermilk or sour milk (see Note)
5 cups whole wheat flour, preferably stone ground
1 to 2 cups unbleached all-purpose flour
2 tablespoons plus 2 teaspoons sugar
1/2 cup (8 tablespoons) shortening or vegetable oil
2 teaspoons baking soda
1 teaspoon salt
2 eggs
1 cup raisins
1 cup walnuts
Flour, for dusting work top

Place the buttermilk in the mixing bowl and add the flours, sugar, shortening, baking soda, salt, and eggs. Pulse by turning the switch on and off quickly until the flour is absorbed and will not be thrown out of the bowl. Mix at the first speed until smooth. Add the raisins and walnuts and mix only long enough to incorporate. If they are overmixed they will be crushed and their color will run into the dough. If it takes more than a few turns, knead them in by hand on the work surface. Proceed as in Shaping and Baking, above, except make 40 rolls.

Yield

Makes 40 rolls.

Note: To make sour milk, combine 2 cups skim milk and 2 teaspoons vinegar. Let stand until clabbered (about 10 minutes).

Chapter Eight

Biscuits and Muffins

Say biscuits and I think South, and Kentucky where I spent several years of my youth.

Brown's Hotel, Louisville, Kentucky, the 1950s—grits, shirred or basted eggs, and hot biscuits right out of the oven. The Blue Boar Cafeteria—fried chicken, biscuits with gravy, okra.

The versatile, ever-popular muffin seems to enjoy a new following in the wake of dietary trends for whole grains, fruits, low sodium, and reduced-fat food products. Included in this chapter are old standards, modern additions, and some original recipes. For large yields double or triple the recipes. Mix with a dough-mixing machine if desired. When mixing muffins add the liquids and mix only until the flour becomes moistened. Do not overmix. The batter should appear lumpy.

Basic Biscuits

These biscuits are quick and easy to make and are best served hot right out of the oven. Biscuits are so easy to mix that it does not warrant using the processor and cleaning up. It is also too easy to overmix biscuits in the machine. And although biscuits can be successfully prepared in a dough-mixing machine, the same applies as for the food processor. The best biscuits are mixed by hand in small batches and served when baked. For mixing large batches you can multiply the recipe by three or four times and use the mixing machine, mixing as little as possible. If necessary finish kneading by hand.

2 cups unbleached all-purpose flour
4 teaspoons baking powder
1/2 teaspoon salt
1 tablespoon shortening, preferably Crisco brand
2/3 to 3/4 cup milk
Flour, for dusting work top
Shortening, for greasing pan

In a large bowl stir together the flour, baking powder, and salt. Cut or rub in the shortening until the mixture resembles course meal. Add the milk and stir with a wooden spoon until the dough begins to come together.

Turn out the dough onto a lightly floured work top, knead a few turns, and pat out to 1/2 inch thickness. The less kneading the more tender the biscuits.

Cut into 12 rounds with a small cutter. Place on a greased baking sheet or iron skillet and bake in a 400°F oven for 10 to 12 minutes. Serve warm.

Yield

Makes 12 biscuits.

BAKER'S SECRET: For flakier biscuits double the shortening and leave larger lumps of shortening when rubbing in.

Variations

Rich Biscuits

Increase the shortening to 2 to 3 tablespoons.

Drop Biscuits

Increase the milk to 1 to 1 1/2 cups, which makes the dough thin enough to drop out by the spoonful onto a greased baking sheet. Bake 8 to 10 minutes.

Onion Cheese Biscuits

These sophisticated biscuits have an unusual flavor. Try them at cocktail time. They are good served with wine.

1 1/2 cups unbleached all-purpose flour
4 teaspoons baking powder
1/2 teaspoon salt
1/4 cup shortening
3/4 cup grated sharp Cheddar cheese
1/4 cup minced green onion
2/3 to 3/4 cup milk
Flour, for dusting work top

In a large bowl combine the flour, baking powder, and salt. Cut or rub in the shortening and cheese until the mixture resembles course meal. Add the onion and enough milk to make a smooth dough.

Turn out the dough onto a lightly floured work top and pat out to 1/2-inch thickness. The less kneading, the more tender the biscuit. Cut into 12 rounds with a 2-inch biscuit cutter or a kitchen glass, or cut half size for 24 cocktail biscuits. Place on an ungreased baking sheet or an iron skillet. Bake in a 400°F oven for 10 to 12 minutes. Serve warm.

Yield

Makes twelve 2-inch biscuits or 24 cocktail biscuits.

Variation

Onion Poppy Seed Biscuits

Add 2 tablespoons poppy seeds to the recipe above. Roll out into a rectangle about 1/2 inch thick. With a wheel knife or sharp blade cut into small squares or rectangles. Brush twice with egg wash (1 egg beaten with 1 tablespoon water). Slip onto a baking sheet with a spatula. Bake as above. Makes 24 biscuits.

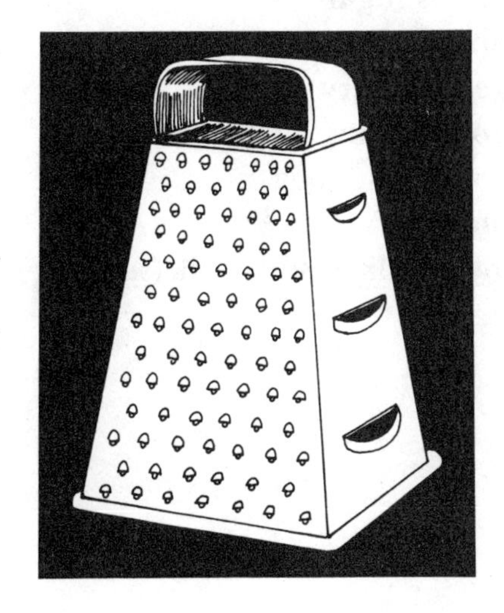

Angel Biscuits

There is a well-known soul food restaurant in New York which makes the most heavenly biscuits (only on Sunday). I never could get the folks there to part with the recipe. Although these treats tasted like baking powder biscuits, they were so light that they seemed to float right up to your lips. Another baker who was my guest for Sunday brunch was sure that there was yeast in the dough, which would account for their being so light. After much searching we determined that they were a version of angel biscuits found throughout the South. There are many versions of this biscuit. Basically the recipes are all very much alike. There are differences in kneading and rising. The method that follows is the one I like best. It is the quickest and in my opinion the best-tasting one. The dough can be refrigerated for a week or frozen for months. You need bake only as much as you can use. More can be ready in 15 minutes anytime you wish. It's like having a hot biscuit factory in your refrigerator. This dough must be made up and refrigerated for one day before its initial use. The longer it stays in the refrigerator, the better it becomes. Defrost frozen biscuit dough overnight in the refrigerator.

4 1/2 to 5 cups unbleached all-purpose flour
3 tablespoons sugar
3/4 cup shortening
1 package active dry yeast
1 tablespoon baking powder
1 teaspoon baking soda
1 teaspoon salt
2 cups buttermilk or sour milk (see Note)

In a large bowl combine the flour and sugar. Cut in or rub in the shortening with your fingers until the mixture resembles coarse meal. Add the dry yeast granules, baking powder, baking soda, and salt; sift the dry ingredients through your fingertips to mix. Add the milk and stir until all the dry ingredients are absorbed. Do not knead. The dough will be heavy and sticky but will become workable when thoroughly chilled. Refrigerate the dough overnight in a covered bowl or plastic bag.

Cutting

The next day take out as much dough as you need and roll out to a thickness of 1/2 inch or less. Cut out with a biscuit cutter or a kitchen glass. The scraps can be rerolled and cut again.

Baking

Place the biscuits on an ungreased baking sheet and bake immediately (without proofing) in a preheated 400°F oven until lightly browned (12 to 15 minutes). Serve warm with lots of butter or jam.

Yield

Makes about 36 2-inch biscuits.

Note: To make sour milk, combine 2 cups skim milk and 2 teaspoons vinegar. Let stand until clabbered (10 minutes).

Variation

Zucchini Biscuits

Add 1/2 cup grated zucchini plus 2 1/2 tablespoons sugar, and reduce the milk to 1/2 cup.

Angel Biscuits

(Food Processor, Steel Blade)

In the work bowl combine the flour, sugar, dry yeast granules, baking powder, baking soda, and salt. Add the shortening and pulse until the mixture resembles course meal. Add the buttermilk slowly while pulsing. Stop as soon as all the dry ingredients are absorbed. The dough will be wet and heavy. If necessary divide the dough in half and process each half separately. Do not knead. Remove the dough and place it in the refrigerator overnight in a covered bowl or plastic bag.

Proceed as in Cutting and Baking, above.

Angel Biscuits

(Dough-Mixing Machine, Flat Beater)

6 3/4 to 7 1/2 cups unbleached all-purpose flour
4 1/2 tablespoons sugar
1 1/4 cups shortening
1 1/2 packages (1 1/2 scant tablespoons) active dry yeast
1 1/2 tablespoons baking powder
1 1/2 teaspoons baking soda
1 1/2 teaspoons salt
3 cups buttermilk or sour milk (see Note)

In the mixing bowl combine the flour, sugar, dry yeast granules, baking powder, baking soda, and salt. Add the shortening and pulse with the on/off switch until the mixture resembles course meal. With the machine running add the buttermilk a little at a time. Stop as soon as all the dry ingredients are absorbed. The dough will be wet and heavy. Avoid kneading. Remove the dough and place in the refrigerator overnight in a covered bowl or a plastic bag. Proceed as in Cutting and Baking, above.

Note: To make 3 cups buttermilk, combine 3 cups skim milk and 3 teaspoons vinegar; let stand until clabbered (about 10 minutes).

Yield

Makes about 4 1/2 dozen biscuits.

Tea Biscuits

Tea biscuits are a bakery shop standard. Most biscuits are best when served warm, whereas tea biscuits can stand out on a bakery shop counter all day and still be wonderful to eat when no longer hot. They have a pleasant, sweet flavor and are best when eaten as a snack or after dinner rather than as an accompaniment to a meal. These biscuits can be kept for several days in the bread box or a plastic bag. When frozen they can be reheated (wrapped in aluminum foil) or lightly toasted. I like them best when served with jam or marmalade and served with hot tea or coffee. When raisins are omitted from the recipe the biscuits can be split and filled with berries, topped with whipped cream, and served as New England-style strawberry shortcake.

3 cups unbleached all-purpose flour
6 tablespoons sugar
4 tablespoons unsalted butter or shortening
1 1/2 tablespoons baking powder
1/2 teaspoon baking soda
1/2 teaspoon salt
1/3 cup skim milk powder
1 cup cold water
1 egg, beaten
3/4 cup dried currants or raisins (optional)
Flour, for dusting hands and work top
1 egg thinned with 1 to 2 teaspoons water, for egg wash
Shortening, for greasing pans

In a large bowl combine the flour and sugar. Cut or rub in the butter until the mixture resembles course meal. Add the baking powder, salt, and milk powder and gently stir to distribute. Add the water and egg, stir, then add the currants (if desired) and stir until all the flour is absorbed.

Lightly dust your hands with flour. Turn the dough out onto a floured work surface and knead only until it all comes together. The less kneading, the more tender the biscuit.

Cutting

On a clean, floured surface press out or roll out the dough 1/2 to 3/4 inch thick. Cut out with a 2 1/2-inch biscuit cutter or a kitchen glass. Knead the scraps together, roll out, and cut more biscuits. You should have 9 to 12 rounds.

BAKER'S SECRET: Save 1/4 of the freshly kneaded dough before rolling out. Incorporate with the scraps for a more tender biscuit.

Baking

Space the rounds evenly on a lightly greased baking pan and brush the tops with the beaten egg mixture. Let dry for a few minutes, then brush a second time. Bake at 400°F until well browned (about 15 minutes).

Yield

Makes 9 to 12 biscuits.

Variation

Whole Wheat Tea Biscuits

Substitute 2 cups whole wheat flour, preferably stone-ground whole wheat, for 2 cups of the white flour (3 cups in the dough-mixing machine recipe). Add 1 tablespoon sugar (1 1/2 tablespoons in the dough-mixing machine recipe).

Tea Biscuits

(Food Processor, Steel Blade)

In the work bowl combine the flour, sugar, baking powder, salt, and milk powder. Add the butter and pulse until the mixture resembles coarse meal. Combine the water with the beaten egg; with the machine running, slowly add all of the liquid. Run the machine only long enough for the dough to come together.

Turn out onto a floured surface. Add the currants (if desired), kneading them in as little as possible. Proceed as in Cutting and Baking, above.

Yield

Makes 9 to 12 biscuits.

Tea Biscuits

(Dough-Mixing Machine, Flat Beater)

6 cups unbleached all-purpose flour
3/4 cup sugar
4 tablespoons baking powder
1 teaspoon salt
2/3 cup skim milk powder
8 tablespoons (1 stick) unsalted butter or margarine
2 cups cold water
2 eggs, beaten
1 1/2 cups dried currants or raisins (optional)
Flour, for dusting hands and work top
1 egg thinned with 1 to 2 teaspoons water, for egg wash
Shortening, for greasing pans

In the mixing bowl combine the flour, sugar, baking powder, salt, and milk powder. Add the butter and mix until the mixture resembles coarse meal. Add the water and eggs. Pulse with the on/off switch until all the ingredients are absorbed so that the flour will not be thrown out of the bowl. Mix only until the dough becomes cohesive. Knead in the currants (if desired) by hand. Proceed as in Cutting and Baking, above.

Yield

Makes 18 to 24 biscuits.

Scones

Traditional British fare, these rich biscuits are served at teatime with clotted cream (a good substitute is crème fraîche) or just buttered and spread with marmalade. At home we use Dundee brand orange marmalade from Scotland, made with Seville oranges, or Chivers brand conserve, or British ginger marmalade (it has a bite). Richer and less sweet than tea biscuits, scones are best served warm. They can be frozen and reheated.

3 cups unbleached all-purpose flour (see Note)
4 tablespoons sugar
6 tablespoons unsalted butter or margarine
1 1/2 tablespoons baking powder
1/2 teaspoon baking soda
1/2 teaspoon salt
1/4 teaspoon ground cardamom, preferably freshly ground (optional)
1 cup light cream, evaporated skim milk, or plain yogurt
1 egg, lightly beaten
3/4 cup dried currants or raisins (optional)
Flour, for dusting hands and work top
Shortening, for greasing pans

In a large bowl combine the flour and sugar. Cut or rub in the butter until the mixture resembles course meal. Add the baking powder, baking soda, salt, and cardamom; gently sift through the dry ingredients with your fingers. Add the cream and egg. Stir, then add the currants (if desired) and mix only until the flour is absorbed.

Lightly dust your hands with flour. Turn the dough out onto a floured work surface and knead only until it all comes together. The less kneading, the more tender the biscuit.

Cutting

On a clean, floured surface press out or roll out the dough 1/2 to 3/4 inch thick. Cut out with a 2 1/2-inch biscuit cutter or a kitchen glass. Knead the scraps together, roll them out, and cut more scones. You should have 9 to 12 rounds.

BAKER'S SECRET: Save 1/4 of the freshly kneaded dough before rolling out. Incorporate with the scraps for a more tender scone.

Baking

Space the rounds evenly on a lightly greased baking pan. Bake at 400°F until lightly browned and the top does not yield to light pressure from a fingertip (about 15 minutes). Check that the bottom has color.

Yield

Makes 9 to 12 scones.

Note: For whole wheat scones substitute 1 cup whole wheat flour, preferably stone ground.

Variation

In Making, above, separate the dough into 2 balls (4 balls in the dough-mixing machine recipe). Roll or press out into 1/2-inch-thick rounds. Place on lightly greased baking sheets and cut each round into eight wedges. Proceed as in Baking, above.

Scones

(Food Processor, Steel Blade)

In the work bowl combine the flour, sugar, baking powder, baking soda, salt, and cardamom. Add the butter and pulse several times until the mixture resembles coarse meal. Combine the cream and beaten egg; with the machine running, slowly add all of the liquid. Run the machine only long enough for the dough to become together.

Turn out the dough onto a floured surface. Add the currants (if desired), kneading them in as little as possible. Proceed as in Cutting and Baking, above.

Yield

Makes 9 to 12 scones.

Scones

(Dough-Mixing Machine, Flat Beater)

6 cups unbleached all-purpose flour (see Note)
1/2 cup sugar
3 tablespoons baking powder
1 teaspoon baking soda
1 teaspoon salt
1/2 teaspoon ground cardamom, preferably freshly ground (optional)
12 tablespoons (1 1/2 sticks) unsalted butter or margarine, at room temperature
2 cups light cream, evaporated skim milk, or plain yogurt
2 eggs, lightly beaten
1 1/2 cups dried currants or raisins (optional)
Flour, for dusting hands and work top
Shortening, for greasing pans

In the mixing bowl combine the flour, sugar, baking powder, baking soda, salt, and cardamom. Add the butter and mix until the dough resembles coarse meal. Add the cream and eggs. Pulse with the on/off switch only until the flour is absorbed and will not be thrown out of the bowl. Knead in the currants (if desired) by hand. Proceed as in Cutting and Baking, above, except you should have a total of 24 rounds.

Yield

Makes 24 scones.

Note: For whole wheat scones substitute 2 cups whole wheat flour, preferably stone ground, for 2 cups of the all-purpose flour.

Singing Hinny

This is a colorful British name for an offbeat scone. Scones are similar to tea biscuits or shortcakes. A small amount of rice flour makes for an unusual flavor. Literally made up in minutes, these scones can be eaten at breakfast with butter and jam. They also go well with stews. Serve warm.

3 cups unbleached all-purpose flour
1/4 cup rice flour (see Note)
1/4 cup sugar
2 tablespoons baking powder
1/2 teaspoon salt (optional)
2 tablespoons shortening
1 cup milk, evaporated skim milk, or light cream
1 cup dried currants or raisins (optional)
Flour, for dusting work top
Shortening, for greasing pan

In a large bowl combine the flours, sugar, baking powder, and salt (if desired). Cut in the shortening or rub between the fingers until the mixture is grainy. Add the milk and currants (if desired) and mix only until absorbed.

Turn out the dough onto a floured surface and knead once or twice. Cut the dough in half and roll out each half into a circle 1/4 inch thick. Score into 8 pie-shaped wedges. Prick holes all over with a fork, then transfer to a greased skillet or griddle.

Bake on the stovetop over medium heat. Turn and bake until browned on both sides.

Yield

Makes 16 scones.

Note: Rice flour can be purchased in Asian markets and natural foods stores. You can grind your own in a spice mill or blender. Grind very fine.

Variation

Replace the milk with 1 cup buttermilk or yogurt and add 1/4 teaspoon baking soda.

Basic Muffins

2 cups unbleached all-purpose flour
4 teaspoons baking powder
1/2 teaspoon salt
4 tablespoons sugar
4 tablespoons shortening, butter, or margarine, at room temperature
1 egg, beaten
3/4 cup milk
Shortening or butter, for greasing pans

In a large bowl combine the flour, baking powder, salt, and sugar. Cut or rub in the shortening until the mixture resembles coarse meal. Add the egg and milk and mix only until absorbed. Drop out into greased or buttered muffin tins, making each cup about two-thirds full.
Bake in a preheated 375°F oven until browned and the center springs back when gently pressed with the fingers (15 to 20 minutes).

Yield

Makes 9 to 12 muffins.

Variations

Raisin Muffins

Fold in 1/2 to 3/4 cup raisins.

Chocolate Chip Muffins

Fold in 1/2 cup semisweet or sweet chocolate bits.

Nut Muffins

Fold in 1/2 cup coarsely chopped nuts.

Streusel Muffins

Spread with Streusel Topping (recipe follows) before baking.

Streusel Topping

This sweet, crumblike mixture is used to top muffins and coffee cakes before baking.

2/3 cup unbleached all-purpose flour
1/4 cup firmly packed brown sugar
1/4 cup granulated sugar
1/2 teaspoon ground cinnamon
2 tablespoons unsalted butter or margarine, cut up
2 tablespoons vegetable shortening

In a medium bowl mix or rub together, do not cream, all the ingredients until the mixture resembles pea sized or larger granules. If the streusel appears to be too moist, rub in several teaspoons flour. Sprinkle on top of batter and bake as directed in recipe.

Peach Muffins with Streusel Topping

1 1/2 cups unbleached all-purpose flour
1/4 cup granulated sugar
1/4 cup firmly packed brown sugar
1 1/2 tablespoons skim milk powder
4 teaspoons baking powder
1/4 teaspoon salt
1 teaspoon ground cinnamon
1/2 cup shortening, butter, or margarine, at room temperature
1 egg, beaten
1/2 cup water
1 1/4 cups coarsely diced peaches (fresh or canned) or fresh berries
Shortening or butter, for greasing pans

In a large bowl combine the flour, sugars, milk powder, baking powder, salt, and cinnamon. Cut or rub in the shortening until the mixture resembles coarse meal. Add the egg and water and mix only until absorbed. Fold in the peaches. Drop out into greased or buttered muffin tins, making each cup about two-thirds full. Spread with Streusel Topping (page 277). Bake in a preheated 375°F oven until browned and the center springs back when gently pressed with the fingers (15 to 20 minutes).

Yield

Makes 9 to 12 muffins.

Variation

Apple Pecan Muffins

Substitute 3/4 cup diced fresh cooking apples (such as Granny Smith) for the peaches and add 1/2 cup lightly chopped pecans. Spread with Streusel Topping mixed with additional pecans, or top with pecans and dust with granulated sugar or coarse crystal sugar.

Berry Muffins with Streusel

Sustitute fresh or frozen berries for the peaches.

Blueberry Muffins

1 1/2 cups unbleached all-purpose flour
4 tablespoons granulated sugar
4 tablespoons firmly packed brown sugar or granulated sugar
1 1/2 tablespoons skim milk powder
4 teaspoons baking powder
1/2 teaspoon salt
1/2 cup butter (1 stick), margarine, or shortening, at room temperature
1 egg, beaten
Grated zest and juice of 1/2 lemon
1/2 cup water
3/4 cup blueberries, preferably fresh, dredged lightly with flour
Shortening, for greasing pans
Granulated or confectioners' sugar, for dusting

In a large bowl combine the flour, sugars, milk powder, baking powder, and salt. Cut or rub in the butter until the mixture resembles coarse meal. Add the egg, lemon zest and juice, and water; mix only until absorbed. Fold in the berries. Drop out into greased muffin tins, making each cup about two-thirds full. Dust with granulated sugar.

Bake in a preheated 375°F oven until browned and the center springs back when gently pressed with the fingers (15 to 20 minutes).

Yield

Makes 9 muffins.

Variation

Cranberry Muffins

Substitute 1 cup cranberries (fresh or frozen) for the blueberries. You can freeze your own cranberries in plastic bags for use throughout the year. Simply place them in the freezer in the plastic pouch in which they are sold.

Blueberry Corn Muffins

1 cup unbleached all-purpose flour
1 cup cornmeal, preferably stone ground
1/3 cup sugar
2 1/2 teaspoons baking powder
1/2 teaspoon salt
6 tablespoons shortening, butter, or margarine, at room temperature
1 egg, beaten
1 cup buttermilk
1 1/2 cups blueberries, dredged in a little flour
Shortening or butter, for greasing pans

In a large bowl combine the flour, cornmeal, sugar, baking powder, and salt. Cut or rub in the shortening until the mixture resembles coarse meal. Add the egg and buttermilk and mix only until absorbed. Fold in the berries. Drop out into greased or buttered muffin tins, making each cup two-thirds full.

Bake in a preheated 375°F oven until browned and the center springs back when gently pressed with the fingers (15 to 20 minutes).

Yield

Makes 9 to 12 muffins.

Adele's Bran Muffins

These low-fat, low-sodium, high-fiber muffins are quick and easy to make and take only 20 minutes to bake. The recipe contains no added fat and, if made with 2 egg whites or an egg substitute and without nuts, there is no cholesterol and no fat. There is also no refined sugar; I prefer the tang that molasses imparts. Unbaked batter can be kept in the refrigerator for a week, then the muffins baked as directed in the recipe.

1/3 cup skim milk powder
1 1/3 cups water
2 egg whites, or 1 egg, beaten, or egg substitute
2 cups unprocessed bran
1/2 cup molasses or honey
1 cup unbleached all-purpose flour
1 teaspoon salt (optional)
1 teaspoon baking soda
1/3 cup raisins, or more to taste
1/3 cup walnuts (optional)
Flour, for dredging nuts raisins and nuts
Shortening, for greasing pans

In a large bowl dissolve the milk powder in the water. Mix in the egg, bran, and molasses, and let stand for several minutes while the bran absorbs the liquid.

In another bowl combine the flour, salt (if desired), and baking soda. Gently stir together with your fingertips. Add to the molasses mixture and mix with a wooden spoon only until the dry ingredients are absorbed. The mixture will be thick. Lightly dredge the raisins and nuts (if used) in flour and fold into the batter.

Drop out the mixture into greased muffin tins, making each cup two-thirds full. If you like larger muffins, fill each cup almost to the top.

BAKER'S SECRET: Place 1 to 2 tablespoons water in any empty muffin cups to keep them from scorching in the oven.

Baking

Place the muffin tins on a baking sheet in a preheated 375° oven and bake until the muffins develop a dark brown color (15 to 20 minutes); a light touch with your finger in the center of a muffin should not leave a depression; the muffin should have a firm feel and spring back. Test several muffins in case your oven bakes unevenly. If necessary bake for an additional 5 minutes. Let cool for 5 minutes in the tins, then remove from the tins and let cool completely on a wire rack. The muffins can be refrigerated or frozen. They will keep for several days in a plastic bag in the bread box.

Yield

Makes 12 regular muffins or 9 jumbo muffins.

Variations

Buttermilk Bran Muffins

Substitute buttermilk or sour milk in place of water and skim milk powder. (My favorite!)

Chocolate Bran Muffins

For a unique flavor, add 4 heaping tablespoons cocoa powder to the dry mixture.

Orange Bran Muffins

Add 2 tablespoons orange marmalade to the liquid mixture. I like Scottish marmalade made with Seville oranges.

Adele's Bran Muffins

(Food Processor, Steel Blade)

In the work bowl combine all the ingredients. Pulse several times but only until all the ingredients are blended.

Drop out the mixture into greased muffin tins, making each cup two-thirds full. If you like larger muffins, fill each cup almost to the top.

Proceed as in Baking, above.

Yield

Makes 12 regular muffins or 9 jumbo muffins.

Adele's Bran Muffins

(Dough-Mixing Machine, Flat Beater)

1 cup skim milk powder
4 cups water
6 egg whites, or 3 eggs, beaten, or egg substitute
6 cups unprocessed bran
1 1/2 cups molasses or honey
3 teaspoons baking soda
3 teaspoons salt (optional)
3 cups unbleached all-purpose flour
1 cup raisins
1 cup walnuts (optional)
Flour, for dredging raisins and nuts
Shortening, for greasing pans

In the mixing bowl dissolve the milk powder in the water. Mix in the egg whites, bran, and molasses, and let stand for several minutes while the bran absorbs the liquid. Gently stir the baking soda and salt (if used) into the flour using your fingertips, then add to the molasses mixture. Pulse with the on/off switch only until absorbed. The mixture will be thick. Lightly dredge the raisins and nuts (if used) in flour, then fold into the batter.
Drop out the mixture into greased muffin tins, making each cup two-thirds full. If you like larger muffins, fill each cup almost to the top.
Proceed as in Baking, above.

Yield

Makes 36 regular muffins or 27 jumbo muffins.

Rich Bran Muffins

These muffins are better than cake. Baking them in paper-lined mini-muffin tins turns brunch or breakfast into party time. Serve with miniature corn muffins for a decorative table. Unused batter can be kept in the refrigerator for a week and muffins baked as desired.

3/4 cup vegetable oil
1/2 cup beaten egg
1/4 cup beaten yolks
1/2 cup water
3/4 cup sugar
1 1/3 cups unprocessed bran
1 teaspoon vanilla extract
1 cup cake flour
1 tablespoon skim milk powder
3 teaspoons baking soda
1 teaspoon salt
1/3 cup raisins
Shortening, for greasing pans
Flour, for dredging raisins

In a large bowl mix together the oil, egg, egg yolks, water, sugar, bran, and vanilla; let stand for several minutes while the bran absorbs the liquid.

In another bowl combine the flour, milk powder, baking soda, and salt; gently stir with the fingertips. Add to the egg mixture and stir until absorbed.

Dropping

Lightly dredge the raisins in flour and fold into the batter. Drop out the batter into a greased or paper-lined muffin tin, making each cup two-thirds full. If you like larger muffins, fill each cup almost to the top.

BAKER'S SECRET: Place 1 to 2 tablespoons water in the empty cups to keep them from scorching in the oven. Use minimuffin tins for party-sized muffins.

Baking

Place the muffin tins on a baking sheet in a preheated 375° oven and bake until the muffins are browned (15 to 20 minutes). A light touch with your finger in the center of a muffin should not leave a depression. Let cool for 5 minutes in the tins, then turn out of the tins and let cool completely on a wire rack. The muffins can be refrigerated or frozen. They will keep for several days in a plastic bag in the bread box.

Yield

12 regular muffins or 9 jumbo muffins.

Rich Bran Muffins

(Food Processor, Steel Blade)

In a medium bowl combine the oil, egg, egg yolks, water and vanilla. In the work bowl combine the sugar, bran, flour, milk powder, baking soda, and salt; pulse to combine. With the machine running slowly, add the egg mixture and mix just until absorbed. Do not overmix.

Proceed as in Dropping and Baking, above.

Yield

12 regular muffins or 9 jumbo muffins.

Rich Bran Muffins

(Dough-Mixing Machine, Flat Beater)

2 1/4 cups vegetable oil
1 1/2 cups beaten egg
3/4 cup beaten egg yolks
1 1/2 cups water
2 1/4 cups sugar
4 cups unprocessed bran
1 tablespoon vanilla extract
3 cups cake flour
3 tablespoons skim milk powder
3 tablespoons baking soda
1 tablespoon salt
1 cup raisins
Shortening, for greasing pans
Flour, for dredging raisins

In the mixing bowl combine the oil, egg, egg yolks, water, sugar, bran, and vanilla, and let stand for several minutes while the bran absorbs the liquid. In a separate bowl combine the flour, milk powder, baking soda, and salt; gently stir with the fingertips, then add to the egg mixture and mix only until absorbed. Proceed as in Dropping and Baking, above.

Yield

Makes 36 regular muffins or 27 jumbo muffins.

Corn Muffins

These muffins bake up into beautiful golden-colored cakes with a slightly gritty texture that makes them so distinctive and popular. They can be baked in muffin tins or as sticks in special corn-shaped pans. If you prefer corn bread, an 8-inch square pan will be perfect for one recipe; bake as directed for muffins. These muffins are not as sweet as store-bought. On a recent visit to New England I was served corn bread that had the sugar completely omitted; I learned that many New Englanders prefer their corn bread this way.

1 cup yellow cornmeal, preferably stone ground
1 cup unbleached all-purpose flour
1/4 cup sugar
1/3 cup skim milk powder (omit for nondairy recipe)
1 teaspoon salt
4 teaspoons baking powder
2 tablespoons unsalted butter, margarine, or shortening, at room temperature
1 egg, beaten
1 cup water
Shortening, for greasing pans

In a large bowl combine the cornmeal, flour, sugar, milk powder (if used), salt, and baking powder. Cut or rub in the butter until the mixture resembles coarse meal. Add the egg and water; stir only until absorbed. Do not overmix.

Dropping

Grease muffin tins or corn-stick pans. (You can use an 8-inch square cake pan instead.) Cast iron pans should be prewarmed, then greased and filled. Drop out the batter into the tins, making each cup three-quarters full.

Baking

Bake in a preheated oven at 425°F until browned (about 20 minutes). The centers should feel firm and spring back when lightly touched with a fingertip. Let cool for 5 minutes in the tins, then remove to a wire rack to cool completely. The muffins can be refrigerated or frozen. They keep for several days in a plastic bag in the bread box.

Yield

Makes 9 to 12 muffins.

Corn Muffins

(Food Processor, Steel Blade)

In the work bowl combine the cornmeal, flour, sugar, milk powder (if used), salt, and baking powder. Mix in the butter until the mixture resembles coarse meal. While pulsing add the egg and water and mix only until they are absorbed. Do not overmix.

Proceed as in Dropping and Baking, above.

Yield

Makes 9 to 12 muffins.

Corn Muffins

(Dough-Mixing Machine, Flat Beater)

This recipe can be doubled if desired. The batter can be refrigerated for up to a week, but the muffins won't puff up quite as high when baked.

2 cups yellow cornmeal, preferably fine stone ground
2 cups unbleached all-purpose flour
1/2 cup sugar
2/3 cup skim milk powder (omit for nondairy recipe)
2 teaspoons salt
8 teaspoons baking powder
4 tablespoons unsalted butter, margarine, or shortening, at room temperature
2 eggs, beaten
2 cups water
Shortening, for greasing pans

In the mixing bowl combine the cornmeal, flour, sugar, milk powder (if used), salt, and baking powder. Mix in the butter until the mixture resembles coarse meal. Add the eggs and water slowly and mix only until absorbed. Do not overmix. Proceed as in Dropping and Baking, above.

Yield

Makes 18 to 24 muffins.

Crunchy Corn Muffins

These muffins bake out sweet and crunchy. Use medium-coarse or coarse cornmeal, if available.

Shortening, for greasing muffin tins
1/2 cup medium-coarse yellow cornmeal, plus more for dusting muffins
1 1/2 cups unbleached all-purpose flour
4 teaspoons baking powder
1/2 teaspoon salt
4 tablespoons sugar
4 tablespoons unsalted butter, margarine, or shortening, at room temperature
1 egg, beaten
3/4 cup milk or water

Prepare well-greased muffin tins. Place 1 tablespoon cornmeal in each cup. Cover, invert, and shake so that the cornmeal coats the bottom and sides of each cup. Tap out any excess.

Drop out the batter with a spoon, filling each cup two-thirds full. Dust the tops of the muffins by sprinkling lightly with extra cornmeal. Proceed as in Baking, above.

BAKER'S SECRET: When making a double batch, place the cornmeal in each cup of the first muffin tin. Invert a second greased tin over the first. While holding the tins together, turn over and shake. Both tins will become coated. Tap out the excess.

Yield

Makes about 9 muffins.

Cajun Corn Muffins

Add a bit of Louisiana spice to your barbecue with these zesty muffins.

1 cup yellow cornmeal
1/2 cup unbleached all-purpose flour
1 tablespoon sugar
1 teaspoon salt
3 teaspoons baking powder
1/2 teaspoon baking soda
2 tablespoons vegetable oil
2 eggs, beaten
1/2 cup kernel corn, fresh cooked or canned and drained
1/4 cup chopped green onion
1/4 teaspoon Louisiana Hot Sauce, or more to taste
3/4 cup buttermilk
Shortening, for greasing pans

In a large bowl place the cornmeal, flour, sugar, salt, baking powder, and baking soda; stir to combine. Add the oil, eggs, corn, green onion, hot sauce, and buttermilk; mix until absorbed.

Dropping

Grease muffin tins or corn-stick pans. (You can use an 8- or 9-inch square cake pan instead.) Cast-iron pans should be prewarmed, then greased and filled. Drop out the batter into the tins, making each cup three-quarters full.

Baking

Bake in a preheated oven at 425°F until browned (about 20 minutes). The centers should feel firm and spring back when lightly touched with a fingertip. Let the muffins cool for 5 minutes in the tins, then remove to a wire rack to cool completely. (Serve the bread from the pan.) The muffins can be refrigerated or frozen. Serve warm.

Yield

Makes 9 to 12 muffins.

Cajun Corn Muffins

(Food Processor, Steel Blade)

In the work bowl place the cornmeal, flour, sugar, salt, baking powder, and baking soda; stir to combine. Mix in the oil, eggs, corn, green onion, and hot sauce. While pulsing add the buttermilk; mix only until absorbed.

Proceed as in Dropping and Baking, above.

Yield

Makes 9 to 12 muffins.

Cajun Corn Muffins

(Dough-Mixing Machine, Flat Beater)

3 cups yellow cornmeal
1 1/2 cups unbleached all-purpose flour
3 tablespoons sugar
1 tablespoon salt
3 tablespoons baking powder
1 1/2 teaspoons baking soda
6 tablespoons vegetable oil
6 eggs, beaten
1 1/2 cups kernel corn, cooked fresh or canned and drained
3/4 cup chopped green onion
3/4 teaspoon Louisiana Hot Sauce, or more to taste
2 1/4 cups buttermilk
Shortening, for greasing pans

In the mixing bowl place the cornmeal, flour, sugar, salt, baking powder, and baking soda; stir to combine. Add the oil, eggs, corn, green onion, hot sauce, and buttermilk; mix until absorbed. Proceed as in Dropping and Baking, above.

Yield

Makes 27 to 36 muffins.

Corn and Molasses Muffins

1 cup cornmeal
3/4 cup unbleached all-purpose flour
3 tablespoons skim milk powder
3 teaspoons baking powder
1/2 teaspoon baking soda
1/2 teaspoon salt
1 tablespoon unsalted butter, margarine, or shortening, at room temperature
1 egg, beaten
1/4 cup molasses
3/4 cup water
Shortening, for greasing pans

In a large bowl combine the cornmeal, flour, milk powder, baking powder, baking soda, and salt. Cut or rub in the butter until the mixture resembles coarse meal. Add the egg, molasses, and water. Mix with a wooden spoon only until absorbed. Drop out the mixture into a greased muffin tin.

Dropping

Grease muffin tins or corn-stick pans. (You can use an 8-inch square cake pan instead.) Cast-iron pans should be prewarmed, then greased and filled. Drop out the batter into the tins, making each cup three-quarters full.

Baking

Bake in a preheated oven at 375°F until browned (about 20 minutes). The centers should feel firm and spring back when lightly touched with a fingertip. Let cool for 5 minutes in the tins, then remove to a wire rack to cool completely. The muffins can be refrigerated or frozen. They keep for several days in a plastic bag in the bread box.

Yield

Makes 9 to 12 muffins.

Corn and Molasses Muffins

(Food Processor, Steel Blade)

In the work bowl place the cornmeal, flour, milk powder, baking powder, baking soda, and salt. Stir to distribute. Add the butter and pulse until the mixture resembles coarse meal. While pulsing add the egg, molasses, and water and mix only until they are absorbed. Do not overmix.

Proceed as in Dropping and Baking, above.

Yield

Makes 9 to 12 muffins.

Corn and Molasses Muffins

(Dough-Mixing Machine, Flat Beater)

This recipe can be doubled if desired. The batter can be refrigerated for up to a week, but the muffins won't puff up quite as high when baked.

2 cups cornmeal
1 1/2 cups unbleached all-purpose flour
6 tablespoons skim milk powder
2 tablespoons baking powder
1 teaspoon baking soda
1 teaspoon salt
2 tablespoons unsalted butter, margarine, or shortening, at room temperature
2 eggs, beaten
1/2 cup molasses
1 1/2 cups water
Shortening, for greasing pans

In the mixing bowl combine the cornmeal, flour, milk powder, baking powder, baking soda, and salt. Mix in the butter until the mixture resembles coarse meal. Slowly add the eggs, molasses, and water and mix only until absorbed. Do not overmix. Proceed as in Dropping and Baking, above.

Yield

Makes 18 to 24 muffins.

Adele's Oat Bran Muffins

These muffins bake out light and fluffy, taste sweet but contain no refined sugar, and are low in sodium. Oats have much greater nutritional value than wheat or most other grains. They are higher in protein and contain significant amounts of vitamins and minerals. Oat bran is high in fiber. This recipe contains no added fat and, if made with 2 egg whites or an egg substitute and without nuts, has no cholesterol or fat.

1 1/3 cups buttermilk or sour milk (see Note)
2 egg whites, or 1 egg, beaten, or egg substitute
2 cups oat bran
1/2 cup molasses
1 cup all-purpose flour
1 teaspoon baking soda
1/3 cup raisins
1/3 cup chopped walnuts (optional)
Flour, for dredging raisins and nuts
Shortening, for greasing pans

In a large bowl combine the buttermilk, egg whites, oat bran, and molasses. Allow to stand for several minutes while the bran absorbs the liquid.

In a small bowl combine the flour and baking soda. Gently stir together with your fingertips. Add to the buttermilk mixture and stir with a wooden spoon only until the dry ingredients are absorbed. Dredge the raisins and nuts (if used) in the flour and fold into the batter.

Dropping

Drop the mixture into greased muffin tins, making each cup two-thirds full.

Baking

Bake in a preheated 375° oven until browned (about 20 minutes). A light touch with a finger in the center of a muffin should not leave a depression. It should have a firm feel and spring back. Let cool for 5 minutes in the tins, then turn out cool completely on a wire rack. The muffins keep well in a plastic bag and can be refrigerated or frozen.

Yield

Makes 12 muffins.

Note: To make sour milk, combine 1 1/3 cups skim milk and 1 teaspoon vinegar. Let stand until clabbered (10 minutes).

Variations

Whole Grain Oat Bran Muffins

Substitute 1 cup whole wheat flour (preferably stone ground) for the 1 cup all-purpose flour. (Substitute 3 cups whole wheat flour for the 3 cups all-purpose flour in the dough-mixing machine recipe.) This will result in a whole grain muffin of exceptional flavor and high fiber content. We prefer this version in our house and it might become your favorite.

Adele's Oat Bran Muffins

(Food Processor, Steel Blade)

In the work bowl combine the buttermilk, egg whites, oat bran, and molasses. Pulse until blended. Add the flour and baking soda and mix only until absorbed. Dredge the raisins and nuts (if used) in the flour and fold into the batter.

Proceed as in Dropping and Baking, above.

Yield

Makes 12 muffins.

Adele's Oat Bran Muffins

(Dough-Mixing Machine, Flat Beater)

4 cups buttermilk or sour milk (see Note)
6 egg whites, or 3 eggs, beaten, or egg substitute
6 cups oat bran
1 1/2 cups molasses
3 cups all-purpose flour
3 teaspoons baking soda
1 cup raisins
1 cup chopped walnuts (optional)
Flour, for dredging raisins and nuts
Shortening, for greasing pans

In the mixing bowl combine the buttermilk, egg whites, oat bran, and molasses. Allow to stand for several minutes while the bran absorbs the liquid. Add the flour and baking soda and gently stir together with your fingertips, then mix only until the dry ingredients are absorbed. Dredge the raisins and nuts (if used) in the flour and fold into the batter.

Dropping

Drop out the batter into greased muffin tins, making each cup two-thirds full. For jumbo muffins, fill each cup to the top. Proceed as in Baking, above.

Yield

Makes 36 regular muffins or 27 jumbo muffins.

Note: To make sour milk, combine 4 cups skim milk and 3 teaspoons vinegar. Let stand until clabbered (10 minutes).

Oatmeal Muffins

Oats and raisins are used in cereal and in cookies, why not muffins? These have a good flavor, they stay soft and moist, make a nutritious breakfast accompaniment, and stand well by themselves as a snack or dessert.

1 cup unbleached all-purpose flour
1 cup rolled oats (not instant)
1/4 cup firmly packed brown sugar
1 teaspoon baking powder
1/2 teaspoon baking soda
1/4 teaspoon salt
1/3 cup skim milk powder
1/3 cup unsalted butter, margarine, or shortening, at room temperature
1 cup water
1 egg, beaten, or egg substitute
1/2 cup raisins
Flour, for dredging raisins
Shortening, for greasing pans

In a large bowl combine the flour, oats, brown sugar, baking powder, baking soda, salt, and milk powder. Cut or rub in the butter until the mixture resembles coarse meal. Add the water and egg and mix with a wooden spoon only until the dry ingredients are absorbed. Dredge the raisins with the flour and fold into the batter.

Dropping

Grease muffin tins or corn-stick pans. (You can use an 8-inch square cake pan instead.) Cast-iron pans should be prewarmed, then greased and filled. Drop out the mixture into the greased tin, making each cup two-thirds full. If you like larger muffins fill each cup almost to the top. Add a little water to the empty cups to prevent scorching.

Baking

Bake in a preheated oven at 375°F until browned (about 20 minutes). The centers should feel firm and spring back when lightly touched with a fingertip. Let cool in the tins for 5 minutes, then remove to a wire rack to cool completely. The muffins can be refrigerated or frozen. They keep for several days in a plastic bag in the bread box.

Yield

Makes 12 regular muffins or 9 jumbo muffins.

Variation

Oatmeal Muffins with Cooked Oatmeal

These muffins are made with leftover cooked oatmeal. Substitute 1 cup cooked oatmeal for the 1 cup rolled oats (2 cups in the dough-mixing machine recipe). Decrease the water to 3/4 cup (1 1/2 cups in the dough-mixing machine recipe). Decrease the milk powder to 1/4 cup (1/2 cup in the dough-mixing machine recipe).

Oatmeal Muffins

(Food Processor, Steel Blade)

In the work bowl combine the flour, oats, brown sugar, baking powder, baking soda, salt, and milk powder. Mix in the butter until the mixture resembles coarse meal. While pulsing add the water and egg and mix only until the dry ingredients are absorbed. Do not overmix. Dredge the raisins with the flour and fold into the batter. Proceed as in Dropping and Baking, above.

Yield

Makes 12 regular muffins or 9 jumbo muffins.

Oatmeal Muffins

(Dough-Mixing Machine, Flat Beater)

2 cups unbleached all-purpose flour
2 cups rolled oats (not instant)
1/2 cup firmly packed brown sugar
2/3 cup skim milk powder
2 teaspoons baking powder
1 teaspoon baking soda
1/2 teaspoon salt
2/3 cup unsalted butter, margarine, or shortening, at room temperature
2 cups water
2 eggs, beaten, or egg substitute
1 cup raisins
Flour, for dredging raisins
Shortening, for greasing pans

In the mixing bowl combine the flour, oats, brown sugar, milk powder, baking powder, baking soda, and salt. Mix in the butter until the mixture resembles coarse meal. Add the water and egg and mix at slow speed only until the dry ingredients are absorbed. Dredge the raisins with the flour and fold into the batter. Proceed as in Dropping and Baking, above.

Yield

Makes 24 regular muffins or 18 jumbo muffins.

Chapter Nine

Quick Breads

Quick breads are breads and loaves that are raised with baking powder and/or baking soda. They range from true breads, such as Irish Soda Bread (page 301), to sweet tea cakes and loaves, such as Rich Carrot Loaf (page 325) and Zucchini Bread (page 341). These quick breads are so named because they are mixed and baked immediately, requiring no fermentation or rising time. Most recipes will make two loaves when using 8- to 9-inch loaf pans. Fill the pans two-thirds to three-quarters full. Any leftover batter can be dropped out and baked in muffin tins, and baked for a shorter time.

Quick Bran Bread

A nutritious, whole-grain quick bread, Bran Bread is made with buttermilk and molasses, which results in a zesty flavor. Nut meats enrich the flavor and add crunch to the bread. Here's a loaf that can enrich your family's diet while they enjoy a tasty treat.

2 cups unprocessed bran
1 1/3 cups buttermilk
1 egg, beaten
1/2 cup molasses
2 tablespoons unsalted butter or margarine, melted
1 cup unbleached all-purpose flour
1/2 teaspoon salt
1 teaspoon baking soda
1/2 teaspoon grated lemon zest
1/2 cup chopped walnuts or pecans (optional)
1/2 cup raisins (optional)
Flour, for dredging nuts and raisins
Shortening, for greasing pans
Flour, for dusting pans

In a large bowl combine the bran, buttermilk, egg, molasses, and butter. Allow a few minutes for the bran to absorb the liquids. In another bowl combine the flour, salt, baking soda, and lemon zest. Add to the bran mixture, mixing only long enough to incorporate. Dredge the nuts and raisins (you may wish to use either or both) in a little flour and fold into the batter. Grease two 8- or 9-inch loaf pans, then line them with parchment or waxed paper and grease and flour-dust the bottom. Turn out the batter into the prepared pans.

Baking

Bake in a preheated 350°F oven until browned (45 to 60 minutes). The center should feel firm when gently pressed with your fingertips. Let cool for 5 to 10 minutes in the pan, then remove to a wire rack to cool completely. This bread is best when used fresh, although it freezes well. It can be toasted for extra crunch.

Yield

Makes 2 loaves.

Variation

Oat Bran Bread

Substitute oat bran for the unprocessed bran.

Quick Bran Bread

(Food Processor, Steel Blade)

Bran Bread is so easy to make by hand that it may not warrant using and cleaning the food processor. If you choose to do so, follow these directions.

In the work bowl combine the bran, buttermilk, egg, molasses, butter, flour, salt, baking soda, and zest. Pulse only until combined. Dredge the nuts and raisins (if used) in the flour and fold into the batter. Grease two 8- or 9-inch loaf pans, then line them with parchment or waxed paper and grease and flour-dust the bottom. Turn out the batter into the prepared pans. Proceed as in Baking, above.

Quick Bran Bread

(Dough-Mixing Machine, Flat Beater)

4 cups unprocessed bran
2 2/3 cups buttermilk
2 eggs, beaten
1 cup molasses
4 tablespoons butter or margarine
2 cups unbleached all-purpose flour
1 teaspoon salt
2 teaspoons baking soda
1 teaspoon grated lemon zest
1 cup chopped walnuts or pecans (optional)
1 cup raisins (optional)
Flour, for dredging nuts and raisins and dusting pan
Shortening, for greasing pan

In the mixing bowl combine the bran, buttermilk, eggs, molasses, and butter. Allow a few minutes for the bran to absorb the liquids. Combine the flour, salt, baking soda, and lemon zest and add to the bran mixture. Mix only long enough to incorporate.

Dredge the nuts and raisins (you may wish to use either or both) in the flour and fold into the batter. Grease four 8- or 9-inch loaf pans, then line them with parchment or waxed paper and grease and flour-dust the bottom. Turn out the batter into the prepared pans. Proceed as in Baking, above.

Yield

Makes 4 loaves.

Buttermilk Whole Grain Bread

1 1/2 cups unbleached all-purpose flour
1/2 cup whole wheat flour, preferably stone ground
1/2 cup wheat germ
1/2 teaspoon salt
1 teaspoon baking soda
1 tablespoon sugar
1 tablespoon unsalted butter or margarine, melted
1 egg, beaten
1 1/2 cups buttermilk
Grated zest and juice of 1/2 lemon
1/2 cup chopped walnuts (optional)
Flour, for dredging nuts and dusting pan
Shortening, for greasing pan

In a large bowl combine the flours, wheat germ, salt, baking soda, sugar, and butter. Add the egg, buttermilk, and lemon; mix only until absorbed. Dredge the nuts (if used) in the flour and fold into the batter. Grease an 8- or 9-inch loaf pan, then line it with parchment or waxed paper and grease and flour-dust the bottom. Turn out the batter into the prepared pan.

Baking

Bake in a preheated 350°F oven until browned (35 to 45 minutes). The center should feel firm when gently pressed with your fingertips. Let cool in the pan for 5 to 10 minutes, then remove to wire racks to cool completely.

Yield

Makes 1 loaf.

Buttermilk Whole Grain Bread

(Food Processor, Steel Blade)

In the work bowl combine the flours, wheat germ, salt, baking soda, sugar and butter. Add the egg, buttermilk, and lemon; mix only until absorbed. Dredge the nuts (if used) in the flour and fold into the batter. Grease an 8- or 9-inch loaf pan, then line it with parchment or waxed paper and grease and flour-dust the bottom. Turn out the batter into the prepared pan and proceed as in Baking, above.

Buttermilk Whole Grain Bread

(Dough-Mixing Machine, Flat Beater)

3 cups unbleached all-purpose flour
1 cup whole wheat flour, preferably stone ground
1 cup wheat germ
1 teaspoon salt
2 teaspoons baking soda
2 tablespoons sugar
2 tablespoons unsalted butter or margarine, melted
2 eggs, beaten
3 cups buttermilk
Grated zest and juice of 1 lemon
1 cup chopped walnuts (optional)
Flour, for dredging nuts and dusting pan
Shortening, for greasing pan

In the mixing bowl combine the flours, wheat germ, salt, baking soda, sugar and butter. Add the egg, buttermilk, and lemon; mix only until absorbed. Dredge the nuts (if used) in the flour and fold into the batter. Grease two 8- or 9-inch loaf pans, then line them with parchment or waxed paper and grease and flour-dust the bottom. Turn out the batter into the prepared pans and proceed as in Baking, above.

Yield

Makes 2 loaves.

Irish Soda Bread

When Irish soda bread comes to mind, I picture a fireplace with a crackling flame and bread being baked in a heavy iron pot sitting on a bed of coals directly on the hearth, the recessed lid of the pot covered with a shovel full of hot ash. There is a hearty aroma of meat and potatoes. Whenever the mood comes upon me, it is easy to whip up a batch of Irish Soda Bread. This recipe is simple to make: It is done in one step—all the ingredients are mixed in one bowl.

4 cups unbleached all-purpose flour
2 tablespoons sugar
4 tablespoons unsalted butter or shortening
1 teaspoon baking soda
1 teaspoon salt
1 1/3 cups buttermilk or sour milk (see Note)
1 egg, beaten
3/4 cup dried currants or raisins
1 tablespoon caraway seeds (optional)
Flour, for dusting work top and bread

In a large bowl combine the flour and sugar. Cut in the butter or rub between the fingers until the mixture resembles coarse meal. Add the baking soda and salt and gently stir with your fingers. Add the buttermilk, egg, currants, and caraway seeds (if used); mix until smooth. Turn out the dough onto a floured work surface.

Shaping

Shape the dough into a ball, smooth side up, and gently press the top down. Sift or dust flour over the top and place on an ungreased baking sheet, an 8-inch pie pan or cake pan, or a cast-iron skillet. Cut two 1/4-inch slashes from end to end in the form of a cross. The cuts will expand in the oven and give the bread its traditional shape.

Baking

Bake in a preheated 375°F oven until the crust feels firm when touched lightly in the center with your fingertips (about 45 minutes). Be careful not to penetrate the crust with your finger. If the center is still soft, continue baking for 5 to 10 minutes more.

Yield

Makes 1 loaf.

Note: To make sour milk, combine 1 1/3 cups skim milk and 1 teaspoon vinegar.

Irish Soda Bread

(Food Processor, Steel Blade)

In the work bowl combine the flour, sugar, baking soda, salt, and butter. Pulse several times until the mixture resembles coarse meal. Add the milk and beaten egg and pulse until all is absorbed (about 30 seconds). Do not overmix.

Turn out the dough onto a floured surface, sprinkle with the currants and caraway seeds (if used), and shape into a ball. Proceed as in Baking, above.

Irish Soda Bread

(Dough-Mixing Machine, Flat Beater)

2 2/3 cups buttermilk or sour milk (see Note)
2 eggs, beaten
8 cups unbleached all-purpose flour
4 tablespoons sugar
1/2 cup (1 stick) unsalted butter or shortening
2 teaspoons baking soda
2 teaspoons salt
2 tablespoons caraway seeds (optional)
1 1/2 cups dried currants or raisins
Flour, for dusting work top and bread

In the mixing bowl combine the buttermilk and eggs; add the flour and baking soda and stir gently with your fingertips. Add the sugar, butter, salt, and caraway seeds (if used). Pulse by turning the switch on and off quickly until the flour is absorbed and will not be thrown out of the bowl. Mix at the first speed until smooth. Add the currants and mix just long enough to incorporate. If they are overmixed they will be crushed and their color will run into the dough. If it takes more than a few turns to incorporate the currants, knead them in by hand on the work surface.

Turn out the dough and divide in half. Proceed as in Shaping and Baking, above.

Yield

Makes 2 loaves.

Note: To make sour milk, combine 2 2/3 cups skim milk and 2 teaspoons vinegar.

Whole Wheat Irish Soda Bread

Irish Soda Bread made with whole wheat flour is nutritious and has a sweet, nutty flavor. Try it for yourself and decide which one you prefer.

2 cups whole wheat flour, preferably stone ground
2 cups unbleached all-purpose flour
3 tablespoons sugar
4 tablespoons unsalted butter or shortening
1 teaspoon baking soda
1 teaspoon salt
1 1/3 cups buttermilk or sour milk (see Note)
1 egg, beaten
3/4 cup dried currants or raisins
1 tablespoon caraway seeds (optional)
Flour, for dusting work top and bread

In a large bowl combine the flours and sugar. Cut in the butter or rub between your fingers until the mixture resembles coarse meal. Add the baking soda and salt and gently stir with your fingers. Add the buttermilk, egg, currants, and caraway seeds (if used) and stir until smooth. Turn out the dough onto a floured work surface.

Shaping

Shape the dough into a ball, smooth side up, and gently press the top down. Sift or dust all-purpose flour over the top and place on an ungreased baking sheet, an 8-inch pie pan or cake pan, or a cast-iron skillet. Cut two 1/4-inch slashes from end to end in the form of a cross. The cuts will expand in the oven and give the bread its traditional shape.

Baking

Bake in a preheated 375°F oven until the crust feels firm when lightly touched in the center with your fingertips (about 45 minutes). Be careful not to penetrate the crust with your finger. If the center is still soft, continue baking for 5 to 10 minutes more.

Yield

Makes 1 loaf.

Note: To make sour milk, combine 1 1/3 cups skim milk and 1 teaspoon vinegar.

Whole Wheat Irish Soda Bread

(Food Processor, Steel Blade)

In the work bowl combine the flours, sugar, butter, baking soda, and salt. Pulse until the mixture resembles coarse meal. Add the milk and beaten egg and pulse until all is absorbed, then pulse for 30 seconds. Do not overmix. Turn out onto a floured surface and sprinkle with the currants and caraway seeds (if used). Proceed as in Shaping and Baking, above.

Whole Wheat Irish Soda Bread

(Dough-Mixing Machine, Flat Beater)

2 2/3 cups buttermilk or sour milk (see Note)
2 eggs, beaten
4 cups whole wheat flour, preferably stone ground
4 cups unbleached all-purpose flour
6 tablespoons sugar
1/2 cup (1 stick) unsalted butter or shortening
2 teaspoons baking soda
2 teaspoons salt
1 1/2 cups dried currants or raisins
2 tablespoons caraway seeds (optional)
Flour, for dusting work top

In the mixing bowl combine the buttermilk, eggs, flours, sugar, butter, baking soda, and salt. Gently stir the flours and baking soda with your fingertips to distribute. Mix by pulsing until the flour is absorbed and will not be thrown out of the bowl. Mix at the first speed until smooth. Add the currants and caraway seeds (if used) and mix just long enough to incorporate. If the currants are overmixed they will be crushed and their color will run into the dough. If it takes more than a few turns to incorporate the currants, knead them in by hand on the work surface.

Turn out the dough and divide it in half. Proceed as in Shaping and Baking, above.

Yield

Makes 2 loaves.

Note: To make sour milk, combine 2 2/3 cups skim milk and 2 teaspoons vinegar.

Quick Irish Soda Bread

Authentic and easy, Irish soda bread in its simplest form is made up of milk, flour, soda, and salt. It contains no added sugar or fat. Here is a treat that is guilt free. Caraway seeds give the bread its distinctive flavor.

2 cups buttermilk or sour milk (see Note)
4 cups unbleached all-purpose flour
1 teaspoon baking soda
1 1/2 teaspoons salt
3/4 cup dried currants or raisins
1 tablespoon caraway seeds (optional)
Flour, for dusting work top and bread

In a large bowl combine all the ingredients and stir until smooth. Turn out the dough onto a floured work surface.

Shaping

Shape the dough into a ball, smooth side up, and gently press the top down. Sift or dust flour over the top and place on an ungreased baking sheet, an 8-inch pie pan or cake pan, or a cast-iron skillet. Cut two 1/4-inch slashes from end to end in the form of a cross. The cuts will expand in the oven and give the bread its traditional shape.

Baking

Bake immediately in a preheated 375°F oven until the crust feels firm when lightly touched in the center with your fingertips (about 45 minutes). Be careful not to penetrate the crust with your finger. If the center is still soft, continue baking for 5 to 10 minutes more. Cover the loaf while it cools.

Yield

Makes 1 loaf.

Note: To make sour milk, combine 2 cups skim milk and 2 teaspoons vinegar.

Quick Irish Soda Bread

(Food Processor, Plastic Blade)

This recipe is so simple that it is hardly worthwhile to use and clean the processor. However, the following is included if you wish to try it.

In the work bowl combine the buttermilk, flour, baking soda, and salt. Pulse just long enough to make a smooth dough (about 30 seconds). Turn out onto a floured surface and sprinkle with the currants and caraway seeds (if used). Proceed as in Shaping and Baking, above.

Quick Irish Soda Bread

(Dough-Mixing Machine, Flat Beater)

4 cups buttermilk or sour milk (see Note)
8 cups unbleached all-purpose flour
2 teaspoons baking soda
3 teaspoons salt
1 1/2 cups dried currants or raisins
2 tablespoons caraway seeds (optional)
Flour, for dusting work top

Place the milk in the mixing bowl and add the flour, baking soda, and salt. Mix by pulsing until the flour is absorbed and will not be thrown out of the bowl, then mix at the first speed only until all is combined. Add the currants and caraway seeds (if used) and mix just long enough to incorporate. If the currants are overmixed they will be crushed and their color will run into the dough. If it takes more than a few turns to distribute the currants, knead them in by hand on the work surface. Turn out the dough onto a floured work surface and divide the dough in half. Proceed as in Shaping and Baking, above.

Yield

Makes 2 loaves.

Note: To make sour milk, combine 4 cups skim milk and 4 teaspoons vinegar.

Mondelbrot

This distinctive Old World loaf tastes like part cookie, part cake. No other dessert or tea cake is comparable. When sliced and oven toasted it tastes like biscotti. Enjoy making this quick, no-sift bread.

1/2 cup sugar
4 tablespoons almond paste or kernel paste (see Note)
6 tablespoons (3/4 stick) unsalted butter or margarine
2 eggs, beaten
2 cups unbleached all-purpose flour
1/2 cup cake flour
1 teaspoon baking powder
1/4 cup milk or water
1/2 teaspoon salt
1 teaspoon almond extract (optional)
Flour, for dusting work top and pans
Shortening, for greasing pans
1 egg beaten with 2 teaspoons water, for egg wash
Sugar, for sprinkling (optional)

Fruit and Nut Filling

2 cups chopped nuts, such as walnuts or filberts, preferably toasted
1/2 cup diced citron or raisins
1/4 cup halved or chopped maraschino cherries (optional)

In a large bowl combine the sugar and paste; rub together as fine as you can. Cream with the butter only until the sugar no longer feels gritty. Add the eggs, one-third at a time, and mix until absorbed. Add the flours, baking powder, milk, salt, and almond extract (if used); stir to combine.

BAKER'S SECRET: Scrape down the sides and bottom of the bowl with a spatula, then continue mixing until well blended. Keep your hands floured. This will be a soft, sticky dough. Turn out onto a well-floured work top.

Filling

You can cut the dough in half and prepare each half with a different filling (see Variations, below). Combine the filling ingredients, then spread on top of the dough. Divide each piece of the dough in half and place one piece on top of the other. Press together, cut in half, and repeat several times so that the filling is evenly distributed. Place in a floured pan and refrigerate for at least 2 hours to facilitate handling.

Shaping

Divide into 2 pieces and lightly mold each into a loaf shape. Place on a greased baking sheet. (In the bakery we use double baking sheets, one inserted into the other, so that the bottom of the Mondelbrot does not burn.) Leave room for the loaves to spread in the oven. Brush with the egg wash. Sprinkle the sugar (if used) in a thin line down the length of each loaf.

Baking

Bake in a preheated 350°F oven until evenly browned and the center feels firm when gently pressed with a fingertip (about 40 minutes). Let cool on wire racks. This bread keeps well for several days and can be frozen.

Yield

Makes 2 loaves.

Note: Kernel paste is made from ground apricot kernels and might be available in a local bakery. Almond paste is available in supermarkets and specialty food shops or make your own (see page 15).

Variations

Chocolate Mondelbrot

Prepare as above but replace the Fruit and Nut Filling with this Chocolate Filling:

8 ounces semisweet chocolate bits, plus more for topping (optional)
1/2 cup (1 stick) butter or margarine

Melt the chocolate and butter together in a double boiler, in a microwave oven, or with a flame tamer; allow to cool. Use as in Fruit and Nut Filling, above. Before baking, brush with the egg wash, as above. The loaves can be topped with chocolate bits, if desired. In the bakery we drizzled additional melted chocolate over the tops of the loaves after baking and cooling.

Toasted Mondelbrot (Biscotti)

Bake the Mondelbrot with the Fruit and Nut Filling, then let cool thoroughly. Cut into 1-inch slices. Arrange the slices, cut side up and touching each other, on a clean baking sheet and bake in a preheated 350°F oven until lightly browned.

Mondelbrot

(Food Processor, Steel Blade)

In the work bowl blend the sugar and paste. Cream with the butter. Add the eggs, one third at a time, and pulse until absorbed. Add the flours, baking powder, milk, salt, and almond extract (if used) and pulse only until blended. Avoid overmixing. This will be a soft, wet dough. Turn out and proceed as in Filling, Shaping, and Baking, above.

Mondelbrot

(Dough-Mixing Machine, Flat Beater)

1 cup sugar
8 tablespoons almond paste or kernel paste (see Note above)
3/4 cup (1 1/2 sticks) unsalted butter or margarine
4 eggs, beaten
4 cups unbleached all-purpose flour
1 cup cake flour
2 teaspoons baking powder
1/2 cup milk or water
1 teaspoon salt
2 teaspoons almond extract (optional)
Flour, for dusting work top
Shortening, for greasing pans
1 egg beaten with 2 teaspoons water, for egg wash
Sugar, for sprinkling (optional)

Fruit and Nut Filling

4 cups chopped nuts, such as walnuts or filberts, preferably toasted
1 cup diced citron or raisins
1/2 cup halved or chopped maraschino cherries (optional)

In the mixing bowl combine the sugar and paste until smooth. Cream with the butter only until the sugar no longer feels gritty. Add the eggs, one third at a time, and mix until absorbed. Add the flours, baking powder, milk, salt, and almond extract (if used); mix until absorbed.

> ***BAKER'S SECRET:*** **Scrape down the sides and bottom of the bowl with a spatula, then continue mixing until well blended. Keep your hands floured. This will be a soft, sticky dough.**

Turn out the dough onto a well-floured work top. Proceed as in Filling, Shaping, and Baking, above, except cut into 4 pieces and bake 2 to a baking sheet.

Yield

Makes 4 loaves.

Wine Loaf

Here is a quick, no-sift recipe for an old standby that can serve as the baker's stockpot. The loaves can be refrigerated for up to a week and can be baked plain or with various additions (variations follow). You will find references to this loaf in other recipes. Drop this mix into muffin tins for cupcakes, or mix with assorted nuts, raisins, or fruits for quick muffins. Thicken with extra flour for bakery Black & Whites (page 311). Mastering this recipe can give you an entire bakery repertoire limited only by your own imagination. For example, substitute lemon or orange flavoring for the vanilla, or substitute butter for the shortening, or add toppings. Have fun with this recipe!

1 1/2 cups shortening
2 cups sugar
5 1/3 cups cake flour
4 teaspoons baking powder
2 teaspoons salt
7 eggs, beaten
2 teaspoons vanilla extract
2/3 cup water
Shortening, for greasing pans
Flour, for dusting pans

In a large bowl cream the shortening with the sugar, 1 1/3 cups flour, baking powder, and salt. Beat in the eggs, one third at a time. Mix in the vanilla. Alternately mix in the remaining 4 cups flour and the water.

BAKER'S SECRET: Scrape down the sides and bottom of the bowl with a spatula, then continue mixing until smooth.

At this point the batter can be stored in clean containers in the refrigerator for up to a week.

Grease four or five 8- or 9-inch loaf pans, then line them with parchment or waxed paper and grease and flour-dust the bottom. Turn out the batter into the prepared pans.

Baking

Bake in a preheated 350°F oven until evenly browned and the center feels firm when gently pressed with a fingertip (30 to 40 minutes). Let cool on wire racks. This bread keeps well for several days and can be frozen.

Yield

Makes 4 or 5 loaves.

Variations

Walnut, Chocolate Bit, Raisin Loaves

Fold in 1/2 to 3/4 cup of any of the above fillings to each loaf cake. Sprinkle additional nuts or chocolate bits on top and bake as above.

Dutchess Loaf

Fill the prepared pans with Wine Loaf batter. With a fingertip dipped in vegetable oil, draw a line lengthwise down the center of the loaf. Bake as for Wine Loaf. Let cool, then remove from the pans. While cooling prepare Vanilla Icing and Chocolate Icing.

Vanilla Icing

1 cup confectioners' sugar or prepared fondant
2 tablespoons unsalted butter or margarine, melted
1/8 teaspoon vanilla extract
1 cup hot water

In the top of a double boiler, combine the sugar, butter, and vanilla; add 1/2 cup of the water. Stir until dissolved. Add the remaining 1/2 cup water 1 to 2 tablespoons at a time as necessary until the icing is smooth and lump free. It should be spreadable but thick, and warm to the touch. Spread the icing while warm on half of the Dutchess Loaf, staying on one side of the vegetable oil line you made with your finger. If need be, the icing can be rewarmed in a double boiler or in a microwave oven, but do not overheat. Reserve some Vanilla Icing to make the Chocolate Icing, below.

Chocolate Icing

2 ounces semisweet chocolate bits

Melt the chocolate bits in a double boiler or in a microwave oven, then let cool. Add to the remaining warm Vanilla Icing and stir quickly and thoroughly. Reheat as in Vanilla Icing, above; if necessary, thin with hot water, 1 teaspoon at a time. When the Vanilla Icing on the Dutchess Loaf is dry to the touch, spread warm Chocolate Icing on the opposite side of the loaf. Serve the Dutchess Loaf within 1 to 2 days of baking. It can be refrigerated but the icing could become runny in humid conditions. This loaf can be frozen, but apply the icing before serving, since the icing may become runny or cracked as the cake defrosts.

Black and Whites

To make these drop cakes, to the prepared Wine Loaf batter slowly fold in enough sifted cake flour to thicken the batter. Prepare 1 or 2 baking pans, either parchment or waxed-paper lined, or greased and flour dusted. With a pastry bag and a large plain tube, drop out the batter into 2 1/2- to 3-inch rounds. Leave space for the rounds to spread in the oven. You may want to test-bake 1 drop cake on a pie pan. If it spreads out too thin, add more flour to the batter; it should hold a perfectly round shape with a domed center. Bake in a 350°F oven until browned and the center is firm when gently pressed with a fingertip (about 15 minutes). Let cool.

The drop cakes can be frozen for later use. Finish on the bottom side by frosting with half chocolate, half vanilla icing, as in the Dutchess Loaf, above.

French Crumb Coffee Cake

Drop out Wine Loaf mix into a greased 9 x 9 baking pan or a 9-inch round layer pan filled 2/3 full. Sprinkle a heavy layer of streusel (recipe, page 277) on top to cover. Bake as above.

Wine Loaf

(Food Processor, Steel Blade)

3/4 cup shortening
1 cup sugar
2 2/3 cups cake flour
2 teaspoons baking powder
1 teaspoon salt
3 1/2 eggs, beaten
1 teaspoon vanilla extract
1/3 cup water
Shortening, for greasing pans
Flour, for dusting pans

In the work bowl combine the shortening, sugar, 2/3 cup of the flour, baking powder, and salt. Beat in the eggs, one third at a time. Add the 2 remaining cups flour; with the machine running pour in the water. Mix only until completely blended.

Grease two or three 8- or 9-inch loaf pans, then line them with parchment or waxed paper and grease and flour-dust the bottom. Turn out the batter into the prepared pans. Proceed as in Baking, above.

Yield

Makes 2 or 3 loaves.

Wine Loaf

(Dough-Mixing Machine, Flat Beater)

2 1/4 cups shortening
3 cups sugar
8 cups cake flour
2 tablespoons baking powder
1 tablespoon salt
10 eggs, beaten
1 tablespoon vanilla extract
1 cup water
Shortening, for greasing pans
Flour, for dusting pans

In the mixing bowl cream the shortening, sugar, 2 cups of the flour, baking powder, and salt. Beat in the eggs, one third at a time. Add the vanilla.

BAKER'S SECRET: Scrape down the sides and bottom of the bowl with a rubber spatula, then continue mixing until smooth.

Mix in the remaining 6 cups flour until absorbed. Add the water a little at a time, then beat until smooth.

Grease six to eight 8- to 9-inch loaf pans, then line them with parchment or waxed paper and grease and flour-dust the bottom. Turn out the batter into the prepared pans. Proceed as in Baking, above.

Yield

Makes 6 to 8 loaves.

Sour Cream Loaf

Here is a rich, sweet coffee cake that is sure to please your guests and enhance your reputation as a baker. This can easily become a family favorite.

1/2 cup (1 stick) unsalted butter or margarine, softened
1 cup sugar
2 eggs, beaten
1 cup heavy sour cream
1 teaspoon vanilla extract
2 cups unbleached all-purpose flour
1 1/2 teaspoons baking powder
1/2 teaspoon baking soda
1/2 teaspoon salt
Shortening, for greasing pans

Filling

3/4 cup firmly packed brown sugar
2 teaspoons ground cinnamon
1/2 cup chopped pecans
1/2 cup semisweet chocolate bits

Blend the Filling ingredients together and set aside.

In a large bowl lightly cream or rub together the butter and sugar. Add the eggs, one at a time, and mix thoroughly. Add the sour cream and vanilla; beat until smooth. Add the flour, baking powder, baking soda, and salt; stir gently with your fingers to combine the dry ingredients, then beat thoroughly.

Turn out half the batter into 2 well-greased loaf pans. Sprinkle on half the Filling (reserve the rest), then add the rest of the batter.

Baking

Bake in a preheated 350 degree F oven for 15 minutes, then carefully top with the reserved Filling. (Leftover Filling can be stored in a tightly closed container.) Bake the loaves until browned and the center feels firm when gently pressed with your fingertips (about 30 minutes). Take care not to burn yourself on the hot topping. Let cool for 5 to 10 minutes in the pans, then transfer to wire racks to cool completely.

Yield

Makes 2 loaves.

Sour Cream Loaf

(Food Processor, Steel Blade)

In the work bowl cream the butter and sugar. Add the eggs, one at a time, then add the sour cream and vanilla. Mix until smooth. Add the flour, baking powder, baking soda, and salt; mix thoroughly.

Turn out half the batter into 2 well-greased loaf pans. Sprinkle on half the Filling (reserve the rest), then add the rest of the batter. Proceed as in Baking, above.

Yield

Makes 2 loaves.

Sour Cream Loaf

(Dough-Mixing Machine, Flat Beater)

For half the yield (2 loaves), use the recipe above.

1 cup (2 sticks) unsalted butter or margarine, softened
2 cups sugar
4 eggs, beaten
2 cups heavy sour cream
2 teaspoons vanilla extract
4 cups unbleached all-purpose flour
3 teaspoons baking powder
1 teaspoon baking soda
1 teaspoon salt
Shortening, for greasing pans

Filling

1 1/2 cups firmly packed brown sugar
4 teaspoons ground cinnamon
1 cup chopped pecans
1 cup semisweet chocolate bits

Blend the Filling ingredients together and set aside.

In the mixing bowl cream the butter and brown sugar. Add the eggs, one at a time, then add the sour cream and vanilla. Mix until smooth. Add the flour, baking powder, baking soda, and salt; stir gently with your fingers to combine the dry ingredients, then mix thoroughly.

Scrape down the sides and bottom of the bowl with a rubber spatula. Mix until smooth.

Turn out half the batter into 4 well-greased loaf pans. Sprinkle on half the Filling (reserve the rest), then add the rest of the batter. Proceed as in Baking, above.

Yield

Makes 4 loaves.

Wonder Loaf

Although this recipe appears to be long and complicated, it's really not hard to make. Just follow along one step at a time. You will end up with a wonderfully light and tasty cake.

1/2 cup plus 1 tablespoon sugar
1/2 cup plus 1 tablespoon (1 stick plus 1 tablespoon) unsalted butter or margarine, softened
1 3/4 cups cake flour
2 eggs plus 2 egg yolks
1 1/4 teaspoons baking powder
1/2 teaspoon salt
1/4 cup milk or water
1/2 teaspoon vanilla extract
1/2 cup egg whites
1/4 cup sugar
Pinch cream of tartar (optional)
6 ounces (about 1 cup) semisweet chocolate bits
Shortening, for greasing pans (optional)
Flour, for dusting pans (optional)

In a large bowl lightly cream or rub together the sugar, butter, and 1/2 cup of the flour. Beat in the eggs and egg yolks one at a time. Mix in the remaining 1 1/4 cups flour, baking powder, and salt. Slowly add the milk and vanilla, then beat thoroughly.

In a separate bowl beat the egg whites into soft peaks. Slowly add the remaining 1/4 cup sugar and cream of tartar (if desired). Beat until stiff peaks form and the egg whites are shiny. Gently fold the whites into the cake mixture.

Making

Meanwhile, melt the chocolate in a double boiler, in a microwave oven, or over a flame tamer. Let cool, then drizzle the melted chocolate in spirals over the top of the finished batter in the mixing bowl. With a spatula quickly swirl the chocolate down through the batter to marbleize. Do not overmix.

BAKER'S SECRET: You want to keep some chocolate from blending fully into the batter. When the cake is being eaten, folks are supposed to wonder how it was baked with strands of rich unmelted chocolate on the inside.

Grease two 8- or 9-inch loaf pans, then line them with parchment or waxed paper and grease and flour-dust the bottom. Carefully scoop the batter into the prepared pans, filling them two-thirds full. In the bakery we drizzled extra melted chocolate over the tops and ran some thin lines with a knife lengthwise through the batter, creating a marbleized design.

Baking

Bake in a preheated 350°F oven until browned and the center feels firm when gently pressed with a fingertip (45 to 60 minutes). Don't burn your finger on any hot melted chocolate that may be on the top. (If you forget, welcome to the club.) Let cool for 5 to 10 minutes in the pans, then remove and let cool completely on wire racks.

Yield

Makes 2 loaves.

Wonder Loaf

(Food Processsor, Steel Blade)

In the work bowl lightly cream or rub together the sugar, butter, and 1/2 cup of the flour. Beat in the eggs and egg yolks one at a time. Mix in the remaining 1 1/4 cups flour, baking powder, and salt. With the machine running, slowly add the milk and vanilla until thoroughly mixed. Transfer the batter to a large mixing bowl.

In a separate bowl beat the egg whites into soft peaks. Slowly add the remaining 1/4 cup sugar and cream of tartar (if desired). Beat until stiff peaks form and the egg whites are shiny. Gently fold the whites into the cake mixture. Proceed as in Making and Baking, above.

Wonder Loaf

(Dough-Mixing Machine, Flat Beater)

For half the yield, use the recipe above.

1 cup plus 2 tablespoons sugar
1 cup plus 2 tablespoons (2 sticks plus 2 tablespoons) unsalted butter or margarine, softened
3 1/2 cups cake flour
4 eggs plus 4 egg yolks
2 1/2 teaspoons baking powder
1 teaspoon salt
1/2 cup milk or water
1 teaspoon vanilla extract
1 cup egg whites
1/2 cup sugar
Pinch cream of tartar (optional)
12 ounces (about 2 cups) semisweet chocolate bits
Shortening, for greasing pans (optional)
Flour, for dusting pans (optional)

In the mixing bowl lightly cream or rub together the sugar, butter, and 1 cup of the flour. Beat in the eggs and egg yolks one at a time. Mix in the remaining 2 1/2 cups flour, baking powder, and salt. Stir lightly with your fingers and mix until absorbed.

BAKER'S SECRET: Stir down the sides and bottom of the bowl with a rubber spatula, then mix until smooth.

Slowly add the milk and vanilla, then beat thoroughly.

In a separate bowl beat the egg whites into soft peaks. Slowly add the remaining 1/2 cup sugar and cream of tartar (if desired). Beat until stiff peaks form and the egg whites are shiny. Gently fold the whites into the cake mixture. Proceed as in Making and Baking, above, except use 4 pans.

Yield

Makes 4 loaves.

Hazelnut Raspberry Loaf

1 cup plus 1 1/2 teaspoons sugar
4 tablespoons praline paste (praline butter) or almond paste (see Note)
3/4 cup (1 1/2 sticks) unsalted butter or margarine
6 eggs, beaten
1/2 teaspoon salt
1/2 teaspoon vanilla extract
1/2 cup all-purpose flour
1 cup ground roasted hazelnuts (filberts)
1 cup Wine Loaf batter (page 310)
1 1/2 cups fresh cake crumbs or bread crumbs
Shortening, for greasing pan
Flour, for dusting pans
Pure raspberry jam, for topping
Confectioners' sugar, for dusting

In a large bowl cream the sugar with the praline paste and butter. Beat in the eggs, one-third at a time. Add the salt, vanilla, flour, ground hazelnuts, Wine Cake batter, and cake crumbs; mix well. Grease a baking sheet, then line them with parchment or waxed paper and grease and flour-dust the bottom. Turn out the batter onto the prepared baking sheets.

Baking

Bake in a preheated 350°F oven until the crust has color and the center is firm when gently pressed with a fingertip (about 45 minutes). Let cool on wire racks. Refrigerate in the pans for several hours or preferably freeze overnight. Before serving, turn out onto a board or the back of a baking sheet; loosen the sides by inserting a spatula along the edges, then invert and tap lightly to release. You may have to place the pan in a warm oven for several minutes to release. When inverted, remove any paper still clinging to the cake.

Cut the sheet in half, spread half with the raspberry jam, and carefully slide the other half on top. Trim the crusts and crumble them by pressing through a a sieve or coarse grater. Spread raspberry jam on top and cover with the fresh cake crumbs. Cut in half lengthwise. Dust with the confectioners' sugar and serve.

Yield

Makes 2 loaves.

Note: Make praline paste by substituting hazelnuts (filberts) for the almonds in Almond Paste (page 15). Or you can use store-bought praline paste (available in fine European gourmet shops) or kernel paste. Kernel paste is made from ground apricot kernels and may be available in a local bakery. Almond paste is available in supermarkets and specialty food shops or you can make your own (page 15). As a last resort, you can use peanut butter.

Hazelnut Raspberry Loaf

(Food Processor, Steel Blade)

In the work bowl cream the sugar with the praline paste and butter. Beat in the eggs, one third at a time. Add the salt, vanilla, flour, ground hazelnuts, Wine Loaf batter, and cake crumbs; mix well. Turn out into a greased and flour-dusted or parchment paper- or waxed paper-lined baking sheet. Proceed as in Baking, above.

Hazelnut Raspberry Loaf

(Dough-Mixing Machine, Flat Beater)

For half the yield, use the recipe above.

2 cups plus 1 tablespoon sugar
8 tablespoons praline paste (praline butter) or almond paste (see Note above)
1 1/2 cups (3 sticks) unsalted butter or margarine
2 1/4 cups beaten eggs (about 11 eggs)
1 teaspoon salt
1 teaspoon vanilla extract
1 cup all-purpose flour
2 cups ground roasted hazelnuts (filberts)
3 cups fresh cake crumbs or bread crumbs
2 cups Wine Loaf batter (see page 310)
3 cups fresh cake crumbs
Shortening, for greasing pans
Flour, for dusting pans
Pure raspberry jam, for topping
Confectioners' sugar, for dusting

In the mixing bowl blend the sugar with the praline paste. Cream with the butter. Beat in the eggs, one third at a time. Add the salt, vanilla, flour, ground hazelnuts, Wine Loaf batter, and cake crumbs; mix well. Scrape down the sides and bottom of the bowl with a rubber spatula; mix until smooth. Grease 2 baking sheets, then line them with parchment or waxed paper and grease and flour-dust the bottom. Turn out the batter onto the prepared baking sheets.

Proceed as in Baking, above, except place one full sheet atop the other and cut the sheet into fourths.

Yield

Makes 4 loaves.

Apricot Nut Loaf

1 cup boiling water
1 cup coarsely chopped dried apricots
1 cup plus 2 tablespoons sugar
2 tablespoons butter or margarine, melted
2 eggs, lightly beaten
1 1/2 cups unbleached all-purpose flour
3/4 cup whole wheat flour, preferably stone ground
2 teaspoons baking powder
1/4 teaspoon baking soda
3/4 teaspoon salt
2 tablespoons orange or apricot liqueur (optional)
3/4 cup milk or water
1 cup chopped walnuts, plus more for topping
Shortening, for greasing pans
Flour, for dusting pans

Pour the boiling water over the chopped apricots and set aside to steep for 15 minutes. Drain, then add the 2 tablespoons sugar and mix together.

In a large bowl combine the prepared apricot mixture with the remaining 1 cup sugar, butter, and eggs. In another large bowl combine the flours, baking powder, baking soda, and salt. Combine the liqueur (if desired) and the milk. Alternatively add the flour mixture and the milk mixture to the apricot mixture. Fold in the nuts.

Grease two or three 8- or 9-inch loaf pans, then line them with parchment or waxed paper and grease and flour-dust the bottom. Turn out the batter into the prepared pans. Top with the additional chopped nuts.

Baking

Bake in a preheated 350°F oven until browned and the center feels firm when gently pressed with your fingertips (45 to 60 minutes). Let cool for 5 to 10 minutes in the pans, then remove to wire racks to cool completely.

Yield

Makes 2 or 3 loaves.

Variation

Apricot Raisin Bread

Steep 1/2 cup raisins (1 cup in the dough-mixing machine recipe) in the boiling water together with the chopped apricots. Omit the nuts. Proceed as per recipe.

Apricot Nut Loaf

(Food Processor, Steel Blade)

Pour the boiling water over the chopped apricots and set aside to steep for 15 minutes. Drain, then add the 2 tablespoons sugar and mix together.

In the work bowl combine the prepared apricot mixture, the remaining 1 cup sugar, butter, and eggs. Add the flours, baking powder, baking soda, and salt. Pulse until blended. Combine the liqueur (if desired) and the milk. With the machine running, slowly add the milk mixture through the feed tube, mixing just until absorbed. Fold in the nuts. Grease two or three 8- or 9-inch loaf pans, then line them with parchment or waxed paper and grease and flour-dust the bottom. Turn out the batter into the prepared pans, and proceed as in Baking, above.

Apricot Nut Loaf

(Dough-Mixing Machine, Flat Beater)

2 cups boiling water
2 cups coarsely chopped dried apricots
2 1/4 cups sugar
4 tablespoons butter or margarine, melted
4 eggs, lightly beaten
3 cups unbleached all-purpose flour
1 1/2 cups whole wheat flour, preferably stone ground
4 teaspoons baking powder
1/2 teaspoon baking soda
1 1/2 teaspoons salt
4 tablespoons orange or apricot liqueur (optional)
1 1/2 cups milk or water
2 cups chopped walnuts, plus more for topping

Pour the boiling water over the chopped apricots and set aside to steep for 15 minutes. Drain, then add 1/4 cup of the sugar and mix together.

In the mixing bowl combine the prepared apricot mixture with the remaining 2 cups sugar, butter, and eggs. Add the flours, baking powder, baking soda, and salt. Stir the dry ingredients with your fingers to distribute, then mix until absorbed. Scrape down the sides and bottom of the bowl with a rubber spatula. Combine the liqueur (if desired) and the milk; add slowly until completely absorbed. Fold in the nuts. Grease four to six 8- or 9-inch loaf pans, then line them with parchment or waxed paper and grease and flour-dust the bottom. Turn out the batter into the prepared pans, top with additional chopped nuts, and proceed as in Baking, above.

Yield

Makes 4 to 6 loaves.

Banana Nut Bread

1/2 cup firmly packed brown sugar
1/4 cup granulated sugar
1/2 cup (1 stick) unsalted butter or margarine
1 cup mashed ripe banana
2 eggs, beaten
2 cups cake flour
1 1/2 teaspoons baking powder
1/4 teaspoon baking soda
3/4 teaspoon salt
1/2 teaspoon vanilla extract
2 tablespoons dark rum (optional)
1/4 cup milk or water
1/2 cup chopped walnuts
Shortening, for greasing pans
Flour, for dusting pans

In a large bowl lightly cream the sugars and butter. Add the banana and beat in the eggs one at a time.

In a medium bowl stir together the flour, baking powder, baking soda, and salt. In a small bowl combine the vanilla, rum (if desired), and milk. Add the milk mixture to the butter mixture alternately with the flour mixture until thoroughly mixed. Fold in the nuts. Grease a 9-inch loaf pan and a miniature loaf pan, then line them with parchment or waxed paper and grease and flour-dust the bottom. Turn out the batter into the prepared pans.

Baking

Bake in a preheated 350°F oven until browned and the center feels firm when gently pressed with your fingertips (45 to 60 minutes). Let cool in the pans for 5 to 10 minutes, then remove to wire racks to cool completely.

Yield

Makes one 9-inch loaf plus 1 miniature loaf.

Variation

Pecan Coconut Loaf

This topping on Banana Nut Bread transforms it into a Pecan Coconut Loaf.

1/3 cup firmly packed brown sugar
1/2 cup chopped pecan pieces
Scant 1 cup loosely packed flaked coconut
4 tablespoons butter or margarine, melted

Prepare Banana Nut Bread as above and bake for 15 minutes. Meanwhile, in a small bowl combine the topping ingredients. Carefully sprinkle the topping over the hot bread and continue baking until done.

Banana Nut Bread

(Food Processor, Steel Blade)

In the work bowl lightly cream the sugars and butter. Add the banana and beat in the eggs one at a time. Add the flour, baking powder, baking soda, salt, vanilla, and rum (if desired). Pulse to blend. With the machine running, slowly add the milk until absorbed. Fold in the chopped nuts. Grease a 9-inch loaf pan and a miniature loaf pan, then line them with parchment or waxed paper and grease and flour-dust the bottom. Turn out the batter into the prepared pans and proceed as in Baking, above.

Banana Nut Bread

(Dough-Mixing Machine, Flat Beater)

1 cup firmly packed brown sugar
1/2 cup granulated sugar
1 cup (2 sticks) butter or margarine
2 cups mashed ripe banana
4 eggs, lightly beaten
4 cups cake flour
1 tablespoon baking powder
1/2 teaspoon baking soda
1 1/2 teaspoons salt
1 teaspoon vanilla extract
4 tablespoons dark rum (optional)
1/2 cup milk or water
1 cup chopped walnuts
Shortening, for greasing pan
Flour, for dusting pan

In the mixing bowl lightly cream the sugars and butter. Add the banana and beat in the eggs one at a time. Add the flour, baking powder, baking soda, salt, vanilla, and rum (if desired). When fully blended, scrape down the sides and bottom of the bowl with a spatula and continue mixing until smooth. Slowly add the milk until completely absorbed. Fold in the chopped nuts. Grease two 9-inch loaf pans and 2 miniature loaf pans, or three 8-inch loaf pans, then line them with parchment or waxed paper and grease and flour-dust the bottom. Turn out the batter into the prepared pans and proceed as in Baking, above.

Yield

Makes two 9-inch loaves plus 2 miniature loaves, or three 8-inch loaves.

Bertie's Date Nut Bread

Although Bertie's Date Nut bread is baked in a loaf pan in this recipe, Aunt Bertie baked it in a round coffee can that was heavily greased and flour dusted and positioned upright in the oven. When cool the can was inverted and the bottom lid cut through with a can opener, then, using the lid, the bread was pushed out onto a platter.

1 cup boiling water
2 cups coarsely chopped pitted dates
1 egg, beaten
1/4 cup granulated sugar
1/4 cup firmly packed brown sugar
2 tablespoons unsalted butter or margarine, melted
1/2 cup unbleached all-purpose flour
1 teaspoon baking powder
1 teaspoon baking soda
1 teaspoon salt
1/2 cup coarsely chopped walnuts
Shortening, for greasing pans
Flour, for dusting pans

In a large bowl pour the boiling water over the dates and allow to cool. Beat in the egg and granulated sugar. Add the brown sugar, butter, flour, baking powder, baking soda, and salt. Stir the dry ingredients gently with your fingers, then mix thoroughly until smooth. Fold in the walnuts. Grease two 8- or 9-inch loaf pans, then line them with parchment or waxed paper and grease and flour-dust the bottom. Turn out the batter into the prepared pans.

Baking

Bake in a preheated 350°F oven until browned and the center feels firm when gently pressed with your fingertips (about 1 hour). Let cool for 5 to 10 minutes in the pans, then remove to a wire rack to cool completely. The bread tastes best when wrapped in aluminum foil and refrigerated overnight before using; it also freezes well. It is delicious when spread with cream cheese.

Yield

Makes 2 loaves.

Bertie's Date Nut Bread

(Food Processor, Steel Blade)

In the work bowl pour the boiling water over the dates and allow to cool. Add the egg, sugars, butter, flour, baking powder, baking soda, and salt. Mix by pulsing until smooth. Fold in the walnuts. Turn out and proceed as in Baking, above.

Bertie's Date Nut Bread

(Dough-Mixing Machine, Flat Beater)

For half the yield, use the recipe above.

2 cups boiling water
4 cups coarsely cut or chopped pitted dates
2 eggs, beaten
1/2 cup granulated sugar
1/2 cup firmly packed brown sugar
2 tablespoons unsalted butter or margarine, at room temperature
1 cup unbleached all-purpose flour
2 teaspoons baking powder
2 teaspoons baking soda
2 teaspoons salt
1 cup coarsely chopped walnuts
Shortening, for greasing pans
Flour, for dusting pans

In the mixing bowl pour the boiling water over the dates and allow to cool. Beat in the egg and granulated sugar. Add the brown sugar, butter, flour, baking powder, baking soda, and salt. Stir the dry ingredients gently with your fingers, then mix thoroughly until smooth. Fold in the walnuts. Grease four 8- or 9-inch loaf pans, then line them with parchment or waxed paper and grease and flour-dust the bottom. Turn out the batter into the prepared pans and proceed as in Baking, above.

Yield

Makes 4 loaves.

Rich Carrot Loaf

1/2 pound (1 1/2 cups) grated or ground carrots
3/4 cup vegetable oil
1/2 cup beaten eggs (2 or 3 eggs)
1 cup sugar
3/4 teaspoon baking powder
3/4 teaspoon baking soda
1/4 teaspoon salt
1/2 teaspoon vanilla extract
1 teaspoon ground cinnamon
1 1/2 cups unbleached all-purpose flour
1/2 cup shredded coconut (optional)
1/2 cup chopped walnuts
1/4 cup raisins
1/4 cup drained crushed pineapple
Shortening, for greasing pans
Flour, for dusting pans

Topping (optional)

1/4 cup (1/2 stick) unsalted butter
3/4 cup plus 1 tablespoon unsifted confectioners' sugar
4 ounces cream cheese
1/2 teaspoon freshly squeezed lemon juice

In a large bowl combine the grated carrot and oil. Beat in the eggs one at a time. Add the sugar, baking powder, baking soda, salt, vanilla, and cinnamon. Mix until thoroughly dissolved. Beat in the flour in small amounts until smooth. Fold in the coconut (if desired), walnuts, raisins, and pineapple. Grease two 8-inch loaf pans or one 9-inch loaf pan, then line them with parchment or waxed paper and grease and flour-dust the bottom. Turn out the batter into the prepared pans.

Baking

Bake in a preheated 350°F oven until browned and the center feels firm when gently pressed with your fingertips (about 1 hour). Let cool for 5 to 10 minutes in the pan, then remove to a wire rack to cool completely.

Yield

Makes two 8-inch loaves or one 9-inch loaf.

Topping

Cream the topping ingredients and spread over the cooled cake.

Rich Carrot Loaf

(Food Processor, Steel Blade)

Place the carrots and oil in the work bowl. With the machine running add the eggs one at a time through the feed tube. Add the sugar, baking powder, baking soda, salt, vanilla, and cinnamon. Mix until thoroughly dissolved. Add the flour one cup at a time and mix until smooth. Fold in the coconut (if desired), walnuts, raisins, and pineapple. Turn out and proceed as in Baking and Topping, above.

Rich Carrot Loaf

(Dough-Mixing Machine, Flat Beater)

3 cups grated or ground carrot (about 1 pound carrots)
1 1/2 cups vegetable oil
1 cup beaten eggs (about 5 eggs)
2 cups sugar
1 1/2 teaspoons baking powder
1 1/2 teaspoons baking soda
1/2 teaspoon salt
1 teaspoon vanilla extract
2 teaspoons ground cinnamon
3 cups unbleached all-purpose flour
1 cup shredded coconut (optional)
1 cup coarsely chopped walnuts
1/2 cup raisins
1/2 cup drained crushed pineapple
Shortening, for greasing pans
Flour, for dusting pans

Topping

1/2 cup (1 stick) unsalted butter
1 1/2 cups plus 2 tablespoons unsifted confectioners' sugar
8 ounces cream cheese
1 teaspoon vanilla extract
1 teaspoon freshly squeezed lemon juice

Place the carrots and oil in the mixing bowl. With the machine running beat in the eggs one at a time. Add the sugar, baking powder, baking soda, salt, vanilla, and cinnamon. Mix until thoroughly dissolved. Add the flour and pulse with the on/off switch until the flour is absorbed so that it does not fly out of the bowl. Mix until smooth.

Scrape down the sides and bottom of the bowl with a spatula. Continue mixing until smooth. Fold in the coconut (if desired), walnuts, raisins, and pineapple. Turn out and proceed as in Baking and Topping, above, except use four 8-inch loaf pans or two 9-inch loaf pans.

Yield

Makes four 8-inch loaves or two 9-inch loaves.

Cinnamon Citron Bread

1/2 cup (1 stick) unsalted butter or margarine, softened
1/4 cup firmly packed brown sugar
1/2 cup granulated sugar
2 eggs
1 tablespoon molasses
1 3/4 cups unbleached all-purpose flour
2 teaspoon baking powder
1/2 teaspoon baking soda
2 teaspoons ground cinnamon
1/2 teaspoon salt
1/4 cup milk or water
3/4 cup raisins plumped in hot water or dark rum
1/3 cup mixed diced citron or candied orange or lemon peel
Shortening, for greasing pans
Flour, for dusting pans
Sherry Glaze (recipe follows) or confectioners' sugar, for dusting bread

Sherry Glaze

1/2 cup sugar
1/2 cup water
1 ounce sherry or brandy

In a large bowl lightly cream the butter and sugars. Beat in the eggs, one at a time. Beat in the molasses.

In a medium bowl combine the flour, baking powder, baking soda, cinnamon, and salt. Stir gently, then add to the butter mixture alternately with the milk; mix until smooth. Fold in the raisins and citron. Grease a 9-inch loaf pan, then line it with parchment or waxed paper and grease and flour-dust the bottom. Turn out the batter into the prepared pan.

Baking

Bake in a preheated 350°F oven until browned and the center feels firm when gently pressed with your fingertips (about 1 hour). Let cool for 5 to 10 minutes in the pan; then remove to a wire rack. Drizzle with the Sherry Glaze while the cake is still warm, or let the cake cool completely and dust with the confectioners' sugar.

Yield

Makes 1 loaf.

Sherry Glaze

Prepare a simple syrup by combining the sugar and the water, bringing to a boil, and boiling for 3 minutes. Stir in the sherry.

Cinnamon Citron Bread

(Food Processor, Steel Blade)

In the work bowl lightly cream the butter and sugars. Beat in the eggs, one at a time. Beat in the molasses. Add the flour, baking powder, baking soda, cinnamon, and salt. With the machine running add the milk. Fold in the raisins and diced citron. Grease a 9-inch loaf pan; then line it with parchment or waxed paper and grease and flour-dust the bottom. Turn out the batter into the prepared pan and proceed as in Baking, above.

Cinnamon Citron Bread

(Dough-Mixing Machine, Flat Beater)

1 cup (2 sticks) unsalted butter or margarine, softened
1/2 cup firmly packed brown sugar
1 cup granulated sugar
4 eggs
2 tablespoons molasses
3 1/2 cups unbleached all-purpose flour
4 teaspoons baking powder
1 teaspoon baking soda
4 teaspoons ground cinnamon
1 teaspoon salt
1/2 cup milk or water
1 1/2 cups raisins plumped in hot water or dark rum
2/3 cup mixed diced citron or candied orange or lemon peel
Shortening, for greasing pans
Flour, for dusting pans
Sherry Glaze (recipe above) or confectioners' sugar, for dusting bread

In the mixing bowl lightly cream the butter and sugars. Beat in the eggs one at a time. Beat in the molasses. Add the flour, baking powder, baking soda, cinnamon, and salt. Stir the dry ingredients gently, then mix until absorbed.

Scrape down the sides and bottom of the bowl. Add the milk slowly, mixing until smooth. Fold in the raisins and diced citron. Grease two 9-inch loaf pans, then line them with parchment or waxed paper and grease and flour-dust the bottom. Turn out the batter into the prepared pans and proceed as in Baking, above.

Yield

Makes 2 loaves.

Cranberry Loaf

1 cup cranberries, rinsed
1 1/4 cups water
1/2 cup unsalted butter or margarine
1 cup sugar
3 eggs
2 cups unbleached all-purpose flour
3 teaspoons baking powder
1/4 teaspoon salt
1/8 teaspoon ground cloves
1 teaspoon ground cinnamon
Shortening, for greasing pans
Flour, for dusting pans

Boil the cranberries in the water only until the skins pop (8 to 10 minutes). Set aside to cool.

In a large bowl cream the butter. Gradually add the sugar. Beat in the eggs one at a time; then blend in the cooled cranberries.

In a medium bowl combine the flour, baking powder, salt, cloves, and cinnamon; add to the butter mixture and beat thoroughly. Grease two 8- or 9-inch loaf pans, then line them with parchment or waxed paper and grease and flour-dust the bottom. Turn out the batter into the prepared pans.

Baking

Bake in a preheated 350°F oven until browned and the center feels firm when gently pressed with your fingertips (50 to 60 minutes). Let cool for 5 to 10 minutes in the pans; then remove to a wire rack to cool completely.

Yield

Makes 2 loaves.

Cranberry Loaf

(Food Processor, Steel Blade)

Prepare the cranberries as above and set aside to cool. In the work bowl cream the butter; then gradually add the sugar. Beat in the eggs one at a time. Add the flour, baking powder, salt, cloves, and cinnamon; mix thoroughly. Stir or fold in the cooled cranberries. Grease two 8- or 9-inch loaf pans; then line them with parchment or waxed paper and grease and flour-dust the bottom. Turn out the batter into the prepared pans and proceed as in Baking, above.

Cranberry Loaf

(Dough-Mixing Machine, Flat Beater)

2 cups cranberries
2 1/2 cups water
1 cup (2 sticks) unsalted butter or margarine
2 cups sugar
6 eggs
4 cups unbleached all-purpose flour
2 tablespoons baking powder
1/2 teaspoon salt
1/4 teaspoon ground cloves
2 teaspoons ground cinnamon
Shortening, for greasing pans
Flour, for dusting pans

Prepare the cranberries as above and set aside to cool. In the mixing bowl cream the butter; then gradually add the sugar. Beat in the eggs one at a time. Add the flour, baking powder, salt, cloves, and cinnamon; mix thoroughly. Stir or fold in the cooled cranberries. Grease four 8- or 9-inch loaf pans; then line them with parchment or waxed paper and grease and flour-dust the bottom. Turn out the batter into the prepared pans and proceed as in Baking, above.

Yield

Makes 4 loaves.

Cranberry Orange Bread

2 tablespoons unsalted butter or margarine, softened
1 cup sugar
Juice and grated zest of 1 orange plus enough water to make 3/4 cup
1/4 cup dry sherry
1 egg, beaten
2 cups unbleached all-purpose flour
1 1/2 teaspoons baking powder
1/2 teaspoon baking soda
1/2 teaspoon salt
1 cup coarsely ground or chopped cranberries
1 cup coarsely chopped walnuts
Shortening, for greasing pans
Flour, for dusting pans

In a large bowl lightly cream the butter and sugar. Beat in the juice mixture, sherry, and egg until smooth. Add the flour, baking powder, baking soda, and salt. Stir the dry ingredients gently, then mix thoroughly. Fold in the cranberries and walnuts. Grease two 8- or 9-inch loaf pans; then line them with parchment or waxed paper and grease and flour-dust the bottom. Turn out the batter into the prepared pans.

Baking

Bake in a preheated 350°F oven until browned and the center feels firm when gently pressed with your fingertips (50 to 60 minutes). Let cool for 5 to 10 minutes in the pans, then remove to a wire rack to cool completely.

Yield

Makes 2 loaves.

Cranberry Orange Bread

(Food Processor, Steel Blade)

In the work bowl lightly cream the butter and sugar. Add the juice mixture, sherry, and egg; pulse to blend until smooth. Add the flour, baking powder, baking soda, and salt; mix thoroughly. Fold in the cranberries and walnuts. Turn out the batter into the prepared pans and proceed as in Baking, above.

Cranberry Orange Bread

(Dough-Mixing Machine, Flat Beater)

4 tablespoons unsalted butter or margarine, softened
2 cups sugar
Juice and grated zest of 2 oranges plus enough water to make 1 1/2 cups
1/2 cup dry sherry
2 eggs, beaten
4 cups unbleached all-purpose flour
1 tablespoon baking powder
1 teaspoon baking soda
1 teaspoon salt
2 cups coarsely ground or chopped cranberries
2 cups coarsely chopped walnuts
Shortening, for greasing pans
Flour, for dusting pans

In the mixing bowl lightly cream the butter and sugar. Add the juice mixture, sherry, and eggs; blend until smooth. Add the flour, baking powder, baking soda, and salt; mix thoroughly. Fold in the cranberries and walnuts. Grease four 8- or 9-inch loaf pans; then line them with parchment or waxed paper and grease and flour-dust the bottom. Turn out the batter into the prepared pans and proceed as in Baking, above.

Yield

Makes 4 loaves.

Orange Pecan Bread

2 tablespoons unsalted butter or margarine, softened
1/2 cup firmly packed brown sugar
1/2 cup granulated sugar
Juice and grated zest of 1 orange plus enough water to make 3/4 cup
1 egg, beaten
1 1/2 cups unbleached all-purpose flour
1/2 cup whole wheat flour, preferably stone ground
1 1/2 teaspoons baking powder
1/2 teaspoon baking soda
1/4 teaspoon salt
1 cup coarsely chopped pecans
6 pecan halves, for topping (optional)
Shortening, for greasing pans
Flour, for dusting pans

In a large bowl lightly cream the butter and sugars. Beat in the juice mixture and egg until smooth. Add the flours, baking powder, baking soda, and salt. Stir the dry ingredients gently, then mix thoroughly. Fold in the pecans. Grease two 8- or 9-inch loaf pans; then line them with parchment or waxed paper and grease and flour-dust the bottom. Turn out the batter into the prepared pans. Place 3 pecan halves (if desired) in a line down the center of each loaf.

Baking

Bake in a preheated 350°F oven until browned and the center feels firm when gently pressed with your fingertips (50 to 60 minutes). Let cool for 5 to 10 minutes in the pans, then remove to a wire rack to cool completely.

Yield

Makes 2 loaves.

Orange Pecan Bread

(Food Processor, Steel Blade)

In the work bowl lightly cream the butter and sugars. Add the juice mixture and egg; pulse to blend until smooth. Add the flours, baking powder, baking soda, and salt; mix thoroughly. Fold in the pecans. Grease two 8- or 9-inch loaf pans; then line them with parchment or waxed paper and grease and flour-dust the bottom. Turn out the batter into the prepared pans. Place 3 pecans halves (if desired) in a line down the center of each loaf. Proceed as in Baking, above.

Orange Pecan Bread

(Dough-Mixing Machine, Flat Beater)

For half the yield, use the previous recipe.

4 tablespoons unsalted butter or margarine, softened
1 cup firmly packed brown sugar
1 cup granulated sugar
Juice and grated zest of 2 oranges plus enough water to make 1 1/2 cups
2 eggs, beaten
3 cups unbleached all-purpose flour
1 cup whole wheat flour, preferably stone ground
1 tablespoon baking powder
1 teaspoon baking soda
1/2 teaspoon salt
2 cups coarsely chopped pecans
12 pecan halves, for topping (optional)
Shortening, for greasing pans
Flour, for dusting pans

In the mixing bowl lightly cream the butter and sugars. Add the juice mixture and egg; blend until smooth. Add the flours, baking powder, baking soda, and salt; mix thoroughly. Fold in the pecans. Grease four 8- or 9-inch loaf pans; then line them with parchment or waxed paper and grease and flour-dust the bottom. Turn out the batter into the prepared pans. Place 3 pecan halves in a line down the center of each loaf and proceed as in Baking, above.

Yield

Makes 4 loaves.

Roman Apple Ring

1 tablespoon unsalted butter or margarine
1/2 cup plus 2 tablespoons granulated sugar
1/2 cup plus 2 tablespoons firmly packed brown sugar
1 tablespoon vegetable oil
4 eggs
3 cups cake flour
1/2 cup skim milk powder (omit for nondairy recipe)
4 teaspoons baking powder
2 teaspoons baking soda
1 1/2 teaspoons salt
1 1/2 teaspoons ground cinnamon
1/2 teaspoon freshly ground nutmeg
1/2 cup water
2 tart apples (such as Granny Smith), peeled and sliced
Shortening, for greasing pans
Flour, for dusting pan
Sliced almonds, for sprinkling (optional)
Granulated sugar, for sprinkling

In a large bowl cream the butter to soften and mix in the sugars and oil. Beat in the eggs one at a time.

In a medium bowl stir together the flour, milk powder (if used), baking powder, baking soda, salt, cinnamon, and nutmeg. Alternately beat small amounts of the flour mixture and the water into the butter mixture until smooth. Add the apples and stir once or twice.

Grease two 8-inch layer cake pans or a ring pan. Fill with the batter and sprinkle with sliced almonds (if desired). Sprinkle with the granulated sugar. Alternately, sprinkle the greased pan (bottom and sides) with sliced almonds, fill with batter and invert after it is baked.

Baking

Bake in a preheated 350°F oven until browned and the center feels firm when gently pressed with your fingertips (about 1 hour). Let cool for 5 to 10 minutes in the pan, then remove to a wire rack to cool completely. Wrap in aluminum foil or plastic and chill overnight before cutting. This cake freezes well.

Yield

Makes 2 cakes.

Roman Apple Ring

(Food Processor, Steel Blade)

In the work bowl lightly cream the butter; mix in the sugars and oil. Beat in the eggs, one at a time. Add the flour, milk powder (if used), baking powder, baking soda, salt, cinnamon, and nutmeg. With the machine running slowly add the water. Add the apples and stir for 1 or 2 turns or fold in by hand.

Grease two 8-inch layer cake pans or a ring pan. Fill with the batter and sprinkle with sliced almonds (if desired). Sprinkle with the granulated sugar. Proceed as in Baking, above.

Roman Apple Ring

(Dough-Mixing Machine, Flat Beater)

2 tablespoons unsalted butter or margarine
1 1/4 cups granulated sugar
1 1/4 cups firmly packed brown sugar
2 tablespoons vegetable oil
8 eggs
6 cups cake flour
1 cup skim milk powder (omit for nondairy recipe)
8 teaspoons baking powder
4 teaspoons baking soda
1 tablespoon salt
1 tablespoon ground cinnamon
1 teaspoon freshly grated nutmeg
1 cup water
4 tart apples (such as Granny Smith), peeled and sliced
Shortening, for greasing pan
Flour, for dusting pan
Sliced almonds, for sprinkling (optional)
Granulated sugar, for sprinkling

In the mixing bowl lightly cream the butter; mix in the sugars and oil. Beat in the eggs, one-third at a time. Add the flour, milk powder (if used), baking powder, baking soda, salt, cinnamon, and nutmeg. With the machine running slowly add the water. Add the apples and stir for 1 or 2 turns or fold in by hand.

Grease four 8-inch layer cake pans or ring pans. Fill with the batter and sprinkle with sliced almonds (if desired). Sprinkle with the granulated sugar. Proceed as in Baking, above.

Yield

Makes 4 cakes.

Skabana Nut Bread

1 1/2 cups unbleached all-purpose flour
1/2 cup whole wheat flour, preferably stone ground
1 tablespoon baking powder
3/4 teaspoon baking soda
1/2 teaspoon salt
2 tablespoons sugar
2 tablespoons honey
4 tablespoons unsalted butter or margarine, melted
1 egg, beaten
1 1/4 cups milk
1/2 cup chunky-style peanut butter
2 medium-sized ripe bananas, mashed
1 teaspoon banana extract
Shortening, for greasing pan
Flour, for dusting pan

In a large bowl stir together the flours, baking powder, baking soda, salt, and sugar. Blend in the honey, butter, egg, milk, peanut butter, mashed banana, and banana extract; beat until mixed thoroughly. Grease two 8- or 9-inch loaf pans; then line them with parchment or waxed paper and grease and flour-dust the bottom. Turn out the batter into the prepared pans.

Baking

Bake in a preheated 350°F oven until browned and the center feels firm when gently pressed with your fingertips (45 to 60 minutes). Let cool for 5 to 10 minutes in the pans, then remove to a wire rack to cool completely. This bread is best eaten the next day; wrap in aluminum foil or plastic wrap and refrigerate overnight. Try it thinly sliced and toasted. It also freezes well.

Yield

Makes 2 loaves.

Variation

Peanut Bread

Omit the banana.

Skabana Nut Bread

(Food Processor, Steel Blade)

In the work bowl stir together the flours, baking powder, baking soda, salt, and sugar. Blend in the honey, butter, egg, peanut butter, mashed banana, and banana extract. With the machine running slowly, add the milk until mixed thoroughly. Grease two 8- or 9-inch loaf pans, then line them with parchment or waxed paper and grease and flour-dust the bottom. Turn out the batter into the prepared pans. Proceed as in Baking, above.

Skabana Nut Bread

(Dough-Mixing Machine, Flat Beater)

3 cups unbleached all-purpose flour
1 cup whole wheat flour, preferably stone ground
2 tablespoons baking powder
1 1/2 teaspoons baking soda
1 teaspoon salt
1/4 cup sugar
1/4 cup honey
1/2 cup unsalted butter or margarine (1 stick)
2 eggs
4 medium-sized ripe bananas, mashed
1 cup chunky-style peanut butter
2 teaspoons banana extract
2 1/2 cups milk
Shortening, for greasing pan
Flour, for dusting pan

In the mixing bowl stir together the flours, baking powder, baking soda, salt, and sugar. Blend in the honey, butter, eggs, mashed banana, peanut butter, and banana extract. With the machine running slowly, add the milk until mixed thoroughly. Grease four 8- or 9-inch loaf pans; then line them with parchment or waxed paper and grease and flour-dust the bottom. Turn out the batter into the prepared pans. Proceed as in Baking, above.

Yield

Makes 4 loaves.

Tea Ring

4 tablespoons unsalted butter or margarine, softened
1/2 cup sugar
1/2 cup molasses
2 eggs, beaten
2/3 cup water
1 carrot, ground or shredded
1 1/2 cups unbleached all-purpose flour
1 cup whole wheat flour, preferably stone ground
1/3 cup skim milk powder (optional)
2 1/2 teaspoons baking powder
1/2 teaspoon baking soda
1/2 teaspoon ground cinnamon
1/2 teaspoon freshly grated nutmeg
1/2 teaspoon ground allspice
1/4 teaspoon salt
1 cup coarsely chopped walnuts
1/2 cup raisins, plumped in hot water or overnight in rum
Shortening, for greasing pan
Confectioners' sugar, for dusting (optional)

In a large bowl lightly cream or rub together the butter and sugar. Beat in the molasses, eggs, water, and carrot until smooth. Add the flours, milk powder (if used), baking powder, baking soda, cinnamon, nutmeg, allspice, and salt. Stir the dry ingredients gently to combine, then beat thoroughly. Fold in the walnuts and raisins.

Turning Out

Turn out into a well-greased 9-inch bundt pan or removable-bottom pan with a ring in the center.

Baking

Bake in a preheated 350°F oven until browned and the center feels firm when gently pressed with your fingertips (about 1 hour). Let cool for 5 to 10 minutes in the pan; then remove to a wire rack to cool completely. Dust with the confectioners' sugar, if desired.

Yield

Makes 1 cake.

Tea Ring

(Food Processor, Steel Blade)

In the work bowl lightly cream or rub together the butter and sugar. Add the molasses, eggs, water, and carrot and process until smooth. Add the flours, milk powder (if used), baking powder, baking soda, cinnamon, nutmeg, allspice, and salt. Pulse until thoroughly blended. Fold in the walnuts and raisins; then proceed as in Turning Out and Baking, above.

Tea Ring

(Dough-Mixing Machine, Flat Beater)

1/2 cup (1 stick) unsalted butter or margarine, softened
1 cup sugar
1 cup molasses
4 eggs, beaten
1 1/3 cups water
2 carrots, ground or shredded
3 cups unbleached all-purpose flour
2 cups whole wheat flour, preferably stone ground
2/3 cup skim milk powder (optional)
5 teaspoons baking powder
1 teaspoon baking soda
1 teaspoon ground cinnamon
1 teaspoon freshly grated nutmeg
1 teaspoon ground allspice
1/2 teaspoon salt
2 cups coarsely chopped walnuts
1 cup raisins plumped in hot water or overnight in rum
Shortening, for greasing pan
Confectioners' sugar, for dusting (optional)

In the mixing bowl lightly cream the butter and sugar. Add the molasses, eggs, water, and ground carrot and mix until smooth. Add the flours, milk powder (if used), baking powder, baking soda, cinnamon, nutmeg, allspice, and salt. Stir the dry ingredients gently with your fingertips to combine, then beat thoroughly.

Scrape down the sides and bottom of the bowl with a rubber spatula. Mix until smooth. Fold in the walnuts and raisins; then proceed as in Turning Out and Baking, above, except use 2 pans.

Yield

Makes 2 cakes.

Zucchini Bread

2 cups sugar
1 1/2 cups vegetable oil
3 cups grated unpeeled zucchini
4 eggs
3 cups unbleached all-purpose flour
2 teaspoon baking powder
2 teaspoons baking soda
1/2 teaspoon salt
1 teaspoon grated lemon zest
1 teaspoon ground cinnamon
1/2 teaspoon ground cloves
1/2 teaspoon freshly grated nutmeg
1/2 cup chopped walnuts
Shortening, for greasing pans
Flour, for dusting pans

In a large bowl combine the sugar, oil, and grated zucchini. Beat in the eggs one at a time.

In a medium bowl combine the flour, baking powder, baking soda, salt, zest, cinnamon, cloves, and nutmeg. Beat into the zucchini mixture until smooth. Fold in the nuts. Grease three 8- or 9-inch loaf pans; then line them with parchment or waxed paper and grease and flour-dust the bottom. Turn out the batter into the prepared pans.

Baking

Bake in a preheated 350°F oven until browned and the center feels firm when gently pressed with your fingertips (about 1 hour). Let cool for 5 to 10 minutes in the pans; then remove to a wire rack to cool completely. Wrap in aluminum foil or plastic and chill overnight before cutting. This bread freezes well.

Yield

Makes 3 loaves.

Zucchini Bread

(Food Processor, Steel Blade)

1 cup sugar
3/4 cup vegetable oil
1 1/2 cups grated unpeeled zucchini
2 eggs
1 1/2 cups unbleached all-purpose flour
1 teaspoon baking powder
1 teaspoon baking soda
1/4 teaspoon salt
1/2 teaspoon grated lemon zest
1/2 teaspoon ground cinnamon
1/4 teaspoon ground cloves
1/4 teaspoon freshly grated nutmeg
1/4 cup chopped walnuts
Shortening, for greasing pans
Flour, for dusting pans

In the work bowl combine the sugar, oil, and grated zucchini. With the machine running add the eggs one at a time. Add the flour, baking powder, baking soda, salt, zest, cinnamon, cloves, and nutmeg. Mix thoroughly. Fold in the nuts. Grease two 8-inch loaf pans; then line them with parchment or waxed paper and grease and flour-dust the bottom. Turn out the batter into the prepared pans and proceed as in Baking, above.

Yield

Makes 2 loaves.

Zucchini Bread

(Dough-Mixing Machine, Flat Beater)

2 cups sugar
1 1/2 cups vegetable oil
3 cups grated unpeeled zucchini
4 eggs
3 cups unbleached all-purpose flour
2 teaspoons baking powder
2 teaspoons baking soda
1/2 teaspoon salt
1 teaspoon grated lemon zest
1 teaspoon ground cinnamon
1/2 teaspoon ground cloves
1/2 teaspoon freshly grated nutmeg
1/2 cup chopped walnuts
Shortening, for greasing pans
Flour, for dusting pans

In the mixing bowl combine the sugar, oil, and grated zucchini. With the machine running add the eggs one at a time. Add the flour, baking powder, baking soda, salt, zest, cinnamon, cloves, and nutmeg. Pulse with the on/off switch until all is absorbed so that the flour does not fly out of the bowl. Mix until smooth.

Scrape down the sides and bottom of the bowl with a spatula and continue mixing until smooth. Fold in the nuts. Grease three 8- or 9-inch loaf pans; then line them with parchment or waxed paper and grease and flour-dust the bottom. Turn out the batter into the prepared pans and proceed as in Baking, above.

Yield

Makes 3 loaves.

Chapter Ten

Twelve Menus: A Morning of Baking

The professional time management required for a baker to produce three or four varieties of bread in the time normally required to make one is adapted here for the home cook. This chapter contains twelve menus, including suggestions for breakfast and lunch using the baked goods you are preparing. Some special recipes are included, such as sourdough pancakes and variety toasts.

Although the bread-baking process takes several hours from start to finish, the actual working time is rarely more than 30 minutes, including the preparation time and measuring and kneading. Most of the time is taken up waiting for the dough to rise and bake; since neither of these steps requires full-time supervision, you can go about other tasks.

In the bakery, in order to complete the required production we must utilize the baker's time to the fullest extent. This is accomplished by starting new dough timed to rise and be made up while the first breads are baking. An experienced baker keeps busy all day, preparing one dough after another so that the dough will be ready as required for the oven or refrigerator. While the first breads are baking, other doughs are in various stages of completion. This way the work keeps moving forward with no time lost.

In rural households bread is often baked once a week, making enough to last until the next baking. This can be a fun way to spend part of a day, either alone or as a group or family activity. Many working couples and singles who enjoy cooking and baking often complain that they never have time to cook, so they dine out or bring prepared foods home. Here is a way to spend part of a free day both cooking and baking, perhaps with family participating, and still have time for an afternoon or evening out.

This series of baking programs is designed to lead you from beginning to end in one morning of baking. The menus allow you to complete several days' worth of breads and sweet doughs in little more time than is required to make and bake one recipe from start to finish. Some of the menus contain hints for quick breakfasts and lunches using the fresh baked goods that are emerging from the oven as you work. By taking advantage of the freezer and refrigerator, you can prepare either doughs or finished breads, baked or unbaked, to be used as you choose throughout the week. In a short time you will find that you can easily devise these menu plans for yourself, based on your personal preferences.

A Morning of Baking, Program 1

Time

2 1/2 to 4 hours, or one morning

Yield

6 loaves of bread and 2 dozen muffins

Milk Bread (Sponge Method) (pages 38-39)
Muffins (Your choice) (pages 277-295)
100% Whole Wheat Bread (page 154)
Italian Bread (page 109; see Toasts, page 30)

Breakfast: Hot muffins with cheese, jelly, and assorted spreads.

Lunch: Soup and sandwiches (using freshly baked Milk Bread).

Assemble the recipes and all ingredients, preferably the evening before.

1. Preheat the oven to 375°. Mix the sponge for Milk Bread and set aside. (15 minutes)
2. Mix a double batch of muffins and bake when the oven reaches temperature. (20 minutes)
3. Mix the Milk Bread when the sponge is ready, then allow to rest. (30 minutes)
4. Shape and proof the Milk Bread. (10 minutes)
5. Prepare a whole wheat sponge. (15 minutes)
6. If you waited for breakfast, now is the time for the hot muffins you just made, served with assorted spreads.
7. Bake the Milk Bread when proofed. (5 minutes)
8. Mix the Whole Wheat Bread, let rest, then shape and proof. (30 minutes)
9. Mix the sponge for Italian Bread and set aside to rise. (20 minutes)
10. Bake the Whole Wheat Bread when fully risen. (5 minutes)
11. Mix, rest, then shape the Italian loaves when ready. Allow to proof and bake. Or, after shaping, refrigerate the dough to bake later or the next morning. Or freeze the dough to be baked fresh later in the week. (20 minutes)

A Morning of Baking, Program 2 (Nondairy)

Time

2 1/4 to 3 1/2 hours.

Yield

4 breads, 3 Potatonik, 4 Mondelbrot.

Cinnamon Raisin Bread (page 85, omit milk powder for nondairy recipe)
Mondelbrot (page 307)
Potatonik (page 60)
Challah (page 73)

Dinner: Potatonik and Challah with a fish entree. Mondelbrot for dessert.

Preheat the oven for the Potatonik.

1. Mix the Cinnamon Raisin Bread. (For nondairy, substitute margarine or oil for butter and omit the skim milk powder.) Set aside to rise. (15 minutes)
2. Mix the Mondelbrot. Refrigerate. (20 minutes)
3. Prepare the sponge for Potatonik. (15 minutes)
4. Make up the Cinnamon Raisin Bread when risen and allow to proof. (10 minutes)
5. Mix the Challah dough. Set aside to rise. (25 minutes)
6. Mix the Potatonik and drop out into pans. Bake (do not proof). (15 minutes)
7. Bake the Cinnamon Raisin Bread when ready. If the Potatonik and Cinnamon Raisin Bread are ready at the same time, bake together at 370°F.
8. Shape the Mondelbrot. Set aside and bake when the oven is empty. Or refrigerate to bake later or the next morning, or freeze unbaked to be used another day. (10 minutes)
9. When the Challah dough is ready, make into the desired shapes. (20 minutes)
10. Proof and bake the Challah or set aside as in Mondelbrot, above.

A Morning of Baking, Program 3

Time
3 1/2 to 4 hours.

Yield
8 breads (more when using the dough-mixing machine).

Psomi Bread (page 151)
Whole Wheat Irish Soda Bread (page 303)
Potato Rye Bread with Onion and Caraway (page 54)
Semolina Bread (page 119)

Lunch: Warm Irish Soda Bread with assorted cheeses, salad, or soup.

Assemble the recipes and all ingredients, preferably a day in advance.

Preheat the oven to the temperature for the Irish Soda Bread.

1. Prepare a sponge for the Psomi Bread; set aside to rise. (15 minutes)
2. Mix a double recipe of Whole Wheat Irish Soda Bread and bake when the oven is ready. (20 minutes)
3. Prepare the potato and sauté the onion for the Potato Rye Bread. (15 minutes)
4. Mix the Psomi Bread dough, then shape and proof. (20 minutes)
5. Mix the Potato Rye Bread, then set aside to rise. (10 minutes)
6. Take a break.
7. When the Potato Rye Bread has risen, punch, let rest, shape, and proof. (20 minutes)
8. Bake the Psomi Bread when proofed. (5 minutes)
9. Mix the Semolina Bread and set aside to rise. (20 minutes)
10. Bake the Potato Rye Bread when proofed. (5 minutes)
11. Shape the Semolina Bread when risen. Refrigerate to bake for dinner or for the following morning. Or freeze for baking later in the week. (15 minutes)

A Morning of Baking, Program 4

Time

2 3/4 to 4 hours.

Yield

6 breads and 2 dozen muffins (more when using the dough-mixing machine).

Cheese Bread (page 82)
Cracked Wheat Bread (page 91)
Peach Muffins with Streusel Topping (page 278)
Irish Raisin Bread (page 106)

Assemble the recipes and all ingredients, preferably a day in advance. Cook the cereal for the Cracked Wheat Bread, preferably the evening before.

1. Preheat the oven for the Peach Muffins. Mix the sponge for the Cheese Bread; set aside. (10 minutes)
2. Prepare the Streusel Topping for the Peach Muffins. (15 minutes)
3. Mix a double recipe for the Peach Muffins and bake. If desired, use a different fruit for the second dozen. (15 minutes)
4. Mix the Cheese Bread dough. Let rest for 10 minutes. (30 minutes)
5. Mix the sponge for Cracked Wheat Bread; set aside to rise. (10 minutes)
6. Shape and proof the Cheese Bread. (10 minutes)
7. Take a break, or have breakfast and serve the hot muffins you just made. (30 minutes)
8. Mix the dough for Cracked Wheat Bread. (20 minutes)
9. Bake the Cheese Bread when proofed. (5 minutes)
10. Mix the Irish Raisin Bread; set aside to rise. (20 minutes)
11. Shape the Cracked Wheat Bread when raised. Proof and bake, or refrigerate for later baking, or freeze for baking later in the week. (5 minutes)
12. When raised, proof and bake the Irish Raisin Bread, or refrigerate for later baking or leave overnight to bake the following morning. Or freeze for baking later in the week.

A Morning of Baking, Program 5

Time

2 3/4 to 4 hours.

Yield

8 or 9 breads (more when using the dough-mixing machine).

Fougasse (French flat bread) (page 97)
100% Whole Wheat Bread (page 154)
Cornmeal Bread (page 43)
London Bloomers (page 124)

Lunch: Cornmeal Bread or Fougasse with a salad of your choice.

Assemble the recipes and all ingredients, preferably a day in advance. Prepare the sponge for the Fougasse a day in advance.

1. Preheat the oven for the Cornmeal Bread. Mix the Fougasse dough; set aside to rise. (20 minutes)
2. Mix the sponge for the Whole Wheat Dough. (10 minutes)
3. Mix the Cornmeal Bread batter and bake when the oven reaches temperature. (15 minutes)
4. When the Fougasse is risen, shape and proof. (10 minutes) (If step 5 is ready first, reverse steps 4 and 5.)
5. When ready, mix the Whole Wheat Bread.(20 minutes)
6. Bake the Fougasse when proofed. (5 minutes)
7. Mix the London Bloomers; set aside to rise. (20 minutes)
8. Shape and proof the Whole Wheat Bread. (10 minutes)
9. Have lunch. (45 minutes)
10. Bake the Whole Wheat Bread. (5 minutes)
11. Shape the London Bloomers. Proof and bake, or refrigerate for later baking or leave overnight to bake the following morning. Or freeze for use later in the week.

A Morning of Baking, Program 6 (Nondairy)

Time

3 to 4 hours.

Yield

6 breads, 1 or 2 French coffee cakes.

Cracked Wheat Bread (page 91, omit milk powder for nondairy recipe)
French Crumb Coffee Cake (see Wine Loaf, page 311)
Anadama Bread (page 41)
French Bread (page 94)

Assemble the recipes and all ingredients, preferably a day in advance. Cook the cracked wheat cereal in advance and refrigerate until morning. In the morning preheat the oven for the French Crumb Coffee Cake.

1. Mix the sponge for the Cracked Wheat Bread. (For nondairy Cracked Wheat Bread, use margarine and omit the milk powder.) Set aside to rise. (10 minutes)
2. Mix the Streusel Topping (page 277) for the French Crumb Coffee Cake. (10 minutes)
3. Mix the Wine Loaf for the French Crumb Coffee Cake; bake. (20 minutes)
4. Mix the Cracked Wheat Bread dough and allow to rest (10 minutes). Shape and proof. (35 minutes)
5. Mix the Anadama Bread and set aside to rise. Set the oven for the Cracked Wheat Bread. (20 minutes)
6. Bake the Cracked Wheat Bread when fully risen. (5 minutes)
7. Take a break. (30 minutes)
8. Shape and proof the Anadama Bread when fully risen. (10 minutes)
9. Mix the sponge for the French Bread and allow to rise. (10 minutes)
10. When the French Bread sponge has risen, mix the French Bread dough and set aside to rise. (15 minutes)
11. When proofed, bake the Anadama Bread.(5 minutes)
12. Shape the French Bread when ready, then allow to proof and bake. Or refrigerate to bake later or the next morning. Or freeze, baked or unbaked, for later use. (10 minutes)

A Morning of Baking, Program 7 (Nondairy)

Time
4 to 5 hours.

Yield
2 or 3 pizzas, 2 breads, 1 to 2 dozen each egg rolls and bagels.

Italian Bread (page 109)
Pizza (page 116, use nondairy toppings)
Egg Rolls and **Garlic Knots** (page 240)
Bagels (page 228)

Lunch: Pizza and salad.

Assemble the recipes and all ingredients, including toppings for the Pizza, preferably a day in advance.

1. Preheat the oven for Italian Bread. Mix the sponge; set aside to rise. (10 minutes)
2. Mix the Pizza dough; set aside to rise. (20 minutes)
3. Mix the Italian Bread dough, let rest, shape, and proof. (35 minutes)
4. Take a break. (30 minutes)
5. Bake the Italian Bread when proofed. (5 minutes)
6. When the Italian Bread is finished baking, increase the oven temperature as per Pizza recipe, roll out the Pizza dough, add the toppings, and bake. (45 minutes) Try Foccacia toppings (page 114) for nondairy recipes.
7. Mix the Egg Roll dough; set aside to rise. (20 minutes)
8. Eat the freshly baked Pizza for lunch. (45 minutes)
9. Mix the Bagel dough; set aside to rise. (20 minutes)
10. Make up the Egg Rolls and proof to bake, or refrigerate overnight and bake the next day. Or freeze, unbaked, for later use. (15 minutes)
11. When the Bagels are ready, shape and proof or refrigerate for up to 1 day. (20 minutes)
12. Boil the Bagels and bake when ready. (45 minutes)

A Morning of Baking, Program 8 (Nondairy)

Time

2 3/4 to 3 hours.

Yield

6 breads, 1 or 2 Zucchini Breads.

Corn Bread (page 190)
Zucchini Bread (page 341)
Laszlo's Sourdough Potato Rye Bread (page 171)
Sourdough Bavarian Pumpernickel Bread (page 181)

Prepare the Rye Sour (page 163) 24 to 48 hours in advance. Make a ready sour in three stages, as per recipe. You will need a minimum of 6 cups sour. Prepare all of the recipe ingredients and cook the rye cereal; refrigerate it until morning.

In the morning preheat the oven to the temperature required for the Zucchini Bread.

1. Mix the Corn Bread. Set aside to rise. (15 minutes)
2. Mix the Zucchini Bread and bake, then set the oven temperature for the Corn Bread. (25 minutes)
3. Mix the Sourdough Potato Rye Bread. (15 minutes)
4. When risen, shape the Corn Bread and bake it, then set the oven for the Bavarian Bread. (10 minutes)
5. When the Sourdough Potato Rye Bread is ready, shape and proof it. (15 minutes)
6. Mix the Sourdough Bavarian Pumpernickel Bread and bake. (15 minutes)
7. Shape the Potato Rye Bread when it is ready. Bake when proofed. (15 minutes)
8. Mix Stage One of the Rye Sour (first of three stages). (10 minutes)
9. Mix Stages Two and/or Three Rye Sour and refrigerate for later use.

A Morning of Baking, Program 9 (Nondairy)

Time

2 to 3 hours.

Yield

4 breads, 4 1/2 dozen rolls, 1 to 2 dozen muffins.

Pumpernickel Bread (page 178)
Rich Bran Muffins (page 283), see Note below
Seven-Grain Bread (page 174)
Hungarian Salt Sticks (pages 223-225)

Note: For nondairy menu omit milk powder.

Prepare the Rye Sour (page 163) 24 to 48 hours in advance. Make a ready sour in three stages, as per recipe.

In the morning preheat the oven to the temperature required for the Rich Bran Muffins.

1. Mix the Pumpernickel Bread and set aside to rise. (15 minutes)
2. Mix the Rich Bran Muffins (omit the milk powder for nondairy); then bake. (25 minutes)
3. Mix the Seven-Grain Bread and allow to rise. (15 minutes)
4. When risen, shape and proof the Pumpernickel Bread. (10 minutes)
5. Shape and proof the Seven-Grain Bread when ready. (15 minutes)
6. Bake the Pumpernickel Bread when ready. (5 minutes)
7. Mix the dough for Salt Sticks and set aside to rise. (20 minutes)
8. Bake the Seven-Grain Bread when ready. (5 minutes)
9. Shape the Salt Sticks when ready and bake or refrigerate for later baking or overnight for use the next day. Or freeze, unbaked, for hot rolls baked when desired.

A Morning of Baking, Program 10 (Nondairy)

Time

3 to 4 hours.

Yield

4 breads, 1 or 2 Date Nut Breads.

Raisin Pumpernickel Bread (page 179)
Bertie's Date Nut Bread (page 323)
Laszlo's Sourdough Potato Rye Bread (page 171)
Foccacia (pages 112-115)

Lunch: Date Nut Bread with salad.

Prepare the Rye Sour (page 163) 24 to 48 hours in advance. Make a ready sour in three stages, as per recipe. Assemble the recipes and all ingredients, preferably a day in advance. In the morning preheat the oven to the temperature required for the Date Nut Bread.

1. Mix the Raisin Pumpernickel Bread; set aside to rise. (20 minutes)
2. Mix the Date Nut Bread and bake. (20 minutes)
3. Sauté the onions and prepare the potatoes for the Potato Rye Bread. (15 minutes)
4. Mix the Potato Rye Bread; set aside to rise. (20 minutes)
5. Shape and proof the Pumpernickel Bread when ready. (15 minutes)
6. Prepare and mix the Foccacia. Set aside to rise. (15 minutes)
7. Shape the Potato Rye Bread when ready. Bake the Pumpernickel Bread when proofed. (15 minutes)
8. Mix Stage One of the Rye Sour (first of three stages). (10 minutes)
9. When proofed, bake the Potato Rye Bread. (5 minutes) If the Foccacia rises first, reverse steps 9 and 10.
10. When risen, shape the Foccacia. Allow to rise and bake. Or refrigerate to bake later or the next morning. Or freeze, baked or unbaked, for later use. (10 minutes)
11. Mix Stage Two and/or Three of the Rye Sour and refrigerate.

A Morning of Baking, Program 11

Time

3 3/4 to 4 hours.

Yield

6 breads, 1 or 2 quick breads, flapjacks.

San Francisco Sourdough Bread (page 209)
George's Sourdough Pancakes (see below)
Murray's Kashi® Bread (page 132) or **Honey Oatmeal Bread** (page 45)
Sourdough French Bread (page 193)
Quick bread (your choice)

George's Sourdough Pancakes

Mix the night before:

1 cup unbleached all-purpose flour
1/2 teaspoon salt
1 cup buttermilk or sour milk
2 tablespoons sour

Mix until smooth. Refrigerate overnight.

In the morning add:

1 egg, lightly beaten
1 tablespoon unsalted butter or margarine, melted
1 teaspoon baking powder
1/2 teaspoon baking soda

Bake on a hot greased griddle or heavy skillet. Additional milk can be added if the batter is too thick.

Prepare the starter 24 to 48 hours in advance. Make a ready sour in three stages, as per recipe. Cook the Kashi® cereal. Refrigerate for use the morning of baking.

In the morning remove the starter from the refrigerator. Preheat the oven.

1. Mix the sponge for the San Francisco Sourdough Bread; set aside to rise. (15 minutes)
2. Mix George's Sourdough Pancakes. Cook and serve for breakfast. (45 minutes)
3. Mix the San Francisco Sourdough Bread; set aside to rise. (15 minutes)
4. Mix the sponge for Kashi® or Honey Oatmeal Bread. (10 minutes)
5. When ready, shape and proof the San Francisco Sourdough Bread. (15 minutes)
6. Mix the quick bread of your choice and bake. (20 minutes)
7. Mix the Sourdough French Bread (using the starter, above) and set aside to rise. (15 minutes)
8. Shape and proof the Kashi® or Honey Oatmeal Bread. (10 minutes)
9. Bake the San Francisco Sourdough Bread when proofed. Shape the French bread when ready. (20 minutes)
10. Bake the Kashi® or Honey Oatmeal Bread when proofed. (5 minutes)
11. Refrigerate or freeze the French Bread for later baking. Refresh the starter as per recipe.

A Morning of Baking, Program 12 (Nondairy)

Time

2 1/2 to 4 hours.

Yield

5 to 8 breads, 2 dozen muffins or biscuits.

Corn Bread (page 190)
Russian Health Bread (page 187)
Biscuits or muffins of your choice (use nondairy recipe)
Sour Rye Bread (page 168)

Breakfast: Hot muffins.

Prepare the Rye Sour (page 163) 24 to 48 hours in advance. Make a ready sour in three stages, as per recipe.

In the morning preheat the oven to the temperature required for the muffins or biscuits.

1. Mix the Corn Bread; set aside to rise. (15 minutes)

2. Mix the Russian Health Bread and allow to rise. (20 minutes)

3. Make a double recipe of biscuits or muffins, using a nondairy recipe if desired, and bake. (15 minutes)

4. When risen, shape the Corn Bread and bake as soon as biscuits are done. (10 minutes)

5. Shape and proof the Russian Health Bread when ready. (15 minutes)

6. Mix the Sour Rye Bread when the fresh sour had risen. Shape into rounds and let the dough rest for 15 minutes. (15 minutes)

7. Shape the Sour Rye Bread when ready. Bake the Russian Health Bread when proofed. (15 minutes)

8. Mix the Rye Sour for the next starter. (10 minutes)

9. Shape the Sour Rye Bread, proof and bake, or refrigerate for later baking. Refrigerate overnight for baking the following morning; unbaked Sour Rye Bread does not freeze well. (20 minutes)

Glossary

Almond Paste: Nut paste made from ground almonds. Expensive. See also Kernel Paste; Macaroon Paste.

Black Seeds: Black caraway, Russian black seeds, sometimes called *chernushka.* These little black bits have an unusual and distinctive flavor. Especially good on rye or corn bread when used for deli or hot meat sandwiches. They are sometimes seen on challah breads. Difficult to obtain; try ethnic sources. May be found as in Indian spice shops as onion seeds or black cumin seeds. Don't buy them if they have little white bits mixed in.

Blind: When a design on a bread or roll is cut in, added on, or braided, and it sinks back into the loaf when baked and is hardly discernible, it is said that the bread or roll came out "blind."

Bloom: When bread, such as French bread, is slashed prior to baking, as the bread rises in the oven the cut opens and "blooms," forming a thick swollen edge along the slash that is very crusty and especially tasty.

Cut In: To blend together shortening and flour or sugar without creaming or aerating the two. To cut in with two knives or a pastry blender or to rub between the fingers until the mixture is thoroughly distributed and grainy in appearance.

Enriched Flour: Flour that has certain vitamins and iron added. Required by federal law.

Hearth: The floor of the oven. Baking on the hearth refers to baking without a pan on the oven floor or on a steel shelf, tiles, or special oven stones set inside the oven.

Kernel Paste: Commercial bakery product made from ground apricot kernels. Used as a substitute for Almond Paste. See also Macaroon Paste.

Knead: A process of continued stretching, pressing, and pulling of a mass of dough, either by hand or machine, causing the gluten (protein) in the flour to develop a network of elastic strands capable of forming and containing individual cells of gas, which allow the dough to expand or rise.

Macaroon Paste: Commercial bakery product. A combination of Almond Paste and Kernel Paste.

Peel: A board or pallet with a handle on which breads are placed for insertion into and removal from the hot oven.

Praline Paste: Nut paste made from roasted hazelnuts.

Proof: The final rise of the loaf prior to baking.

Proscuitto: Naturally processed Italian ham.

Punch: As in to punch down—to press out and expel all the gases from a risen dough.

Ready Dough: A dough that has risen to its optimum size and is ready to be punched down.

Roll-in: Butter or other fats that are layered into yeast dough by rolling out and folding to make it very light and flaky.

Sheave: A baker's term meaning to shove or shovel baked goods off a peel onto the oven hearth.

Sponge: In yeast dough, combination of the liquids, yeast, and a portion of the flour, a soft mixture allowed to ferment and rise up, forming a soft, spongelike mass. In effect, pre-fermentation of the dough before the final mixing and kneading.

Stipple: To dock. To pierce the skin of the bread or pastry with a thin skewer, nail, or blade. To punch a series of small holes in the bread to allow the gases to escape from the loaf as it rises in the oven and to prevent the crust from bursting. This procedure is used on breads for which it is not desirable to slash or cut the tops with a blade.

Wash: A liquid used to brush (paint) bread; also, when used as a verb, to brush the top of a bread or rolls with a pastry brush dipped in water or other liquid.

Sources for Bakers

A. Lilie.
(609) 655-0970
P.O. Box 126
Jamesburg, NJ 08831
Mail-order bakers' supplies, clear flour, rye flour, sourdough bread mixes, bread machine mixes, specialty flours, etc.

Arrowhead Mills, Inc.
(806) 364-0730
Box 866
Hereford, TX 79045
Mail-order grains and flours.

Ener-G Food
(800) 331-5222
P.O. Box 84487
Seattle, WA 98124
Mail-order bread mixes, egg substitute (powdered), milk substitute, flours.

Garden Spot Distributors
(800) 829-5100
438 White Oak Rd.
New Holland, PA 17557
Mail-order grains, flours, cereals, organic products.

King Arthur Flour Bakers Catalogue
(800) 827-6836
RR2, Box 56
Norwich, VT 05055
Mail-order flours, grains, and many other items.

Morgan's Mills
(207) 785-4900
RD2, Box 4602
Union, ME 04862
Mail-order stone-ground flours, cereals, organic items.

Paprikas Weiss Food Importers
(212) 288-6117
1572 2nd Ave.
New York, NY 10028
Retail / mail-order flours, spices, bakers' supplies, imports.

Pete's Spice
(212) 505-5660
174 1st Ave.
New York, NY 10009
Retail and mail-order herbs and spices, flours, etc.

Vermont Country Store
(802) 362-4647
P.O. Box 3000
Manchester Center, VT 05255
Mail-order and retail stone-ground flours, cereals, etc.

Walnut Acres
(800) 433-3998
Penns Creek, PA 17862
Mail-order organic farm, flours, grains, etc.

List of Recipes by Chapter

Index

R

S

T

V

W

Y

Z